*The contents of this book have been written entirely by the author and all proof reading and grammar are also down to me, apologies for any errors but I am an angler first, and writer second, hopefully this will not detract from your enjoyment of the book. Dedicated to my family without whom I would achieve little xxxx*

# Contents

# Contents continued

# Fishtytwo weeks of the year

Introduction

I cannot remember the first moment that the idea of spending a year trying to catch as many different species as possible entered my head but sometime around the summer of 2017. As an avid angler I am always thinking of the next challenge I want to set myself, maybe a new personal best weight for a Shark or a much sort after Carp with its own name or my own Holy Grail a large freshwater eel. Whatever challenge I set myself I have to have the conviction and passion to dedicate the time, finances and effort into achieving that goal.

I have over the years been fortunate enough to succeed in many of these challenges with only a couple eluding me to this day. So, by setting myself a target of 52 species in 52 weeks while celebrating my 52nd birthday year it never occurred to me I could fail. Once I had added to the pressure by supporting and raising money for the Stroke Association charity, failure was most definitely not an option. So why the Stroke Association? Quite simply strokes are something that had been brought to my attention in recent times firstly with my Dad having a mini stroke and secondly when friend and angling pal Andy suffered a huge and debilitating stroke.

Unlike many diseases where you start becoming ill and get diagnosed with a condition that gets worse over time, the suddenness's of a stroke means you could go off to work fit and well and return home no longer able to walk, talk or feed yourself.

I know this is in the extreme but in my friend Andy's case it was that sudden and that extensive, truly shocking if you have not had friends or family effected by a stroke. The fact that Andy has fought tooth and nail every day since to recover has been a real inspiration to me. I would go as far as to say it was life changing, not in regard to improving my diet and fitness but in wanting to achieve things in my life daily in case I didn't get a chance tomorrow. The first year 2017 after Andy's stroke I fished at least twice a week and made no apology for the fact that's what I wanted to do, quite selfish and tough on my family. It was for this reason that I wanted to do something that I could be proud of and that would raise money for a great charity supporting Stroke victims like Andy on their road to recovery. So, 2018 is the year I try and give something back and with the support of great friends and a truly wonderful family I am not going to fail.

This isn't the sort of challenge that I could just rock up next to the nearest beach and start hauling species after species, there was a great deal of planning required. I contacted the charity to ask for their views and advice, with my daughters training I set up a website, blog and Twitter account. That all sounds quick and easy but in reality, it took a few months and more than a little verbal abuse of the Laptop stopping short of giving it a dam good thrashing! I considered myself techno savvy having been brought up with the Sega Mega drive, Sony Walkman's and the first wireless television remotes.

It's only when I tried to link the social media data streams do I realize I could be out of my depth, I'm sure the Ghostbusters stated, "never cross the streams"! Regardless of my techno phobia it all got sorted and once live I was ready to post, and tweet to my heart's content. The blog entries are the basis of the chapters of this book so all being well there should be at least 52 chapters!

*Above the poster design and below the link to the webpage where you can read the blogs and see the full gallery of fish.*

https://stevedawe189.wixsite.com/fishtytwochallenge

## Chapter 1, I hope the 1st was the worst!

Well what a start to the challenge that was, a day of one disaster after another it all seemed so simple when we came up with a plan B! So, Chris picked me up at 10.30 and we headed to Plymouth after some of the smaller Wrasse, arriving at our chosen pier at low water. Eager to get started and with the sun shining I baited my micro rod with fresh rag and flicked it seaward, splosh the handle from the reel flew into the sea and scuppered the use of that rod! So, I reached for my trusty Abu spinning rod and quickly set up and cast again, a small bite and I struck to find the rig snagged, I flicked the rod a couple of times to free the rig and then crack! The rod snapped, and the broken tip disappeared beneath the waves no doubt fairly close to the lost reel handle. I was also still snagged and that broke so I lost all of that, as I turned to say to Chris it can't get worse my bait box lid flew past me like a Frisbee and into the sea. So, I was now rod less and struggling to see how we could turn this around. Chris hadn't been having that great a trip either and was losing tackle as quick as he could tie it, his pair of scissors fell to bits and his bait box lid also blew out to sea!

We decided not to be beaten and fish on sharing Chris's rod, we were struggling but the young lad who turned up with his mum and nan to try his first ever effort at angling was heading for his own disaster. The young boy had been nagging his mum to take him fishing for years and this year she had bought him a rod reel and bit of tackle.

The lad had watched an episode of river monsters and arrived with soap as bait, this wasn't the legendary Blue Vundu catfish soap but a bar of Dove. We happily advised him that maybe he should try some ragworm, Chris spent some time rigging him up and generally giving him some pointers not that we were in a position to advise anyone. It is however great to see youngsters keen to get into angling and well-done Mum and Nan for sitting there freezing to make your lads Christmas. It must have been good karma as soon Chris had a good bite and the first fish was landed a very welcome rockling.

So, I was now back on the rod and hoping to quickly land a rockling myself to get a fish on the board, I soon had a bite and the fish got to the sanctuary of the rocks, bugger! More lost tackle then the heavens opened up. I quickly retrieved the pakamac waterproof coat from the bottom of the rucksack and realized I had picked up my wife's one, as I stood there getting soaked bursting out of the little jacket like a geriatric hulk I really thought I'm going to be beaten. The rain cleared, my numb fingers thawed, a finger of sunlight stretched downwards eventually touching the sea's surface and the angling spark was re-ignited. I stuck with it and as the light faded and the sea rose I finally got that fish we had worked so hard for, a Three Bearded Shore Rockling not huge but to me splendid in its reddish hue. There is another couple of Rockling species to go for this year, the Three Bearded Rockling that is large and orange and the much smaller 5 Bearded Rockling. Hopefully I will get a chance at them during the following 12 months.

My aspirations for this trip had not been realized but providing I can scratch out a result when things are tough then it's all positive plus looking back on this episode it is rather amusing and a degree of fun must go hand in hand with each trip successful or not. Thanks Chris for sticking it out today and for the share of the rod, it didn't go the way we planned but fishing rarely does, I truly hope that the 1st was the worst, and things get a little easier. Well 51 more species to go and things can only get better, or can they?

*Shore Rockling starts the ball rolling*

## Chapter 2 Has my luck changed?

Well another weekend arrived and due to calamities of the previous one it was going to be a two-pronged approach, to try and get a couple of species on the board, when planning this challenge, I probably should have taken into account Sickness, Holidays, Work, Weather and bad angling! So, this trip was to be off to South Devon and try for a few small species again fishing light tackle against some submerged structures. The targets were the Corkwing Wrasse, Goldsinny Wrasse and a Pouting all small yet obliging species with the wrasse being very attractive little fish. The nature of their habitats is extremely rocky and tackle losses were inevitable but hopefully not on the scale of the previous trip.

I got up at 05.00 am to find everything frozen solid and so the car had to be defrosted, by the time I had achieved this Chris had walked down to my place and we loaded up and drove gingerly southwards with an air temp of -3, brrrr. Once on the duel carriageway I felt confident enough to drive a bit faster and even managed to overtake a lorry, halfway through this maneuver the rear passenger door flew open like an airplane door blowing out, cold air rushed in and the Citroen Picasso flashed a warning light for anyone stupid enough to not realize the door was open at 70mph. Chris was on it in a flash and slipped across and managed to pull the door back and the car soon re-pressurized. This is the sort of incident that you really don't need at the start of a trip, but if that's the only disaster of the day it won't be too bad.

Well that certainly woke us up but no damage was done and so before long we arrived at the multi-story car park, I so hate an empty car park I took ages to find a suitable space out of the dozens of empty ones then still parked badly anyway.

We hiked down the pier to the very end then straddled the wall leading to a sheltered little spot with concrete steps down to the water, as I climbed over my flask fell from the side of the rucksack. Donk, donk, donk the flask bounced from step to step heading towards the sea closely followed by a frantic me screaming "NO"! Incredibly as the flask rolled to the edge of the last step it stopped teetering halfway between oblivion and safety. Got it! My hand gripped the flask and I raised it triumphantly in the air towards Chris, "this is a good omen" I exclaimed. So maybe this was to be a lucky day, best get a bait in the water, the bait was lowered down as the sun begrudgingly started to climb skyward, but the icy air still attacked any skin we had failed to cover. The rod arched over as a fish grabbed the bait and I reeled in the first fish of the day a welcome little pouting.

Chris wasn't far behind and another Pouting was soon caught then released, things were indeed looking up and soon we had caught several of these obliging little fish and it was time to try for something different. We tried inside the harbor in attempt to catch some of the target wrasse, but they weren't interested. A couple more anglers arrived, and I recognized one of them as Cephalopod George so called for his love of catching Squid, Octopus and Cuttlefish.

George was very helpful giving us some pointers on how to target the various small species in the vicinity of the pier, it was appreciated. We decided to climb back over the wall and try our luck on the seaward side once again, joined by George and his pal. Soon Chris had a good bite and after a short battle swung in a fishing reel, this sounds crazy especially after losing part of my rod and reel the week before. The reel had no corrosion on it and had been hooked fair and square, luckily, we had witnesses, or we might have even doubted our own sanity.

I forgot to mention in all the excitement of catching the fish, earlier Chris had told me he had seen a penguin swim past and that when I turned it had dived under, I watched for 5 minutes and no penguin surfaced so I put that down to him sniffing to much of his fish attracting spray. It was a few hours later when George's buddy shouted Penguin! I just managed to see the bird paddling off before diving again. " That's no Penguin", I exclaimed "it's a juvenile Razorbill", " NO it's a Penguin" the two were adamant, Chris has since conceded it did look just like a razorbill but having not seen one of those he assumed it must have been a penguin.

Well the fishing was becoming frustrating as Chris lost a good Ballan Wrasse in the rocks and then I hooked a good wrasse that I couldn't stop on the light tackle and once again it was lost, I really could have done with that fish. The next one we hooked was once again Chris and this one also found a hole but by putting the rod down and waiting the fish was soon back swimming and Chris was able to get the fish to the surface and we netted it, didn't count for my tally but I was pleased that Chris had got one.

So, the trip was shaping up ok, but I really needed another species and perhaps a slice of luck, it wasn't a very productive day and the other guys were also struggling on what is normally a very productive mark. I spotted another strange item in the water floating slowly past in the tide, a Christmas cracker fortune fish, had someone took it to the sea and released it, very weird but I shouldn't really be surprised. I decided a change of tactics was required to try for another species and cast out a pulley rig loaded with squid, this was soon taken by something and I struck and quickly pulled in the second of my species for the day a very welcome little Whiting. Chris managed a Dogfish and a Mackerel, but the cold NE Wind and colored water really made it a struggle for the mini species we were after. Sunday afternoon and we had another crack and tried for some coarse fish species at my lakes, the wind was bitter, and boy did we struggle. It's a bit like fishing my home ground as I know the lakes and fish inside out, but we tried everything and only saw one fish move on the surface. It looked like the first blank was looming as the light began to fade when a couple of tiny Perch saved the day.

So, species 4 is on the board the humble Perch and it's refreshing not to be hung up on the size of the fish, already during this challenge I am finding a greater respect for these smaller species and also the fish that may not be specimens but have saved the day. Thanks once again Chris for sharing the experience, pain, cold, laughs and stress it's really appreciated. Got a few good trips coming up in the next 7 days so hopefully a few more species will make the gallery, tight lines everyone.

Chapter 3 For Cod's sake!

Week three and things are really heating up as the southwest goes tropical, the reality is the lakes were frozen this Friday, and the Ilfracombe Spurdog trip was blown off Saturday, and someone forgot to book the Cod for Sunday. So, January is shaping up to be something quite forgettable and even the best laid plans are once again proving fishing is far from predictable. Sometimes no matter how much effort you put in you return home to spend the evening scratching your head. Fishing wise January and February can be real gruler's although this is more due to adverse weather conditions as opposed to a lack of fish.

So, let's have a look at what went in to today's Cod quest and then when I read it back maybe I can see where it went wrong.

- First thing is research where's a good venue to catch Cod? The Bristol Channel, check!
- When's the best time to catch them? Jan, Feb check!

- Get myself on a trip with a group of good anglers targeting Cod, check!

- Find out the best rigs and spend an afternoon tying them, check!

- Get advice on the best baits and spend the morning preparing them, check!

So now I know, when, where, how and what with, easy peasy just need to dig out the big hand on a stick so I can pat myself on the back as the Cod throw themselves at me! If only it was that easy I just need to remember it's a challenge not a given, I'm still confident it will work out in the end.

The bait preparation alone could have caused some domestic repercussions and the timing is crucial.

Step 1 wait for lovely wife to say she is going shopping.

Step 2 gather all the items required to prepare the bait secretly before her departure

Step 3 Unleash the products on the kitchen as soon as the door closes.

Ensure you marinade your selection in some foul-smelling gunk that promises to attract fish. Finally undertake a deep clean of the kitchen before the good lady returns and catches you in the act. With everything planned, prepped and packed I was awoken by the alarm at 03.30am I remember thinking I cannot find any positives in stumbling around at this time of the morning. I thought I would take the dog out before leaving and even he couldn't see the sense in it, turning his back and huffing at me when I switched on the light. So, I hit the road at 04.15 and spent the journey imagining just how big the Cod would be while humming along to Simon and Garfunkel.

The journey took 1.5hrs and incredibly the sunshine town of Minehead was still black as ink, I met one of the Happy Danglers who advised me of a parking discrepancy we could exploit which I duly did, makes a change! We boarded Steve Webbers excellent charter boat Osprey and headed out into the dark calm waters of the Bristol Channel. The guys I was out with today really are a smashing bunch rightly living up to their name the Happy Danglers, Mike, Toby, Nick, Troy and Dave! The skipper Steve and deckhand William, had kept us supplied with hot drinks and bacon rolls but I have to say I really felt the cold today, getting to the stage where I need to take a blanket and water bottle. Fish wise a few whiting started to appear, and I managed a small one, but I've already had one so no points for that one. Nick was flying on the species taking, dogfish, whiting, thornback and spotted rays but sadly lost his conger. Finally, another bite for me and I managed to straighten my fingers enough to grab the rod and after no battle whatsoever I swung in a Lesser Spotted Dogfish, yes, a species on the list, probably the only time I will be pleased to see one this year

The skipper tried a number of areas and despite the previous day producing some great Cod on the boat they never materialized for us. I managed to lose a Ray while bringing it in and that was a species I was hoping for. With about 10 minutes to go I had a good bite and this resulted in species 6 the Conger Eel, again not the biggest but on a rock-hard day that had taken a lot of effort I was very grateful to catch and return that eel. There it is, a tough weekend and hopefully one day things will come together as per the plan.

## Chapter 4 Dab spelt backwards is bad!

The weeks seem to be flying by and before I know it I'm back updating the blog; this weekend's instalment was my first species failure but that is inevitable with a sport that contains so many variables. What I will say is this weekend has been totally entertaining and despite the challenge I must continue to enjoy my hobby in the good times and bad. The plan A had been a boat trip aboard Bluefin out of Ilfracombe chasing a Spurdog, think this was my third attempt at this trip and like the previous trips Mother Nature flexed her muscles and agitated the sea.

So, having learned from previous challenge weekends I had a plan B and C ready formulated and plan B was instigated, shore fishing for *Limanda Limanda* better known as the Common Dab. The Dab is one of our smaller flatfish species, meaning small hooks and baits were in order, the location I chose was a north Devon beach where I have caught Dabs previously. We planned to fish over the low tide period and with the wind set to pick up and come from a North Westerly direction it could get a bit damp.

The beach in question has an initial 50 to 80 meters of large boulders that can twist an ankle in a heartbeat, after the boulders the ground turns to sand with the odd rock. The dabs like the sand so by fishing over the low water period your actually always on the sand. Dabs are a tasty sweet fish but the ones we normally get of this beach are a little too small and are quickly returned to grow bigger.

Chris picked me up at 11.00 am and upon opening the door I could see that the tooth ache he had been moaning about had now manifested itself into a golf ball in the side of his mouth. I enquired into his wellbeing secretly concerned that if he became nauseas or dizzy while we were fishing I might have no one to take photos, fortunately he put my mind at rest by stating he was on anti-biotics and it was mainly cosmetic. He was right with the cosmetic bit and I was a little concerned in case we ran into any families with young children, he could have terrified them.

It was a full ten minutes before we left as my Dental Nurse wife had to give a consultation on what Chris should be doing, the main one being to regularly rinse his mouth with salty water. Finally, we arrived at the beach with a thick mist and warm drizzle there to meet us, I managed to pick my way through the tank trap sized boulders down to the water's edge and drop the tackle without it disappearing into the crevices surrounding us. The tripod was erected as secure as possible and the rods cast, time for a coffee and to admire the view, it's always a special moment when the rods are cast, and you relax and for the first time appreciate the vista

The drizzle and mist cleared and despite the freshening North Westerly it was a really pleasant afternoon, just needed to add a fish or two. Abscess Boy was off to my right and in the process of recasting while situated close to the water edge, crash! A huge wave smashed into the boulders adjacent to where the afflicted one stood, he took it full on, hilarious, I quickly pointed out that it was an extreme way of having a saltwater mouth wash!

My chuckling was interrupted by a rattle on the right-hand rod and I struck to nothing as the little fish out smarted me, a quick re-bait of the tiny hooks and I launched the rod skyward with maximum effort to punch through the strong breeze. "Oh bugger" I may have used too much effort and not enough technique as a huge bird's nest in the spool grew rapidly towards me like an expanding bowl of spaghetti. Suddenly it was Chris whose face broke into a growing smile clearly visible despite the deformity, "oh no what's happened mate" Chris asked sarcastically, my silence was deafening.

Twenty minutes of tugging, unwinding and cursing, two grown men qualified as engineers had that little tangle sorted and the rod was once again cast seaward. I must have put it on the right spot as the rod tip bounced straight away a quick strike and the first fish of the trip was landed, unfortunately not the species I was after but one I've already had the Whiting.

The rocks were becoming like lumps of pure ice following the earlier drizzle and I lost count of the number of tumbles I took, they are so much more painful at our age. With the low tide I was able to rid the sea of some of snagged lines and tackle, it's just a case of following the bright line down to the gaps in the boulders and retrieving the snagged rigs. There are several anglers that make a hobby out of tackle retrieval, I guess it's the same for the golf ball forages.

*Lumpy after taking a saltwater mouthwash to the body!*

Chris was next to check his bait, the wind was getting up and bites were pretty hard to detect so it was best to check the bait every 20 minutes to ensure there was bait still on the hook. As soon as I saw the trace come out of the water I knew Chris had caught our target species a Dab as the little brown fish swung in like a large tree leaf. This was Chris's first ever Dab and therefore a personal best, so I was chuffed for him, but I was starting to think my challenge should have been I take pictures of my mates catching 52 species. It did prove that we were doing everything right, so it was surely just a case of keep doing what we are doing.

The afternoon was more of the same for me with a collection of missed rattling bites and Whiting and I landed 8 of them with not a single Dab. To add to my woes my tripod blew over and the screw holding the rod rest disappeared down one of the crevices, teach me to take the cheap tripod out on a windy day. Once again, our engineering skills sprang into action and I was able to strap the rod rest to the tripod using one of Lumpy's rod straps. This ad-hoc repair was far from perfect but enabled me to continue fishing so that was one positive.

As I sat watching the waves crash into the rocks I remembered fishing the very same spot at dead low tide some 20 years previously although it was in the night and winter. I was fishing with my sister Sarah and about 300 yards off the beach a trawler was working, I remember thinking that's ruined the night. Then the rod pulled over and I was into a large fish that turned out to be a 10lb Cod an awesome fish that I will never forget.

The tide soon came in and it was time to retreat to the safety and shelter of the pier, we set up and cast out commenting how nice it was out of the wind and spray, Crash! A huge wave smashed into the side of the pier causing a huge wave to break over the top of the wall and over a now dry Chris, "still using the extreme mouth wash then mate"? Think I may have been close to getting a few lumps of my own at this point, I decided to keep quiet when he was hit by another wave some 10 minutes later after moving further along the pier. It was about now that a couple of mates arrived, Ian Hooper and Nick Job, both had been catching Dabs with impunity recently, so I would pick their brains for some tips. Ian cast out and came over for a chat, he gave me some great advice but basically what we were doing was the way to go. He then went off to check his bait and low and behold what did he reel in!

Dab followed by another Dab, clearly Mr. Hooper is a Dab whisperer so although I learned a lot about catching them for me on this trip I learned Dab spelt backwards is bad like my results. I will be back at them in a few weeks and even the most obliging of our little fish can be elusive if your lucks not in. It was a really enjoyable session with great guys that I really look forward to fishing with again soon. I also bumped into an old fishing pal John who managed a personal best shore conger last night with a 12lber so well done. Thanks Chris for pushing through the pain caused by that great lump in your mouth, hopefully it will have gone down by next week or the children of Birmingham will think Halloween has come early. Minnows next week with a man who knows a thing or two about tiddlers, I can't wait for what will be a mad weekend filled with curry, beer and maybe a few species of fish.

# Chapter 5 Yabba Dabba Do!

Having been beaten at the weekend by the species I was after I felt determined to get back as soon as possible to get the species in the bag. The difficulty was juggling work and family commitments around a window in the weather something so many of us have to contend with. So, I decided to have a go last night fishing 1 hour up and 2 hours down, this time using all the advice I had been given. Chris didn't take much convincing and with his face having returned to just plain ugly we were soon at the mark, a couple of anglers were already setup fishing, and everything seemed good for a fish. We asked the anglers how they had done, and they had managed a few Whiting and a solitary Dab, this spurred me on knowing the little flats were feeding. I cast out the rigs armed with tiny hooks which were loaded with Black lug tipped with squid then I sat back to wait with everything crossed. It wasn't long before the left-hand rod tip shook violently indicating some interest, upon striking I found myself snagged. Chris had noticed my predicament and exclaimed "hold on mate I will get the glove" he then pulled out he's 1970s snooker referee glove which he had decided was suitable for pulling for breaks. However, as luck would have it the line didn't break and came free, I reeled in to find a 3 Bearded Shore Rockling looking somewhat annoyed under the beam of the headlight. There was also a bunch of line tangled in the rig, the cause of the snag no doubt, it's always nice to remove that from a beach. We debated the species of 3 bearded rockling that I had caught and decided it was the Shore Rockling and one I had already had, so a quick snap and back into the sea with him.

Next it was Chris's turn as he decided to reel in and check the bait, as he swung the rig over the wall there on the bottom hook sat a Dab! I was starting to feel cursed as once again everyone around me were catching Dabs, to add to my paranoia I started catching dogfish and whiting on the tiny lug baits. Sometimes you feel that Neptune isn't ready to give you the fish you desire and no matter what you do will change it, we fished on into the ebb tide and just after midnight with the fat lady climbing her podium my rod tip trembled very gently. I pointed it out to Chris, "this is different, very gentle" at this point the rod bent over demanding a strike and I promptly obliged. There was definitely a fish on, but I was unsure of what species, the problem fishing over a wall with a high parapet it's like the lucky dip at the fete you don't know what you've got until it is your hand. Boom! A beautiful little Dab sprung into view and a little Irish jig followed as both Chris and I were elated. We quickly took the pictures and I ran the fish down the steps to the water's edge to release the little guy carefully and thanked him for showing up in the nick of time. Chris wanted to put out a big bait for the last hour and I just wanted to cast out and enjoy the ambience of this beautiful little harbor. We started to pack up when Chris's whole Whiting was grabbed by something and the steady pulls seemed very eel like, sadly the fish found the rocks and we never got to see it the last action of the night. So, it's onto the next species as this was a bit of an extra blog there should be the normal Sunday one after the midlands trip. Thanks, so much Jon Patten, Pete Gregory and Ian Hooper for the tips it really is appreciated and without doubt helped me get this species. Cheers as usual Chris for driving, photographing and sharing the experience.

*Above the much sort after Dab, just one of the smaller species that really put me to the test this year.*

## Chapter 6 A face full of Anthony Joshua!

The original title of this blog was going to be the Monster Minnow Midlands Mashup however due to a lack of minnows of any size there was no monsters or mashup and a title just stating midlands didn't sound exciting enough, nothing against my mates in Brum.

We had arranged this trip a few weeks previous and while the southwest had been battered by strong winds the midlands had suffered freezing temps, snow and flooding. I hadn't considered that anything could affect a minnow hunt, so obliging are these little fish that they have often been caught using just an empty bottle. The guide I had conned / cajoled into helping me on this task was long term friend and my Eel angling hero Nick Rose aka El Presidente! I asked Nick to guide us to a plethora of mini freshwater fish to include Minnow, Gudgeon, Bleak and Dace, a task Nick appeared happy to do. So, the weekend of the trip arrived, and we decided to leave on the Friday to have a steady trip up to Birmingham, size 16 to 20 hooks to nylon and various pints of maggots were obtained. Nick messaged with the news the rivers were unfishable and most had burst their banks, I knew at that point deep down we had just lost the minnows! Like any professional guide worth his salt El Presidente had formulated another plan and other species were on the cards so it was game on. The Citroen Picasso Desire made short work of the M5 while still remaining within the legal speed limits and before we knew it we pulled up onto the Presidential palace our home for a couple of days.

We had a quick brew and a team talk before heading out after a target for the cameraman, Chris I'm after 53 species Hodgson. Chris hadn't had a Zander in the United Kingdom, so we would target them on one of the labyrinth of canals in the area, stopping on route at one of the countries great tackle shops, now owned by a national chain. We also stopped and tried a tiny stream exiting a lake that may have thrown up a Gudgeon. The tiny stream was in fact pushing through at a rate of knots and chocolate brown in color, we assembled our whips and thrashed the water into a foam. For non-anglers a whip is a small carbon pole used for catching mini species quickly or in our case amusing the local commuters as two grown men perch precariously on a narrow bridge over a flooded ditch with children's rods.

Despite our best efforts we didn't manage a bite, I had a feeling the bait wasn't popular as I observed the myriad of water beetles bringing the maggots we chucked in back to the surface as if they were cleaning their little homes. So, we moved on to the Zander spot and a lovely section of canal that produces small school Zander quite regularly. I need a Zander for my challenge, but I have a great trip arranged for them later in the year with good friend Steve McDonald where I will be hoping for one of the big ones. We cast out the rods and waited, it wasn't long before Chris managed his first Zander, taking several in quick succession, my rods on the right-hand side remained motionless despite the bait and rigs being the same. Chris had a 3lb zander that a Pike had tried to eat, and its side showed a big bite mark still fresh, it did however swim away fine. Chris ended his zander session with a lovely fish just under 8lbs.

The temperature had dropped dramatically, and a frost had formed on the grass and our rods were sparkling in the moonlight, I finally got a turn when a small Zander took the bait, fingers crossed I get a bigger one later in the year. By now we were all freezing, hungry and achieved our goal so Nick took us back home for a well needed curry and cider, quite literally Cider with Rosie! We soon polished off the food and drink and with my species challenge still firmly in my mind I decided to try and pull a fast one, El Presidente has a presidential sized koi pond in his garden and as he was the guide he should cater to his client's wishes. I quickly set up the mini pen rod with a float and tiny hook and went out into the garden in the total darkness, nicks security light flicked on as I walked past illuminating the pond. Much of this big pond is shrouded in thick weed and there are some stunning Koi over 7lbs in weight, not something I would want to hook on the mini rod. I threw in some maggots and the other two stood laughing as I tried to cast the float to the right spot, just as I did the light went off. I had to jump and wave my arms to get the light on again this was an ongoing procedure and the neighbor's must have assumed that Nick was running angler Zumba classes. Once we had the timing sorted of casting, dancing and baiting with maggots the fish finally got used to the float. Suddenly it disappeared as a fish took the bait, the tiny rod bent double as I battled with some type of golden beast, "net, net" I shouted remembering what the challenge was all about. Nick appeared at my side brandishing a child's beach dipping net " it won't fit in there" I laughed as the ghillie struggled to get the fish head first in the tiny net.

Amazingly we got the stunning fish a Golden Orfe in the net and landed it, the tiny pen rod had tamed the beast and what's more it was species number 9! The next morning, I woke and decided that there was enough light filtering through the curtains to get dressed by, I reached for my Christmas present deodorant spray, essence of Joshua. A gift from my wonderful mother in law that I thought would be perfect for the road trip, problem was I hadn't used a spray deodorant for many years preferring the simplicity and efficiency offered by a roll on. I fumbled with the grenade shaped device unable to find a button or trigger as I got more annoyed I found myself staring closer at the device, it did not seem to have an exit point for the spray, suddenly I had twisted the top and a button flicked up which in my excitement I jammed my thumb on, whoosh a powerful jet, the essence of Joshua filled my lungs, nose and eyes, clearly the same substance used in a riot. Hence the title of the blog and apologies for digressing but this is a warning that like the great boxer who endorses this spray it can knock you off your feet.

We were soon fed and watered by our wonderful host and being delivered to our next venue, due to the cold temperatures and high-water levels Nick had decided to fish a tiny back water that joins the canal from a nearby lake. The little spot could throw up several species and Nick who had put himself under a bit of pressure to help me with this challenge really hoped it would come good. We approached the swim and I noticed a sign floating in the canal, it read "No fishing on this side", reminding me of the sign in the film Jurassic Park, "This way to the dock" and that sign swiveled in a number of directions.

This sign could have floated from the other side or from further up the canal, so I wasn't sure if we were pushing boundaries or not. We arrived at the spot and I'm sure they filmed the Swamp Beast at this bayou like location, the rain was pouring, and the small body of water appeared devoid of life, well accept the odd Gator. We had walked past many lovely comfy looking swims to get to this jungle but at times like this you must go with the guide's advice and we got the rods in the water like we were told.

Chris suddenly exclaimed "Gudgeon on "as he swung in the first shimmering little fish which was indeed a gudgeon. I was then into a fish which headed for the snags great fun on a whip and I soon landed species 10 a small Chub what a start. I added another Chub straight away and then a Perch before finally getting my first of many Gudgeon. I swapped tactics to the quiver tip and swim feeder to try for something bigger. It wasn't long before the rod tip bounced and swung round, I played and landed another different species in the shape of the Bronze Bream incredible from this little patch of water. Chris was next with a fish on the quiver tip landing his first ever Chub again not huge but great fun on the light tackle and in difficult conditions. I switched back to the whip in an effort to target a Roach and by regularly feeding maggots I was soon getting quick bites that were really hard to strike. Finally, my reactions caught up with one of these lightning bites and finally a Roach made an appearance, fantastic species fishing. I should say that this little spot appeared to have been used recently by a bunch of toe rags leaving litter and beer cans everywhere, Nick bagged this all up and disposed of it, a true angler!

We continued catching Perch and Gudgeon, but no further Roach or Chub appeared, I tried a Pike rod just in case a predator had moved in but that was it for the day. We were off to the pub to celebrate a fantastic day of light tackle fishing in a little backwater that could easily be ignored, Nicks experience gifted us that day without a doubt. Nick had a final treat for us on that damp but great day to visit a local hostelry to see the big Eel over the fireplace, I love my eels, so I was genuinely excited to see this eel. We entered the bar which you could hardly fit one man and a guitar in, only to find a man with a guitar sat there, however directly above the scruffy haired musician hung a huge eel in a case. I say eel as I can only assume it was once an eel but had sadly died and been stuffed with Duplo bricks as the eel was contorted as if fed through a mangle then bleached. Such a shame and I would class the poor beast of more of a zombie eel than any resemblance of a real eel.

We finished our pints just as Bustin Jeber started his set, photographer Chris jumped up stating "vocals mate, don't worry I'm a sound engineer", he then proceeded to fiddle with the guys sound mixer before claiming it was now sorted. We left the pub prior to the start of the act and I had visions of a massive squealing feedback disaster occurring for the poor lad, of course I could be wrong, and Chris could indeed be the sound man's version of Robin Hood going from pub to pub taking from the talented and giving to the tone deaf. So back to Nicks for the final night, Chinese takeaway, cider and maybe another pond raid!

It had indeed turned into another pond raid and the Pen Rod once again doing the business as I managed to stalk one of the elusive Goldfish and persuade it to eat the pink maggot. So, there it was species number 14 what a great weekend. The next day we had a few hours before I was meeting my daughter for lunch in Bristol and Nick took us to a tributary off the River Severn that could produce Pike, Bleak and Dace so we headed off with a fair bit of confidence.

That was the plan and there was still a lot of water pushing through the river which in fact is normally a 2m wide stream, despite a few hours effort it was a session to far and nothing showed. Time had sadly come to end on what had been a fantastic weekend and I was itching to catchup with my little girl, so we packed up happy and planning our return in the summer for a few other species. We cannot thank Nick enough a truly wonderful host and dear friend whose company I enjoy immensely. Thank you so much mate from us but more importantly from the Stroke Association who you have helped immensely this weekend, p.s don't put my Nash Hoodie on and eat onions! Cheers Chris for the usual and for any frustrated musicians you may help or hinder over the course of this challenge. Thanks to my wonderful wife who let me go off for the weekend chasing minnows. I wish a speedy recovery to all effected by or suffering from a Stroke including the family's involved.

# Chapter 7 Spur of the moment!

It's not really time for another blog but a Spur of the moment chance to get on a trip after Spurdog came up, having had 3 similar trips already cancelled this year I jumped at the chance. The window in the weather was only for a day so I was delighted to hear from John the skipper that the trip was on. Chris wanted to get his first Spur and offered to drive which was perfect after my drive over the weekend.

The morning arrived, and the phone alarm started its welcome to the morning soothing tune rising in volume the more it was ignored, why is it that the alarm tune you choose sounds great the night before you get up. It was 5.15am and still pitch black, I once again forced the dog to get up and come for a walk, the cars all sparkled in their cloaks of frost and a super bright full moon surely meant a big tide. The drive to Ilfracombe was a tad dicey with a few large patches of ice waiting for the unwary, however we arrived by 07.15 and kitted up for a day afloat. We stepped aboard John Barbery's Ilfracombe based charter boat Bluefin and exchanged pleasantries with the rest of the anglers on board, John swung the boat to face the sea and as the sun rose we headed out into the channel.

There were 7 anglers on board including Chris and I and it was great to meet up with Pete Gregory for the first time this year, we have a few trips chasing different species this year.

Pete suffers from the same affliction as I with respect to being blind as bats without our reading glasses and at one point while we found our lines tangled neither of us could see to untangle the mess and called 70-year-old skipper John to be our eyes. Pete genuinely left his reading glasses in his van by accident, I however am still in denial and purposely forget mine, this getting old is starting to affect my fishing, I might soon need size 6/0 hooks to nylon! A couple of half decent Bullhuss made an appearance to the other guys rods and when my rod signaled a good bite I assumed another species would be added to the list, it was indeed a Bullhuss but far from decent, however it still ticked the box, so a quick photo was taken.

Once the tide started to ease we were able to steam out towards the Welsh coast and try and find a Spurdog or two, the weather was chilly but still a glorious day. The new mark still had a fair tide running and our 1lb leads were off to Milford Haven, so we moved up to 2lb leads and were then at least able to keep the leads on the bottom. Congers and Huss started appearing, but still no Spurs this was worrying I only needed one, I changed the bait to a whole whiting and this was taken instantly by a feisty Conger which used the tide to give the impression it was possibly a Spurdog, very sneaky.

John then rustled up one of his infamous hot drinks in rather fetching festive cups, the bright patterns however did not cover the fact that the drinks were awful. I am sure John uses seawater to make his non-descript beverages and maybe someone cynical could say he makes them awful, so you don't ask for another.

Finally, the first Spurdog arrived to one of the guys but no pack attack followed, a bit strange for a voracious pack fish, the Congers however were on fire and I had a couple more in quick succession as did Chris. Photographer Chris had moved to the other side of the boat, he said it was as there was more room, but I think he was fed up of me saying " Chris can you take a picture of this", it's difficult when you're trying to fish yourself, so I wouldn't have blamed him. I decided to change my bait to a Mackerel head and lengthened the trace, the difference was instant with the rod bouncing sharply as the lead reached the seabed. I struck as the fish headed uptide I was sure it was a Spur as the fight is different from that of the Conger, after a few good dives the fish broke the surface a huge Spurdog that I thought could be a new personal best. John seeing the size quickly grabbed the net and scooped my armor-plated fish up and into the boat. We put the fish in the sling and she weighed an incredible 19lb beating my best by 2lb, I was over the moon and the added bonus was this was species 16.

The tide was now at slack water and the eels were really starting to feed unlike the pesky Spurdogs, Andrew Atkinson had a couple of beauty's the best going 40lb see below, some great eeling today. Pete stood next to me was getting plenty of Huss but as soon as they saw his face they seemed to spit out the bait and dive back to the comfort of Davey Jones and his locker. This is a bit of a trait with this species and I think we all suffered from the Huss dropping the bait when they got to the surface and I don't think Pete was to blame for all of them.

The tide was once again streaming away and the 2lb anchors were once again attached to the rigs, not the best thing when your using 12lb to 20lb test tackle. John pointed out we were going to move back inshore in 10 minutes as the tide would be too strong to stay any longer, Chris could hear the fat lady starting to sing when he had a violent bite. Sure, enough a Spurdog had decided to reward his perseverance by making an appearance, he was delighted and once again fishing gave out another one of its rewards.

We moved to the new mark, the tide strength was much lower close to the North Devon cliffs and we were once again able to drop down the size of the leads. This inshore mark was also full of eels and I landed 5 in a row before picking up another Spurdog, Pete managed a couple of spurs from this mark before the weather closed in and it was time to head in. It had been a fantastic if not somewhat opportune day and once again John on Bluefin delivered a fantastic days fishing and the festive coffee cups were something new. We set out today with the hope of getting a Spurdog, me for my challenge list and Chris for his first ever, so it was job done and what a bonus the big spur was. It wasn't only the Huss that didn't seem to like the look of Pete, as on our journey to the harbor gulls dropped a crab leg and a large hermit crab shell from the sky narrowly missing Pete's head.

Thanks to the boat crew today, great banter and help, I hope to fish with you all again aboard Bluefin fairly soon.

Chapter 8 Rock Lobster

Tricky to follow on from that new personal best Spurdog in the week but not every trip is going to produce monsters, this time the plan was to take it down a notch and try for some of our smallest sea fish, Lenny the Blenny and Toby the Goby. Most people have run into this pair of guys as children while out dipping nets in rock pools, it's these bad boys that dart off as you approach but secretly they control the tidal ponds with a voracious appetite and an equally aggressive manner to outsiders.

I need both the Goby and the Blenny for my challenge and there are a several species of both none of them growing very large so butt pads and harnesses were not required. This expedition was one for the pen rods coupled with size 18 hooks and maggots, a floating bead acted as my indicator. We chose a North Cornwall beach mark based on the fact that Chris had caught some type of small fish from a rock pool at this spot when he was 9, on hindsight maybe some more up to date info could have been an advantage.

So, we arrived at the beach with the tide falling for a further 2 hours, this is the safest way knowing that you are not going be cut off and providing you stick to these times. The weather conditions were bright and sunny but with a bitter North Easterly wind, it was time to cover all exposed skin.

The beach was nice and easy to traverse, so too was the broken stones punctuated by the odd seaweed covered boulder, the weed covered rocks however were lethal like green ice. I think it was about the third group of rocks that had me on my backside with a crash, although the abundant seaweed acted like a slimy airbag cushioning my fall if not my dignity. Chris not far behind asked "is it slippery mate"? My curt reply was "no mate I was just checking I could still get my feet above my head at short notice"!

It should at this point be pointed out as an issue of safety, don't go climbing over slippery rocks unless accompanied by a responsible adult. I had made the mistake of taking someone who after witnessing a painful slip would first use his phone to film the incident to claim £250 from Harry Hill. Luckily no damage was done, and we yomped onwards looking for the honey hole, the perfect lair of the rock pool mafia.

Despite searching dozens of likely looking pools and dropping a variety of tasty morsels into them not so much as an anemone moved, I know now that the winter rock pools contain the same as Chris's tacklebox, nothing but saltwater. So, it was now heading towards the afternoon and I needed a plan B and C, plan B was simple create something in the sand to make it worth travelling to the beach for, there really was only one option "Rock Lobster"! While Chris became smaller and smaller disappearing amongst the moonlike surface of the foreshore I started a mini construction project, creating my very own Rock Lobster a tribute to one of my favorite bands the B52s or in this case B-fishty 2s.

Once I had got that act of total frustration out of my system Chris arrived and after scratching his head for a bit and looking at my creation he enquired had I caught anything, "no mate but I did make a Rock Lobster"! I knew the B52s really weren't Chris's genre, but I could tell he thought I had made better use of the last 30 minutes than he had. So, I broke plan C to him which involved straddling the weed and rock obstacle course back to the car and heading to the lakes to try and catch a few Rudd to save the day. I was confident in getting a few Rudd fairly quickly and I hadn't had one for my challenge yet so that's where we headed. It didn't seem long, and we were on the top lake scattering handfuls of maggots across the surface in the hope to attract a shoal of the plentiful little fish. The small float darted under and the first Rudd saved the day, and also became my species number 17, within an hour I landed a net full of the greedy little tykes. Chris was having the same results but added a Skimmer Bream to his own list.

We only planned a short day as we were going to fish around the last 2 hours of the ebb tide so before we knew it the afternoon was over. We still had a great few hours by saltwater and fresh, and at the very least it beats sitting in front of the box, I also learned some important lessons. Goby's and Blenny's don't live in rock pools all the time, you're never too old to play in the sand, a clump of seaweed may not protect your rump as much as you had hoped it would and finally it's never over till it's over!

## Chapter 9 A little Ray of Sunshine

The weather has been playing havoc with boat and shore anglers alike, I've had several boat trips cancelled this year and also a few guided shore fishing trips with top Bristol Channel guide Jansen Teakle. It was actually last autumn that we set a date to try for Conger and Huss and that was cancelled as the weather kicked off, the next trip was to be Thornback Rays and the weather put the kibosh on that one. So, it was great to finally get the news that a good tide and weather were in unison giving us the conditions we needed to go and search for a Thornback Ray.

The Bristol Channel with its chocca mocca frothy water is perfect for the Thornback Ray who love to roam the mud flats in search of their favorite food, shoals of frozen Bluey's. The Bluey better known as the Pacific Saury is an oily fish found in the freezers of most tackle shops and the high oil content helps the Rays locate the bait in the most colored of channel water. Having messaged Jansen, I knew he would be bringing the bait, so I didn't have the embarrassment of asking the shop if they had any Bluey's under the counter! The day arrived, and it was once again an early start as I was to meet Jansen in our special place, under the clock tower and he would be wearing a pink carnation in his salopettes to help recognize him.

I left home at 5.45 and there was a southerly wind already building something I discovered when I unhooked the frost protection screen from the windscreen as it blew down the road.

The frost protection screen was another one of my dear wife's magic bean moments whereby she has been sold something we will neither need or use, a thin piece of shiny plastic like that found at Roswell New Mexico with frost deflecting organozomes. She very kindly fixed it to the windscreen the previous night to deflect the frost particles but with no frost and a strong wind that it definitely does not deflect, I now found myself chasing it like an escaped dog and all at 5am. Once it was caught and stored I was on my way still somewhat perturbed by the fact that my wife bought not only one but two of the darn things, time for some Paloma Faith and chill for the rest of the drive.

I arrived in plenty of time and stepping outside the bitter wind hinted at a degree of easterly, hopefully this would swing Southwesterly as the morning progressed. I dressed for the cold, bought my parking ticket and started the assent to base camp, a few steps up the hill and a luminous lycra clad runner emerged from the gloom and I pulled in to let him pass. His face looked like he was going to explode bright red with steam rising from his soaked mop of hair "morning" I said, " yes good morning off fishing"? I thought I might reply with "no just fly tipping" but he rapidly disappeared. I struggled onwards when the same crazy fool came back down towards me, "morning" I said, no response that time. This continued happening all the way to the summit and I even asked if he wanted to carry my rucksack on the next pass he made, and people think our sport is mad! The summit was reached, and I dropped the kit and looked back across the beach as the light grew stronger, yellow streaks from behind the clouds reflected on the expanse of sand below, stunning start to the day.

The view from the other side of mount Jansen was not only less stunning but lacking the main ingredient, water! The Bristol Channel mud was clearly visible, and I know rays only need a few inches of water to move around in but even they would struggle in that, the Bristol Channel however can fill and recede with lightning speed. The strength and speed of the tides are one of the main reasons I use the services of Jansen, an experienced angler with many hours spent learning the ways of this infamous body of water.

I marched towards the meeting point and could see Jansen had just arrived, it was now I realized what a rugged handsome chap Jansen actually was, having only ever met him in the dark on previous expeditions. Clearly healthy and fit Jansen reminded me of myself 18 months ago, when I say months I actually mean years obviously, we are only as old as we feel but this walk always makes me feel old. So, with re-introductions made we yomped the downhill section and discussed the tactics, Jansen was confident as the fishing conditions were good and no doubt would improve further with the arrival of the water. By the time the rods were setup the water was charging up the beach to our right and so the first casts were made with the hooks loaded with the bait of choice.

I started getting a few rattling bites that we put down to small Whiting and sure enough one of the small critters manage to hook itself, nice to see fish feeding but that isn't what I'm after.

It was a fair while before the first proper bite but when it came it was unmistakable with the line going instantly slack as the Ray swam off downtide. I wound down until I felt resistance then kited the fish towards where Jansen had done his mountain goat descent to meet the fish. It wasn't a monster but as far as my challenge goes its species 18 and I was really happy to get the Thornback Ray, I'm a real fan of rays and hope I can get several different species of them during this challenge. The photos were taken, and Jansen climbed back down the rocks to release the ray back to the sea, nice to see it waving its wings at us as it slid down beneath the waves although Rays don't have fingers, so it might have been a bit ruder than a wave!

Time to re-bait the rod and I noticed Jansen was keen for me to do the baits, so I was involved and doing them in the sizes I wanted them, of course it could also be that now it had thawed out it was considerably messier, surely not. So, baits all done, and we were fishing again, it wasn't long before the next bluey bait got scoffed by a Ray and this one came up on the surface a long way out so no surprise at what it was. It was another male Thornback and a quick picture before sending Jansen down the rocks for the release, much easier in the daylight, and with a man servant.

It was a bit of a wait before the next ray made an appearance and we tried a few different things to instigate bites, casting further out, bigger baits, chanting and eventually I had another enquiry.

This turned into the third Thornback of the session and Jansen unhooked it at the water and released the Ray to grow bigger. It wasn't too long to wait for another bite and Thornback number 4 was safely landed and it was another male fish, another picture and this time I asked if I could climb down and return the Ray to the sea.

Jansen looked a little bit concerned by my request but seeing the excitement on my little face he conceded. He pointed out the safest route down to the water and in normal conditions with the correct footwear I would have breezed it. However, I had forgot my walking boots and so had to do with what I had in the car, my muck boots, waterproof but smooth soled. I held the Ray carefully with one hand and gingerly climbed from rock to rock, Jansen urging me to turn for a quick snap of me putting a bit of effort to return the prize. My right foot slid away causing the left to give way, I landed with a crunch on my thigh but like a glass of wine the Ray was held aloft and protected. "Ouch that hurt" I yelled, Jansen inquired to my wellbeing while secretly checking he still had the signed accident waiver tucked in his pocket.

This was two weeks in a row I had ended up on my backside, appropriate footwear is essential, note to myself! The Ray seemed amused by my predicament flapping its wings during the fall as if to reduce the velocity of the impact. It's a shame those wings weren't considerably bigger as it might well have had an effect then.

While lying on my back looking up at the sky, I noticed the Ray which was I was now holding directly above me had a droplet of slime forming at the corner of its mouth and with every passing second the droplet grew. My body was still in self diagnostic mode and not quite ready to trust my legs, but this was now a race against time, I had to escape the impending mucus before it reached me. With only seconds to spare and with a thin trail of slime now descending towards me like a glass blowers bottle. In a split second I rolled sideways and jumped to my feet while pushing the Ray away. Disaster avoided I can't begin to imagine having to deal with that gunk in my mouth. The remainder of the descent seaward went largely to plan and despite the Rays best effort to make me ingest toxic Ray slime I still released him carefully. The tide was ebbing rapidly as the session was coming to an end everything had gone eerily quiet on the fish front, it was looking like 4 rays was going to be the final tally and that's a great day session and mission accomplished as far as the fishtytwo challenge was concerned but as an angler I secretly wanted just one more. Looking across the channel I could see the sun shining brightly over in Wales and I realized just how close we were to the welsh coastline.

A small finger of sun crept from the welsh side and touched the water a little ray of hope and sure enough as I wound in the final rod to pack up a last and 5th Thornback was attached, great way to end a fantastic days fishing with a truly inspirational guy, I learned a lot, caught several and we both got home safely.

Jansen runs the guiding service The Gambling Angler and I can't recommend him highly enough. Out again on Saturday after species 19 with a bit of luck, if not I'm sure there will be a tale or two.

*Above one of stunning Thornback Rays, Jansen helped me to catch.*

# Chapter 10 Raining, Cats and Dogs

You can't predict the weather and when Chris and I planned this weekend's trip we needed to purchase tickets in advance, so come the day of the trip it was obviously forecast for heavy rain and strong winds. Getting used to these 5am fishing starts as is the dog, and now I only have to drag him for the first 100yds. The venue for this weekend's sortie was Tiverton Canal a 12-mile local canal fairly shallow and allegedly full of jack pike, these being the target species. Having never visited this canal before we opted for a mobile approach, with a float fished dead bait and light lure rod to fish small jelly grubs. During the week I done as much research as possible and looked at the various bridges via google which allowed a glimpse of these sections of canal. The intended fishing areas were marked on a plan of the canal which hopefully will also come in useful for the summer Tenching trips.

Chris arrived in the pope mobile as a fine drizzle started only visible in the headlights of the vehicle, I knew this was the driest that the day would be. We had taken a light roaming approach to packing the kit and I had a rucksack, net and the two rods, plus some heavy duty waterproof clothing to keep out the forecast monsoon. Within the hour we pulled into the first chosen areas car park and set about rigging the rods and layering up the clothing, a raft of ducks quacked angrily as they drifted past us in the emerging dawn. The canal looked good and a few quick casts highlighted just how weedy this waterway really is, it was still too dark to see into the water but with every second the light grew.

We leapfrogged each other down the canal to cover as many areas as possible but please don't think we actually played leapfrog as that would have been dangerous in the low light and just plain wrong. This first area seemed perfect for a pike or two but after the first hour it was decidedly quiet, I changed lures and bait frequently in order to try and find a fish hopefully before the heavy rain started. I scaled everything down just in case the fish were being decidedly picky and finally a small red and white grub instigated some interest as a pike swirled just under the lure, as I lifted it out of the water, " darn it I've missed one Chris"! Not sure if he was interested in hearing that bit of news or not, but just in case that was the highlight of the day I wanted it registered with another human. I checked the hook to ensure it wasn't blunt and re-covered the same section of water, this time a Pike grabbed it instantly, well I say Pike maybe I should call it a Pikelet as it really was incredibly small. It was so small that when Chris looked over he thought I had just put a bigger lure on, "trying something new"? Chris had asked "no mate this is actually the first Pike of the day, and incredibly species number 19"!

This might not be the best advert for the great predator *Esox Lucius* but very reminiscent of the baby crocodiles it was still armed with razor sharp teeth and the attitude of a hunter. The rain started becoming heavy and the wind not wanting to be outdone raised its game and blew wildly, I pushed on down the canal looking for the Pikelets father's mother. The next leapfrog Chris made he informed me he had one drop off while trying to hand it out of the water, at least we were finding a few fish now.

The weather was fast becoming darn annoying and at one point I thought Chris had decided to warm himself up by fishing directly below the electric power lines, fortunately he only has a small rod.

We covered about 2 miles of this section of canal and both lost another fish a piece but the area we now found ourselves just didn't seen pikey, the section had recently been worked on with much of the removed weed now adorning the bank edges. The water was crystal clear and the bottom clean not a great habitat for an ambush predator, we decided to go back to the car and move to spot 5 miles further along the canal. We arrived at the next area and it wasn't until I went to put the waterproofs on that I realized just how wet we had got, the coat now weighed twice as much as it did. There's also something sole destroying about climbing into waterproofs that have exceeded their saturation level, I would be lying if I didn't think at this point I will take that little pike as a result and run. However, angler's love a bit of self-abuse in pursuit of something in a bigger size and besides Chris hadn't landed one so we had to soldier on for a least a bit longer. This sentiment was short lived when Chris stated he was swapping to hat number two, having worn a flat cap all morning he now placed a cowboy hat on his head, being neither from the north or a cowboy I felt I had to interject. We started walking towards the next section of canal and I couldn't contain it anymore, "do you know what I'd love to put in room 101"? Chris seemed confused with the random context of my statement "no I don't go on"!

I gestured towards his head " people who wear cowboy hats, that aren't actually cowboys" Chris was clearly not expecting that topic to be raised but still managed a reply " well a lot of people consider I'm a cowboy". He had a point, so I said no more and trudged onwards protected by the ever-growing sponge bob square coat on my back, the rain was now cold and wet as opposed to just wet. This section of the canal had some cracking looking spots and once again we whipped the water to a foam with our frenzied repeated casting.

In the distance a woman's voice bellowed "Ziggy no"! I glanced down the canal, but a bend prevented me seeing the lady in question but once again the woman shouted this time with more urgency" Ziggy no"! The only Ziggy I know owns Anglers Paradise and he doesn't strike me as the type of person to be running amok on a canal towpath that is of course unless he was sat on a big game boat steaming down the canal with a glass of homemade wine in his hand! The culprit soon became obvious as a large black dog dove into the canal a few yards down from where Chris had just cast his lure, "Ziggy no, please Ziggy no", screamed the perturbed women. The dog carried on oblivious to her frantic requests for obedience as it searched excitedly in the area it observed the splash, Chris had retrieved the line out of harm's way, but Labrador Ziggy carried on regardless. Eventually the dog tired of this game and climbed from the water the lady thinking the dog had heeded her instructions went forward to attach him to a leash.

Ziggy had other ideas and bolted up the path towards me, the owner once again running behind "Ziggy no"! Part of me thought maybe the dog was actually called Ziggy No, it was something amusing on a dreary day and now the dog included me in his act of defiance. He bounded straight towards me, soaked, sweaty, overweight and slobbering but that's enough about me. I braced for impact as the inbound Ziggy seemed focused on knocking me into the canal, at the last second, he swerved and instantly stuck his head into my cool bag. "Ziggy no" I yelled, but too late he had grabbed a prize and was off along the towpath to consume it, what tasty item did the super intelligent Ziggy steal, Rudd, Mackerel or maybe a section of lamprey? The clearly out of breath owner had managed to pounce on the dopey hound as he lay mouthing the contraband, she removed it from him and passed it to me, my spool of bait elastic, clever dog that one!

That turned out to be the highlight of that section of the canal and our lures received no attention from any pike and it was time for a final move to the end of the canal. We pulled into the last carpark as the driving rain signaled it was going to get seriously wet, this final push really was under duress with neither of us wanting to signal time and go home and get warm. This area of the canal was the deepest we had witnessed and did look really good, on another day I would start here and work back but today at this time, stood drenched, cold and underwhelmed I struggled to re-bait the rod with fingers that refused to work. I stood staring at the motionless float while all the time feeling new areas that the water had penetrated my clothing and in my heart of heart I now knew the rain had reached my pants, time to go!

I then noticed a large cat mincing towards me down the path, I find cats arrogant at the best of times, but this was the first cat that has ever smirked at me. It quite literally came over to my landing net, looked into it, sniffed it and walked off smirking and in one expression it had summed up my day, no fish been in that net mate!

That really was enough for me and it had felt a long and torturous day for extremely slim pickings, a day of rain, cats and dogs but no matter how small that fish was it is still number 19 so from that perspective it's a job done.

Well done Chris for getting a soaking with me and for heeding my room 101 warning and removing the Cowboy hat at the last venue, hopefully next week's effort will be drier, warmer and a tad more productive. If I take into account the tickets, bait, fuel and parking the little pike was worth about £50 per pound so a valuable little guy, be nice to meet it again when it's all grown up. Thanks everyone who reads, likes and offers support to me on this challenge it really is appreciated.

# Chapter 11 The Cod, the Bread and the Ugly

Here we are again it's time for this week's blog and this time is going be a double one as next weekend I am banned from not only fishing but even talking about fishing will be taboo, it's the wife's special birthday and her foot is firmly down. The first part of this week's challenge was an opportunity to get back up the Bristol Channel heading out from Watchet aboard Reel Deal Charters. This trip had actually been booked for the 1st Jan and was meant to be the very start of my 52-week challenge, the weather has conspired on a number of occasions since. When I saw skipper, Dan Hawkins had posted spaces for a Friday Cod sortie, in one of these rare weather windows I put our names straight down.

The weather remained settled as predicted and once again a hard frost greeted the dog and I when I opened the porch door, luckily the frost protection device was on the screen! I loaded the kit in the car and went to remove the screen protector, unfortunately a heavy shower of rain had fallen during the night soaking the material and causing it to freeze to the screen. I started the engine and after a bit of pulling I managed to rip the screen protector free from the screen, it did leave a fair bit of the material still attached, glad my wife had bought two. Chris was waiting out on the side of the road like a great pile of refuse, with his assorted mish mash of bags and containers, I think I will refer to him as bag boy during this adventure.

The anthem for our 80-mile journey was a blast from the past, quite literally, Jeff Wayne's War of the Worlds, what a classic album this really is and both bag boy and I imagined ourselves as brave souls heading out for codling onboard the Bristol channels very own Thunder Child!

We arrived safe and sound despite the Martians, at Watchet Marina and this was another venue I've never fished which is another one of the positives of doing this species challenge, I'm getting to try new methods from new areas. Despite being by the coast it was - 0.1 but other than the chill in the air it looked like a stunning morning, blue skies, and chocolate water the Bristol Channel looking truly radiant. We managed to get the marina code from another angler and carefully negotiated the frosty steps down to the pontoons, a short walk and we were welcomed aboard the borrowed dive boat Obsession 2. This boat was on loan for the winter period while skipper Dan's new purpose-built Reel Deal 3 was being built, although a dive boat, Obsession 2 was more than adequate for angling with plenty of room on board.

Skipper Dan Hawkins quickly introduced himself and stated that I had put him under a bit of pressure today with my challenge being for such a good cause, he went on to ask, "how big a Cod do you need"? That was simple "any size Dan, I don't care if it's only 6 inches long it's all about the species", Dan replied "that's good you might get one like that today".

I had heard good things about Dan and in one instance while fishing from Pembrokeshire a group of very loud welsh anglers had claimed he was the best skipper they had ever been out with, furthermore they are happy to travel from wales to north Devon to fish with him. Straight away I knew he was exactly what it said on the tin, the fact that he was determined to help me get a Cod of any size was proof enough.

He also enquired what else I needed that may be possible and straight away it had to be the Spotted Ray, Dan stated that they had been coming out to fish baits. Typical I had done mini Sandeel and Squid wraps for the Spotty's but didn't bring fish, Dan pointed to the café on the harbor and stated that they sell mackerel. Bag Boy kindly offered to go and grab a pack of their finest Mackerel fillets, really annoying when we both have freezers full.

While I started tackling up on the boat more characters started emerging and not wishing to sound derogatory it really reminded me of the scene from the Pirates of the Caribbean where Davey Jones's ship The Flying Dutchman rose from the sea and her crew spawned from the ships structure all covered in seaweed and barnacles! This group of elderly gentlemen appeared from various parts of the boat to introduce themselves and clearly, they were a smashing bunch of friends and regulars aboard Dan's trips. It didn't seem very long before the banter and abuse started, and I wondered if their lack of teeth was the result of banter gone bad, I doubt if they had a full set of teeth between them.

It was about this time my phone started ringing and I chose to ignore it, I was fishing what could be more important, it began ringing again. I removed the phone from my pocket and checked the screen, 2 missed calls from Bag Boy, I glanced towards the quayside café but couldn't see him, he must be wanting to know if I want fillets or whole mackerel bait, I decided to leave it to him.

We were waiting in the marina for quite some time and I was wondering if my compatriot had maybe fallen in or even worse might be having a full English. Eventually he arrived with a soggy bag of the oldest mackerel fillets I've ever seen, clearly, they had mistaken bag boy for a harbor side crab lining tourist. "Why didn't you answer your phone" enquired bag boy," didn't hear it mate, why what was the problem"? "I was shut out of the gate and couldn't remember the code", oops how bad did I feel. I quickly changed the subject "what the hell is that", I gestured to the bag of warm fillets. " a long long time ago they were Mackerel but if it gets you a Spotted Ray it would be worth it don't you think"! He had a point and I'd rather have a bad bit of Mackerel than no Mackerel, but I really felt that Crabs wouldn't touch it.

We carefully negotiated the Harbor gates which is quite a maze and something different to see on the way out to sea, I quickly fired off some pictures much to the amazement of the Dutchman's crew.

Once out of the harbor we headed off towards Minehead and hopefully a few Codling, I opened my bait box proudly revealing my Lugworm and Squid pre-prepared wraps, the old fella next to me chuckled as he threaded small lugworm onto a rig of multiple tiny hooks. I quickly gazed around at the rest of Bristol channel diehards and sure enough the same rigs hung from their rods like a myriad of Christmas decorations, I looked over to Bag Boy who was tying his 6/0 pennel rig, " mate think we might be going too big with the rigs". He also surveyed the boat and came to the same conclusion, we changed our hooks down to a more sensible 1/0 on a pulley rig.

Dan appeared and advised to take off the pulley and use a zip slider which he passed to me, he added "keep the trace really short while the tide is running so the bait stays nailed to the bottom". This is what makes a great skipper ensuring their anglers have the best chance to catch and not just leaving you to find out the hard way, if you ignore this type of advice more fool you!

The sea was lovely and flat, I knew bag boy wouldn't be needing an extra bag today and to be fair I think he has got the sea sickness thing sorted, it was definitely worth him soldiering on through the early chunder episodes. The day really was glorious and its days like this that just being out on the sea is reward enough, the sea air fills your lungs as the boat rises and falls, edging ever closer to the anticipation filled fishing mark.

The skipper swung Obsession 2 into the tide and released the chunk of iron that would be our umbilical for the next few hours, fishing the channel allows you to still feel part of the landscape as you're never really far from land. Today was no exception and the white tent like towers of Butlins glistened in the winter sunlight, I couldn't help but feel they didn't really fit in with the rest of the stunning Somerset coastline. The boat settled into her position and a flurry of casts sent the baits shooting off in all directions like the legs of a spider.

This is the first time I have set out to uptide and I am extremely impressed with the system, I will be investing in an uptide rod in preparation for next autumn. The basic idea is to cast a gripper lead out from the boat higher up the tide, as the lead lands line is paid out to allow the wires on the lead to dig into the mud, the line in effect has a large bow in it. When a fish picks up the bait the lead is pulled out of the mud and the rod indicates a slack line bite, the fish is normally hooked at this point but retrieving the slack line rapidly is the priority. The channel is shallow and the tides strong without the use of uptiding, fishing would not be as effective and would also lead to the use of heavy leads, uptiding allows a 6oz lead to hold in a strong tide. It wasn't long and angler Paul on the far side reeled in a brace of small Codling, multi hook Mike next to me was next and he pulled in a pair of small Codling. The toothless wonder up the front then shouted he had opened his account with a small Codling, I was surrounded by Codling and anyone of those fish would have made my day.

I reeled in and shortened my trace to less than a foot, changed the bait to a small piece of black lug minus the squid and fired the bait back uptide. Dan appeared with the first of the many cups of welcome steaming hot coffee and enquired how it was going, stating once again "don't worry we will get you one", you can't beat a confident skipper.

I watched the rod tip intensely and noticed a few small rattles, could it be the codling I so desired, the rod tip straightened and rattled again but very slightly. I was sure this was a bite but without the clearly visible slack line I didn't want to take it too early.

The skipper tapped me on the shoulder, "try this, bait all three hooks with worm and stick with it", he had made me a rig what an absolute legend. I baited the hooks with small lugworms and grabbed the rod to retrieve it and change the rig, I could feel something kicking at the other end remembering the earlier suspect bite. As the rig approached the boat I could clearly see my target species heading towards me, I was praying inside" stay on, stay on", and as I swung the fish aboard the crew cheered species 20! It was another of those great moments resulting from a small but significant fish, it may seem crazy that I get so excited over such small fish, I know however that the little fish will achieve big things in this particular challenge. Skipper Dan was clearly delighted and relived to see me land one and Bag Boy stepped up to do a great job of the pictures, small but perfect, future super Cod.

What now, well it was straight on with a Spotted Ray bait, manky fish held together with a strip of Squid and lashings of elastic. The skipper decided to make a move as the tide started to pick up and we soon found ourselves on an area of broken ground, this area also had a better chance of a Ray, so fingers crossed.

Once again small Codling started coming aboard and the rest of the boat were taking part in the Cod competition, so every small fish was measured prior to release. I then noticed a hard rattle on the rod tip and the line slackened off indicating the lead had been freed from its grip, I wound in the slack line rapidly hoping that I had now found the Spotted Ray I was after. I could feel a fish but wasn't convinced it was the fish I was after, however it was spotted, being a Lesser Spotted Dogfish. I swung the fish in and it was quite a good size LSD but with some striking markings I decided to get a new picture for the gallery.

Sadly, Bag Boys rod had been pretty quiet, and he was desperate to get his first ever Cod, frustrating when you see so many around you, he did say he was hanging it out for a big one. This didn't quite pan out as he landed the obligatory dogfish and a whiting with the latter fooling him it was a codling right till the end. The skipper then cooked up bacon rolls for the dentally challenged who had brought the raw ingredients with them, Dan pointed out though how entertaining it was, watching them trying to eat the rolls with so few teeth. He actually stated it was like being at a sawmill with the toothless wonders one front tooth resembling the saw blade, joking aside the frying bacon was demoralizing to those without and my cheese dipper just didn't have the same appeal.

It was however somewhat amusing when the skipper served them the rolls to be told by one, they couldn't eat it as they had a raging toothache, how unlucky to have toothache in your only tooth, soup next trip perhaps!

The fishing really slowed up during the flood tide and despite my best effort for the Ray I only managed another dogfish, there were over 30 small Codling caught and released by a group of very experienced channel anglers. I must say a big thank you to these guys for all their help and support on the day and the great banter they really are a hilarious bunch of guys, god willing I'm still doing what they are doing at that age. Finally, a massive thank you to Dan Hawkins skipper of Reel Deal Charters, you are indeed a top skipper and Dan added a donation to the pot so thanks for that too. Chris and I learned a great deal about fishing the channel today and will be back next autumn a bit wiser, I however will be trying to get out with Dan on one of his Porbeagle trips in April.

The second species targeted this weekend was to be the King Carp and with a little bit of sun forecast the method was to be floating bread crust, my favorite method of stalking Carp. The Carp in Sanctuary lakes respond well to crust and despite the early morning frost I still felt we could raise a few fish. I headed over to the lakes at 11.30 in the morning and arranged to do a few hours fence construction before having a go for the Carp. I arrived at the top lake to see the biggest ugliest Cormorant I've ever seen, like a huge black Heron, I showed it the door, but it probably explains why this lake has been out of sorts lately.

I made a start wiring up the electric fence when Chris arrived, no longer Bag Boy he turned up armed with crusty loaves so today he was to be known as Baguette Boy. We spent a few hours fixing connectors and running wires eventually finishing at the compost toilet, a good few hours work and now half the land has the new fence installed. We stopped for coffee and in baguette boy's case, ginger tea his new favorite drink. The lake then had chunks of bread dropped into key locations and we sat back to fish float fished corn while awaiting the first slurp of a feeding Carp

It didn't seem to be too long before a small carp swirled just under our feet in the thick bed of rushes, this was literally 3 feet from baguette boys float fished corn. Sure, enough this fish dropped down onto the corn and Chris was hooked up on his light tackle, the feisty little common led him all over the place but eventually capitulated and rolled into the net. The little fish was in great condition and was clearly one spawned in the lake being smaller than any we had stocked.

It was time for another hot drink and wait for a sign of a feeding fish, although it was no longer than 20 minutes before another Carp swirled for some bread over on the dam bank, "I'm going have a go for that" I told baguette boy. There now followed about 40 minutes of frustration and missed opportunities as the fish spat out my crust at least 3 times, the water was really clear with visibility of 3 feet meaning they were really flighty.

I cast the bread and let it drift down towards the fish and remained low and still like a scarecrow and as the fish slowly rise to look closer at the bread, your heart beats become deafening in the silent bubble you've have put yourself. Suddenly the vacuum like mouth of the carp sucked in the crust and like a coiled Viper I struck, well more like a coiled Slow Worm. The fish was off across the surface clearly fuming at its lapse in concentration, despite the cold water the fish fought well and reminded me how much I enjoy summer stalking. Chris slid the net under the fish a gorgeous looking Common Carp and species 21, what a lovely fish to hit 21 with, some quick pictures and the fish was returned. I did notice the top of the tail had been taken most likely an old Otter injury that had healed very well, a lucky fish I think.

I told baguette boy I thought there was another fish further down taking crust and as if it heard us, a great swirl emanated from the dam wall once again. " Go get it" I said to Chris and he was off in a shot, however he too suffered the frustration that accompanies early season crusting, the fish swirling and blowing the baits with a take it or leave it attitude. The light was beginning to fade, and the thousands of starlings made it even darker as they headed to roost their squawks and chirps becoming deafening. Then a huge splash as baguette boy connected with a Carp, I grabbed the landing net and headed over to him, a short battle and I slid the net under a lovely winter Mirror Carp not a bad few hours with a couple of baguettes and a few slices of bread, the simplest of rigs, a single hook. Chris was clearly chuffed to get a couple of fish after a gruella the previous day and it was nice to do two completely different styles of angling.

Well that's the two last sessions covered, and I'm delighted to be on species 21, that's probably it for this month although I may have something in the pipeline for the end of the month to knock off another. Thanks again to the boat crew, Dan and Chris and as ever thanks to my wife for the support and if only she liked fishing her birthday would be so much more special.

## Chapter 12 There's fish on deck and he's stuck in the wreck!

March should surely herald the start of spring, but no, not for us here in good old blighty we have a blizzard combined with spring tides, result chaos! The last weekend in Feb and it was my wife's surprise party and her birthday etc, etc the long and short "No Fishing"! That's all fine and dandy and luckily, I had a few species in the bag to act as a buffer so onwards and upwards. Roll on to the start of the month, 1st March 2018 and the white magic begins to fall from the skies. I am referring to the Snow as white magic as it has an incredible ability to make things disappear, firstly people's patience, then their common sense, and finally their will to get to work. The white magic then moves onto transport, with trains, planes and buses all disappearing before our very eyes, finally it targets our foods with milk and bread vanishing from the supermarket shelves.

It seems that every year it takes less and less snow to cause more and more chaos, from my perspective it was the end of the weekends species challenge. I then went on to add a serious cold to my woes and the worse a patient I become the less caring my marital nurse becomes, I clearly remember the "In sickness and in health" bit of our contract even if the "obey" bit has slipped my mind. So, a few weeks had elapsed for all the above reasons and I really needed to get out and catch something, but it also had to be something I hadn't had yet.

Once again, the weather was doing its worst with strong winds and big tides striking the South Devon coastline with enough fury to remove roads and sea defences, the beaches of Slapton and Beesands receiving the brunt of this damage.

Then a little ray of hope, another of those little weather windows that skippers and anglers alike prey for after such a long fishless spell. First of the skippers I follow, to post a trip was Chippy Chapman from Bite Adventures based in Penzance, a simple post stating 6 spaces Wrecking and Sandbanks. This surely meant Pollack and possibly a Ling, both species are on my list, so I messaged straight away asking for a space, once this was secured I then asked my good lady if I was able go, she will say no one day and that will be awkward!

I alerted Chris who was equally frustrated at the lack of any opportunities of late and he also rapidly secured a space, he also offered to drive the pope-mobile which was great in my poorly condition. I advised him of the necessary baits and lures that we should take as he hadn't done much if any wreck fishing. The morning arrived, and it was the now standard 5.15 alarm call to leave at 6am, the weather was calm and even lacked the morning chill so common lately. Chris arrived at 5.59 and once the 7-point turn was completed the clock hit the magic 6.00am, time to hit the road! It was a nice steady drive down and I couldn't help but think that maybe one trip I should sit in the back on a chair, wearing a white gown to really get the full Pope experience, not sure the side windows would stop a rotten tomato let alone an assassin's bullet though!

We pulled up near the harbor side and Chris managed to find the last remaining free space, the reason quickly became apparent as we had a huge pond of water to wade through to get to the boot. It was at this point I realized I had bought the wrong tip for my rod and as I couldn't fish with the 2-foot butt section it was a bit of a disaster. I decided to take the tip less section and reel as I knew Chippy is sponsored by Fin Nor and would have a spare tip, the cost would be a slight bit of ribbing, but I could cope with that. So, we assembled by the steps looking down at the lovely Bite Adventures Charter Boat, holder of the British Catch and release Blue Shark Record and a boat I have enjoyed some great trips on. First mate and newly qualified skipper Kieran Faisey started carrying kit down the steps and before long we were all aboard and grateful to be afloat. Fellow Shark Club member Alex Mckay was also on the trip and it was great to have a catch up with another lover of the Shark.

Bite Adventures twin outboard engines churned the water to foam and thrust us seaward on a glorious sunny day that seemed impossible a few days earlier. The plan was to target a few wrecks for Pollack and as the tide dropped off head inshore for some of the flatfish species on the numerous sandbanks. The sea was flat and the sun warm, the perfect tonic for a group of anglers starved of fishing opportunities and on days like this being out afloat is reward enough, fish are truly a bonus. Chris seemed to be spending a lot of the journey looking thoughtfully out to sea like a scene from a great Hemingway novel, the truth was a little more like an 18 to 30s holiday video with some excessive chundering.

Strange he seems to be affected early on in the day and recover in time for lunch, I'm only glad I've never suffered the affliction as you don't find much sympathy on a boat full of anglers. The engines slowed as we approached the site of the rusting hulk of the ship wreck, now home to an abundance of sea life. As I look at the gently rippling water surface I am reminded of just how incredible the skipper's equipment is in the modern charter world, plotters, sidescan digital sounders and GPS can find these sunken hulks, but only an experienced skipper can interpret the data and position the boat according to the conditions on the day. Tide, temperature, wind and type of species are all fundamental in boat positioning. Fortunately, we were in good hands and soon Chippy shouted for us to drop the lines, the wreck wasn't that deep and soon we were working our various fish imitation lures over the ironwork. Within 20 minutes we knew the wreck was not fishing well and it was time to try another wreck a few miles away, there's no shortage of sunken ships in the sea around the Penzance peninsula.

Within no time we were back fishing another barnacle covered sunken ship, this one was in a bit deeper water, evident as the line rapidly emptied from the spool. A shout from the stern of the boat "fish on" the first Pollack had grabbed the imitation fish and soon a few more made the same mistake. As I counted each turn of my reel handle, I noted at 23 turns a definite pluck on the lure, but this was a chance missed. I dropped the lure again and counted getting to the 20th turn when the lure was grabbed, the fish dived hard for the wreck taking line which is typical of the fighting prowess of the Pollack.

Soon my first fish circled up to the surface virtually exploding out of the water assisted by air pressure. This was fantastic I had managed species 22 fairly quickly in the trip so now it was time for some fishing sport with these hard fighting fish. I took a few pictures and got back into position for the next drift over the wreck, the lure reached the sea bed but there was no time for counting turns as a fish grabbed it instantly and once again a fighting Pollack was slowly brought to the surface. Chris seemed to be battling a real monster as his rod was bent double with line streaming off but as strong as he is there was no way he was pulling in the ship he was now attached too!

His line gave way and his lure was lost, unfortunately this is a risk while fishing these degrading chunks of steel with their twisted rails and crumbling superstructure. The next drift I was into a fish again and Chris was once again fighting the wreck only pausing to clear his stomach, I was starting to think that Neptune takes a dim view of seasickness and he was exacting a high price on Chris today as another lure became part of the ship. I managed to lose a few fish after they spat the hook fairly rapidly but still ended up with several Pollack before the tide started to ease off. Chris was having a nightmare and lost 5 lures to Davey Jones Locker but took comfort in the fact that he had used the ones from my tackle box, and there I was thinking I hadn't lost a thing! With the tide dropping off Chippy suggested I try for a Ling with a bait, I do like fishing for Ling they are like a Conger Eel with morale's no sneaky wrapping their tails around pipes and through portholes.

I decided to use a baited pirk a method I've caught Ling on before, the dangerous thing is the Ling sit tight on the wreck and so the bait needs to be right in there too. Chippy advised me to use a mackerel flapper and Kieran quickly obliged and prepared me a mackerel bait fit for a King, or in this case a Ling. I lowered the baited pirk down into the darkness and once on the bottom I slowly raised the rod tip up and down to imitate a dead chunk of fish pretending to swim. Within seconds the ploy worked as a hungry Ling pounced on the bait, back on the surface this was indicated by the rod suddenly arching downwards. I knew I had my second species of the day and species 23 of the challenge so I played the fish steadily praying it didn't come off on the journey to the surface. The ling appeared on the surface at the same time as the smile on my face, it's great when a plan comes together, strangely we never had any more Ling so good fortune indeed. We now headed in for a bash at the sandbanks and secretly I was hoping for a Weaver fish a toxic spined fish that would be a real bonus for the challenge. Chris was happy with the arrival of the sand fishing as it brought an end to the tackle grabbing wrecks!

The water clarity inshore was pretty poor and both Chippy and Kieran feel it can be the kiss of death for the bait fishing over the banks. This indeed turned out to be the case and the skipper undertook several moves before finding an area with a few fish feeding, with a few Huss, Dogfish and Whiting appearing. Chris suddenly struck a rattling bite as a fish arrived to save a blank and this fish was possibly a personal best being a big Pouting, this species is not popular and other than Conger Eels no one are ever pleased to see them.

It was nice for Chris to get some penance for the tough day he had suffered, and he followed the big pouting up with another for good measure. I made the mistake of saying even a Dogfish would be nice and like magic one appeared to remove a bit of my skin and mess up the rig, still I'd hate to have a sea without them in it. That was it for the trip and it was a great day with the usual banter, several fish including two more species off the list, highlight was the appearance of an 8lb Coalfish to one of the other anglers, a stunning fish. Thanks to Chippy Chapman and Kieran Faisey for all their help and the loan of a rod, look forward to the next trip. Great to fish with the rest of the guys and Alex has promised to take me fishing for Turbot and Seatrout sounds more like fine dining!

The final part of any Penzance trip is a 3-piece variety meal at the local KFC but upon reaching the door a sign greeted us "Limited Menu" so this meant the variety meal had no variety. They managed a few bits of chicken before closing the drive thru and ending the chicken altogether, Kentucky Fried Chips only! Sad times if we cannot get Chicken to Penzance how will we ever get men to Mars.

Mother's Day, so not really appropriate to slope of fishing for a day but that doesn't mean a few hours are out of the question, especially as I made homemade Pasty's for lunch. So, once I had visited my mum and given her the card and standard plant I decided to go somewhere for a couple of hours just to cast a line. It would have to be somewhere where I would have a chance to catch another species but with a falling tide, cold easterly wind and no bait the choices weren't exactly obvious.

The forecast was sunshine and showers with the afternoon looking to improve so a plan was hatched and after speaking with Chris we decided to head down to Torquay for a couple of hours after a Wrasse. The species of Wrasse I was really after was the Ballan Wrasse, a tough rugged master of the kelp a species that broke my line on our last visit to this mark. I picked Chris up at 14.30 and we were in the excellent tackle shop Hookz by 15.30, I asked for a quarter of their finest Ragworm the best bait for the day. They then burst our bubble, stating they had sold out of Rag and Crab and added that the area we were going to fish had been fishing awful and a local competition had been cancelled. So, things were not looking great, but we were determined to give it a go, we bid farewell to the shop assistant and were about to set off when he called us back.

The guy explained he had some Ragworm that was dead and so couldn't be sold but we were welcome to have it if we wanted something that was better than nothing, we gratefully accepted. Now we were in business and we made our way to the rocky mark to try for a Wrasse and lose a bit of tackle.

The sea was extremely colored still and there was a fair swell crashing into the rocks below us as we prepared our rigs. The time was against us a bit, as Wrasse don't seem to feed in the dark, probably due to the fact they are one of the few fish species that actually sleeps. The multitude of Wrasse species is renowned for their striking markings and colors with the males usually the brighter of the sexes, similar to humans then! We both set off using different methods with Chris using a float set up and me using a simple leger rig, nice and cheap to replace, Wrasse tend to have a bolt hole and once encamped you just can't get them out without losing your tackle.

The wind was pretty bitter, and the swell was buffeting the rigs against the rocks, but we fished on with our dead Ragworm and an air of bloody mindlessness. Then I noticed a quick rattle on the rod tip and I picked up the rod to feel any movement through the braid, the fish returned with a far more aggressive bite and I struck and held tight. The Wrasse tried relentlessly to reach the snags littering the sea bed, but I gave no quarter and soon the fish saw sense and was lead steadily to the surface. It is incredible how tough these fish are when giving an account of themselves and it's not until they reach the surface do you realize they are half the size you estimated.

Chris really loves Ballan Wrasse and would quite happily fish exclusively for them, I do have to agree they are one of the most stunning of our inshore species. The fish may have weighed a little under a 1lb but at species 24 it was gratefully received, a few pictures and then the little Rottweiler was safely returned. The Wrasse had some stunning markings and some amazing blue streaks within the fins although the photos just don't do it justice, I had to get a close up of the markings as they are all individual like a fingerprint. Chris then had an enquiry with his rod rattling sharply, but the lead had snagged causing the fish to spit out the hook and make good its escape. The next bite was mine again but this time the wrasse found sanctuary and cut me off, despite the strong kit the habitat these fish reside in is brutal to even the strongest of lines. The bites dried up, but the weather didn't and the sky's opened up depositing sheets of chilled rain into us on this exposed point.

We both felt it was time to knock it on the head, we were getting heavier and heavier with the onset of the rain and the sky looked dark and foreboding, sometimes you know it's time to cut and run. The journey home was dreadful with driving rain and spray and it backed up our decision to leave when we did. The trip had been short and not so sweet, but the target had been achieved largely down to the generosity of Hookz tackle for the free bait but also because we were determined to wet a line. My target of getting to the halfway stage of the challenge by April is well on track but as an angler I know you can't count your chickens until they have hatched and its tough fishing at the moment. Cheers Chris for the photos and sharing the soaking this afternoon, until the next one.

# Chapter 14 Somewhere over the Rainbow, Trout!

Here I am writing the latest of my challenge blogs which was going to have a strong spring is here theme but today its chucking it down with snow again and the War of the Bread has started. Luckily, I had managed a couple of hours the previous day to attempt species 25 to bring me ever closer to the halfway point. The fish I decided upon was the Rainbow Trout and although it's been a while since I got the fly rod out I was confident it would soon all come back to me, especially after I snagged a few trees and snapped some leaders. The time was limited as I only had a half day to spare and although the weather was changeable the showers were set to be light.

The venue I chose was Simpson Valley fishery a complex of lakes not far from our own lakes, the venue is managed by Andrew Moore's and fellow Holsworthy Sea Angling Club member Paul Cozens. I made a quick call to Paul for some advice on which lake to target for the chance of a Rainbow Trout, and to book a space. Paul advised me to try the smaller Trout Lake, Jenny Wren and on this lake during certain times you can use LRF methods which stands for Light Rock Fishing but covers much of today's lighter lure angling. This excited me as I hadn't had a chance to test out my LRF kit yet and the thought of a big trout slamming into a small lure is somewhat appealing. I asked Paul if it was okay to fish the lake catch and release, which it was, and Paul went on to offer the trip free of charge to support the good cause, so many thanks to Simpson Valley Fishery for this.

The kit was packed in the car and the thing with LRF fishing it's extremely compact with only a Rod, Reel, Net and Bag required, I did get the fly rod ready but left it at the last-minute opting to stick with the plan. When I arrived at the lake the sun was shining, and the breeze was fairly light, a fish rose only feet from where I stood signaling maybe a chance of a fish. While I threaded the line through the small rod rings I was reminded how poor my eyes are and although I had capitulated and started bringing glasses I still hadn't gone the whole hog and put them on. Unfortunately, this always leads to missed rings on the threading of the line and much frustration but eventually my stubbornness got the line through and a red and white curly tail was tied to the end of the line. The selection of lures I had chosen for the day were all small and bright and the plan was to start largish and scale down if necessary.

While setting up the kit several more fish had topped, and they seemed to be spread evenly across the lake. Before making the first cast I crushed down the barb to help with the catch and release of any trout hooked, Rainbow Trout are pretty fragile and need to be unhooked quickly. I then worked my way around the lake casting long, short and retrieving fast then slow, I cast onto topping fish and tight to the snags but with not so much as a pluck on the line. It was time for a rethink and with several fish actively feeding there had to be a food source on or close to the surface.

At this point I had a wander without the rod, examining the water margins in several spots and discovered several small insects bouncing around the surface also frogs in the process of spawning. These couple of obvious food sources could be preoccupying the trout and I now had that sinking feeling when you know you should have brought along a bit more kit, in this case the fly rod. Well I needed another plan using the equipment I had with me and it needed to be a little more refined.

I decided that with the brightness of the sun and the frog element I would go with a black and green grub, I trimmed this down to fit nicely with a size 6 barbless carp hook. I then tied a 4lb fluorocarbon leader in the hope of disguising the line in the clear water, and after tying on the modified grub I pinched an AA Split shot to assist with casting. The final part of the cunning plan was to swap from the Fishtytwo winter hat to the summer peaked cap.

With the changes instigated I set off to find a fish and it didn't take me long as a fish rolled 20 yards to my left, I flicked the modified grub in the direction of the dissipating ripples, positioning it perfectly just a foot in front of the fish. The first couple of turns and a bow wave broke the surface as the fish locked on to its prize, sure enough the flimsy LRF rod doubled over as the fish and lure made contact. The surface of the water erupted as the angry trout strived to fling the piece of rubber back to me, no you don't I thought, and I gingerly played the fish to the margins and waiting net.

It shows that by making a few small changes you can really make a difference to your chances but more importantly you cannot beat matching the hatch, find what your target is eating and replicate it. I wouldn't say the cut down grub imitated the prey of the trout, but it was an improvement on everything I had used. I took a few quick pictures of this stunning Rainbow Trout which has got me too species 25 and then ensured it swam off strongly by keeping it upright in the net for a few minutes.

The time had flown by and I had a couple hours left before I had to be home, so I made the decision to leave the Trout and nip back over to our lakes and try for a LRF caught Perch. While driving the few miles over to Sanctuary Lakes the heavens opened up and the black sky deposited hail and driving rain, what a great bit of timing that was. Dodging that hail storm and catching the Rainbow made me think my luck was in and as I pulled up to the lakes it was highlighted further by the stunning pair of Rainbows now glowing in the sky above the lake, a day of rainbows.

This must be an omen I thought and after a quick check of the electric fences I grabbed the LRF rod and set about jigging the little grub along the bottom of the lower lake in the hope of a Perch. Second cast and by a bed of sunken lily's the popular little grub was nailed by a very aggressive fish, not the intended Perch but a feisty little Pike.

The little pike led me a merry dance and while it wallowed in the margin waiting to be scooped in the net another much bigger Pike attempted to steal it narrowly missing the floundering fish. The sudden appearance of this bigger fish made me jump backwards and slip on the greasy grass, fortunately staying attached to the first pike.

Once I regained my composure I was able to scoop the lucky little Pike up and after checking he was unmarked and taking a picture, I released him in another swim out of the sight of the bigger fish. Now I wanted to catch the bigger Pike it would be great to update my charity challenge Pike picture as that was the smallest Pike ever. I didn't fancy using my LRF rod although it would I'm sure handle a good size fish, I opted for a stronger rod and float fished Rudd. Luckily, I keep spare tackle in the lock up at the lakes for just this situation, within 10 minutes I was back fishing with less than an hour to go.

While watching the rod I noticed the abundant frogs swarming in the margins no doubt attracting pike to this area, I took a couple of pictures as there was Frogs spawn and Toads spawn in the same weed bed. Being pre-occupied with the spring watch I almost missed the float moving off slowly to the right, I struck, finding out instantly this was a bigger pike as the Pike erupted out of the water. This would have been fun on the light rod, but I was grateful to have a wire trace and 8lb mono to get the fish subdued with no disasters. The fish was netted first time and the single treble was just in the scissors of the fish and quickly popped out.

The Pike was definitely the same fish that tried to eat its smaller brethren a short time before, it is incredible what a pike will attempt to eat, they are a strike first think later predator. The fish was in great condition and following a check over and few pictures she swam off to terrify some more amphibians. It had been a busy, yet productive half days fishing spread over two venues with a few different methods and I should have returned home happy with species 25 in the bag.

Just before heading for home I received a message from fishing pal Billy informing me of the sudden death of a fishing friend of ours. Des was a similar age to me and fit and healthy and although I am not yet aware of the circumstances of his passing I am shocked and saddened. Death does come to us all but when it's unexpected and of a person with so much life to live it is so much harder to come to terms with. I enjoyed my time fishing with this generous, kind, and thoughtful man, he will be missed immensely by his friends, family, and members of the SACGB, rest in peace Des mate.

## Chapter 15 Something stunning captured!

With only two weekends to go before Easter and my target of hitting the halfway mark, there was a little bit of pressure to try and secure species 26. The period we are in at the moment is a real tricky one with the departure of winter species and the arrival of summer species making it very hit and miss. This is compounded further by my overzealous species catching thus far and maybe if I had paced myself, I would at this period of transition, still have some easier fish choices. So, the plan was to try for some spring / summer species, perhaps a few weeks too early, in the hope that one of them slipped up, after all they are only fish! The year before the Tench fishing at Sanctuary Lakes had started well in early April

Saturday morning was spent taking the old electric fence down from the top lake at Sanctuary Lakes, but only after a little bit of pre-bait was added to the bottom lake to stir up the Tench. My accomplice on this cold drizzly morning was none other than, constant coughing Chris and his bottomless flask of ginger tea. I have formed the opinion that the tea isn't ginger it's in fact rust from the flask and over the last few months it's been slowly poisoning him to the point he is coughing incessantly.

Of course, I wouldn't be much of a friend if I didn't try and ease the pain, so I sent him the opposite way around the lake from me, in the hope as he retreated so did the relentless spluttering!

Despite this week's infliction we got on well with the fence removal and upon returning to the designated storage spot I noted that Chris had neatly coiled his wire into neat spools, dam his anal tendencies. I however had dragged my huge tangled mess to the spot and now felt pressured to do it properly, I remember thinking he can't be that sick if he has time to wrap all that fencing up. Eventually everything was broken down and stacked perfectly like a Supermarket shelf, although my side of the pile was maybe still a tad Lidl-ish.

Time for some Tench fishing, by now however the rain was heavier and the breeze several degrees colder it really couldn't be further from those perfect Tench days. We cast our floats baited with corn and proceeded to relax and enjoy the ambience of the afternoon. Well I say ambience, what I mean is listen to the honking of the Canada Geese, the chugging of the farmers tractor, the booming of shotguns in the wood and to top it all the gurgling death rattle of constant coughing Chris! A combination of good angling, and bad luck in equal measure saw a few ruddy Rudd make an appearance followed by a few Perch to brighten the day.

Chris had to head off as his lad's band, the three-piece known as Quorum had a gig to do at one of the most hi-Tec of our local venues Hatherleigh Community Centre. Unfortunately, there was to be no such glamour for me as I was on a mission and with the departure of Chris I was determined to stay till I got to see a Tench.

Eventually 3 hours later, after sitting stationary, aside from an occasional throw of some corn I spotted a Tench, as a nice fish rolled 20 yards out. Despite the cold and wet I knew if I stuck it out I would get that fish, well that theory was pants and despite staying into dark not so much as a frog moved the float. So that was to be that for the early Tench effort, but it was a tad cold, and I only saw one fish roll, onwards for tomorrows plan of an early Small Eyed Ray.

Sunday was a very different day with the great golden ball in the sky arriving with enough strength to allow the removal of one of the layers of clothing, this combined with the clocks going forward an hour it should make the evenings Ray fishing quite spectacular. The north Devon beaches of Saunton, Pustborough and Woolacombe are not only some of my favorite places to fish, but they provide some of the most stunning of sunsets.

To secure a few brownie points, I cooked breakfast and made pasties for an early tea, in-between stirring the gravy I was nipping out to the garden to tie up Sandeel squid wraps. Fortunately, I didn't get the two mixed up as that would surely have led to a world of pain from Mrs. D, especially if she found a Sandeel head in her pasty. Coughing Chris arrived and sadly his cough hadn't become any less annoying, but he did man up enough to drive the Popemobile on tonight's jaunt. The hour-long journey up to the beach in the north of the county was full of the usual anticipation and stark reality that it's always a gamble to target something that's barely arrived, but on such a wonderful evening would it really matter.

We approached the narrowing road to the beach and were suddenly confronted by a moped with a surfboard as a sidecar coming towards us, incredible how resourceful these Surfers can be. Chris managed to miss the surfboard sidecar dude but not the tank trap pothole and the pope-mobile shuddered under the impact, luckily the ridiculously high roof prevented us from suffering a double lobotomy. If you live in Devon, you get used to pothole avoidance and maybe on another day we avoid the pothole but destroy surf dude's surfboard sidecar! We finally rounded the corner and the beach expanded in front of us like a huge slice of Dutch cheese but with considerably more appeal. Time to don the waders and yomp far enough along the beach to make us feel truly alone, and it also prevents quite so many people from pointing and laughing. The beach looked glorious with the still bright sun radiating onto the exposed low tide sand, it reminds me of an untouched canvas awaiting natures surf powered paint brush to finish the masterpiece.

Splat, Chris slapped his tripod onto the pristine sand sending ripples back towards the sea and yet further desecration came in the form of his size 9s stomping around like a Sasquatch summoning rain. Chris stated, " this will do me right here", strangely I set up right next to him, which considering we both only brought one rod was a bit daft, we could have used one tripod. The rods were quickly assembled, and I headed out for the first wade into the sea, I love this way of fishing you truly feel part of the environment when you're out in the surf casting your rod skyward.

We have a rule that we take turns wading to ensure one of us is always out of the water, wading can be extremely dangerous and having been trained in water rescue I've had to experience being pulled under water into rapids, disorientation is an understatement. Both of us had soon cast our Sandeel / Squid wraps and it was now time to stand back and relish the pure beauty of the view with the sun slowly setting.

With every passing minute the view became ever more dramatic and the best camera in the world cannot deliver the full sensory experience bestowed upon you, with the crash of the waves, the screech of the gulls, the taste of salt on your lips and the naked guy in the distance. Wait a minute " there's a naked guy in the distance", I couldn't believe what I was saying but sure enough like Reggie Perrin a guy had rocked up, abandoned his clothing and ran seaward in an action reminiscent of the 70s comedy "The rise and fall of Reginald Perrin"!

This beach is 3 miles long why, has he got too become one with nature in front of us, incredibly this guy swam around for a bit then walked calmly back up the beach to a rucksack of a similar size to himself. We seem to attract these strange activities but maybe it's us who are the strange ones and I guess if you spend a lot of your time in the dark, and sheltered from civilization like we do, this is what you will encounter. Luckily this was the last of the evening's strangeness and we were able to once again concentrate on the motionless rods and setting sun.

The setting sun was truly incredible and despite the lack of fish I would come back time and time again for the views that mother nature provided, you can keep your full HD 360 3D TV, and give me the North Devon beach sunset every time. We stuck it out for nearly 3 hours into the flood tide but unfortunately, we didn't capture a single fish, but I did capture some stunning scenic pictures that will inspire me to get back out for a Small Eyed Ray right through April.

*Above yet another stunning Putsborough sunset, who cares if you blank with this sort of view.*

Despite the two blanks and no species 26, this weekend I did get a bit of good news in the form of a positive plug for my challenge in the excellent national magazine Saltwater Boat Angling this month, many thanks Tim Macpherson, appreciate the support. Constant Coughing Chris and I do have a plan for this week that just might get me that species 26 before Easter, it's a plan that means going back to our childhood days, watch this space it just might pay off!

## Chapter 16 Roaming the Retro River

So that plan I mentioned at the end of the last blog, to try and get species 26 before Easter took place last night and what fun it was. As a spotty youth and while still at school one of my favorite pastimes was wandering the moorland streams that pass through our little town and try to catch the flighty wild Brown Trout that resided there. From March the 15th onwards I would dash home grab my spinning rod and shoulder bag and head to Fatherford woods and the gorgeous River Okement, meandering down from Dartmoor above. The little river at this point was shallow, foamy and strewn with boulders, the bulk of the river was rapids punctuated with shallow glides and swirling pools.

*The stunning Dartmoor, River Okement a place of great memories*

My memories of this river are all fond ones and I can still remember all the times when elusive 10"+ Brownie's were encountered, although rare they were there. It was only these biggest of fish did I ever consider taking for the table and most times I was happy to return the Trout quickly to the river, my fishing shoulder bag had a measure printed on the side, no need to estimate the size with this bag. My parents must have thought that, the fishing bag with the measure on the side was the safest option when they chose it, to prevent me falling foul of the law.

The same logic must have occurred when they chose my school shoes, all my mates had Doctor Martins with 10 holes, but not I, my mum bought me Clarks Commandos! If the shoes name, lack of laces and clumpy style wasn't embarrassing enough, the fact that on the heels they had a raised backward facing arrow built in, that left a track for you to follow home should you ever get lost was a playground bashing for sure.

However now as a grown up, I feel that both the bag and the Clarks Commandos were a flipping good idea and if I still had them id use them both. The plan was to have my roast dinner and meet Chris by the old viaduct and try and relive our old schooldays by working our way up the river towards the moor using LRF rods armed with worm and cheese. The tactics we used as youngsters were size 14 hooks, one large split shot, cheese, worms and bread for making dispersals, so we stuck to the retro style and kept it simple.

Upon my arrival the river looked lovely and the gurgling, roaring of the water tumbling across the extensive granite boulders instantly took me back to my youth. The walk up this section of the river is largely devoid of walkers and runners especially during the week and even more so during the evening. Chris arrived and seemed remarkably cough free which was a good thing for both of us, although with the river rumble he would have been drowned out, maybe literally! We set off each finding our own preferred spots and continued the retro theme by touch ledgering the bait down through the pools, straight away my line was pulled from my fingers as a savage grab at the worm occurred. My strike was like the average British train, considerably late and the hook returned wormless. It took a few more missed bites before I finally got my act together with brain and arm coordination finally becoming symbiotic, my first tiny fish in forty years from this river was now landed.

The stunning little fish writhed and jumped with an attitude way above its station and upon early examination it was identified as a Salmon Parr, the young stage of a salmon and as the size shows, very early stage. This future king of the river was quickly returned, and I was so pleased to see that the river I grew up with still contained the eco system it did 40 years ago. The next pool and once again a couple of missed superfast snatches with the greedy little fish beating me to the prize, Chris was undergoing the same frustrations and every now and then I heard the shout" darn it", as his bait was nabbed!

With the amount of bites, I was getting even a Brazilian three toed Sloth would eventually connect, and soon yet again I battled a tiny future Salmon as another little Parr was swung in and quickly returned. I knew Salmon used to make it up this far and it's great to see they still do with so much against them, this really is the limit of their journeys.

Chris finally connected with a fish, well I say fish it was possibly grabbed by the worm as it swam past, Chris looked suitably embarrassed. My eyes weren't good enough to see for sure, but it did look like another Parr. We walked further up the valley looking for the perfect run for a Brown Trout and eventually I connected with one, great fun on the LRF gear.

Sadly, Chris was once again double booked and had to head off to a band practice, he must have been crazy the fishing was constant, the scenery breath taking, school boy Chris would have stuck with the fishing. Maybe the worm food he had caught had pushed him over the edge and the worry of catching something smaller hung over him like a really tiny cloud. My plan was to keep going and keep reliving those memory's each of the most attractive pools I reached had fish memories or camping and swimming memories.

Then my bubble was burst for a minute, as on the ground before me, sat a plastic bag full of dog poo, this is my pet hate, why, oh why, does someone pick up the dog poo in a bag then dump the bag in a beauty spot. The dog mess as annoying as it is would have degraded, the plastic bag wont!

The low point of this ignorant thoughtless act is that 300yds back towards the viaduct is a supplied, maintained dog bin, unbelievable! I decided to grab that on the way back and deposit it in the bin for the sake of my peace of mind, I quickly found a waterfall to get my chakra back inline and sat for a minute enjoying a naturally created radox like show of foam.

Once suitably calm I continued up the river revealing more and more of my old stomping grounds and at one point discovered the standard, slaughtered sheep. The slaughtered sheep were common place when we were younger, and I remember the stories of the Monster of the Moors, a creature that sucked the life from these dozy woolen animals. It made me chuckle the thought of how terrified we used to be cowering under a slither of canvas and while the Monster of the Moors could tear a sheep to bits, it couldn't get through the cheapest of nylons!

The further I climbed, the more trout there seemed to be, and it was getting to the stage where I could get a bite from anywhere, I moved up to a tiny side stream that I had fished as a lad and soon found the whirlpool I considered my own holy grail. This was a spot to fish when times were hard, as it would always produce, and here it was I couldn't wait to cast and as I did I knew as the line swirled into the right spot it would go in seconds.

Bang a fish hit the bait hard in the little stream and in no time, it was swung to my hand, I looked at the trout and thought are you the relative of the trout I used to catch, most likely and what a thought. The second cast was also quickly taken, and this pool was still the theatre of dreams where Dartmoor stream trout are concerned. The time had gone on, and I had been so engrossed in casting and walking I now found myself an hour's walk back to the car, with the light dropping and no head torch it was time to make tracks, if only I had those Clarks Commandos! The thick woods increased the feeling of gloom and as I passed the slaughtered sleep not only was I no longer chuckling about the Monster of the Moor I was thinking about the landlord's warning in American Werewolf in London ", "stay off the moors and beware the moon"!

Now with this thought firmly in my mind every shadow looked beast like, every snap of a twig sounded like the stomping of huge feet, the owl screech just had to be a wolf howl! How can something so benign and beautiful, suddenly change into the set from a classic Hammer Horror. Eventually I made it back to the bag of dog doo and knew I was only 300 yards from the carpark and civilization, at least I could beat any beast off with the bag of dog waste! Once I reached the car I could relax, even though it's at this point most horror movies deliver the big shock as the star of the movie are seconds from safety. Despite the final judders it was a great couple of hours and if it wasn't for doing the challenge it's unlikely I would ever have fished this river again, but now I will be back, and I won't be waiting another 40 years.

## Chapter 17 Heads & Tails

Apologies for the frequency of the blogs lately but if I don't get things down in print not long after they happen I soon forget, and I promised myself that even the failures need to be included to keep this all real. With Easter being early this year, I knew I would have a couple of chances of targeting species 28 although what it would be was still a mystery. The first opportunity was to be on the Thursday afternoon and with some sunshine and heavy showers I didn't fancy going too far. Finally, I made the decision to try for a Grey Mullet, a tricky fish at the right time of year, so with the recent cold spell and heavy rain it wasn't the best of plans, but my choices are still limited.

I messaged Chris who was happy to give his wife a break from the constant coughing, although he also agreed it wasn't the most cunning of our plans. The venue I chose was an area I've wanted to try for Mullet for some time and I know that during the summer this section of river can be black with them.

We drove for about 45 minutes before finally relenting and asking the I phone for some help, I'm sure the female map assistance is condescending when I ask her for help. It turned out we were only 2 miles from the spot on the river, and I done that with my natural sense of direction, I Phone Woman!

This is a wonderful comfy spot to fish and it really doesn't feel like your sea fishing, but this section produces Flounder, Bass, Seatrout and Mullet. You can park for free right in front of your rods and what more could you ask for, well maybe if the numerous pond life that turn up and tip the contents of their cars onto the grass, could actually drag their sorry backsides the 20 yards to the bin! Chris picked up the rubbish and walked it over to chuck it in the bin, it's this sort of thing that gets fishing a bad name and anglers banned, its unfortunately far to common nowadays. Once the beautiful spot was returned to the way it should have been, we got out the bread that was to be mashed up to create the attractor for the mullet, added to this would be some rotten mackerel and fish oil.

You need plenty of bread to create a good trail for the mullet to home in on, we were going to use bread flake for bait, fished below floats. With Mullet being a wily, finicky feeder, we chose to use 4lb fluorocarbon traces with a size 14 hook, reducing the chances of the fish spooking.

It transpired that our refined techniques were not required as the flooding tide brought only groups of hungry Canadian Geese honking happily as they feasted on our chum trail of bread. The Mullet no doubt, still grouped further down the estuary waiting for the spring to finally arrive and I can't say I blame them, the rain had started falling heavily and the temperature dropped along with our spirits. The highlight of the trip was when a magnificent White Swan arrived like Ray Winston at a Morris Dances convention, the Swan put down a serious beating on those Geese and I was more than happy to see that guy polish of the bread.

So that was the first blank of the weekend out of the way and the next effort would be a solo mission after Fridays fencing work. Chris wasn't available Good Friday due to attending band camp, he would however pop out Saturday to help with the final part of the post installation. I arrived at the lake to find a light frost, with the water in the barrel iced up, there was no breeze and it was a great temperature for driving posts into the ground.

The installation of the new predator fence has been going on for months and that is the consequence of doing it yourself, although I have had some genuine offers of help, it's nice to have done it ourselves.

The first 3 hours it felt like I put a ton of posts in, but they were all level and at the correct height for the wiring, so now it was time for a couple of hours fishing. Once again, I would try for a Tench although a cold breeze had arrived, and the skies were darkening, it was surely only a matter of time before the rain arrived. This time I decided to change tactics for the Tench and scale things down, so I opted for the quivertip rod with a size 16 hook to nylon and open-end feeder. I mashed up a loaf of bread and mixed in a tin of Sweetcorn, then deposited a few handfuls a rod length out from the bank. The second rod would be popped-up corn on a scaled down carp rig that would be cast out to the deeper water.

The rods were cast, and I sat back to await the impending rain while sitting as motionless as possible for a couple of hours. I think about 40 minutes passed and by steadily putting in a few grains of corn every 10 minutes I had managed, to keep occupied and entice some interest into the area, with groups of pin bubbles now rising to the surface. The quivertip was showing small pulls and tweaks as fish were clearly hoovering up the free offerings, surely any second now. A large group of bubbles popped on the surface directly above the baited spot and finally the tip swung round as a fish grabbed the single grain of corn, the light gear strained as this now hooked fish tried to keep its head in the silt. The powerful judders and short runs pointed towards the fish I was after and species 28, sure enough the emerald beauty of a *Tinca tinca* the Green Tench rolled over for the net. I took a quick picture of the infamous red eye of the Tench, then popped the fish in the keep net just in case I went on to catch another and I could then get a brace shot.

I re-baited the rod and introduced some more corn and mashed bread to the swim, then poured myself a celebratory cuppa as the pressure was off, well until the next time. The rain was now overhead, and the droplets were punctuated by spots of sleet and with an air temperature of just 2 degrees it was hardly surprising that my breath was visible in the air. Just in time to give me a morale boost a huge tail pattern boiled on the surface, again right above the bait, a tail pattern is generated when a fish puts its head on the bottom of the lake to feed and the waving of the tail causes a vortex in the water.

The rod tip once again shot round and this time the strike was met with a very different fish, as a huge bow wave appeared on the water's surface. The light line squealed as the fish headed out across the lake, this was clearly one of the lakes 3 Carp and possibly the big Ghostie. Several nervous minutes passed as I convinced the big fish to return to the bank where I waited with the net, the fish was now circling deep and the lighter rod lacked the stiffness to raise the fishes head. I applied a little more side strain and the inevitable happened, the tiny hook popped out. There then followed the numbness associated with the loss of a good fish, you find yourself staring at the water's surface in the hope the fish reappears. Why hadn't the fish picked up the other rod with a stronger setup and larger hook, isn't that always the way, I went for a stroll around the lake with a big stick to hopefully whack a mole, (that's a joke by the way they are far too fast).

Once the fresh air, freezing rain and wet feet had taken my mind off the lost fish I was ready to start again. The rod was back out and within 20 minutes there was activity as feeding fish were once again evident, the rod tip shaking as fish passed close to the bait or moved the feeder.

At last a fish picked up the grain of corn and I was again playing a much more sensibly sized Tench, the fish was soon netted with no mistakes. Now with the brace of Tench I was after and the weather deteriorating I decided to call it a day, still gutted about the Carp I decided after tomorrows' fencing work I would try for a Carp on the top lake, to hopefully get even.

The weather came in even worse on my journey home with snow now falling on the higher sections of the journey, beast from the east 3? Saturday was to be my final chance for an hour's fishing this weekend, but only after completing the last field full of fence posts. Fortunately, Chris came out to give me a hand for a couple of hours but couldn't stay as the lure of the Gods of Rock were once again calling, and another gig was on the agenda.

We started ramming the posts with the giant blue post educator and Chris watched me do a few of the posts before stating, "now let me have a go on the big post"! Every fourth post is a large 8 foot by 6-inch post and they do take some driving in, especially to get them down to the right height, Chris however sees them as an extension to the gym and relishes the challenge.

This particular post was in some hard ground and Chris raised the post pounder above his head and slammed it into the post although it caught the post wrong and veered off coming down on his head with a resounding donk! He immediately dropped the tool and staggered off clutching his head, I then done exactly what I hate people doing to me when I've just injured myself, I asked "are you all right mate"? Chris replied yes but as he stood up a spurt of blood pumped from the top of his head. I am not good with seeing my own blood and this extends to people bleeding in front of me I was now in fight or flight mode with a strong urge to keel over.

Fortunately, I didn't, and I quickly got clean water and some paper tissue to help clean the wound, I insisted Chris sat down and drunk some water. He was determined to get on and finish the job and I can only put this down to the years he spent head banging at concerts, this small bang on the head was nothing to a hardened rocker! Despite the flesh wound and the concussion Chris battled on and we got the posts in the ground and level within 2 hours. I did cheekily grab a picture of the wounded soldier, only for the purposes of the blog, stating that if anything happened he would at least make the latest instalment.

Chris headed off to go and bang his drums and give his head a rest, leaving me to do a few minor maintenance jobs and grab an hours fishing. First thing I did was break up some crusty bread and distribute it at different points around the top lake, I then left this for a while why I cleared the other lakes outlets, of debris.

Once I returned I stealthily crept around looking for feeding fish, I spotted a nice Common cautiously mouthing a piece of crust hard against the margin. I sat on the grass and waited while it grew in confidence, eventually hoovering up any bread within its proximity; I then went and got my rod and net. I attached a 1-inch square of bread crust to the hook and flicked it out just passed the feeding Carp, I slowly inched the bait back to the hot zone and instantly a loud slurp indicated the carp had taken the bait.

I lifted the rod connecting with the shocked fish and it rapidly left the margins opting to fight out in the center of the lake. This time with the right gear and decent hook the fish was only going one way and that was in the net. The fish was a gorgeous conditioned Common Carp and although it had no large gut, coming out of the winter, it was long and thick enough to warrant a weigh. The Carp came in at 16lb 4oz which was great to see and be nice to see this fish in October with a bit of an autumn stomach.

As I returned the fish to the lake I noticed some more swirls over in the far margin and a quick bit of reconnaissance confirmed a further 3 nice Carp were now taking bread with two of them being very nice fish. I glanced at the watch and I knew I had to get back for my tea, it wasn't one of those times I felt like pushing my luck with Mrs. D, it was Easter after all. So, I packed up and chucked the rest of the bread in, reluctantly watching the group of fish now confidently wolfing down the offerings, next time! The Tails in the title of this blog refers to the lost carp's tail patterns on the water's surface and the Head well that's obvious. I've since checked that Chris made it through the night and despite his head bleeding off and on for several hours, he will be there for me to take the mickey out of on our next instalment. I might have to start calling him Sick note, as in the last three months he had the flu, an abscess, constant cough and split head! This is a man that watches his diet, regularly attends the gym and respects his body, I however have been ailment free while eating buckets of KFC, drinking Cider every night and only exercising while trying to get in my dry suit, I'm just saying!

## Chapter 18 The Dawn of New Species

It's another weekend into the challenge and the target for this week was to be the Plaice, this fish's arrival generally signifies the start of spring. The wonderful tasty Plaice is extremely popular with anglers and Social Media quickly comes alive with reports of the red spotted beauty's appearing from the east coast to the west. For me I think the Plaice can be a stunning looking fish with the leathery brown skin sporting vibrant red spots like an attractive case of the measles. The location was to be Dartmouth, fishing aboard African Queen with the lads from the Holsworthy Sea Anglers, last year, the same trip produced some cracking plaice. Of course, it couldn't be that simple and by Friday the trip was cancelled due to strong winds, in addition, despite Saturday and Sunday looking perfect, the water would be too colored to target plaice so that plan was scuppered.

Saturday Chris and I spent the day working out at the lakes but of course we did manage a couple of hours fishing for fun and landed 4 Carp on floating breadcrust, with a couple of real stunning previously uncaught fish

Luckily there were no accidents this Saturday, but Chris was still coughing like a Donkey and had added to his list of ailments by coughing so much he fainted, fell of the couch and received carpet burns to the face! It sounded like one of those ridiculous stories made up to cover the real reason, Chris however is sticking with his story.

So, it was late Saturday afternoon and the frustration of the cancelled trip was still needling me, it was certainly looking like it would be a no score weekend, I then spotted a post from Anglo Dawn skipper, Andy Howell. He had put a post on social media stating he may run a half day trip on Sunday and would probably be anchoring up, I fired off a message straight away, as a plan now rattled around the vacuum created by my ever-reducing brain.

Andy replied soon after and knowing the charity challenge I am undertaking asked if I fancy trying for a Red Band Fish and Cuckoo Wrasse? Well that was like offering a particularly tasty chunk of cheese to an unusually skinny Mouse, the result was inevitable, cheese filled Mouse. It was now a case of running around to sort out all the light tackle for a species hunt and as the trip was to be for the morning I thought we could have a crack at the crafty Grey Mullet in the harbor during the afternoon. Luckily my wonderfully supportive wife gave me the green light, this was good as I don't think either of us wants to test the no permission scenario. I arranged a doctor's certificate for Sick boy and just hoped that his sore head, burned face and constant coughing wouldn't affect the photographs.

Due to the nature of his condition and he's recent bouts of fainting at the site of a rough carpet, I decided to drive, it would be slightly safer. I checked the phone alarm and sure enough the 05.15 was still there, and so it was set, no need to worry about snow and ice it was going to be a cracking day, well according to the weather men!

So, it wasn't quite tropical in the morning and the car was frozen up but the weekend before, it had been snowing so beggars can't be choosers, I still managed to pick Chris up by 6am for the journey down to Falmouth. We arrived at the marina where the charter boat Anglo Dawn is berthed, great location with free parking is always a bonus for us anglers, it does mean the costs are more expensive for the skipper. We quickly suited up and walked over to the security gate leading to the boat pontoons, we sat and supped an early coffee as the morning mist slowly dissipated. While we discussed the coming days fishing, friend and inspirational angler John Locker arrived with a trolley just in time to load all our stuff on it. John had just returned from his Oil Rig work abroad and was keen to wet a line, we spend a lot of time bouncing ideas of each other and fish as part of a 4-man team in the Conger festival.

We managed to sneak through the gate behind a poor sighted Uncle Albert type hobby sailor and made our way through the maze of boats towards Anglo Dawn, we paused several times to admire the shoals of cruising mullet, seemingly oblivious to our presence. Andy was already aboard the boat prepping her for our departure and shortly the rest of the crew arrived, Sharking Simon, lucky Vicky and bait supplier Smithy, the magnificent seven! As we negotiated the mooring and headed out of the River Fal, we were met by the child like cry of the gulls, the gurgle of the turbulent water as the props spun at slow speed and finally the choking rasping of sick boy Chris echoing across the bay.

Once we arrived at the first mark a couple miles out of the river mouth, we all excitedly dropped the tiny strings of Sabikis (small sets of sparkling lures) to the sea bed in the hope of attracting any number of species. I was going straight after one of my favorites of smaller sea fish, the Red Band Fish, skipper Andy had told me that he had caught Red Bands here before. The Red Band fish is a stunning small eel like fish, part of the ribbon fish family, they live in mud burrows with just their heads sticking out grabbing any small fish or shrimp swimming past. I had managed to catch my first ever ones with Andy the previous year and knew that the tiny lures worked right on the bottom offered the best chance. "Fish on" was shouted by Smithy and sure enough a gorgeous Red Band fish was brought aboard, its undulating body similar to that of a sound wave.

Now being re-acquainted with one of these stunning little fish I was even more determined to get one and fished hard on the bottom with only the smallest of twitches. Simon, Vicky and Fish Locker all managed to pull in Herrings, what was going on, all around me species were coming in as Vicky brought in a pair of Mackerel. It was then I noticed Andy and John laughing, "what's going on" I enquired," they replied, "what's that you got in your seatbox""? I immediately glanced to my box and there like a neon beacon sat a BANANA! There are many anglers, boatmen and skippers that believe that the presence of a banana on-board a boat is bad luck and, in this case, bad luck for the angler whose box the ferocious fruit sits in!

Needless to say, the offending fruit was removed and returned to the culprit, John the fish Locker, he would then be destined to suffer the curse of the Banana! With the curse lifted I continued my quest for the Red Band and within minutes I felt the rod judder as a fish was fooled by the imitation shrimps. I knew by the way the fish was fighting it wasn't the Red Band but whatever it was, would surely be a new one off the list. Sure, enough the shimmer of a circling Mackerel rose to the surface and was carefully swung aboard, species 29! With the first fish in the bag I dropped down again just as the boat drifted off the edge of the muddy ground onto sand, once again the rod tip rattled, and my trap had been sprung. The fish definitely felt different and was in the mini species category, the serpent like shape of large Sandeel broke the surface better known as a Launce, species 30. This was more like it two species in quick succession, and all since Banana-gate had been exposed and how was the conspirator doing, we'll all I will say is you reap what you sow!

Right no more messing about I needed my Red Band fish, only one had been boated thus far and we were off the spot they called home, it was time for a re-position of the boat. Andy positioned Anglo Dawn back in Red Band central and informed me it was the last chance before we moved inshore and tried some rough ground. I dropped the line of lures and bounced them in such a way that no Red Band could resist, all the time using my mind to will the fish out of its muddy burrow in the name of charity. Tap tap on the rod and I just knew it was the target, I lifted the rod and sure enough I could feel tiny shakes through the braid and I proceeded to slowly and calmly bring the fish to the boat.

I found myself trying to see down through the water, to identify the fish but I was still so sure, so sure I made the brave decision to call for the net, I didn't want the ruby red prize falling off at the side of the boat. Then a glimmer of pink as a Red Band Fish writhed onto the water's surface, the skipper retrieved the prize and the quest was done, species 31 and one of my favorite's and as a bonus, a new personal best for that species.

The skipper shouted, "okay bring them up everyone he's got the fish let's have a move" Andy then told me he knew a small spot I could get a Poor Cod, another on my list. This was turning out to be a great day for the challenge and with such a great bunch of anglers it would also be day of good banter. Chris was still struggling with the chest infection and although no seasickness affected him the constant cough clearly was, I knew we would shortly be targeting Wrasse one of his favorite's, hopefully it would perk him up. Within 10 minutes we were over the little rock that sheltered a population of Pouting and Poor Cod, back down with the Sabiki's and straight away the lures attracted a bite, unfortunately this turned out to be a Pouting followed by a few others.

Chris was finally into a fish although he probably wouldn't want to brag about it being a very small Poor Cod. The next drop was successful for me with species 32 spinning its way up to the surface, sick boy had found his mojo and added another Poor Cod to his own tally, so a brace shot was in order.

With another species secured it was time to go and catch a few Wrasse from a section of reef only 10 minutes steam, hooks were baited with fresh Ragworm and this time I needed a Cuckoo Wrasse and a male would be even better with their striking color's.

*Above the awesome Red Band Fish one of my favorite's*

Within seconds of dropping the lines we were all getting bites with a few small Ballan Wrasse getting to the baits first. Vicky brought in the first Cuckoo Wrasse and it was a lovely looking Male exactly what was on my list, and at least I knew they were down there, not that I doubted the skippers word of course. Chris who was now in full Wrasse mode was getting a few fish and then landed a bright orange female Cuckoo Wrasse, where as I could still not get past the Ballan's. John with the curse of the banana hanging over him had decided to go big or go home and fish a live launce for a huge Ballan or Pollack, he did get a take, but it dropped the bait.

Finally following a quick re-position of the boat, I hooked the male Cuckoo Wrasse I was after, incredible when these fish appear on the surface it's like the Las Vegas strip in a fish form. What a fantastic looking creature to make species 33, Neptune was certainly sending me the jewels of the sea on this trip. Typical with fish species you struggle to get one then two come along at once and that was the case with the Cuckoo Wrasse as the very next drop down resulted in another incredibly marked cuckoo although a little smaller, they do have some crazy teeth though!

With everybody having their fill, of some hectic sport with the Wrasse it was time to try an area with a large mud bank in the hope of a Sole or Ray. I changed to a three-hook boomed rig with weights at either end to pin everything to the bottom, again live ragworm was the bait of choice.

Straight away the rod tip bounced and the first fish from the new bit of ground was about to appear, another male cuckoo wrasse! I was being haunted by them now, had they followed me to this new spot? You can never tire of seeing them but when your chasing species you want something else to appear.

John the fish Locker had put out two large baits in the hope of a large Thornback Ray and the use of the bait dropper had encouraged some interest as both of his rods signaled a bite simultaneously. The Demon of the banana decided to punish him further and after missing several good takes offered him only a lesser spotted dogfish as penance. Chris seeing the dogfish appear, quickly switched to small fish baits and promptly caught one claiming it was not what he was after, he has a dogfish fetish I'm sure. The free mackerel chunks attracted the dogfish in and I soon had one on my nice little Sole rig, roughing up the traces and blunting the hooks. Chris had a final highlight of the trip when he hooked and landed his first ever and now personal best Starfish, although he felt cheated when we explained that just because there's a fish in the name it doesn't mean it's actually a fish.

Time to head in and what a mornings fishing, the weather had been like a summers day, the company excellent, the skippering top drawer and the species sublime. Although I didn't want to push my luck I did feel that Neptune had definitely supported my challenge today so maybe I could squeeze one more species out of him.

We arrived back at the marina and said our farewells, we had a special treat as John's family met us at the gate wife Hannah and inspirational little lad James. I had heard so much about this little lad from proud dad and Banana smuggler John, it was great to finally meet him.

Fairly soon it was just Chris and I, plus crowds of people, a Swanage of Swans, a flotilla of boats and a rapidly dropping tide, not the best conditions for stalking Grey Mullet with bread. We swapped the tackle over and took off a few layers as by now it was roasting, we setup our stall over in the corner of the carpark as fishing from the marina isn't permitted. Chris set about making a concoction of mashed bread, sardines and rancid mackerel, this was then chucked in the water to create an impressive cloud of particles. The stinking gunk seemed to attract every swan from the river Fal and also had the effect of pushing any cruising mullet away to the safety of the pontoons, we tried in vain for around 40 minutes. The mullet that did cruise past seemed to swim around the bread reef Chris had created and even the Swans got fed up and left, it did seem that this was where my luck ran out.

We decided to knock it on the head and I picked up my stuff and as I started to walk back to the car, I noticed out of the corner of my eye a Mullet come out from the shelter of the pontoon, swim out to an area of open water and suck in a single piece of bread that had drifted down through the gauntlet of swans. I quickly unhitched the float and hook and molded on a small chunk of bread flake around the size 14 hook, a quick flick and the float landed 6 feet from the mullet in his direction of travel.

The un-weighted line allowed the bread flake to sink slowly through the water into the Mullets line of site, to my disbelief the Mullet sped up and took the flake on the move. For a second, I didn't know whether to strike or not but opted to just hit it, crash the Mullet clearly caught out threw itself out of the water, before diving for the safety of the pontoons. Chris was still packing up when I shouted, "I've only bloody gone and hooked one ", I played the fish gingerly on the 4lb mono and it fought all the way to the margin.

The tide had receded considerably and directly below us there was no longer any water, just large clumps of seaweed and mud. The wall we were perched on was probably 12-foot-high and our landing net was 6 feet, what a dilemma, well not really, Chris needed to take one for the team and get down in that mud with the net.

Chris clearly not keen on this idea and with a recent track record of nasty accidents suggested we hand line the fish up the wall, I explained to him that Mullet are not like a Wrasse their mouths are soft and the hook was tiny. He eventually conceded it was the only option, and like the star he is, he went down in the quagmire to retrieve this lovely grey mullet. I would, and have done, the same for him on many occasions and also have been there to net many of his personal bests, that's part of fishing together, and it's what makes fishing such a team venture.

The Grey Mullet is not something I have set out to fish for before this challenge, and although I have caught one before by mistake it wasn't as big as the fish in the net, so double bubble species 34 and another personal best.

*Above Thick Lipped Grey Mullet ending an epic species day.*

Mullet are a crafty fish with its unusual mouth coupled with an incredible ability to sense line and hooks, it can be a testing species to catch, this particular day the Mullet were not interested in feeding, and positively shy'd away from any free offerings'. For this solitary fish to decide to take the bait in the manner it did, and just as we were about to leave, signifies more than a slice of luck, something I'm sure I wouldn't have been blessed with, if that bloody Banana had remained undetected. It has been a fantastic weekend, 6 species including 2 personal bests, thanks in no small measure to the hard work of Chris, Andy Howell, John Locker and the rest of the boat crew. When I informed Mrs. D of the good news that I had achieved 6 species she immediately responded with " so that's 6 weeks you can stay at home now then" has she learnt nothing in the last 30 years, it never ends, if it's not for the challenge it's for fun!

As a footnote when I pulled up at Chris's to drop him and his gear off he once again had one of his moments, he had got out of the car and as he went around the back I heard a crash. I got out and upon reaching the rear of the car, there he was on his back covered in gravel, " what are you doing down there" I asked, "Another fainting spell was his reply. I don't think he will be going Ray fishing later this week, can't have him fainting 100 yards out in the surf.

## Chapter 19 A plaice in the sun?

It's been a few weeks since the last blog and following that last 6 species day was always going to be tough, the cushion these fish had provided allowed me to gamble on an early Small Eyed Ray. The first attempt had been a total blank and the second crack at the sunset beach wasn't to be much better, Chris was too ill to make the trip and so it was a solo effort. The weather was fairly calm and the seas small, so I was still happy to fish the venue on my own, the wading would be to thigh height only. When I arrived, I could see a few anglers in the center area where I would have like to go but I plumped for the left-hand side, at the risk of a dogfish or two. I soon had both rods out and as the darkness engulfed the beach the first bite was indicated by the rattling of the rod. I struck to find the dull bottom dragging of a dogfish and soon the eye shine out in the surf confirmed the first dogfish of the night. As I walked past the tripod to go out to return the dogfish I noticed the other rod bouncing and once the fish was away I dealt with the next rod. This time it felt a bit weightier and although largely suppressed I could start to feel the hope building, was this to be the Ray I needed, no it was two dogfish one on the main hook and one on the tiny stinger hook baited with ragworm.

This was to be the order of the night and upon reeling in the eighth dogfish I had decided it wasn't going to happen, and maybe it's better to live and fight another day. The next trip was to be an early morning attempt, at one of my favorite eating fish, the spotty Plaice, and I was once again joined by sick boy.

We had decided to a go at 5.30am and Chris was picking me up, to save time I decided to carry all my kit and meet him up the top of the road. I had been in position sat on the bucket for 5 minutes, when Chris appeared bang on time, I raised my hand in a friendly gesture, but Chris carried on past. I now found myself running by the side of the car and unfortunately. I still failed to get any acknowledgement, eventually I ran out of steam as the red lights disappeared down the road. I now had to go back for my gear and then get back to my house all before Chris banged on the door and woke up the rest of the family. I managed to intercept him halfway along the garden path and by using the medium of harsh whispering, I conveyed my disappointment. I guess that's another of the poor guys growing list of ailments, blind and deaf he had the dumb covered years ago.

The long journey to the south Devon beach started with an amazing sunrise signifying the start of a warm day and reminded me of the west country saying, "red sky in the morning, more bloody grockles arriving"! We then came across another famous Devon landmark that had only just been on west country news. The strange thing was that this huge pothole that had made the news, was permanently repaired by the time we made our return journey just a few hours later, the power of the media. We arrived at the beach and there were already 4 anglers set up and fishing, such is the draw of the tasty flat fish, we found a space around the center of the beach and quickly cast our sparkling attracta rigs. The water was far from clear and the recent storms had managed to spoil what was an improving fishing situation, but we know you definitely won't get them fishing from the couch.

It really was a cracking morning and before we knew it anglers were appearing from everywhere, filling every available space, a trawler was also now working just off the beach and the earlier anticipation had turned into an air of disappointment. The baits were coming back untouched and the whole beach had a circus like feel, with 3 more anglers setting up in the 50-yard gap between me and the next guy. Time to get out of there, I will give this beach a miss for the rest of the year. Chris cast as long as he could and that particular set of gear for the last time, he managed to find a snag in the sand and lose the lot. So now, that's 3 blanks in a row, species wise and it soon eats into the luxury of the buffer zone I had created. This was compounded further when a string of work emergencies meant I was unable to attend my first shark trip of the year, aboard Dan Hawkins stunning brand-new Reel Deal charter boat. Fortunately, by getting everything sorted out at work by Thursday evening, I was allowed to take the Friday off, as luck would have it there were spaces on a Plaice trip aboard African Queen out of Dartmouth.

I messaged the skipper Alan Hemsley and sure enough there were still a few spaces, so I grabbed the chance to have another go at the Plaice. I had been out with Alan the previous year along with the Holsworthy Sea Anglers and we managed a great catch of plaice, so it was worth a go. When I spoke to the skipper again on the final weather check he told me the fishing was going to be tough with the easterly wind and furthermore there was only two of us due to drop-outs.

One of the frustrations of being a charter boat skipper is when people drop out at the last minute and now with just two anglers the trip would be a loss for Alan. However, with the forecast being good and two very keen guys the skipper to his credit decided to go anyway, I think that shows the character of the man. I did try to drum up a few more anglers but being short notice and a work day, it was unsuccessful, even Chris had a rock gig to attend. It was another early start and after struggling to find a space in Dartmouth town center, I opted for the park and ride, which for anyone going out on a boat is a pretty good option, the bus stops right by the pontoon and all-day parking for £5. I arrived at the boat a bit early, and Alan made me a nice fresh cup of coffee while we waited for the second angler Paul to arrive. The gear I had brought was nice and light having learned the year before that the Plaice give a great account of themselves on light tackle. The rigs were extremely blinged in the hope of attracting the predatory plaice, and inspire them to rise from their sandy lairs, the method was to drift slowly over the sandbanks with hooks baited with prawn and squid.

Paul arrived and with the introductions quickly made the skipper started up African Queen and pushed out to the Skerries against the tide, it's a lovely mark to fish as before you know it you're out there. We dropped down with that initial anticipation, as the tide pushed us into our first drift over the banks, the water was almost chocolate and skipper Alan felt we could struggle because of it.

I think the first hour past and the skipper decided to try and catch a few Launce for fresh baits, he wasn't feathering for long when he picked up a Herring. A short time later he hooked another Herring and I then mentioned I was yet to have a Herring on my species quest, straight away he offered me the rod to try and put that right. The sabikis touched the bottom and after a couple of vigorous jigs with the rod I felt the juddering of fish, sure enough it was mission accomplished as I brought up 3 Herring. The photo was quickly taken, and the fish dropped into the live bait tank for possible use later, this tiny Tarpon was species 35 and one I was delighted to cross off the list.

The skipper told us that a few Plaice had been caught the previous day once the tide had changed but as we were approaching slack water maybe we should try something different, by putting down the anchor and try for a Small Eyed Ray. Well I didn't take a lot of convincing I love all Rays and Small Eyed are one of my favorites, I've managed to land them on light tackle in the past so there were no worries there. Alan recommended using a small circle the same as I was using for Plaice with a small chunk of fresh Herring as bait.

With the anchor in position and the boat now on the edge of the bank we dropped our baits, the water was deeper and clearer, and it suddenly felt right for it. My rod tip rattled hard as a fish grabbed the bait, I waited, but the bite didn't develop, Paul then had a bite and connected with a nice fish that was clearly a Ray. The fish was fighting well on his light gear and having been hooked literally within 5 minutes of arriving at the spot, things were really looking positive for a fish or two.

The Ray surfaced and indeed was a nice male Small Eyed and first ever one for Paul who was rightly chuffed, I retrieved my tackle to find it baitless, no doubt down to the missed bite. As the tide continued to slacken we were both having a few finicky bites that never developed and things went decidedly quiet for an hour. Once the tide started to push again the bites returned and Paul rapidly landed a couple of dogfish, I then had a typical dogfish bite and pulled in my first doggy. The skipper then informed us that the tide was starting to push, and we will need to get ready to get back on the bank for the Plaice drift shortly, we decided a quick cuppa then head for the bank. We freshened our baits for the last few minutes and my bait hadn't long reached the bottom when I noticed some gentle pulls and bounces.

The sensitive rod and light braid showed the slightest of movements and I said to the skipper I think that a Ray has settled on that, a few second later the rod pulled down slowly into an arc and the fish was off and running. I picked up the rod as the fish stripped braid from the reel stopping only to shake the rod violently venting its anger. With steady pressure I managed to get the fish away from the bottom and up into the tide, once again the fish dived taking a good deal of braid, I knew this was a tidy fish but couldn't imagine what sort of Small Eyed Ray would be capable of these types of runs.

Eventually the dives became short and despite the murky water the golden shape of a large Blonde Ray approached the surface.

The skipper netted the big Ray as soon as it broke through to the light, quite a feat to get that big old Ray straight in.

*Big Blonde Ray crashed the party*

As the net was brought back over the rail, I knew instantly this was a new personal best, with my previous best Blonde Ray being 9lb. The large claspers indicated this was a male and that sort of explains the aggressive fight, this is very often the case with members of the shark family. The little circle hook was positioned perfectly in the corner of the huge mouth and these hooks continue to impress me in a variety of fishing disciplines. The fish was quickly unhooked and weighed, achieving 20lb, WAS, weighed at sea, which clearly blew my previous best out of the water. What a wonderful, wonderful specimen to make species 36, thanks Neptune!

Once a few pictures were taken I carefully lowered the fish over the side and watched as with a flap of his wings he rolled over and downwards out of site. We then up anchored and made the short steam to the other side of the sand bank to begin the drift for Plaice. The water was once again very coloured and it was definitely affecting the fishing, I know how productive these trips generally are and we just weren't getting any bites. Then out of the blue I distinguished a slight difference in the plucks created by the ripples in the sand with a more pronounced spring around, I released my finger from the spool and allowed the braid to offer no resistance for the count of 20 seconds. I then slowly tightened and could feel that there was a bit more weight, I carefully retrieved the line and sure enough the outline of a Plaice came up towards the surface.

As the fish was 3 feet below the boat I could see it was holding on to the strip of squid and wasn't hooked, before the skipper could get the net, the fish had decided that no squid is worth fighting those ugly geezers for, spat out the bait, and shot off out of sight. NO! I yelled, all day we had tried for that little bugger and there he was gone! I was so close to getting one, but that was to be our last opportunity of the day and the fishery was definitely out of sorts, I will be back in a few weeks to right this wrong.

The weather had been sublime and the sea was as flat as I've ever seen, just a shame about the murky water but how could I complain having boated such a gorgeous fish. I loved the company of Paul and Alan, and I'm under no illusions that I wouldn't have caught that fish without the help and guidance of the skipper, fact! I'm definitely going to do a few more trips out with Alan and African Queen this year, its an excellent, historic fishery, but with the added knowledge of an experienced skipper, a few not so well-known gems can be unlocked. Doing this challenge, I have received so much support on the water from skippers and anglers, some I have met for the first time, the brotherhood of angling is indeed a great one. The final part of the blog refers to this weekend, and another failure, to be honest it was a shot in the dark, I was going to try for one of the few Ghost Koi we have at sanctuary, they are a tricky fish to target. The problem is twofold, firstly there are very few of them with only one in the bottom lake and possibly 3 of them in the top lake, secondly, they are extremely cautious at our lakes and once spooked it's pretty much over for that day.

Following another morning of hard work by Chris, my dad and I we had managed to finish the fence and postcrete one of the new gate posts in position. Chris and my dad couldn't stay for the afternoon, but I planned to try and track down one of the Koi. I started on the top lake and after putting in 4 or 5 broken slices of bread I soon had 7 Carp hoovering the bread up, and after another 20 minutes they were swirling on the bread at only an arm's length out.

The Koi were absent at this point, but I know they are partial to mixers as opposed to breadcrust and I think it's probably down to their smaller mouths. I threw out a scattering of mixers and despite the king carp gulping them down, a few had drifted into the heavy weed. Sure, enough it wasn't long before I spotted a Koi lurking below the mixers.

The Koi started picking off the odd mixer away from the pack, so it was time to bait the rod, I had side hooked a mixer colored pop up and trimmed it to a dog biscuit shape. I lowered the bait onto the surface and straight away a Mirror Carp swooped in for the bait, just as it gulped the bait I lifted it clear. The look of surprise on the carp's face was amazing it clearly was perplexed why it had no food in its mouth and swam in circles trying to locate the food item. The last thing I wanted was to hook a Carp and spook the Koi, this process was repeated no less than 10 times with a myriad of different Carp all seeming to be confused to have missed the bait.

I was actually finding it quite amusing to have turned the tables on the normally suspicious fish. Finally, by creating a diversion of bread further along the bank I was able to target the flighty Koi as it gained confidence picking off the dog biscuits. I lowered the little floating bait onto the surface in the area holding the Koi and crouched down.

The glowing whiteness of the approaching Koi was easy to spot and I'm sure this adds to their wariness, the fish hovered below and gently sucked down the bait. I swept the rod rapidly upwards only to see the bait fly free into the air and the eruption of the surface signalled the Koi knew it had be duped. That was it, chance over and I knew I might as well call it a day, so like the Plaice they will have to wait for another day, and when I return, that day, it will be my turn. That's another blog done, two more species in the bag, neither of which I expected at this point, but that's fishing. My target is to get to 40 species by June and with 4 species required in 5 weeks, it is achievable, if, I can get the Plaice, Small Eyed Ray, Freshwater Eel and a Corkwing Wrasse. I will of course be grateful to get anything else that should happen by, like a Haddock or Red Bream.

Thanks to everyone who helped me get the species this month and thanks to Neptune for throwing me the occasional P.B to get my old legs shaking!

Chapter 20 Goby or not Goby

This week I had decided to have another attempt at some of the UKs Mini species, having failed miserably on the previous few efforts. It would be nice to try a different area and perhaps get some local knowledge, as luck would have it, good friend John Locker had just messaged me regarding a recent species trip. John had been fishing a shore mark down in Falmouth and landed a number of mini species and some of these I would have liked to knock off my list. We made arrangements to meet up on the Saturday afternoon and John would take us to a few marks where these species are known to reside. The art of LRF, light rock fishing has really taken off in the last few years, and its opened up a whole new category of fish species, too small to have been hooked previously. The tackle is quite obviously light, and hooks and lines are more in keeping with a match coarse angler, sometimes as small as a size 18.

The British mini species list contains a multitude of tiny little characters, many with vibrate colors and elaborate fins, some inhabit the smallest of pools. I was keen for my challenge to include a wide spectrum of native species and these mini fish deserve to be up there with Sharks, Pike and Conger Eel. Chris was keen to join me on another quest and any possibility of a Wrasse will wet his appetite, I had my own Wrasse to try to catch, the stunning Corkwing Wrasse and if really lucky the Goldsinny Wrasse. We met John down in Falmouth and followed him to the first spot, this mark was a low water mark and could throw up the odd Giant Goby, that would be a real bonus species.

We parked up, loaded ourselves up with the kit and headed off down the track to the jagged, largely exposed rocky shoreline, this area screamed Wrasse and the wrasse whisperer was champing at the bit to get started on this stunning mark. The spot John had brought us was glorious and as we made our way up the rocks we met a group of divers, they told us all they had seen was some Pouting and a solitary Spider Crab, not very inspiring! We soon found some great looking gully's and prepared to fish, John had dug some fresh harbour Ragworm and this was to be the main bait around these rocks.

It wasn't too long until we started getting bites as the small abundant fish made mincemeat of the fresh worm baits, connecting with them was another matter. When you go from one fishing discipline to another it takes a little while to get tuned in to the next species and John was first to connect, landing a lovely Corkwing Wrasse.

 Next it was my turn and no worries about getting tuned in as the rod nearly jumped from my hand, a good scrap ensued but the hook popped out while the fish wallowed on the surface, it had been a Ballan Wrasse. Then it was the Wrasse whisperer's turn as he swung in a lovely little Common Blenny, 3 different species in a matter of minutes. Chris took a close-up photo of his first and personal best Blenny before holding it up for a trophy shot, Blenny Henry had other ideas and decided to sink its teeth into Chris's finger. This aggressive attitude paid off, as Chris immediately dropped the toothy tadpole into the sea and shouted, " it bit me", the lack of sympathy was deafening as both John and I found it highly amusing.

Finally, I managed to connect with another fish and this time there was no mistakes and even better, it was a Corkwing Wrasse and species 37, happy days and this was followed by a Corkwing male. The beauty of having rockpools all around you can keep a few fish safe and in water, while you setup the camera, then retrieve them for photograph.

John the fish Locker had 3 Ballan Wrasse in quick succession, signally the tide had started to flood and time to move to our next mark, as great as the Ballan Wrasse are we were after different species and these fish quickly bully the smaller fish away. Chris hadn't had a Wrasse yet and getting him to move spots, was like prising a limpet from a rock with only a stick of celery! We drove the 30 minutes to the next mark, a small stone jetty nicely tucked away and despite the strong breeze, it was comfy fishing.

This time it was a case of dropping down the face of the wall and try to encourage the fish living in the multitude of cracks and holes to grab the bait. Once again John was quickly into a fish, landing a Corkwing then followed it up with a Black Goby, this was a fish I wanted, and I was confident id get one. The rod then bounced frantically as something grabbed the wriggling bait, sure enough a fish had been hooked, this time a pretty little Ballan Wrasse.

Chris was clearly having a little bit of Wrasse envy and hoped that at some point during the day his appetite would be satisfied.

As we sat there absorbing the ambience the bellowing of an impromptu sea chanty erupted from the mouths of a group of old sea dogs, tying flags to a rope, to our rear. Luckily the second verse was cut short by the howling of some type of fog horn only yards from our location, I'm not sure which of the two noises grated worse. We managed a few more Ballan's before the Ben Ainsley appreciation society decided it would be fun to turn their sailing boats as close to the little structure we were sat on, as possible. This definitely finished the fishing from this spot today and we packed up and headed to the next and final mark, Chris hoping for a Wrasse and I for a Goby.

The next spot was a pier made up of multiple construction methods with the first section being a standard stone-built structure, this changed around halfway to a timber and steel structure sat on pillars like your typical seaside pier. The weather was hot, and the pier was full of the public, shuffling around like giant tree sloths in shorts, and carrying ice creams. This is my worst nightmare and I would normally avoid this sort of spot like the plague. Our guide Sherpa Locker was adamant this was the spot to try and he ran through the method for success, I must admit to missing much of the lesson as the obscenity's being voiced by a group of local oiks next to us, largely drowned him out. We split up to cover various areas of the pier and I think about 30 minutes had elapsed before I realised some type of droning noise was actually making me feel despondent. I glanced toward the direction of the white noise to see, Two String Tony, the most depressing Pier based musician Truro had ever spawned.

The whining aimless strumming now emanating from this double denim clad man, could only be described as torture, clearly apparent by the 50-yard exclusion zone the sloths had created around him. I had an overbearing sensation to quit this pier of despair and rapidly packed up the rods and headed off to find the others. I caught up with Chris and he told me about his epic battle with a huge Black Goby, unlike Blenny Henry this chap never sunk its choppers into Chris's finger and was no doubt the specimen of the trip.

John had also managed a few more fish and was now on 5 species, he really does know how to fish these spots. Spotting my packed-up rods, he asked why, I explained the lack of bites coupled with an overbearing feeling of dread brought on by an under-zealous guitarist were to blame.

He convinced me to have another hour as there was still time to get that Goby, his northern positively worked wonders and I was soon re-threading the line. While re-tackling I noticed the Pirate Jack Sparrow, looking worriedly out to sea, filling in the dots I assumed he was going on the party boat later, and was now concerned his mates had told him it was fancy dress when it wasn't. I know exactly how he feels having once burst into a pub dressed as the incredible hulk, complete with green face, only to find out no one else was in fancy dress.

With my kit once again ready for action I made my way down the steps under the pier as advised by John, I cast the ragworm close to the weed green timbers and gently bounced the rig along the bottom. I continued this process for around 30 minutes, each cast was closer to the corroding structure. Then finally the fine tip of the rod juddered, as a micro fish pounced, I gingerly retrieved the line knowing something was on the end. Yes, wriggling at the end of the line was a Black Goby, even in XS, I was delighted and ran up the steps to show my prize to the others, as I went to grab the little fish it swung out over the water, for a second I thought disaster may ensue but it swung right round and safely back to my hand

As I held the fish up for the photo I could see the Pirate Jack Sparrow was now surrounded by a bevvy of beautiful piratese's and I knew, we both got what we were after. With the Black Goby caught, it was time to head back to the marina to pick up my car and start the long journey home. Chris was still keen to have a crack at the marina Mullet and we decided if after chucking in some bread we attracted some Mullet we would stay for a while and have a go. Sure, enough the bread proved very attractive.

So, with every Swan in Falmouth now attending the Chris Hodgson's all you can eat bread buffet, it really was time to hit the road. It was a really enjoyable afternoon with great company and I learned a lot from talented angler John, so good of him to support this cause with his time and help. From challenge perspective two more species added to the pot and if the weather remains good this week, I'm sure another is on the cards Thursday, fingers crossed.

## Chapter 21 New beginnings and happy endings

As I write the latest blog I'm still recovering from a bout of self-inflicted Sun Stroke a condition I suffer from if I don't take appropriate precautions, in fact last night I was too ill to even consider doing the blog. It's worth reminding ourselves as anglers, we may be surrounded by water, but the sun can get us from multiple angles, and while pre-occupied with the act of fishing the skin burning can go largely unnoticed. I have a real concern that the wonderful flavours and aroma of many of the sun creams on the market is a real turn off for the super scent abilities of the fish. I think its high time we had some Calamari Cream or Lug Lotion, just to give us anglers some sun protection, of course I could always ask Chris to rub on my cream, but I think I'd rather burn! Now back to this week's update, incredibly we were approaching a bank holiday with a fantastic weather forecast, so skippers could finally announce trips with a large degree of confidence. I was particularly relieved as my first trip since the previous blog was going to be doubly exciting, and although only a half day trip the weather looked spot on.

The trip was to be newly qualified charter skipper, Kieren Faisey's first paying customer trip and I was delighted to be supporting this inspiring young skipper as he starts his new venture. Kieren has previously been working as first mate aboard the excellent Bite Adventures, and with Chippy Chapmans tutorage and support, he has now started his own path with Lo-Kie Adventures.

The trip was to target the Haddock residing in the deep water off Penzance, this was a species I had never fished for and never caught so the prospect of a new personal best is always an exciting one. Rapidly improving Chris would once again join me and was just as keen to support Kieren as I, but with the trip only being a half day we decided to get there early and try for a Blenny.

The departure time from my place was crazy, being 4am but we wanted to get to the pier for first light and give ourselves a few hours mini species fishing before our 9am start aboard Lo-Kie. To mark the start of the summer I had ordered a new shirt and being Hi-vis it was certainly going to make the challenge and charity stand out!

We arrived at the pier at 5.30am and set up the light rods to target the little critters that live in the walls, unfortunately we only had maggots as bait. We tried a multitude of rigs, lures and spots but nothing seemed to be working today, I know this pier is normally productive, so we must have just been fishing badly. I guess the pea green shirt could have spooked them, in fact Kieren said to me later that morning while on the boat "nice to see the bling is on you and not the traces"!

We persisted with the tiny rigs and despite all our best efforts not so much as a crab was landed, we were though visited by a one-legged seagull whom we affectively named sod off!

Before long Kieren arrived to start setting up the boat and he was full of confidence that we would have good morning's fishing and furthermore that I would get my first Haddock. Within the hour we had swapped the cold hard pier for the gentle rocking of the charter boat Lo-Kie, and we were now joined by angling mates John Locker and Sam James. The rest of the charter was made up of first time anglers and with introductions made it was now time for the skipper to start her up and go begin his career!

The boat was a lovely steady ride and was clearly relishing the clean water of the south coast waters having been based up in Minehead, with the chocolate waters of the Bristol Channel. It was great to be fishing with John and Sam again and together we make up three quarters of our Conger Club team, so some team tactics were discussed. Having not fished for Haddock before I had taken a crash course in the basics the previous night, finding out they like small hooks, small baits and can be finicky biters. However, there is no substitute for actual experience and the reality was largely the opposite of what I had read.

The rigs I finally settled on after speaking with the skipper and John who had caught them previously were 3 feet of 50lb mono, zip slider with 10oz flat lead, 3/0 hook with squid strip bound to the shank then a 2-inch strip of squid to tip the hook it doesn't get much simpler.

Within 30 minutes we were on the mark and the plan was to try this spot and if no good we would steam a short distance to a wreck and finish the day there. I could see that wreckaphobic Chris was not keen on attaching a load of his tackle to another Penzance wreck and was clearly praying the skipper hit the hot spot on the first attempt. Kieren dropped the anchor and slowly the boat found her position in what was left of the tide, " ok down you go guys" we sent down the baits with an air of excitement all secretly hoping for the first fish. My Fin Nor lethal shook violently and pulled downwards I lifted into a fish that fought well initially and continued spasmodically up to the surface, I had everything I could cross, crossed in the hope it was the target. Kieren was over in a flash knowing this was to be the first fish for paying customers and sure enough a stunning silvery Haddock circled its way to the surface. I didn't bother hiding my adulation and shouted "yes" as species 39 was swung over the rail.

It was far from the biggest of Haddock but was still a personal best and being the first time, I've seen one close up, it was clear they rely on sight with those large eyes, the telescopic small mouth perfect for grubbing around on the bottom. It's strange I never actually thought I would be in a position to fish for Haddock, what with their dwindling numbers and love of deep water. The Haddock fishing in Penzance has improved year on year and now, it's probably one of the most consistent of fisheries for them, the great news is, that the Haddock seem to be moving east with fish caught in the Bristol Channel and Falmouth. I can recommend having a go for them, lovely looking, great sport and sublime eating quality.

John was too my left and was having bites but not connecting, Chris and Sam on the right were still waiting for some action. A couple more Haddock were caught by the first-time anglers and one of these being a nice fish of around 5lb, Kieren was doing a great job of offering advice, baiting hooks and unhooking fish. Amazingly I was into another fish and I noticed this bite came shortly after lifting the bait up and dropping it back down, it was indeed another Haddock and a bit bigger. Kieren had passed the news to Chippy over the radio that I had caught the Haddock I was after, and his reply was " if he's catching them, there must be bloody thousands of them down there"! Chris then received some interest and struck into the fish, he has a knack of attracting, the dogfish!

John was getting a lot of interest from the angler's lines further up the boat as their lighter leads drifted down tide and onto his. It appeared that I was having a lucky day as once again I was into a Haddock and I couldn't understand how, when I was in-between John and Chris who was also into another dogfish.

It's a funny thing fishing, and it happens time and time again that identical methods a few yards apart can have such differing results. Sam finally had a good bite and we all hoped it would be a Haddock to christen his new rod, but it turned out to be a Whiting and I think the look on his face as he unhooked the whiting conveyed his disappointment.

John the fish Locker just won't be beaten, and after a few modifications and a heavier lead he was quickly into his first Haddock of the morning. This was then followed by a real scrapper and a much better fish just to prove he was still in the game. The angling tourists were keeping Kieren busy and they were getting several fish, in my view totally due to the advice and assistance of the skipper. I decided to push my luck and enquired if Kieren and Chippy were sharing a kettle as catching these Haddock was thirsty work, fortunately he took it well enough and before long he delivered us a lovely brew, another tick. As soon as I picked up the coffee cup the rod bounced as another Haddock sucked up the squid bait and I soon had it on the boat, just as Chris hooked yet another Dogfish.

Kieren, keen for Chris to get his first Haddock asked if he could make some adjustments to the rig and bait setup, only a fool shuns the advice of a skipper and Chris happily agreed. With the changes made it wasn't long before Chris connected with his first ever Haddock, we were all delighted for him, having waded through a sea of dogfish. John and I were still getting plenty of Haddock bites and I made the mistake of saying I'm managing to avoid the Dogfish only for my very next fish to be a Dogfish, Grrrr!
I had a final Haddock before it was time to go and in the 3 hrs fishing landed a respectable 10 fish with 9 of them being Haddock, Chris also had 10 fish with 8 being dogfish and 2 Haddock. John had 6 Haddock with a couple of nice ones and I really felt for Sam who didn't manage one this trip, but still fished really hard, next time mate!

I think the boat tally was 50 Haddock in a half day trip, not a bad start for the fledging skipper and I for one can vouch for the overall skippering skills of young Kieren. I am looking forward to another trip with him soon, he is surely going to have a great career in a tough business.

Saturday morning Chris and I knuckled down to some maintenance at the lakes and it's really starting to take shape with the recent grass cuts and extra planting now showing. We had a couple hours Tench fishing as there were a couple of guys fishing the top lake, they had 5 Carp in the morning including the Koi I was after last week. Sam James and his kids were on the bottom lake and the kids were busy having a Rudd match landing over 120 fish. The Tench fishing was hard and I didn't get a bite until I moved over to the windward side of the lake, whereby I caught a fish within minutes. Like a shark getting the scent of blood, Chris soon moved over to the same area and promptly connected with a Tench another nice fish. I managed one more on the feeder before we called it a day.

We said farewell to Sam and wished him luck for the evening ahead, I think Sam was there to spend a night out with the kids rather than any serious fishing, it's great to see the youngsters enjoying being outside and camping. When I got back from the lake I was reminded of what's just around the corner as my Shark Club festival badge had arrived, looking forward to this annual event and great social.

Sunday, I had managed to find a couple of spaces aboard a boat from Lyme Bay charters, this successful charter business is a father and son team of Phil and Lewis Hodder. The two charter boats they operate are Alice Rose and Pegasus both run out of Lyme Regis Harbour. The trip was another short one and was targeting Black Bream, another fish I've never fished for. Lewis had kindly messaged me a rig diagram and some tips, that's a great way to impress new customers. Chris and I arrived at Lyme Regis and parked up in the top car park and made our way down the lovely walk down the hill. We once again had planned to try and catch a few mini species from the numerous walls and piers that made up the harbour and sea defences.

This time however we decided to call in the local tackle shop and purchase some fresh ragworm, as usual with local tackle shops they are a wealth of knowledge and the owner gave us some great tips and picked out the smaller rag for us, top bloke. As we were early we decided to have a slow walk to the boat to check out some potential spots for later, it all looked very fishy. Before we knew it, we were at the boat, there were already a couple of anglers aboard, so we stepped down and introduced ourselves to skipper Phil, now skipper Phil is the polar opposite of skipper Kieren and told us he was retiring shortly. It seemed strange to have the pleasure of fishing with two great skippers one embarking on his new career and one happily ending it.

The day was a scorcher and it was my first outing for my shorts, something Chris found highly amusing with several cracks about short fat hairy legs. Eventually the boat was full, and we headed out in search of Black Bream, this was another short steam of only 2 miles and once again it was to be fishing at anchor.

We picked up some tips from a few of the guys who clearly new how to bream fish and the first drop down was met with frantic bites, the initial excitement was short-lived as anglers wound in multiple catches of tiny pout. We fished through the swarm of these bait robbing little orange pests and it wasn't until Chris said we should keep a few for conger bait that they ceased! Then a small Black Bream was landed and returned, its spawning time and the fish are quickly returned to preserve the future stocks. A couple more Bream were caught when I received a good rattling bite and upon striking I knew I had a Bream as the small fish bounded around wildly, then it was off.

I was gutted that's two species that have got away recently and despite fishing hard that was my only chance, a small group of Smooth Hound arrived and probably pushed the few Bream out. Two hounds were caught in quick succession before they too disappeared although one was a scraper double, so it lovely to see. For Chris and I it was to be a couple of hours T Barring Dogfish from our hooks as a pack moved in to fill the void created by the departing target species.

I couldn't get out of the sun and I would have gladly used sun cream, if it deterred the skin rasping pack of Rock Salmon, we were soon back in the harbour and I saw enough of the fishery to know I will be back when the Bream move in properly. Our final effort was along the harbour walls, but the quiet little harbour was now like the kick out of a Little Mix concert with people and families filling every available space, even the walls were covered with groups of families engaged in the art of Crab wrangling. We eventually found a few rocks to scramble over and this lead to a nice boulder strewn gully. I flicked out a Ragworm and straight away it was hit by a greedy little wrasse.

I carefully directed it through the dense kelp and boulders, now seeing it was a stunning male Corkwing, a species I had already caught but this one was so vibrant I couldn't not take a quick picture of it.

Chris lost a fish to the snags before I managed another bigger Corkwing only to see it drop off at the edge, the wrasse were beating the smaller species to the bait so with the water receding and the sun getting hotter we decided to call it a day and admit defeat. It was a close, but no cigar on this trip, although I will be back to fish with Phil's son Lewis who will continue to run Pegasus and I will get that Black Bream. Thanks for your company as ever Chris and I couldn't end without mentioning your big fat Gypsy hand towel that you hand crafted rather than pay for the real thing, also your homemade scent feeders that are as close to the real thing as Quorn is to meat! I particular like the fact that you chose Pouting orange as the colour and essence of Doggy as an aroma.

Sort of reminds me of the industrial grade tripods you made, capable of launching Scud missiles, or the plastic sand spikes that wouldn't prop up a bit of bamboo let alone a rod and how could I forget the fact that you squirreled away off cuts of the electric fence wire to create sea booms! You are as tight as old man Steptoe when it comes to tackle, and your innovation is borderline eccentricity, however life would be so less colourful without your totally awesome fishing show derived lunacy and I could never forget my personal best Plaice was attracted by one of your Spoon, spoons, or should I say loon spoon! It's going to be slim pickings next weekend as I'm on call for the week so that limits my fishing somewhat. The following weekend is a National Anguilla Club fish-in, up in Kent which should make a good blog and it will be nice to meet up with some great old friends and maybe even get an Eel or two!

## Chapter 22 Frustrating forty

As I suspected when I started this challenge there were going to be good times and bad times and reaching 39 species with some of the conditions and temperatures over the last 5 months, has been a real bonus. So, when you have a run of good conditions and reports of good numbers of fish, its surely only a case of time by the water equals a result, unfortunately this isn't always the case. Social media is a great tool for highlighting what's being caught around the country, but it also creates a snowball effect, whereby reports of a certain species being caught generate enough interest that more anglers go out and try for them. This can give the impression that these fish are climbing up the beaches or banks and there's never been a better chance of getting them. The reality is that half a dozen, hard core anglers who post and fish regularly, are getting rewarded for all their time and effort, the dozens of blanks, searching out new spots, trying different baits and rigs are not highlighted just the end results.

To be honest who wants to read about blanks, failures and bad luck, we want pictures of big fish being held by grinning anglers beating their personal bests, or do we? It is great to see these wonderful specimen fish and it can be so inspiring too young and old anglers alike, but at the same time it can frustrate and demoralise anglers who strive to replicate these successes. I know an excellent shore angling page, that is run by an extremely good angler who promotes the reporting of big fish, these cover the pages every week, but at the same time he has asked for reports where people haven't caught.

As you can imagine the blank session reports are very rare, although there must be thousands happening weekly, I love to read them, and always give them a like, I just wish there was more of them to create a realistic picture of the true nature of angling. It's like most things you learn in life, we learn by our mistakes, so let's be proud to share them and maybe it will also inspire others. Fishing can be a great leveller and in the last Blog, I couldn't do anything wrong while Haddock fishing, yet a superb angler Sam struggled that day. You really need to take the rough with the smooth in this game and providing it's not always the rough we soon pick ourselves up and get back to it. Hopefully the above will now explain, why I've still done a blog despite blanking several times lately.

The target for species 40 was to be the Smooth hound, a gorgeous member of the shark family and an annual visitor to the beach and rock marks around the country. The Smooth Hounds come inshore to forage for the peeling crabs, although they are just as happy and capable of eating hardback crabs. I have a few boat trips booked in June that I'm sure will throw up a Smooth hound or two and I also have a trip with top shore guide Jansen Teakle in June when I'm hoping to get a new personal best. However, I really wanted to get one myself for the species challenge and from the shore, I did fairly well last season and absolutely loved fishing for them in North Devon. With the target chosen Chris and I set off for a short session that coincided with a rising tide and falling light, normally good conditions from this particular mark.

The tide was at its lowest when we arrived, and we had decided to travel light and use one rod and share a tripod, which was mine, as Chris's monstrosity weighed a ton another downside of saving a penny.

With the rods soon assembled it was time for the bait and as the trip was at short notice I hadn't had time to pick up some of the frozen crab I have in the lakes freezer. Instead I said to Chris I will pick some up from Homleigh, a local garden centre, stroke tackle shop, when I picked up a small packet of Peeler crab I had no idea they were encrusted in precious jewels. Upon reaching the counter I was to find out that for 3 packs containing 3 small peeler crabs, I would need to part with £15, I started having a Jack and the beanstalk moment, maybe they would grow into a giant peeler Crab tree! I think I even considered knocking the trip on the head, it's sort of crazy to spend this money on a few baits to then go and try to catch a fish to raise some money for charity.

Clearly, I could stay home and give the money straight to the charity, but the same could be said for every fish I've had so far, none have been caught for free. I couldn't wait to break the news to Mr Skin Flint, as there was no way he could whittle a crab out of a bit of scrap, however he did miraculously manage to find a crab in his freezer and coupled with a bit of squid would give him enough to make do.

I took out a peeler crab of such value it would not look out of place hanging from the ears of Kim Kardasian, £1.666666 recurring. I appreciate Mr Ammo and Mr Homleigh have a lot of costs involved, with getting the crab from under the rock, packaged, into the freezer and out to the shop, and all in good condition but really £5 for 3, I think Ebenezer Hodgson is rubbing off on me. I guess at the end of the day, I could just get off my backside and go and gather my own fresh peeler crabs, but that's the price of being time deficient. Now the bait issue has been ranted about I really needed to make the most of the baits I had, and to start with I went with only £0.83 worth of crab in the hope that the Hounds would take pity on me.

The peeled crab looks irresistible, and once its bound on, surely no hound in its right mind could resist, tipped off with a nice juicy crab claw, but with plenty of hook still showing. Chris started bravely, going with his only crab, something that could have cost him dear if the bait had been lost, as my golden Crabs now had a street value of £2.50 each. The rods were cast, and the instant action never materialised, so it was sit back and enjoy the ambience, Chris being ever resourceful and fearing having to purchase one of my crabs had a plan. He had cunningly brought along his prawn trap and was now going to unleash it from the beach into the sea, to ensnare hard back crabs. I must admit this was one of Chris's better ideas, it's just a shame the execution was so darn poor.

He loaded the mesh basket with a chunk of squid and huge rock then stood on the shoreline spinning it around like Hiawatha hunting Elk, as he launched it triumphantly seaward the thin cord snapped. Chris turned and despondently remarked " well it's definitely in the feeding zone", knowing full well he would never see it again. It was clear there was only going be one outcome with a rock that size and throwing it out like Thors hammer, I am sure it would have worked though. We sat silently for the next 30 minutes neither wanting to relive the nets last moments and drinking our warm beverages, hot coffee for me and excessively watered-down chicken oxo cube for Chris.

The rods remained motionless for an hour and Chris decided he needed to change baits to see what was out there, this normally means one thing, he wanted to catch a Dogfish to save the blank. Out of the corner of my eye I then noticed an object, just behind the surf, rise like a writhing serpent, the prawn net had returned! I pointed it out to Chris, but it had once again vanished beneath the waves, I walked down to the water's edge and scanned the surface.

Sure, enough I could see a dark shape rolling around on the bottom in the murky water, as I was sensibly wearing waders I decided it was safe enough to go out and try to retrieve it. I timed it, so the waves were at their least disruptive and waded out sinking my arm in the direction of the dark shadow, I felt the broken cord and gripped and lifted rescuing the net from a watery grave.

As I lifted the net up I could see our old friend, Blenny Henry looking somewhat dizzy and confused, now that really takes the biscuit, a species I have tried on numerous occasions to knock of the list and now I've caught him in a net! Unfortunately, the challenge is for all species to be caught on rod and line, so I took a quick picture and released the vicious little troll in the hope we will meet again in the right circumstances. Chris who was re-invigorated by the net rescue had managed to re-bait his rod with squid and was now waiting to " see what was out there". It was about now that the heavens opened up and the driving rain really lowered the temperature and if the truth was known, the morale too. The squid though had bought the expected bites, but after missing several, Chris felt they were caused by some unknown assailant and scaled down hook and bait size. This had the desired effect, as the first Dogfish was soon writhing around on the water's edge, this was followed by a second before the dogfish whisperer conceded that's what was out there.

I had thrown caution to the wind and splashed out on a whole un-shelled crab to try and inspire a Smooth Hound, all £1.66 on a single hook. With just 30 minutes to go I had a sharp but short take and it never returned, Chris had a similar take on crab just before we left but again, it wasn't strike-able, so a big fat blank for me and drenched through to boot. Chris however got his net back and the standard Doggies he needs, so he can count them when he goes to sleep at night. The next trip was a solo effort and once again I stuck to methods that have worked in the past, got to the mark right on low water and fished it right through to high water.

I changed the bait every 30 minutes with whole crabs, spared no expense, in the hope that a passing fish would spot the movement of the crab settling, I cast short, long and in different directions. The afternoon was glorious, but not so much as a burping limpet disturbed the bait, and finally with much disappointment I had to concede defeat yet again. Species 40 is putting up a struggle and I feel that as far as the Smooth Hounds go, they will be relegated to a different number, but at least they are not vexing me as much as Blenny Henry who has turned up multiple times to the rods of others and latterly in the bottom of a net. Which species will move into the top 40 slot, all hopes are now pinned on *Anguilla Anguilla* the common Eel one of my favourite of all the fishes. The eel is incredibly mysterious, long lived, smart, strong and specimens, are without doubt the most testing of species. The eel with its serpentine form cannot even be classed as a marmite species, as the number of anglers who actively seek them out are probably less than 100 country wide.

As one of my all-time favourites, I will be delighted for the Eel to help me reach the 40-species mark, and this coming weekend I will be trying at the National Anguilla Club fish-in over in Kent. One thing is for sure the seats I will be using while eel fishing, are far more comfortable than the seats for shore fishing. Hopefully I haven't disappointed to many blog readers with my ramblings which amounted to zero fish but believe me even the greatest anglers are having them too.

## Chapter 23 Eel meet again

Typing this latest blog while trying to stay awake following a weekend under canvas that included a 600-mile round journey. This weekend the target was the Freshwater Eel and the extra bonus would be if I could catch one during the National Anguilla Club fish-in. The National Anguilla Club are the longest running single species club in the United Kingdom, having been established in 1962. I have been a member off and on over the years also serving as Records Officer and Southwest Regional Organiser, it was an honour to have represented this great club.

During that time, I made some lifelong friends and these hard-core Eeling enthusiasts have my utmost respect, the pursuit of specimen eels is rarely rewarded yet demands a lifetime of effort. As a stranger trying to consider what your average eel angler may actually be like, the preconceptions are no doubt along the lines of, a group of crazy haired, badly dressed, liquor loving, species obsessed, recluses. I would however like to say, nothing is further from the truth, but I can't, that description pretty much covers most of the old school eelers, but if you scratch beneath the surface these guys are some of the most talented of anglers.

Eels are not popular due to their serpentine characteristics, slime and ability to cross land, so it's not surprising that news of their numbers plummeting, falls largely on deaf ears.

The freshwater eel like the eel angler are becoming rarer compared with previous years and the disappearance of a keystone species like the eel will have huge consequences to the greater eco-system. Please respect the Eel and return them to the water as quickly and carefully as possible, just remember a 6lb eel could be 60 years old. I do tend to get on my soap box where eels are concerned I grew up with them in every water course I visited, and I would like that to remain the case for generations to come.

This weekend was based at Nicholls Quarry in Kent, a large gravel pit with a great pedigree for producing good eels, the club had booked most of the lake with 23 members attending. Below the best time to relax and enjoy the ambience of Nicholls is sunset and dawn. I decided to leave at 2am in the morning as I have M25ophobia and didn't fancy joining the 4 lanes of crawling traffic that is a daily occurrence on this slab of tarmac. As per the plan I had loaded the car with all the kit and headed off at 2am sharp, I had decided to get there, setup camp, then catch up on the missing sleep.

It wasn't too long, and I found myself stuck in traffic at 3.00am on the A303, do these people never sleep, where are they all going, surely there not all crazy anglers? It was a case of head down and get there without stopping and I pulled up at the gate at 6.15am, and for once getting my rods cast out was not a priority, sorting the Bivvy and bed however was.

The bailiff had opened the gate and ran through the rules, so it was now a case of finding a spot to set up camp, I had spotted club social officer Nick Duffy AKA the Magnet, as I had driven in. He had acquired this nickname apparently for his ability to attract fish and I'm pretty sure a magnet can work both ways, and I think he is pretty dam good at repelling fish.

*Above a reunion with the Magnet*

We exchanged pleasantries and he convinced me to jump in the swim next to him, he and several others had arrived a day earlier, and there were probably already 10 anglers fishing. Duffy had told me he had 6 eels the previous night but knowing his reputation for wind ups I asked for proof, sure enough like a cheesy magician he produced a group of eels in a net. Wow I didn't know what was more amazing, him telling the truth or him catching eels, either way I was definitely jumping in the swim next to the magnet. I then set about building camp, which was easier said than done having not done a night in a Bivvy for a year, luckily, it's like riding a bike and I'm rubbish at that too.

Maybe the tiredness added to the frustration, but I must have set that flipping thing up 3 times before I remembered to attach the strap across the bottom, crucial to keep the thing rigid. Nick the Magnet brought me over a lovely cup of steaming tea, and I didn't have the heart to say I don't drink tea, however it was just the ticket and I was soon revitalised and ready to continue.

Finally, everything was in place and I just had to go and get my bait the club vice president and great friend Nick Rose had picked up for me, 100 large worms. This little jaunt would end up taking me a couple of hours, every camp required a quick chat with the fellow club member, this is a large part of the event socialising with friends old and new.

I finally made it to El Viceo Presidente's Wild west fort, and it was time for another drink, another cup of tea was lovingly prepared, and I thought Nick knew I didn't drink tea. Of course, I've only stayed with him on numerous occasions and had a holiday in France with him, but he is getting on a bit! With my bait collected and socialising done I made my way back to club Tropicana, our bank was bathed in sun and sheltered from the wind, whereas the other fishable bank was exposed to the worst of the wind and it was pretty dam cold over there.

It was finally time to cast my baits out and I had decided to go with two on modified Dyson rigs, one with worm and the other with dead bait, both cast into the deep gully a few rod lengths out. The third rod I went for something different, a simple running lead set up baited with a fresh Tiger prawn, Mrs D hates me using them as it's not something we can normally afford to buy for tea, let alone feed to fish. I do rate them and by fishing them in the margin against a bed of rushes I could trickle a few freebies in every so often.

With the traps set it should have been sleep time, but I hadn't had any breakfast, so it was firing up the stove time and get half a dozen chipolatas nicely tanned. The cookers nowadays, when combined with the new style toaster pans, make bankside cooking a pleasure and within 10 minutes I had sausage rolls and mug of coffee ready to go.

The venue has a reputation for producing fish in the day with nights not so productive and even knowing that, I had still managed to flitter away most of the day, so these next few hours were crucial. With the breakfast consumed and all the household chores now complete I could finally get my head down, leaving my fishing alarms to wake me should I get a bite. The issue with this particular water is that it is surrounded by houses and new development and has recently had part of the lake filled in for further development. This results in the constant drone of excavators, dozers and dump trucks, added to this are the dulcet tones of a group of builders working on the new builds, result, it's like sleeping in a site office. If that wasn't enough it seems like there is a military shooting range nearby or downtown Hythe has a serious gun culture, constant firing even managed to drown out Bob the builder and his buddies. That's why the nights were so blissful, just the occasional wailing of a Delkim alarm and the distant, haunting moans of a Ray Hammel staggering back from the pub.

Despite this constant racket I was so tired I knew given a comfy bed and being able to stay horizontal for a short time I'd be off to the land of nod. It only seemed like a few minutes when the alarm signalled a bite, as something made off with the margin fished prawn. Due to a total lack of body co-ordination I managed to fall off the bed and onto my cooking stuff, that fish had time to not only eat the Prawn but tie the rig to a sunken snag.

When I finally struck everything was solid, I did manage to retrieve the gear by walking up the bank and changing the angle of the line. Another prawn was hooked up and trimmed to size, before being dropped back in the margin in the hope that the fish returned.

Once again, I shut my eyes just long enough to get the feeling of falling backwards, as deep sleep beckoned, De de de de de! The same rod was once again screaming for attention, this time everything went like clockwork and I struck the rapidly departing fish and was met with the powerful bouncing of an angry eel, jamming its tail into the silty gravel. The Magnets radar was working perfectly, as he emerged from the back of the swim " what did you get that on"? This is what I like about Mr Duffy, no conspiracies, secret investigations, checking bait boxes or spying, just straight out what you using! I quite happily told him it took a prawn and it was the second take in a few minutes, " let's have a prawn" was the Magnets next comment. The fish was fighting above its weight but as this was species 40 I was probably playing it overly careful, Nick netted the fish perfectly earning himself a prawn in the process.

The fish was a 2lber and not huge but gratefully received nevertheless, I decided to get a few pictures as the sun was out and I needed an eel picture for the gallery. I returned the eel to the lake and re-cast the rod to the same spot before hiding the remaining prawns securely, they could become a valuable commodity.

*Above the first eel of the weekend caught on fresh prawn.*

I finally managed to get a couple of hours sleep due largely to the fact I could now relax having landed the 40th species and also the silence of the alarms. It was only to be a couple of hours though, as once again the prawn rod was taken by another Eel of similar size which was unhooked and quickly returned.

Well I started thinking I was onto something here, and as the evening drew in I moved a second rod onto bottom fished prawn dropped into the left-hand margin, the middle rod was also placed in the margin but with a dead bait. Before dark the right-hand prawn rod was off again but I managed to miss that one and strongly suspected the fish would return. As day turned to night I enjoyed watching the awesome fishing skills of the handsome Grebes, I'd love them to visit our lakes and unlike the Cormorant the Grebe would be most welcome. I managed to get a few photos as the lake became calm.

The night was cold and silent, with very few alarms sounding and I was clearly way off the mark with the margin prawns, as they never moved again. The next morning, I at least felt well rested and seeing as it was The Vice Presidents birthday I decided to reel in and go and give him a card and pressie. I decided to have a quick cuppa before heading off and scanning the lake with the camera zoom I could see groups of anglers standing contemplating a pretty disappointing start. I could even hear from across the lake, club President John Davis, trying to come up with a single positive thing regarding carp anglers!

Upon walking round, the lake it was soon apparent that not much had been caught, a couple of 3s, a few Pike and plenty of Bream, the eels that had been caught were all at long range and the consensus was that the pressure of nearly 80 lines in the water had pushed the eels to the far side of the lake. I reached fort Rose to find the weathered old warrior snoring his head off although he may well deny that, I woke him up with his card and pack of beers in return for a cup of coffee. Nick hadn't had an eel yet, but hand managed a carp, he is a closet carper for sure, he will come out one day. We were joined by the Noel Coward of the club the charismatic and totally addictive David O Sullivan, better known as Sully. Weirdly he brought his alarm remote over to us then went back to his Bivvy and fiddled with the alarms making us jump at every squark. Eventually his titillation paid off as one of his rods signalled a fast run, the rod hooped over, and it looked like Sully was into a proper one.

Despite some excellent milking of the situation, the size of the Eel was not representative of Sully's initial responses, we struggled to tell the worm from the Eel The guys were going to the pub later to celebrate the vice president's birthday and a few hard core footy fans were staying for the FA cup. I however decided after a bite less night I wanted to make the most out of the day. Neither a fan of drinking or football the victor mildrew in me declined the offer and looking below I think I would have fared much better at the pub.

Without knowing better, I decided to stick with what had worked the previous day and fished prawn in the margins, on hindsight I should have tried something different as the rods remained motionless all day. With most of the guys at the pub I found intelligent stimulation non-existent which in fairness was the same when Duffy was there anyway. I found an attractive moth to photograph but even he left when I asked for some angling inspiration. After a gruellingly hot and unproductive day even the arrival of the Magnets grinning face was pleasurable, he asked what takeaway I wanted as he was going to get it. The plan was to meet at the lakes club house and have a collective meal, drink and birthday cake presentation, after only talking with Moths, Ants and Grebes, even fellow eel anglers seemed super appealing. We done the social meal and Nick managed to receive two cakes with the second cake being a wonderfully baked Carp cake, once again highlighting a secret interest. I decided to get back and try a different tactic for the final evening, but on the way back ran into a slightly sozzelled sully. We spent a while discussing Sully's forthcoming holiday to Devon and planned a short beach session and fish supper, I really enjoyed the same thing the previous year.

Once I got back to my swim it was all change as the rods needed to be re-rigged and my plan was to use single worm baits cut into 4 small pieces then banged out as far as I could cast them. Everything was pointing to the fish being further out, so I put all my eggs in one basket and put all 3 on worm and at range. With the traps set and coffee made it was time to sit back and watch the unfolding of another of mother nature's fantastic portraits, with a perfect sunset only punctuated by diving Grebes.

The left-hand rod was suddenly sounding a fast take and as I picked up the rod the line was still flying off the reel, I struck and could feel a better fish determined to remain on the spot it was. Slowly I convinced it inwards as Duffy once again noticed the action, he shouted across " that's a better fish isn't it"? I thought it was but didn't want to say and as the fish reached the deep gully in front of the margin the hook came out. So that was my better fish chance over and done, I recast and sat back on the bed to contemplate what I had done wrong, the verdict, nothing! Before I could analyse my loss further the same rod was off again but this time it was a much smaller eel and I soon had it on the bank and unhooked.

The middle rod rollover flipped upwards as another eel grabbed the worms, this one was missed in my haste to get another one landed. Now with two rods out of the water the final rod went off and I hooked up again with an eel of around 2lb 8oz, after another missed run on worms I swapped all the rods to dead baits in the hope of picking up a better fish. That was the kiss of death and I received no further takes that night.

While packing up in the morning I heard from the magnet he had a few smaller eels but nothing decent, then angler Steve Richardson next to Duffy had a screaming run. The magnet went straight over, no doubt to see what bait he was using. As Steve played the eel he made the mistake of telling Nick that he had a 4lb 10oz in the net already, I could only imagine the magnets face when he heard that.. I went over to take a few pictures of Steve's fantastic eel which turned out to be the best fish of the weekend.

I may have been a tad unfair on Nick the Magnet Duffy in this blog, but he has made a career out of stitching fellow members up and I myself have suffered at his hands on a number of occasions. Probably the worst being while eel fishing with mates Glen and Regan in deepest Bridgewater, we were sat listening to the fisherman's blues, radio show when the host stated he had just received a text message from Eel hunter Steve Dawe, direct from the bank. He went on to say, Steve is really excited having broken his personal best eel with a fish of 1lb 4oz, he then added " Steve attributes his recent success due to wearing his wife's lucky pink thong"! This statement was then analysed by the host and guest who came to the conclusion that the wearing of a lucky pink thong probably made no difference and maybe I should keep that info to myself in future! I was shocked beyond belief and couldn't understand who could have done such a thing. It wasn't too long before the culprit was revealed, Duffy, and I will get him back at some point! Having said that I think the world would be a considerably duller place without a Magnet causing chaos and I'm glad to have spent the weekend with him.

The fishing was pretty poor considering how good this pit can be and there were some quality eel specialists working hard and a few others drinking hard, but you get what you want from one of these events and as long as you go home happy it's a success so well-done Nick and the club for a well organised event. I would like to add that the club have supported my charity challenge with a donation of £50, and for a small club that's a very generous and important donation, many thanks to the committee and membership for the support.

Not sure what the next species will be I am still annoyed with a few that haven't materialised yet, the Smoothound, Small eyed Ray and pesky Blenny so it may be one of those next!

## Chapter 24 Take the rough with the Smooth

The pressure has definitely eased now I hit the 40-species mark but it's no good being complacent when who knows what is around the corner. Despite Mrs Ds best efforts in convincing me to relax and do something else for a few weeks, I know only too well that would involve domestic chores. Following several individual donations from members of the Eel club my just giving page has topped £500, I feel truly humbled by the generosity of so many people. With a big chunk of the species caught, it is inevitable that it's going to get tougher to specifically seek out the missing ones, especially while fishing reefs and wrecks.

A few weeks previously I had been in contact with Murray Collins, skipper of the successful Looe based charter boat, Swallow 2. We had discussed the possibility of getting a Coalfish for my challenge list, Murray had been getting several Coalie's during he's recent wrecking / reefing trips so there was a chance. Murray had a space this week and although the tides weren't great I was still keen to have a go so it was confirmed, and the day arrived with a forecast of fine weather.

I got down to Looe by 7.15 and rather than pay to park I opted for the walk down from Hannafore Road, this turned out to be a double mistake. Firstly, as I walked down the steps and along the river to where Murray normally births Swallow 2 I noticed it was in fact on the other side of the river, "oh bugger"!

I carried on along the path and as I drew level with the boat, I could see fellow shark club mate Alex trying to sneak a Mullet out from the side of the boat, " hey Alex" I shouted, " I'm on the wrong side"! That was a pretty obvious comment and clearly Alex thought so too, as he answered with "really"!

There was no choice, I needed to carry on and walk all the way round, as I continued along the path I was suddenly met by a barrier blocking off the footway and with no way past I was forced to go all the way back. Finally, having walked around the obstruction I met Murray who had driven round to pick us up, there were a few more guys on the trip in the same predicament. Great customer service from Murray saving us old fellows from the long walk, but Looe skippers are great at this sort of thing, it's a consequence of mooring on a river.

Once on the boat the usual pleasantries were exchanged and we all set about rigging the rods, it was a day of drifting reefs and pinnacles so lures, and booms were the order of the day. Murray gave me as much advice as he could on targeting the Coalfish that tend to sit above the shoals of Pollack, he went on to give me a Deadly Night shade coloured artificial eel that the Coalfish had taken a shine too. The method of fishing was to drop the rig consisting of a lead weight, long flowing trace and artificial eel down to the reef then retrieve steadily up to around 20 turns of the reel, this is repeated until a fish grabs the lure and make you work to bring him up. The difference with the Coalfish was to reel twice the speed as normal and to twice the height above the reef, this equalled twice as much shoulder ache the next day.

Alex had made the long walk from the other side of the huge cat Swallow 2, to pass me his own words of wisdom and also another secret eel that Coalfish love. This is the sort of support I've been blessed with while doing this challenge, Skippers and anglers alike, doing everything they can to help me get that species, that's why I have reached 40 species already. Murray fired up the twin inboards and they gurgled to life like the purring of two of the Tiger Tanks parked outside the bank in Kelly's Heroes, that surely makes me Oddball! We slowly spun around in the flooding tide only just floating and still just scraping bottom, the beautiful site of the open sea loomed. We were joined to our rear by good friend and Skipper Sharky Pete aboard his charter boat Force 10, looking dapper after her winter spruce up. Pete was out on a similar trip and had landed a Coalfish the previous day, sharing this info with Murray, like these Looe legends so often do. We cleared the harbour and it was pedal to the metal to reach the first mark in time for breakfast, a lovely day with a calm sea probably not the best of forecasts for our type of fishing.

Small tides and flat conditions prevent the long traces required for giving the rubber eel a lifelike movement from extending out, this can lead to frustrating tangles, something I found out fairly quickly. I had started with a Portland rig, normally so good at not tangling, but even this was quickly knotted up, then a boom rig, again lots of knots and finally I went right back to basics with a 3-way swivel, which seemed to cure the problem on this particular day. Once I got everything sorted I set about the fast retrieve fishing with the little nightshade sidewinder lure, it wasn't long before it was hit at 27 turns up.

I knew this was probably a Pollack before it hit the surface and sure enough a greedy little guy had wolfed the sidewinder eel. As this was reef fishing and not at great depth the little Pollack were able to be released and he shot off back to terrorise future chunks of rubber. I managed another small Pollack before we moved to a different mark, a short steam along the coast. There were a few Pollack being caught and Murray noticed they were coughing up Sprat, the large shape showing high up in the water on the fish finder, was no doubt attributed to these shimmering shoals of Sprat.

The ever-industrious Murray sidled over with another lure, urging me to have a go high in the water with this Sprat Pattern lure. I was a little reluctant to change but I'm still not stupid enough to ignore a skipper's advice so, on it went. I let it hit bottom and retrieved it super quick, the Fin Nor reel isn't a slouch in the retrieve stakes and as I got to 37 turns the lure was hit and the fish made a powerful dive. I secretly hoped it was the target, fast retrieve, high in the water and we had matched the hatch with the lure, surely everything has fallen into place. Murray was there in seconds, eyes scanning the depths for the glistening shape of a rising fish, "Pollack", Murray burst my bubble with one word. As disappointing as it is, I was really looking for a needle in a haystack and the Pollack fresh from the sea is undeniably a handsome fish, so there's no complaints from me. The little sprat lure though was doing the business taking several more of these copper reef warriors before the day was out, no Coalfish showed to anyone, although Alex did wind me up with a Pollack draped in a black cloth!

The trip was great and once again I got to fish with a great group of anglers, aboard a superb boat, skippered by a truly dedicated man, who put a lot of effort in, what more can you ask. Before heading home, I dropped my boat stuff off at the car and headed down to the rocks to try for that blasted Blenny, knowing in my heart of hearts it is destined to be species 52! With an hour of rock hopping completed, hunger got the better of me and I decided to make tracks, unfortunately in my haste I left my cool bag on the rocks with a box of squid, baiting elastic and lucky scissors. They were only lucky scissors as I had lost them previously and managed to retrieve them from a lake, this time I fear I may never see them again, unless they turn up bobbing up and down in a chum trail.

The next effort was to be another go at a shore caught Smooth Hound, the first couple of trips after them had been somewhat frustrating and both Chris and I were determined to get one this time. We decided to go to a North Devon beach mark we now call Hooper's Hole, and as it was a glorious evening we expected it to be busy, surprisingly we were on our own. I cast out the half Spider Crab and placed the rod on the rest and knew it may well stay there for a little while being low tide. I had brought the LRF rod, so I could have a go at the elusive Blenny and maybe a 5 beard Rockling at the edge of the boulders.

I had cast the scratching rig baited with fish and squid tight to the edge of the rough ground and propped the little rod in the rocks like a beach casting mini-me, I did feel like an ageing gnome. Surprise, surprise nothing on the Blenny tackle, and eventually it was lost to the rough ground, time to return to the Hound rod.

As I negotiated the tank trap boulders, managing to only slip on every third one, I spotted something shining in amongst the stones, something lost that I had found, Nemo! I carefully picked the heroic little Clown fish up in my hand, only to find out that the Pixar favourite was in fact a Terminator, cyberdyne technology clearly visible from the damaged body! What manner of skulduggery was at play here, was nothing sacred anymore, even a children's character could be sent back in time, to hunt down Sarah Connor. Part of me wanted to crush the little beast, but I decided to keep well out of this fight. The hound rod was recast and upon inspection the crab bait had been sucked clean, glad I checked, Chris found a similar result upon checking his own bait. With the baits retied and back out on the sea bed it was coffee and sunset, and the temperature dropped along with the sun.

The tide was about 2.5 hours into the flood and we were still confident in getting a fish, but with every passing minute, the dark cloud of doubt consumes your thoughts, and you begin to worry about the bait, the rig or snags, Zzzz! Chris had a sharp take on the rod and I could clearly see in the glow of the sunset the line dropping slack, " its swimming towards you" I stated. Chris soon caught up with the slack line and by now the Smooth Hound was heading right, a short battle later the fish was reading for netting and I waded out and scooped her up first go. At last the fish we were after had arrived, lovely to see that first Smooth Hound of the year and this was personal best for Chris so double happy days. Smooth Hounds are a beautiful member of the shark family and I love to see them, they are also very well behaved once landed with no spines, sharp teeth or abrasive skin removing coating.

With the pictures taken it was time to release the fish back to the sea, Chris carried the fish down to the water and released the fish, the hound decided to hang around for a while no doubt confused by the headlights. With the first hound making appearance surely it wouldn't be alone, they are after all a pack fish. Eventually after several cups of coffee and multiple laps of the rocks, the rod signalled a good bite but for some reason the fish dropped it and didn't return.

Chris had decided to put out a, go big or go home bait, to try for a conger and out of the blue it started getting some interest, unfortunately the culprit got into a snag and that was the end of the rig. It was another hour before the rod was off again and this time no messing around it was a full-on rip-roaring run, the strike was met by the wonderful feeling of a Smooth Hound heading off along the beach.

These fish are totally awesome critters and the powerful body and huge paddle like fins give them all the power they need, even the small ones don't capitulate straight away. Chris was quickly out in the surf, and done a grand job of netting the fish, we were both delighted to have got this one out of the way.

With species 41 landed I felt a little sad, I love the Smooth Hound fishing but technically I need to move on to the next species, luckily, I do have some more opportunities in June to possibly catch some bigger ones.

The Smooth Hound may have taken 3 trips to acquire but that only adds to the euphoria of the final capture, it was so much sweeter having both caught as we did put in a bit of effort in the end. As the fish swam off into the inky waters of the channel we decided that despite there being 3hrs of good tide left we should head home as we both had work in a few hours and some sleep is always better than no sleep. If, however I hadn't got that fish, I fear I would still be there now, building rock towers out of pebbles.

Saturday was the standard work day at the lakes and while my Dad cut the grass, only breaking one drive belt, I finished the earth wire and tidied the tackle hut. This was well over due, but as I needed to get some of my kit ready for France next week, it made sense to do it at the same time. Once the maintenance duties were complete my Dad headed home while

I had a wander around the lakes putting in some corn around a few of the bottom lakes lily beds. Incredible how they have sprung up in the last fortnight, it does concentrate the Tench though, so I am always pleased to see them flowering. With the bottom lake baited, I checked out the Carp lake, and within 10 minutes had half a dozen fish fighting over the dog mixers I had thrown in, Carp are too easy, and I decided to go for an hours Tench fishing instead. As soon as I had got to the chosen lily bed with the tackle there was plenty of fizzing going on as the Tench rooted around in the silt looking for more sweetcorn. It didn't take too long to get the first fish and I soon notched up 5 fish, all pristine red eyed Tench, then I hooked into a better fish and the light float rod strained as I tried to keep the fish clear of the lily pads.

Fortunately, the fish decided to try heading away from cover and it was game over, as I sunk the landing net, a golden glow emerged from the murky water. It was one of this lake's few Golden Tench and a real beauty, I thought it definitely warranted a few photos and a place in the gallery.

The only downside was that the super bright fish clashed with my top and would have been better with a darker background, but then I never expected this fish today. I decided to record this fish as 28B, alongside the Green Tench, as technically they are the same species. Well that's another blog over with, and a bit of a mixed bag, all the trips were really enjoyable and another species off the list. I very much doubt I will be doing another blog before I head off to France for a week's fishing, I will of course do a blog on the weeks activities, upon my return, but unfortunately the fish don't count as they are not caught in the United Kingdom. I am putting this blog out on a Saturday night as tomorrow I need to tie Catfish rigs, and start packing the gear, what a pain this fishing debarkle is.

## Chapter 25 Small boat, big result

A bonus trip equals an extra blog and after a cracking day with a top bloke, I am totally shattered, early starts are becoming the norm, but they never get easy. At fairly short notice good friend Sam James and I arranged a trip aboard Sam's small boat fishing a few marks in the area of the Lizard in Cornwall. The weather was forecast to be scorchio and with the predicted good tides, Sam agreed to help me try and knock a species or two off my list. When we spoke the two species that came to mind were the Plaice and the Small Eyed Ray, Sam knew a few marks for both, so the targets were chosen.

I got Mrs D to pick up some fresh prawns, pushing my luck with those now, Sam picked up some King Ragworm, combined with Squid and Sandeel gave us all the options we needed. Sam was keen to leave at 7am to make the most of the day which resulted in an alarm call of 04.15 and departure of 5am, as I was looking forward to this getting up wasn't a chore. The drive down on the empty roads took 1hr 45 minutes and I pulled into the parish church carpark with 15 minutes to spare, just 5 minutes later we had loaded the little boat with all the kit. The boat lay on the shingle like a beached fibre glass whale, desperate to be pushed back into the sea.

The little cove where Sam and his family reside is quite stunning and its truly a lovely place to live, a small boat situated here is all you need to unlock a few inshore secrets.

We placed the plastic tubes evenly upon the shingle and dragged the boat over them like the Vikings launching their dragon headed plunder boats. Luckily, I wore my waders which allowed a good push off from the shore, Sam pulled the chord and the outboard fired first time, like captain Ahab chasing down the Great White Whale, Sam stood at the helm with a day of pressure weighing on his mind.

The boat cleared the rocky entrance to the cove and the time hit 7.01, not bad for hitting our schedule, the morning sun had not quite broken through the cloud, yet it was still a beautiful site. The first mark was a sandbank which we drifted over with Plaice rigs laden with Prawn and Ragworm, a few rattles but nothing to show for our efforts. Sam decided to travel a bit further along the coast and target another sandbank before the tide slackened right off, this drift produced no fish but in fairness we were not really moving. Time to drop the anchor and have a go for a Ray, this meant a change to sand eel / squid wraps for me and a big Bluey bait for Sam.

The sun was now beating down and I was getting hassled by a bumblebee, like a Japanese zero it dived on me time and time again. I think the purple Stroke T Shirt in a sea of grey had pushed it over the edge, eventually the Bee spotted another boat in the distance and buzzed off with purpose. Sam's rod was bouncing, and he managed to miss the first bite, my sand eel was then scoffed by a Lesser Spotted Gremlin and Sam followed this with one of his own.

We prayed this was not the start of a pack attack and when Sam's Bluey bait was off again we feared the worse, the bend in the rod pointed towards a different assailant and to our relief a Bullhuss rose to the surface. I added another Sand eel to my wrap and flicked the bait down tide away from the shadow of the boat, this seemed to do the trick as the light Plaice rod suddenly pulled downwards and wasn't stopping. I lifted into the fish and initially thought, Dogfish but the fish had been swimming uptide. When I finally made contact, the fish stripped the braid from the little Abu reel and made repeated deep dives before Sam squeezed it into the net, a lovely Small Eyed Ray, another species knocked off the list.

It's great to watch these lovely Rays swimming off when you release them, this one swam along the surface before diving sharply back to the seabed. Sam was now able to relax he had done a Stirling job on putting us on the fish and the decision to anchor had paid off, especially when Sam's prawn bait on his second rod produced a lovely red spotted Plaice. This was clearly the area for the Plaice and with the tide slowly starting to flood we gambled and set up for some more drifting for the Plaice. We moved back along the coast and dropped the sparkly enticing traces loaded with perfect baits, Sam had spotted fish on the sounder at mid-water and set up some feathers in the hope it was Mackerel. He had got the feathers to the mid-water level when something grabbed them, both of us assuming some form of baitfish but neither of us expected a Grey Gurnard this high in the water but there it was.

We planned to have a go for Red Gurnard later if I ever pulled my finger out and got the Plaice I needed, Sam now on fire species wise added Mackerel to the days catch with a couple of strings in quick succession. The drifts we had done all seemed pretty poor largely down to the lack of tide, the sounder showed we were drifting slowly in an arc and not covering much ground.

This is not the best thing for successful Plaice drifting but of course the man on fire Sam James proved that even a poor drift can produce if you have the skills, as he pulled in another Plaice on the prawn bait. This fish unfortunately had a body for radio and was pretty ugly for a Plaice with a substance like moss growing on it, clearly it had been waiting a long time to pounce. Sam re-positioned the boat and suddenly we were sat perfectly with plenty of tide now pushing us along, the rod tips vibrating rhythmically as the weights bounced over the sand.

The Plaice really had no excuse now everything was spot on, and at last a Plaice dived on my prawn bait and was safely netted. Incredibly as I was unhooking that one my second rod sprung over as another Plaice grabbed a bait, two in the net at the same time and another species crossed off the list. The first Plaice was a beauty which made the capture even sweeter and their bright red spots almost glowed in the bright midday sun.

*Pictured above a lovely brace of Plaice, just what I needed.*

It was time to move out to deeper water and try for another species the Red Gurnard a fish I had never had so any size would be a best. We steamed out on the now flat sea with the feeling that we could literally keep going out and fish wherever we wanted but soon we stopped on some ground Sam has had Red Gurnard from before. Within 10 minutes we moved again after both picking up dogfish, the final mark was in over 100 feet of water and Sam felt confident.

I baited with a tiny slither of fresh Mackerel and Sam tried multiple baits, as soon as his bait hit the bottom it was taken by a good fish we suspected was a Haddock but sadly spat the hook halfway up. With about 15 minutes to go my rod was suddenly wrenched forward but upon lifting into the fish it seemed stuck on the bottom, steady pressure had the unseen fish on the move. Another fish that stripped plenty of line with multiple dives and eventually the light outfit won the day as a 10lb Small Eyed rolled on the surface, this fish took a tiny bit of bait on a tiny hook.

Once again it was lovely to watch this beautiful male ray swim around before descending down out of sight, a great way to end an awesome day. It has been a long, hot tiring day but I've loved every minute, and now with 43 species caught I can relax on holiday before getting back to it on my return. I cannot thank Sam James enough, he worked his socks off today and delivered exactly what we set out to achieve, great company and I really look forward to doing some more small boat fishing.

## Chapter 26 Thunder, Rain and Lightning but it's the Ants that are frightening!

Seems an age since I have done a blog and the fish in this one doesn't even count towards my fifty-two species as they are caught from outside the UK. Why bother with a blog that doesn't reduce the list of species? well quite simply spreading the word and promoting the Stroke Association has always been as important as catching fish and raising money. The 4-yearly trip across the pond with a group of mates has been a tradition that is timed to coincide with the World Cup, although this year we were slightly premature. We have certain criteria when deciding on venues these include, exclusive use of the lake, a cottage close or adjacent to the lake and of course some nice fish. This year we had booked a 4-acre lake with a large cottage near the town of Vitre, named Etang Bertie, there was also a smaller lake attached to the property that we could use. We booked the ferry from Poole but didn't really take into account travel time and the fact it was my birthday, the result was a 3.00am departure from home after a night celebrating. The amount of gear for these trips seems to grow every time and this is despite the fact we have a house to use and shops to purchase supplies. Just looking at the huge pile of kit showed I had everything, but the kitchen sink included to ensure I covered all eventualities.

Due to the early start we had opted to load Trevor's van the night before and as we were travelling with 1 van and 1 car, space could be a premium.

We needn't have worried as some quality vehicle loading by Jamie and Kevin had all the gear neatly stacked with space to spare. Before we knew it, we were on route towards Poole and the Brittany Ferry to Cherbourg, the journey was uneventful and filled with the anticipation of the following weeks fishing.

Mike was joining us on this trip and although not an angler he was an avid camper and lover of France, we had persuaded him to join us having all grown up with him. He had kindly volunteered to drive his car, taking Kevin, Jamie and I with him, Trevor and his 12-year-old son Tommy followed behind in the van with the kit. The ferry port as usual is a breeze and the staff at Brittany Ferries are well versed in the loading process, we were joined in the queue by a convoy of world war two American jeeps. It's a stark reminder that 74 years previously young men had made the ultimate sacrifice landing on the Normandy beaches to face a well-armed ruthless German force.

 Once aboard ship it was time for breakfast and we headed for the café hoping for a traditional English breakfast, unfortunately the café served continental, so it was orange juice and croissants. As we finished the rather unsatisfactory breakfast we had a message from Trevor who had been loaded separately and was now in the café having a full English! Darn it, we didn't think that there could be two restaurants onboard. That didn't faze Kev and Jamie who were up for breakfast number two and we all headed off to track it down, while in the café we think we may have spotted our first Frenchman.

The 4-hour crossing was pleasant and with the sun beaming down we found a sun trap up on deck and lounged around taking in the ambience of the morning. Soon the huge ferry arrived at the commercial hub of Cherbourg and whatever way you look at it, the port just isn't picturesque, but it does provide the service it was designed for.

We soon disembarked and cleared security before heading south to the town of Vitre around 3 hours' drive. Before arriving at the lake, we stocked up at the local Lidl's which was handy as the store was the same as back home, although much of the food was very different. Finally, 14 hours after leaving home we arrived at the lake and its lovely typical French cottage, first order of service was the walk around.

 The lake was gorgeous with a large central island and around 5 purpose made swims, although these were somewhat overgrown, and the water level was 2 feet higher than it should have been.

Eventually we all selected swims and I chose an area known as deep bay that also included an overgrown arm off to the left, that surely would be an ambush point for Catfish, the species I was after. We set up the camps and were keen to get the rods out and get some sleep, to start properly in the morning, young Tommy was quickly into a fish, a small catfish that made his day.

With the darkness wrapping its inky arms around the lake it was time to hit the sack and get some well-earned sleep, I know I hadn't thought too much about tactics, just pellet out on the far margin. The night was far from peaceful as the deafening screeches of a million frogs did their best to prevent us sleeping, the humid night meant a night on top of the bag. I soon found myself subjected to a multitude of little critters crawling all over me, I flicked on the head torch to reveal a trail of Ants along my arm, across the bed and down the side of my rucksack to the floor. My only option was to climb into the bag and zip up leaving just my face exposed, no doubt to be ravaged by the tiny beasts.

The consequence of covering up was to cook inside a material sauna, the lesser of the two evils, despite the tiredness I slept very little as the constant stomping of tiny feet across my face was somewhat of a distraction. The next morning could not come quick enough and as soon as the light was up I emptied my bivvy to reveal a black mass of ants under every item. I had setup camp on an ant's nest and the residents were none too pleased, I had found some ant powder at the house and created a barrier around the inside perimeter of the tent. This should keep the army of ants at bay for the next evening and maybe I would get some sleep. Jamie and Kevin over the far side of the lake had opened their accounts with a couple of nice fish in the early hours of the morning.

Mike who hadn't fished during the night had enjoyed a nice night's sleep and I felt somewhat jealous that I had lent him my dome tent with a sewn in ground sheet making it Ant proof.

My rods with the Catfish baits had remained silent and I felt that a change of tactics would be in order for the upcoming evening. Trevor had managed a nice 27lber and while he popped back to the house his son Tom hooked into a real beast of a fish, I assisted him as much as possible, but the fish crossed the whole lake to the sanctuary of the marginal weed beds and the hook came out. The little lad followed this up with another monster that took the bait to the edge of the island, this time fearing the fish was snagged I had a go with the rod and after walking slowly backwards the fish was once again on the move and swimming. Tom took back over but the fish found another snag, this was obviously a catfish and after witnessing the fish roll and slapping its tail it was clearly a 40lb+ fish.

Trevor turned up and took over from his frustrated son, he soon had the fish in the open water and passed the rod back to his son. Unfortunately, as can be the case with big fish they will exploit any weakness, and, in this case, Trevor tried to move his left-hand rod from the path of the approaching cat only to find his line snagged, the two taught lines crossed and the inevitable happened the one with the fish on parted. Poor Tom was gutted but not despondent and quickly got his baits back out in the water with my bait boat. I spent the afternoon stalking in the back of the arm with float fished worm in the hope of picking up a catfish. My persistence paid off as a raft of bubbles exploded around the float signifying the arrival of a fish and shortly after the float slid slowly away and a small Catfish was hooked and landed, much to my relief.

The evening plan was to use a large bunch of worms fished on a Dyson rig in the middle of the deep channel entering the arm. As the evening approached so did the grumbling beast of a thunder storm and with the rods out, ants contained, and tea eaten it was time to take cover in the Bivvy and wait out the storm. The rumbles grew deafening, even drowning out the howler monkey like frog chorus, splats of rain impacted on the outer skin of my shelter and lightening lit up the mozzy proof Bivvy front, like an x-ray machine firing repeatedly.

The worm rig was off and running as a catfish chomped on the worms, I couldn't believe how I went from dry to drenched in mere seconds. I landed the catfish and sacked it up as the owner wanted small cats removed and put in the small lake below the main one. I re-cast the worm rod and climbed soaked back into my cosy little camp, removing the wet clothes and firing up the kettle for a warming brew.

Just as I was dried out the worm rod was off again, and, in my haste, I failed to put on my coat and once again found myself instantly soaked in the driving rain. This was another small catfish but bigger than the first and as before was sacked for transfer to the other lake. I returned again to my material house and like the last little pig felt secure once inside, as I know from previous excursions it just doesn't leak. I sat on the bed, now down to just my underpants the only dry item I had on.

My thoughts once again drifted to my neighbour Mike, who chooses not to fish during the night and was tucked up snug and warm in the adjacent tent. The storm was reaching dangerous levels and I was contemplating calling it a night when the worm rod was wailing for attention again, I ran out bare foot and in only my pants which soon met the same fate of all my previous layers. As soon as I struck the fish I knew it was a much better fish and the rod steadily bent over as the fish swam away up the arm on the left. I now realised this was a daft place to catfish as the fish disappeared out of view, my line now heading towards the reeds, 10 minutes of a fairly even tug of war and I had the Catfish in the margin at my feet but stuck solid.

Boom a huge clap of thunder bellowed above my head and the lightening lit the whole lake, I must be stark raving mad I thought as I lay down the rod and waded out up to my waste in the warm lake. I followed the line down to the top of the rig knowing full well my hand will meet the catfish at some point, as I followed the trace to the hook I felt the base of the reed where the hook was now imbedded.

 The fish was gone, I was soaked literally to the skin and with so much static in the air I knew even my remaining hair was probably stood on its end. I didn't feel like recasting the bait and when Jamie called on the walkie talkie to say he was also down to his pants and felt it too dangerous to continue we all reeled in and called it a night.

The storm raged all night and so it was another night of little to no sleep, although I soon warmed up inside the sleeping bag I was relieved to know I wouldn't have to get out again. The next morning our camps looked battered and bruised and it's amazing how good a shower and clean clothes can make you feel. Kevin and Jamie had managed a few more fish during the night leading to them getting a soaking like me, they continued their carp catching in the morning both taking good twenty's.

Trevor and Tom had wisely not fished during the night and were now up and determined to get a fish or two with the sun out there was no excuse. I had, had enough of the back bay it wasn't a sensible place to target Catfish as if they went left like last night it was nearly impossible to get them back to my swim, so it was time to move. With the sun now beating down and my kit nicely dry I walked all the way around to a swim in front of the island where I hoped a hooked catfish could be landed easier.

 The move took me a couple of hours and I made sure that the area was ant free and not too close to trees as more thunder storms were forecast that evening. I got the rods out fairly quickly with one on the Dyson worms and another using a fresh dead bait, the third was on large pellet. The dead bait was taken in no time, and I was surprised to see a Pike on the end of the line. The worms continued to get interest from small catfish and I soon landed a few more of these voracious little predators, they really loved the huge bunch of worms. The bigger cats were remaining elusive although Jamie was getting a few by accidents on his little wafter baits the best going 20lb, typical!

Kevin had managed a 30lb Carp and they were hoping that perhaps the bigger fish were finally going to feed. As predicted the thunderstorms returned and somewhat earlier than predicted it becomes somewhat demoralising night after night of lashing rain and ground vibrating thunder not to mention the hazard that standing with a 12-foot carbon pole creates. Tommy was into a great fish and soon his dad netted him a personal best 27lber and not even the rain could ruin this moment with his dad. The storms arrived early and cleared for a time allowing a brief glimpse of a beautiful sunset and once again we were serenaded by our million-strong frog choir, it seemed a perfect evening.

It wasn't long before the storms returned and fearing a night of soaking I reeled in opting for a good night's sleep and a new plan for the morning. With several days elapsing and I not managing to land anything of any note I decided to try and catch a few carp instead, so the next day I borrowed a couple of the wafters from Kev and Jamie having not brought carp baits.

I made up some ground bait and setup a method feeder in the margin and steadily introduced bait throughout the day. I noticed a lovely green dragon fly sat sunbathing or most likely drying itself out, the wings caught the light in such a way that it resembled stained glass windows, incredible mother nature. I hadn't noticed until afterwards the other creature or Dragonfly larvae sat beneath the wings and this could well have been the empty shell of this insect.

The margin rod let out a scream as a fish had fallen into the trap that I had made throughout the day and Mike finally had something to help me net, it wasn't until it rolled just out of reach that I could see it was the lakes Koi Carp.

*Above the stunning Koi brightened up the week*

Like David Dickinson the orange glow looked totally unnatural in the chocolate coloured water, and for a few heart stopping moments I felt this stunning fish would surely be lost. We couldn't get the net past the marginal weeds and while we struggled the fish rolled repeatedly in its bid for freedom, finally the net reached, and the prize was mine.

The fish wasn't huge, but size is irrelevant on a fish of this beauty and this golden glow punctuated even the dullest of days, and like an arriving sentinel this fish heralded in a change in the weather and my fishing. The next day the weather was cracking, and I said to Mike lets go and check out the weedy pond below the main lake, this 2-acre lake was like something from the lost world. Trees long dead hung over the lakes margins like timber octopuses reaching out into the gloom, the surface of the lake was covered in a layer of moss croutons and thick weed strands rose from the silty lakebed.

 This lake was also very shallow probably only a depth of 3 feet, and due to the dense overgrowth and lush conifers the ambient temperature was several degrees lower than the more exposed higher lake. We grabbed a rod each and went off for a few hours in search of whatever lives there, it's quite exciting casting into the unknown. I opted for the method feeder with a small meaty flavoured pop-up, I could then bury the hook bait in the ground bait and avoid the patches of dense weed.

The rod had only been cast 5 minutes when it tore off and a bow wave formed on the green surface scattering the moss in all directions'. This small Carp went ballistic and was what we call a wild Carp, carp left to their own devices will eventually revert to their wild form, long lean and powerful. The fish of just a couple of pounds was quite stunning due to the clear spring water and was very coppery with a purple hue so common with clear water fish.

Within another 20 minutes I was in again and this one jumped clean from the water like a marlin causing a thousand frogs to chirp wildly for help, an amazing scrap followed with a much better size fish, strangely chunky for this little lake. Mike really needed to get one so the next take on my rod was his, his own rod without the feeder had been incredibly quiet. It didn't take long before my rod was once again attached to a Carp and Mike finally got a fish, although he hadn't hardly fished this week opting to run 10k everyday instead.

It was great to see Mike chuffed with his small wild carp and he was more than happy to end his fishing with that fish and continue watching everyone else. The afternoon continued to produce carp for us and we finished with another stunning looking carp, a nice low double, making it 10 runs in the few hours we did, more importantly it was great to spend quality time with one of my long-time mates.

It was time to get back to the main lake the lads were having a barbecue and watching the England game that evening, for me fishing beats football every day of the week so I would be on the lake myself that night. One of the downsides of the recent bad weather was my bait boat had started to play up and was now not working at all, I think water had got into the handset, but it was totalled for the week. This meant it was back to the old school method of casting out and baiting with a catapult, it's important not to rely on this hi-Tec equipment which is never a substitute for basic water craft.

My plan for the afternoon / evening was one rod cast out to a weedy bay on the left where fish had been showing over the last few days, the middle rod was to be for cats with double 22mm halibut pellet cast in the deep channel and baited with a kilo of big pellet. The final rod was to be cast to the right of the island with a PVA bag of pellet and a small popup. I knew that the catfish liked large beds of pellet and so topped up the channel with 20 baits every 30 minutes, this had the desired effect as soon a huge area of bubbles erupted over the baited area. This sheet of bubbles and froth extended over a large area and patches of silt were also visible across a large square section of the surface, I knew this was a very large catfish, they reach sizes of 130lb in this lake.

Then as expected the catfish rod roared off and the surface of the lake boiled, I picked up the rod and engaged the reel, but the fish was already steaming off down the side of the island. Despite the strong tackle I couldn't stop the fish, all I could do was to keep the pressure on to impede its journey as best I could, then the rod flew back, and the fish was gone. Upon retrieving the tackle, I could see the hook trace had parted, I had been using 30lb Ntrap coated braid, but I normally use heavier quicksilver, looking at the bait bucket the two pre-baited rigs sat on the pellets were both the heavy quicksilver. No excuses there, total angler error, never, never give big fish a weak point to exploit as they will inevitably make a fool out of you. The left-hand rod was now off and running and in a slow dejected sort of way so was I, the fish was hooked and after a short battle Mike netted it first go.

I re-rigged the catfish rod with the appropriate quicksilver trace material and put out another kilo of pellet in the same area, the night began pulling in and the lake felt strangely eerie with the guys all up at the house. It was a perfect fishing night, hot humid with a slight breeze and I relished the company of the frogs, bats and feral cats. We have had dealings with feral cats in the past and I never take any chance with them, as one walked towards the darkened door of my Bivvy I decided to bark loudly in my best Rottweiler voice, it did the trick as the cat left the ground instantly and I didn't see it land!

I must have dozed off to sleep as it was 2am when I was awoken by the screaming of some hideous alien beast with its high-pitched beeping noise, that will be the alarm with the catfish rod then. I ran out and struck to nothing, how frustrating, I clipped on a new trace loaded with pellet and fired it out into the darkness and added 20 baits in the general direction.

It's always difficult to get back to sleep after that sort of incident but eventually I did only to have the same alien encounter an hour later with the rod once again roaring off. This was becoming tiresome, but I lifted into the rod and felt good resistance as the fish kited left towards weedy bay, no you don't I thought and bullied it back right, the fish made repeated runs towards the island and I thought this must be a fairly nice catfish.

The fish was now approaching the margin and as it turned in the red glow of my head torch I was shocked to see a large Carp, I needed to get out past the reeds to net the fish and just waded out fully clothed, the warm water oozed into every void and was not unpleasant in the sticky night. Now I had cleared the rushes I could net the fish properly and after a couple of misses I finally scooped up the fish, a lovely big common of 30lb. I weighed the fish which went 31lb, lovely, jubbly and surely worth getting wet for, problem was no one to take the pictures, I sacked the fish temporarily and went back to the house to change into dry clothes. Despite creeping carefully up the creaky stairs they were awfully loud but maybe that was my intention and sure enough Mike called out " is everything ok"? I explained what I had caught and that I needed to get the fish back as soon as possible and he graciously got dressed and came down and done the photos, what a star! Mike was soon back at the house and I was once again sat in the darkness although somewhat happier after landing that fish.

I made a coffee and decided to sit and watch the arrival of dawn over the lake as the frog chorus changed to the bird's dawn chorus, fish started topping all over the lake. Then the right-hand rod was off next to the island and as I played the fish towards the margin the left-hand rod was also signalling a fast bite, typical two fish at once. I eventually netted the first fish and ran and grabbed the second rod but by now this one had reached the weed and the hook pulled free. The other fish was another lovely common and as luck would have it I spotted Jamie heading back to his Bivvy, he gladly came over and done the obligatory pictures.

Everyone was getting their baits out and young Tommy was keen as mustard rowing out his baits, baiting up and getting rewarded with a bevy of fish in quick succession, including a 30lber. The fish really were on the feed on our last day of fishing and despite Jamie starting well with 10 twenties' in a row his catches had petered out, dad Kevin though was catching up with a 30lb Common and the biggest fish of the trip a 37lb Mirror. The left hand weedy bay continued to show signs of fish and I crept through the overgrowth to grab a few snaps of the fish rolling amongst the weed, I got a shot of the carp but also spotted a big grass Snake heading over to snakeaphobic Kevin and took a quick snap. Just as I returned from the look around weedy bay the rod positioned over there, roared off and I was into another big common carp that used the weed beds to its advantage, determination prevailed, and I managed to get the fish in and landed.

Jamie had decided to have a go down the weedy lake for one of the hard fighting wild carp and was soon radioing that he had caught a catfish, this was quickly followed by another. I couldn't believe it, I was wanting catfish and he was catching them while trying for carp. Then young tommy reported he had just landed a pesky catfish of 12lb, once again on his fruity carp bait. I had enough of carp and seeing as we were packing up today I decided to get all my stuff packed and put away and just go to the bottom lake for the evening and fish for catfish, at least I would feel like I was predator fishing.

Trevor, Toms dad had also done well through the week but unfortunately when I asked him for the pictures of his fish he had caught, I was sent one Carp picture, three black squares and a picture of a lion! With everything dried in what was the hottest day of the week it was time to head down to spend the last few hours on the weedy lake in the hope of a catfish or two. Jamie had managed 3 during the afternoon so there seemed to be a few about and if not, it would still be a relaxing way to finish the holiday.

I walked down ahead of Mike who said he would meet me down there in 5 minutes, it took less than 5 minutes to get the first run and what fun that was hooking a catfish in such shallow water. Mike arrived in time to take the photos and he really is a natural at taking the pictures pointing out if the background isn't great or two bright.

The evening was really enjoyable and a fitting end to a wonderful weeks fishing, testing at times for sure but what fishing isn't. I managed 3 Cats in the few hours on the weedy pond the biggest being 15lb and my total for the week was 11 Carp to 31lb, 15 Cats to 15lb, 1 Pike and 1 Hybrid. The highlight catch of my trip was without doubt the stunning Koi, although the ones that got away may have been nice. The other guys all caught plenty of carp and young Tommy caught the most which was fantastic to see, every fish he caught was earned, he rigged up, baited up and played the fish all himself I look forward to Tom giving us a lesson again on our next trip.

We spent that evening in the cottage and headed off early the next day stopping at a French café for a final taste of France, you can't come to France without sampling their finest creation a drink that sums up the French and the French talent for creation, that's right Oragina! Thanks guys for wonderful memories, some in the face of adversary, you all kept me sane when disaster struck on numerous occasions and I'm proud to call you my mates! It's only going be two years to the next one as we are going during the Euros so roll on then.

*The picture above shows the gang before we leave for home.*

Back to the challenge next weekend with a try for the Tope, joining the Happy Danglers out of Minehead aboard Steve Webbers Osprey.

Chapter 27 Father's Day but the Tope don't play.

This week's blog was to be largely about the mighty Tope one of our most powerful of sea fish and a voracious member of the shark family that inhabits the inshore marks of our coast. As can be typical with fishing and my challenge nothing really goes to plan, and you just can't get fish to follow a script.

The trip was booked some time ago with the Happy Danglers and the boat was skipper Steve Webber's Osprey based in Minehead, so, quality boat, skipper and venue. Due to a cancelation Chris was able to join me on his first trip with the Danglers which would make the long journey to Minehead slightly more interesting. The Saturday we were out working at the lakes during the morning adding a strand of barb wire to the fence. You really have to know what you're doing with this stuff, and as we didn't, we managed to cut each other up worse than a couple of drunk musketeers.

Once patched up and completed we headed off to the beach to gather hardback crabs for the following days trip, if the Tope didn't show it would be Smoothhounds as a backup. Hardback crabs are a far cheaper alternative to buying peeler crabs but if you factor in the fuel and time not sure how much we really saved, especially as they were so elusive. We spent quite a while foraging under rocks and weed before we found a single crab, the really annoying thing was that every pool was full of my nemesis the lesser caught Blenny!

Chris looked at one stage to be praying to the gods of the Crab to bestow a couple of crustaceans upon us as he huddled over a small gap in the rocks, it seemed to do the trick as soon we were both wrangling with the aggressive little crabs. This was just in the nick of time as both Chris and I were getting to the point of robbing some kids of their prized buckets of crabs, which probably wouldn't have ended well.

With the crabs safely caught it was time to get home and sort the tackle, it wasn't an early start in the morning as we weren't heading out to sea until 10am. Chris picked me up and despite a brisk south westerly breeze it looked a great day for a spot of Tope fishing. Our leisurely trip up to Minehead had cost us one of the free parking spaces and that always leaves a bad taste in the mouth, now £6 out of pocket. We walked over to the harbour where everyone else was busy catching crabs from the harbour wall like excited children, we had actually thought of that and brought our crab nets but as there were now plenty of crab we didn't bother. The boats of the Minehead fleet were all getting readied by their respective skippers and it's a sign of the times that there are so many Cats within the charter industry now. This type of boat does provide a large comfortable fishing platform that many anglers choose as their preferred option. Steve picked us up at the steps and we were soon loaded up and heading south in the less than clear water of the Bristol Channel, the white spires of Butlins standing out like a plastic Sydney Opera House slowly grew smaller as we steamed along the coast.

The coastline along the Somerset / Devon borders is quite stunning with huge cliffs clad in dense trees resembling Jurassic Park's Isla Nublea island, and the murky brown waters certainly do hold monsters. I do love the journey to the first mark of the day, the sea air acts like an atomiser of good things in life and I will never tire of this feeling of admiration for the world in which we live. I watched the gulls soaring effortlessly and with such grace, it was hard to imagine that these are the same creatures that steals chips and bombs you with their super accurate doo doos! The image on this morning was of a bird of great aerial skills and it reminded of one of the few books I read through choice, Johnathan Livingstone Seagull a wonderful book giving a different perspective on Gulls. Before we knew it the engines of Osprey fell silent and the large chunk of iron plummeted to the seabed, our umbilical to tether us in the rapid channel tide flow. The boat settled into her position and it was lines down time, incredibly it was only 6oz of lead that was needed to pin the rig to the bottom a rarity in this neck of the woods. The mark we were on was an area frequented by Smoothhounds and it was straight on with the hardback crabs in the hope that a pack would soon arrive. Pete Gregory was soon into the first hound of the day and he proved to be the most consistent Hound catcher on the day despite reluctantly using his supply of peeler crab to achieve it. I was then into a hound that had snaffled one of our hard-earned beach crabs, as per usual the scrap was excellent and eventually a nice hound broke surface, skipper Steve quickly unhooking it at the side of the boat. No photo opportunity that time, I must remember to let the skipper know I'd like a quick picture, a couple more hounds were landed before the tide picked up.

With the increasing tide the wind also picked up and before we knew it we were surrounded by white horses and a misty drizzle arrived to dampen spirits. Skipper Steve decided to move to another mark tight to the protection of the cliffs which would offer a variation of species. With the move made the difference was staggering and even the sun decided to come out, the surface of the water was flat calm, and it was hard to imagine that 20 minutes previously we had been so uncomfortable. With the chance of a Bullhuss now on the cards I decided to try a Mackerel Head on a more substantial trace that was fished on the uptide setup, I have been after a double figure Bullhuss for several years so always have a go for them when I can. I cast this towards the shore allowing the grip lead to lodge properly in the soft seabed before tightening the line. Instantly the rod sprang back as a fish took the bait, this turned out to be a strap Conger, followed by another one and I then changed to half a Mackerel bait.

The rod once again sprang back and this time upon striking it was very different with line peeling off the fixed spool reel steadily, indicating a better fish. The skipper arrived with the net knowing it could be a better fish and a short distance behind the boat the broad snout of a Bullhuss appeared from the gloom, I knew it was a personal best and just hoped it wasn't just holding the bait a trait this species is notorious for. I have lost a few good Bullhuss in the past out with Andy Howell on Anglo Dawn, due to them letting go at the surface after gripping the bait during the whole fight. With the fish safely netted I was keen to see if it would be the double I was after and at 11lb 8oz it certainly was so that was trip made for me.

I have had a Bullhuss on this challenge but as it was smaller than the Lesser Spotted Dogfish in the gallery it was somewhat demeaning to the superior species, at least I can now put this wrong right and update the gallery. Chris was also desperately seeking a Huss having not caught one this year despite trying on a number of occasions and now I hoped it would come together for him, he stuck to the plan, big baits and surely it would only be a matter of time. There were several Huss coming aboard and it was all getting a bit strange with trip organiser and backbone of the danglers Nick Smith hooking a Bullhuss and Lesser Spotted Dogfish on the same hook.

Chris then thinking Neptune had finally heeded his prayers battled a Bullhuss to the surface only to find out that incredibly it was hooked in the tail, super lucky or highly unlucky either way it was like strange forces were at work! Pete then made his day catching a stunningly marked 3 Bearded Rockling which after the mammoth photo session was returned lovingly to the sea, the rockling hadn't been returned long before Pete managed a nice Bullhuss.

Chris was no doubt wondering what he could do to finally get one as several had been landed from all around the boat. We decided to try out a bit further for the Tope in a mark with a bit deeper water, unfortunately this meant stronger tide and It was on with the 1lb 8oz leads, wire trace and big baits. As the slack water arrived so did a scattering of Conger and Chris managed one of the better ones a scraper double, which pleased him no end although it was released prior to a photograph.

The tide soon began to run again, and Nick Smith was soon battling a fish that although initially appeared decent turned into an average Huss, not that he was milking it whatsoever. Several dogfish crashed the party and pulling in a big lead in a strong tide with one of these spotted spinners can be somewhat tiresome. As evident by the title the Tope never showed, and Pete told me from his experience they don't really like the rough sea and overcast days, this sort of rings true with the successful Tope days I've had in the past.

I have neglected to mention the excellent hosting skills of skipper Steve and first mate Will, nothing was too much trouble and I had brought bacon and rolls which were cooked up for a hot breakfast. Also on the trip another Chris, this one a master sausage maker, supplied the afternoons hot snacks with his superior spicy sausages. I hope skipper Andy Howell reads this and adds this to Anglo's facilities for our August sorte, I can imagine the answer will include the words, stuffed, you, get and can! With the Huss back on the feed there was still time for Chris to get one and as both our rods began bouncing we feared that deep below the waves a dogfish may be undertaking a knit one pearl one job on our lines.

Chris seized the moment and struck defiantly hoping to either knock off the dogfish or hook the Huss fortunately it was the latter and sure enough finally he got what he had hoped for.

Seeing we weren't connected to the same fish I thought I should check my bait and this also had a Bullhuss attached although my one was only dogfish sized. We opted to finish off the day with another go at the Smoothhounds on a mark closer to home and up anchored for the 40-minute steam back. I have fished this mark before and it's a great spot for rays, so I was in two minds what to target, as I hadn't got a Smoothound picture, and if I caught a Starry Smoothound it would be specics 44 that was the initial target.

As per the rest of the day Pete was soon in to a decent hound which looked every bit a double figure fish, strangely the fish had taken he's Bluey bait intended for Rays. Tom fishing to my left had simultaneous bites on his two rods landing both fish, a Smoothound and Thornback Ray, good bit of angling that Tom.

Nick also landed a nice Hound on the new mark, but I think sleepy Cider Sam who had slept through at least one mark was having some serious sausage reaction, no doubt curtailing his fishing abilities. I had missed a few bites on the crab and I think they must have been pup hounds as they seemed to drop the bait fairly quickly after the initial rattle. Finally, a proper take on a spider peeler and I was hooked into a hound and my last fish of the day, the skipper kindly netted it, so I could grab a photograph. The fish was indeed a Starry Smoothound and therefore species 44, purists will say that recent genealogy testing points to Common and Starry being the same species, I have always considered them separate and after much discussion that's what I'm going with.

The Starry Smoothhound is so called due to the bright white clusters of spots that cover their backs, the Common has no or very fine spots that are hardly visible. With the day at an end and everyone feeling exhausted, happy and content, and they weren't 3 of snow white's dwarfs, it was time to head for home. Thanks to skipper Steve, first mate Will and big thanks to Nick Smith for all the organising he does for the Danglers. Cheers as usual to Chris for driving, photography and helping gather bait, and to my wife and kids for letting me disappear on Father's Day. Next weekend it's the 2-day Conger festival down in Plymouth and although I've had a Conger for the species hunt I could add a bigger one and I aim to try for that pesky blenny on Saturday evening. Our team name is Longer, Stronger Conger and after coming runners up two years in a row we are hoping this is our year, if not it's still a great weekend.

*The stunning Bullhuss and a new personal best, happy days.*

## Chapter 28 Longer, Stronger, Conger

This weekend it was the British Conger Club annual 2-day festival and despite the fact that I've already landed a Conger I still had a plan to try and sneak out another species. Last year I had come second in the biggest Eel competition with a Conger of 51lb and our team had come second in the team competition for the second year in a row. This year we wanted to win the team event and take the crown from the Gouriet brothers team, a super pair of guys who have been awesome in their Conger wrangling. Our team was Steve Hollyer, Sam James, John Locker and I, bit of a strange old mix and friend Steve Hollyer is not only an inspirational angler but is totally blind. Sam is deaf but manages with the use of hearing aids and I guess as I don't say much I must be dumb! Clearly, I haven't mentioned the whole team as there is also the small matter of John the fish locker, who appears to be the perfect specimen getting his guns out at the slightest sign of sun. Yes, I used to think John was faultless but I'm glad to say that when his wife Hannah posted a video of the interview, following his historic capture of the record Bass I knew he was indeed human and could look as stupid as the rest of us.

So that's our team and we have done okay over the last few years, this year however we had pre- comp team talks, and bounced a few ideas around in the hope that this would be our year. Baits would be key, and it would be crucial to carryout regular bait changes to ensure a good scent.

This year the club had decided to have the AGM on the Friday night following the signing on process in the hope that more members would attend. I managed to extend my accommodation to include the extra night and travelled down Friday afternoon arriving at the George Guest house around 16.30.

Like every other city, as soon as you stop for more than 5 minutes you start paying and Plymouth City Council are just as effective as the rest, with parking meters on every section of road. The accommodation was very impressive, as I had a huge room with two single beds and a double, nice ensuite shower and all for £60 can't complain. I met up with John, Hannah and Tom, Johns friend Tom had just made an epic 8hr journey from up north, to fish the competition for the first time. We all had a bite to eat then headed off to the registration and AGM, the barbican was packed as the good weather drew people of all ages to be by the sea. The AGM went fairly well although there were a few issues with hearing the speakers above the music being played in the other bar. Sam James had made a proposal that I had seconded, that referred to the confusion created by associate and full membership and suggested that we just have membership of the club without the need to catch a large eel. The thought was that with dwindling membership, could we afford to turn away potential members dissuaded by the impression of elitism that the present two-tier system created. This idea was agreed by the membership which surprised both Sam and I but shows how much the existing membership want the club to survive.

The other big issue at the AGM was the standing down of Conger Club legend and President Mike Millman, Mike has been involved with the club for more than 50 years and I remember watching his conger video when video was a thing! Mike delivered a great speech highlighting the difference in numbers attending tonight's meeting compared to the 300 plus that attended the dinner and dance in 1997, once again highlighting the demise of the single species clubs. The club presented Mike an engraved bowl and his supportive wife a bouquet of flowers that clearly moved them and for once Mike was short of words. Following the AGM was the raffle, and I had actually bought a few strips for a fiver which turned out to be my first bit of luck of the weekend as my number was pulled out first, resulting in £50 in cash.

Now with a wedge of cash burning a hole in my pocket I decided to make a b-line for my room as I had an early start planned in the morning, part of my plan to get another species. I had decided as the club had agreed an early start of 6am in the morning to make the most of the tides that I would get up at 4am drive down to Elphinstone carpark, cook sausages, and chuck out my LRF rod for a mini species or two, genius! I got back to the hotel around 10pm and straight away realised that my room was virtually above the pub next door, the revellers outside were having fun and making a lot of noise, but I just needed to move to the single bed away from the window. I must have dozed off but was woken by the couple upstairs directly above my single bed, seemingly playing a noisy game of hopscotch, but they were having fun and all I had to do was move to the other single bed which was not directly below them.

It was at this point I realised why there was 3 beds in the room and eventually I fell asleep, but it seemed unfairly short as the flippin alarm cheerily burst into life. I dragged myself out of bed and made as much noise as possible making my morning brew in the hope the hopscotchers would be disturbed. The sun was already starting to rise as I arrived at the carpark and despite the rigid lines of the urban landscape it was still strangely beautiful. The ridge monkey was loaded with sausages and the little stove roared to life in the chill morning light, the LRF rod was flicked out with a small piece of ragworm dangling enticingly, we could all eat well this morning. The LRF rod was bouncing wildly as some little critter feasted on the hapless worm, juggling sausages, rolls and conger rods wasn't the best way of connecting with these tiny fish and I missed fish after fish, who were no doubt getting fat on the worms. More importantly the sausages were ready, and it was my time to have a nibble, so the little fish would have to wait until later.

I was really glad I made the effort as there was something quite poetic about watching the sunrise over a city while enjoying a freshly cooked sausage bap! I then had a phone call from John telling me to get myself over to the pontoon as everyone was arriving, I finished the rolls and grabbed the conger stuff for the 5 minute yomp to the ferry pontoon. As per usual on the first day of a festival everyone was full of anticipation and hoping for a monster, the one thing that was for sure was there would be no fresh mackerel for bait. Like the previous year the Mackerel were noticeable by their absence and the club had advised us all to bring plenty of bait, we had brought, cuttlefish, octopus and frozen mackerel so were covered.

We sat on the pontoon ready for the 6am start and one by one the other boats loaded up and set off out to sea, around 6.15 Paul Maris rang the skipper of our boat for day one Tamesis, Roy answered and explained he hadn't been told of a 6am start and would be there at 7am!

The 8 of us sat there and remained good humoured and pondered the rumours of possible foul play, we knew the skipper would still give us our designated fishing time it was just annoying about the early start. Before long the sea lock opened and Tamesis appeared like a very welcome white chariot, we loaded up and were on our way as some of the other boats dropped anchor. The eels started biting and we all quickly noticed just how finicky they were with slow pulls and tugs very non-committal, eventually one slipped up and was being pumped steadily to the surface when the rod sprung back, and the eel was gone.

The club had decided to insist on barbless hooks for the first time on this festival and this decision was made for the right reasons but turned out to possibly be a mistake. I lost my first eel after a minute of playing it during a series of violent head shakes, John hooked his annual standard Ling, which he followed up with a chubby pouting, why don't they come off? Eventually eels were starting to get to the surface and I managed to get my first one on-board, I had a problem with the dense red algae building up on the leader knot,

We really seemed to be up against it this weekend with the barbless hooks, algae, lack of bait and finicky eels but at least we were all in the same boat so to speak. Fortunately, both John and I were slowly scraping out a result and the last hour on a new wreck, I managed to land 4 fish giving me 6 for day one and John ended with 7, several fish of 30lb were landed but Paul Maris on our boat had the only weigher that went 42lb on the scales at sea. We had several multiple hook ups when the eels finally came on the feed, but sadly both the last fish threw the hooks on their journey to the surface.

We headed in a little deflated thinking largely about all the fish that were lost and how we could improve the next day. It had been a tough day and the hour steam home, soon had me crashed on the deck dreaming of a smaller species of fish. We found out from team mates Steve and Sam that they had managed 11 eels between them, so all looked good for our team after day one. Once we reached dock I thanked the skipper and his mate and headed straight over to the carpark to settle some unfinished business with the gang of worm robbers. We hadn't got back until 5.15 and Steve's wife Helen had booked a table at an Indian for us at 7pm so I was on the clock, I figured I would spend 30 minutes to try and winkle out another species. It took me about 5 minutes to get some reward for the persistence with the little species, as the first nibble connected with a Goldsinny Wrasse and species 45, it was strange spending the day heaving up Conger Eels to now find myself chuffed by something my conger bait could have eaten.

The next problem I had was finding someone to do a photograph, a rather skinny guy approached clearly under the influence of some type of narcotics, I reluctantly scanned the carpark for anyone else, even a kid or wobbly granny, but no it was Trainspotter guy or nothing. He agreed to take a picture and as he stood there, I really considered if he legged it with the camera could I catch him or not, I surmised that I probably could over a distance of about 20 feet, any further and I would probably collapse. You really shouldn't judge a book by its cover, and the guy was very nice and done a pretty good picture, even better, he passed the camera back, I just had to deal with the awkward minute or so where he thought we were now mates.

Finally, shaky joe ambled off picking up a dog end on the way, and as I thanked him for his help, he shouted I will be back later to see how you have done, I went on to catch 3 Goldsinny's and a token Corkwing, it was then a rush to shower and make the Indian. We had a great evening Steve, Helen, Sam and I but the others didn't want to risk spicy food before a day afloat. I was back at the hotel by 9.30 and asleep 15 minutes later, tomorrow was another day. The alarm didn't wake me up, but hopscotch girl did at 3.30am, as she had forgotten her key, returned to the hotel, and kept her finger on the bell until the owner Nigel let her in. I could clearly hear her giving some drunken excuse, then every stair she climbed, sounded like two builders taking turns to thump a car bonnet with a sledge hammer. Then she set about rowing with someone on the phone for 30 minutes while simultaneously chucking her shoes around the room, I was really going off her!

I couldn't get back to sleep and besides I was worried she may come through the floor with the amount of stomping and hopscotch that had been going on. I decided to get up and check out early, another early start would allow me to cook more sausages and get some traces ready.

The second day we were on Sea Angler and skipper Malcom had us loaded and under way just before 6am and first out of the blocks, the plan was to feather the wreck for a bit of bait prior to starting. John and Tom were situated at the back hatching a plan, they were going to target a Ling while we drifted for bait, I managed to snap their little meeting on film, as it happened their baits were both taken, Johns fish got into the wreck and Toms bit clean through the 200lb trace!

I stuck with the simple Sabiki feathers and managed several nice pouting for bait before randomly catching a stunning female Cuckoo Wrasse I have already had a nice male cuckoo wrasse for the challenge but can add the female under the same number. The really good news was this lovely little fish shot off down to the seabed something they can struggle with in really deep water.

With the tide starting to run the skipper anchored us over the wreck and we once again dropped our baits in the hope of a longer, stronger, conger. We were honoured today with our fellow anglers being the Essex boys Paul, & Dave, Paul Sweetman, Dave Ball and his son little balls, Tom, John and I, a real motley crew.

This was another tough day with lots of lost eels and also a bit of discarded net draped over the wreck that would catch your rigs or eels halfway up, very frustrating. I've been diagnosed with carpal tunnel and by the second day even the splint wasn't really helping but that's a sign of getting old and just another one for the list of defects.

Team mate John was grinding out a few fish and by the end of the day he had amassed 9 Eels to 42lb, I had lost 3 and boated 3 to 40lb and on a hard weekend I can't complain. Team mates Sam and Steve however had really had a tough one with Steve losing a really big eel that just threw the hook during the fight leaving them with one fish a piece, they were on the boat with the other half of our rival's team who had only had one fish.

It was all going to be down to how Andy and Matt had done it was now in the lap of the gods as we up anchored and headed for port. With all the results in we got the news we had been hoping for and our team had finally done it, we won the team event, BCC tankard, and a super Greys boat rod each. John who had done really well on the second day won the Trophy for the most eels caught, so the icing on the cake.

Our team Longer, Stronger Conger landed 38 Eels which were all released safe and well, and it was a triple winning weekend for me, winning the raffle, winning the team event and catching species 45. I feel fortunate to be part of a team of truly inspirational guys, all for their own reasons and I am looking forward to defending our crown next year.

We have been told the festival is moving to Weymouth, this is sad for Plymouth but maybe a change is as good as a rest. Blue sharks next, hopefully my first trip of the year with skipper of Force 10, Pete Davis, I seem to have a little bit of luck when fishing with him.

*Team, Longer, Stronger Conger, Me, John Locker, Steve Hollyer, BCC Chairman Paul Sweetman & Sam James*

Chapter 29 I dream of Ice Cream and Black Bream

Following on from the lovely warm weekend of the Conger festival things have just got hotter and hotter, I really struggle with the heat and had a few heat related dizzy spells during the aforementioned festival. Fortunately, team mate John was on hand to make sure I got in the shade and necked some water, it's very easy to avoid sunstroke and walk straight into heat stroke.

With the temperatures set to top 28 degrees and a couple of boat trips booked I was going to be taking no chances, cover up with light layers, sun block, and constant hydration. The first trip I was really excited about was to be the first shark trip of the year and out with my lucky shark skipper Pete Davis aboard the Looe shark boat Force 10, unfortunately despite the heat the easterly winds scuppered this trip and it was cancelled.

It is disappointing when the trips are cancelled but boat fishing and shark fishing in particular are expensive pastimes and the skippers want you to enjoy your day as safely and productively as possible. So, the first shark of the year will have to hang on for another week, as another chance looms the following weekend again from Looe aboard Dan Gunnows boat Borlewen.

The second trip I had booked was a day inshore fishing aboard Pegasus out of Lyme Regis, skippered by a great young skipper Lewis Hodder, the target for me being the Black Bream. I had lost one previously on a trip in May out with Lewis's dad Phil and really wanted to get my revenge, plus I have never caught a Black Bream. The forecast was similar to the shark trip but Chris, also out for the day messaged Lewis and got the great news back that we were good to go and an 8.00am start.

The difference between a few miles up the coast can be quite amazing but if you include fishing 2 miles offshore with 16 miles offshore the conditions can be like chalk and cheese. With the trip on, we ordered half a kilo of ragworm from the excellent shop the Tackle Box in Lyme Regis, a very helpful chap who opens at 7.30am, which is perfect. Fishing from Lyme Regis is pretty good for us, we can get there in a hour, its £2 all day to park and Lewis has quality, consistent fishing within a short steam. It was a change from the shark rods to the lighter outfits and a great chance to try out my prize from the conger festival, the Greys 6lb to 12lb class rod. Chris volunteered to drive, also offering to walk the big hill at the end of the day to retrieve the car while I watched the gear from the shade, all for the price of the ragworm and an ice cream. The sat-nav lady owned by Chris had clearly climbed out of the wrong side of the glove box, as she proceeded to take us on a scenic tour of the south coasts most narrow lanes. Fortunately, we had left at 6.00am and even with the old bat-nav's best attempts to prevent us fishing, we arrived at 7.00am, plenty of time to drop off the kit, get the bait and amble over to the boat.

We reached the pick-up point just as Lewis pulled Pegasus alongside, we were joined by another angler we named Camp David, a smashing guy keen to copy and use everyone else's rigs. We boarded the boat and were informed that there would only be 5 of us on board today, great for us anglers but not a lot of money for the skipper, it's such a tough, tough business.

I really hope over the year, my blogs highlight just how fantastic our country's charter boat fleet really are, these guys work their socks off, to put us on fish and make our dreams a reality, please, please, get out and support them! We were joined on the boat by the other two anglers, smashing Steve, and Irish international angler Rock Salmon Roy. The sea looked a little choppy as we headed off, back the way we came towards Beer, the further we travelled the flatter the sea became.

The first hour was to be drifting for Plaice and Gurnard, the gurnard was a fish I need, and I would be having a good effort at them during the day. Every time I fish Lyme Bay it amazes me how little lead is needed and the heaviest weight I used all day was 6oz, this is great when using lighter tackle for the smaller species.

Lewis asked who fancied a brew, that's always music to my ears to get offered that first cup of coffee of the trip, unfortunately the invertor had other ideas, and after a strong smell of melting plastic, it packed up.

So, there was going to be no coffee and tea's today, Lewis has just put a door in the side of the boat for the upcoming shark festival, knowing my fellow shark anglers I think the kettle may be just as important! The drift produced no fish and Lewis decided to move to a new area and anchor a section of reef for a variety of species, this was my chance for a Black Bream. With the anchor down, bream rigs on, we were instantly getting rapid rattles on the ragworm / squid baits, the culprits were soon identified as pouting and poor cod.

The pouting can be a pain, but in shallow water when its body and eyes aren't distorted by the rapid ascent from deep water it can be an attractive little fish, as above, and as Camp David found out it's a dam good Conger bait, as he caught a strap Conger after dropping one back down. Then the spotted sandpaper hoovers arrived and apart from the dogfish whisperer Chris, we were all inundated, with Rock Salmon Roy taking the brunt of their wrath. I decided to try a different tactic and baited with a cocktail of ragworm and prawn on my bream rig, it wasn't long before I had a violent take that I missed. I checked the rig to find the bottom prawn missing, I re-baited and dropped back down, straight away another violent take but this time I struck perfectly and connected.

The fish fought extremely well juddering the rod violently as it circled with short powerful beats of its tail, I knew it was the fish I was after having got this far once before.

The skipper was suddenly next to me with the net, stating it was indeed a bream, I once again had that nervous feeling that the hook would pull at any second, but Neptune decided to reward me with another of his gems of the sea. The stunning silver fish went straight into the net and I felt elated at a new personal best and species 46, the pictures were quickly taken as the fish was to be released.

With my first Bream caught I should have perhaps changed tactics and gone for another species, especially as Lewis told me there was a good chance of an Undulate Ray from this mark. However, I decided to try for another of these little warriors and dropped the rig once again baited with prawn but minus the ragworms, straight away I had another Bream on, much to the amazement of everyone else.

This one was a little bigger and turned out to be a female, I didn't worry about a photo opting to release the beautiful fish straight away, I dropped straight down again hoping to be third time lucky. Incredibly it was hit straight away again and this one felt like the pick of the bunch taking line on a couple of occasions and putting a good bend in the rod, then up pops a conger eel on my size 1/0 hook and prawn bait. It would have been a great bream though, that signalled a change of tactic and I put out a squid / mackerel tube bait in the hope of an Undulate Ray. Camp David then brought in a stunning Spotted Ray that I would have loved, a species I needed, and I was torn as to change to a smaller bait again or stick it out, I opted to stick not twist.

The result of persevering with the big bait was another spotted sandpaper hoover that had managed to get the huge bait in its tough little mouth. With the dogs being a pain, it was time for a move to another bit of ground, back towards Lyme Regis a short steam along the coast. The sea had flattened right off, and the sun was beating down unbearably as if a god, was using a magnifying glass to burn us up, like ants trapped on a path.

I had kept as covered as I could and sat myself close to the wheelhouse to utilise the tiny bit of shade the structure created, ice creams filled my head, and I was sure that a boat-based Mr Whippy would make a killing out at sea, maybe I had already had too much sun. The weekend before I had the delight of lovely toffee crunch ice cream with a flake, at the conger festival, but remember my disappointment after thinking I had purchased the jumbo cone, only to see John Locker with a cone twice the size, it's not just bigger fish he gets!

This week however, I would get the best ice cream they sold, and to hell with the cost, we arrived at the new mark just as I was covering my ice cream in imaginary sprinkles. The anchor dropped, and we were once again fishing, it wasn't long before smashing Steve was into a nice fish and Lewis quickly netted an absolutely stunning Red Gurnard a really nice size one too, then Chris was into a fish and he too brought in a Red Gurnard, another stunning little fish, that was a new best for him and made his day.

With two Gurnards in quick succession I swapped over to baited feathers in the hope I could bag one for the challenge, this resulted in more dogfish, the sea must be paved with them. The skipper did manage to locate another bream, but it seemed to be a shoal of one and the hope of a few more bream never materialised. We finished off the day with an hour drifting for Plaice but both Chris and I had neglected to bring our plaice rigs and paid for it, as half a dozen plaice were caught to the other guys. While drifting for Plaice I did retrieve my rig to find it covered in small delicate Starfish another of the seas little wonders.

The day was over and both Chris and I both enjoyed our day immensely, both having new bests and especially getting species 46, the journey back in was an imaginary kaleidoscope of different flavoured ice creams. We bid fell well to Lewis and the guys and while Chris climbed the hill to retrieve the car I went to get the ice creams, Chris arrived just in time to receive his, super, dooper, double, choca, strawberry and candy floss ice cream. That was, and I am sure Chris would agree the best ice cream we've ever had, and I don't think I can remember going to an ice cream shop with so much choice, 12 types of cone alone was mind boggling.

Saturday was a day at the lake and with the stock pond having dropped by 3 feet I really need to get some of the fish out and into the main Carp lake, these fish having never seen bait before are extremely hard to catch and I may need to introduce bait for a week to get them interested.

I had a walk around the lakes and it's incredible the flora and fauna that has made its life on this once barren field, dragonfly's swarm over every water surface, pond skaters dance with one another. The lakes are full of fry with shoals of mini Perch, Orfe and Bream forming black masses just beneath the surface. The multitude of water plants so lost, when first planted now fill every available space, and the multitude of coloured lilies are now self-seeding appearing at new locations across the lakes. One of my favourite plants is the Purple Loosestrife a plant highlighted to me by John Wilson in one of his early carp stalking programs, I literally had to have them because of him.

It's not easy creating a fishery where everything is in balance, and so much work has gone into what we now have, I think every time I see Tadpoles, Newts, Kingfishers, Lizards and a myriad of other water loving creatures it really is a little pat on the back to my dad and I from mother nature and that's tribute enough. The fish are also a product of a healthy un-stressful environment, fin perfect, content and growing well, a lack of angling pressure surely helps. Despite my list of jobs, the fact these fish are there cruising under my nose, means I cannot help but spend an hour stalking, although they are growing ever more cunning.

I still managed to catch several fish on the high tech, hook and bread technique that has been so productive over the years and I'm sure for many more to come. I went to the trouble of taking a few self-timer pictures of a couple of the 5 Carp I had stalking and considering how hot it's been and the recent spawning they are still looking peachy.

So that's the blog for this week done, I'm really made up with the Black Bream so thanks to Lewis on Pegasus for that one, thanks Chris for driving and walking the hill in the heat and well done on that lovely P.B Red Gurnard. Next week it will probably be a spot of Tenching on Saturday morning and Sharking on Sunday, looking forward to it already especially as I will be fishing with my old mate the legend that is the Brumsta.

Chapter 30 The curse of the Grrrnards

This is a Blog that could have been celebrating another two species but once again the fishing gods conspired to ensure that my challenge is no walk in the park. The first trip was targeting the Conger Eels residing in a wreck off the lizard known as the Snake Pit, an invitation to fish with Conger club teammates Sam James and Steve Holyer.

This was to be fishing aboard Steve's own 19-foot boat Freebird launched from the lovely little cove where they live. I have previously mentioned that Steve is totally blind, and I was really looking forward to fishing with this truly inspirational guy once again, combined with Sam and his hearing difficulties they make a quite a pair, incredible to watch them working together. It took me a couple of hours to get down to Sam's and the weather was still flipping hot, hot, hot!

The tides were perfect for conger fishing and the plan was to fish several hours for the Eels and as the tide slackened off try for the elusive John Dory that are also resident on this wreck. That would give a few hours in the afternoon to try for a Gurnard for the species hunt, I still remember both Steve and Sam stating, "Gurnard that will be no problem they are easy", strangely that's what Lewis the skipper of Pegasus had said the week before. We parked down near the little beach, somehow and headed off for the launching process, somewhat reminiscent of the launching of a new ship as the vessel glides down runners and crashes into the sea.

Steve was already on-board sorting out the boat, that's how well he knows his boat and the harbour, I tripped over several times on the abundant rocks, ropes and abandoned lobster pots, yet Steve makes it look easy. With the boat down the runners and in the water, we were joined by Steve's friend and local bass angler Noddy, who having never landed a conger before was hoping for his first.

With the crew aboard, Sam spun Freebird seaward and opened up the engine to send us bouncing over the mirror like surface of the early morning sea. The journey to the Snake pit didn't take long as the wreck is fairly close to shore but still lies in 200 feet of water. Now followed some pretty amazing positioning of the boat where Steve conveyed the exact numbers from his head to Sam for the positioning of the boat, we drifted over the wreck 4 times, during which I dropped down feathers to collect fresh Pouting for bait. Steve was adamant where the boat should sit, and 30 to 40 minutes was spent ensuring this would be the case. Sam put the boat uptide of the wreck and Steve released the anchor putting the boat right on the money, the importance of this accurate position was soon realised as bites were instant.

All the eels we caught were 100% possible because of the time taken to get the boat in the correct spot, and fandango swivels and hooks don't put you on fish, good seamanship does, so thanks guys for your work that day. Steve was soon into an eel and it gave him a good scrap even on his heavy tackle, he knows there are monsters in the Snake Pit and doesn't risk being under gunned.

The eel was a 20lber and Steve grabbed the trace and expertly T barred the eel quickly off at the boat edge. I was soon connected to my first conger of the day which also fought all the way to the surface, seeing the eel was a bigger fish I asked Sam if we could try netting it. The net was a smaller type boat net, but Sam put it down tide and I dropped the eel back into first time, easy peasy, it also contained the eel safely while we weighed it. The fish was just shy of 30lb in the net so around 28lb a nice long eel, a monster of the future I hope. The eel was quickly released and disappeared rapidly to the ships hold to join the writhing mass of eels that gives the snake pit its name. Next up was Sam with his broken finger and an angry eel gave him a good work out before submitting to the superior muscles of the life boat man.

We decided to bring this one in for a quick picture and the eel was relatively well behaved, the thing with conger and small boats it's always tricky to get good photograph's, if you walk back to far you're over the side. I managed to get back enough to get a quick landscape picture of Sam's Eel before it was slid back to the inviting looking water.

The temperature was rising, and the Eel action had been fairly frantic we had landed 5 in quick succession and lost a few that had either got to structure or spat the hooks. There then followed a period of nothing, this mirrored the recent conger festival and you start to question if you have bait on, are you snagged or has the boat moved.

Steve checked the numbers and decided to release a little more rope to put us back in the sweet spot, this soon done the trick as bites began again. I had changed to a smaller bait having pulled out of my last fish, this time two large Octopus tentacles would surely be irresistible. This done the trick as instead of the gentle plucks so typical of congers the rod tip bounced once and swung straight down as an eel down in the dark backed off to the safety of some structure. I bullied it up the important first 20 feet and into open water before it was aware what was happening, now with its fight or flight mode truly in fight mode it shook its head violently. These large head shakes cause the rod to shake violently and the bigger the head shake's the bigger the eel, it then made a dive for the wreck taking line but not enough to get to sanctuary.

Suddenly a scream was let out like someone falling in a mincer, it was Noddy connected to his first ever eel next to me and every head shake of his eel was met with woops of delight. Fortunately, the eels stayed apart and Noddy got his first eel of 25lb up to the surface and quickly unhooked with only a little drama. I had managed to milk my eel battle enough that everyone agreed it must be a fairly nice fish, it's always a little worrying that something smaller may pop up on the surface to plant egg directly on your face. Fortunately, this wasn't the case and Sam once again done a sterling job with the net, with the Eel going straight in with no issues, we both got a hold to swing her in though.

The eel remained calm until we were weighing it whereby the split ring on the scales opened up tipping the net enough for the eel to escape to the deck and unleash hell, Noddy was screaming once again but this time in fear as the eel headed towards him with fury in its face. I jumped on the writhing eel and picked up a gash to the leg for my trouble but soon we had the grumpy fish calm again. The eel weighed 42lb and turned out to be the biggest of the mornings fishing, a nice fish for an inshore wreck and tribute to the skills of Sam and Steve.

We ended up with 12 Conger and lost a few as is the case with conger fishing the odds are largely in their favour it's just a case of how much we can change them. We drifted the wreck and a nearby reef for the needle in a haystack that is the John Dory but to no avail, always worth a go. Then it was inshore for the easy Gurnard, well you can guess how that went, a ton of Cuckoo Wrasse, Dogfish, and Whiting but no Gurnard. Sam of course pulled up a lovely Red Gurnard and the icing on the cake was when Steve said he had a bite on his rod that he believed to be from a gurnard, did I want it? Well Steve had landed 5 dogfish in a row, he must have thought I was born yesterday, " no thanks mate you can bring your own dogfish in I told him". Well of course it had to happen, sure enough he reeled in a Red Gurnard and I really needed a door to bang my head against.

We headed for home having had a great day, no species to add to the list but with Gurnards either side of me surely it won't be long before these "easy little fish stop being so difficult".

Sunday was my first chance at a Blue Shark and I had a trip booked up with Dan Gunnow aboard his new updated Borlewen, great young skipper that I have done well with, in the past. I was to be joined with long term angling pal Glen Patterson, his nephew Mason and mate Martin. The guys had travelled down from the Midlands and London, Glen though was staying in a caravan on holiday for the week. The weather was still dam hot, but the bad news was there was little to no wind and when combined with a smallish tide equals very little drift. The less ground you cover with a drift the less scent is getting to potential sharks, plus they seem lazy and lethargic often choosing to just visit you rather than battle with you. We steamed out 23 miles and the slight breeze was disappearing fast, the feathers were dropped to gather fresh bait and before long we had several fresh Mackerel baits all ready to go. Glen brought up his feathers and shouted, " what's this ugly little red thing"? of course I knew without even turning around, it was another Red Gurnard, this fish is the boat version of the blasted Blenny and is going haunt me all year! It was about an hour when a shark appeared around my bright green float, slapping its tail as it circled tight before disappearing deeper, the anticipation was unbearable.

Glens rod behind mine was off as the shark took his bait, he subdued the fish in fairly short time and it was unhooked at the side being around 60lb It was another hour before the next shark appeared and as predicted it was just milling around chasing gulls, biting floats and taking quick bites of the baits, swimming tantalisingly close to the boat and Masons close in bait.

Eventually when she'd had frustrated us to within an inch of our lives, she took the bait still not convincingly but enough to get the hook connected. Mason done a great job on his first Blue Shark and it made the qualifying length although a somewhat skinny fish. Clearly chuffed Mason's trip was made and it's always great to see someone get their first shark I can still remember mine like it was yesterday. I then spotted a shark around my float and once again it was trying to bite the bright green bottle and generally harassing the top of the rig, it then went down for the bait and the ratchet was screaming that wonderful shark bell noise that forces adrenalin around your body in an instant. I picked up the rod and engaged the drag lever letting the barbless circle do its job, the line tightened instantly as the fish realised something was amiss, it started the initial dive when the rod sprang back with that sickening cut line feeling. That was it gone the line was severed and I can only surmise that the constant harassment to the float of the sharks had damaged the monofilament at that point. I re-tackled somewhat dejected, but the arrival of another shark can lift even the lowest of spirits, I love seeing these fish they are a true apex predator within our world. The fish was another nice size Shark and once again played around sunning itself and showing off in the lovely blue water.

Eventually the fish swam out to Glens float and straight down on to his bait, the float bobbed up again and with no further sign Dan advised Glen to check the bait, as he retrieved the bait the shark worried it was losing its meal grabbed the bait and it was fish on.

Never use a butt pad Glen had a nice little workout with this fish and eventually it was defeated and brought in for the measuring process. This one was also a Shark Club qualifier but with a much bigger girth making around 85lb in weight, really pleased for Glen who is no stranger to monster fish, having some real beasts around the world. I did have another enquiry as a shark took off with the bait, but it was dropped and after inspection 10 minutes later the hook was bait less, another chance missed. So that was that, 3 sharks landed, and a few opportunities missed, but that's fishing. It was great to fish with Dan again and his new boat is mighty impressive, but it still needs a good skipper at the helm and despite not having developed any quirks, yet he is a dam good skipper and a pleasure to fish with. Glen, I and the guys went for a slap-up fish supper and I'm not one to drop anyone in trouble, but Glen could be after this. When we were ordering our fish and chips I decided to go for the Oap portion, that's not an omission on my behalf, Glen chose the standard with added mushy peas and bread and butter.

He then received a phone call from his other half who wanted to know when he would be back to the caravan as she had spent the afternoon cooking a roast dinner, Glen's answer " I am just having a cup of tea love then I will be back for it", incredible and he even complained that he only got one slice of bread and butter. If his good lady does ever read this I hope he gets his backside tanned as I owe him for sneaking up on me while I fished a midlands canal in the dead of night under the guise of a local couple of thugs!

So, no more species this week although I could almost touch them, its shark festival next week so I have 3 more days to try and catch the Blue Shark, I hope this isn't my first festival blank, but the weather is looking pretty poor with light winds.

## Chapter 31 The Shark Club Stresstival

I cannot believe the 2018 annual Shark club festival has been and gone, it seemed so far away back in January when the challenge began, but here we are with two festivals completed. The shark festival has always been a great fun event with a few Sharks thrown in for good measure, once I even won it, proof if needed that anyone can! This year had even greater significance as the capture of a Blue Shark was high on my list of species for my challenge and to get one during the festival would be really special.

The first day arrived and fishing partner Brian had text me the list of boats we had been drawn on over the 3-day festival, they were Top cat, Borlewen and Meercat two boats I've never fished from before. Brian was waiting by the quay and skipper Andre carried out he's boat checks before taking all our kit aboard the large boat Top cat. We were joined on day 1 by Peter and Shark Club chairman Bob Woodman making the 4, Brian and I always fish the festival together and I've fished with Bob on a few previous occasions. The 11 boats were soon fully loaded with their various crews of sharking enthusiast's, proudly sporting their numerous festival patches proving their love of the sport and the actual event. The weather was hot, and the wind was a no show making an effective chum trail very difficult, in these conditions the boat and chum cover little to no ground meaning sharks will struggle to find the scent. We stopped for Mackerel not far off land and soon picked up a few, I hooked a real jumbo Mackerel which actually stripped line from the light outfit.

The skipper pulled in a Red Gurnard, this seemed quite normal to me now, gurnards turning up to everyone around me, except me. We soon had plenty of fresh hook baits and the skipper started the engines and along with most of the shark fleet we headed for the shark grounds some 23 miles west in our case.

With the long steam completed the anticipation was growing, as the boat bobbed slowly in the dwindling breeze we waited patiently for the call on the radio signalling lines down. It transpired that we hadn't heard the call on the radio and were 30 minutes late in starting but the tide and wind were initially so bad we just couldn't get the floats to leave the protection of the boat anyway. Eventually the floats decided it was safe enough to move out into the slick and they were soon joined by our favourite shark alarms, the handsome Fulmar's.

These sea birds love to sit in the slick created by the chopped fish and oil that makes up the chum mix, they wait for little morsels to drift towards them and quickly gobble them up before any of their brethren.

They have a wonderful ability to see / sense sharks in the area and will lift from the water and circle the boat often landing away from the chum trail, sharks very often take an exploratory bite of any unwise seabirds, so it pays for them to remain vigilante.

The fulmars today however remaincd relaxed but then carried out a strange ritual whereby they appeared to paddle vigorously on the spot, this was a technique to bring the fish morsels to the surface. The chum trail was spread wide but not far, and we really were sat in the doldrums' if only a breeze would arrive to save the day, it took an hour before the first shark arrived and the fish powered through the middle of the floats pausing only to smack my float with its tail. Another hour passed when Bobs float was no longer there, no ratchet or any sound, it then returned like one of the barrels in the film Jaws breaching the surface.

Then back down beneath the surface, only to pop up once again, a small fish no doubt mouthing the bait, 20 minutes then passed before the float was down and the ratchet purred. Bob tightened up so the barbless circle hook could do its work and it was fish on.

Bob soon had the fish to the side and it really didn't want to fight much and even remained calm for the measuring process, great start for Mr Woodman but he always does pretty well maybe something to do with his pink trousers. The day remained quiet and with time ticking away I was really doubting the appearance of another shark, even worse I had fished really hard for a Gurnard all day and in 200 feet of water every Whiting is energy sapping. Brian happened to mention it was 15.50 and with only 10 minutes till lines up it was Woodman time as Bob had a knack of a last-minute fish, sure enough right on cue his float disappeared.

The result was a hard fighting fish the polar opposite of his first fish and it took steady Bob a few minutes to get this one to the boat, however it was soon aboard and being measured.

That was the only excitement on day 1 for our boat, it was now the steam back to the harbour and time to check into my hotel, get showered, fed and watch the footy. Well the lack of a shark on day one was the least of my problems as the hotel, The Harbour Moon, informed me they had changed ownership since I booked and no longer dealt with Expedia the company I had booked through and whom had taken £120 in payment. The hotel stated they had no rooms available and I would need to take it up with expedia, not a lot of use 18.30 in the evening while I'm stood in the middle of Looe with my suitcase. I had no choice but to leave, I sat in a nearby carpark deciding whether to knock the festival on the head and go home, I posted my dilemma on Facebook and let Brian know.

The great members of the Shark Club were soon offering me somewhere to kip and Brian and Wife Libby got the short straw, as I headed over to their cottage to take refuge. They were wonderful hosts and really looked after me I cannot thank them enough, like everyone who offered to put me up, thanks so much you really are the salt of the earth. With the stress of the first 24 hrs behind me it was another day and another boat, today we were out on skipper Dan Gunnows lovely new boat Borlewen, we were joined by anglers Beau and Paul Martin.

Paul, I know well as he makes all my wonderful shark traces for me and I owed him a few quid for the last lot, not a lot of places to hide on a boat so I paid as soon as I saw him. We were soon under way and were closely followed by the huge cat Swallow 2 skippered by Murray Collins another of looe's finest skippers, a quick stop for Mackerel for fresh baits and we were once again heading out into the blue. The journey out was full of good banter and that's such an integral part of the festival, getting to fish with other anglers and skippers and making new friendships, not to mention the learning curve you go through. We pulled up into the desired area and straight away we noticed more breeze, the start time had been set for 10.00 and Dan stuck the kettle on to make use of the waiting time.

The bags of chum were then placed over the side at 10.00 on the dot and the trail was started, we draw for positions with 1 being far away and 4 close to the boat, I managed to draw 4 for the second day in a row. I quite like the position by the boat, the chum scent is strongest at its source, the bags tied to the boat, you can also see your bait to check it's still there.

The downside is its normally the rod that needs to be removed if someone hooks a shark as its inevitably in the way. With all the baits set it was now the waiting game, for me this meant more bait fishing, better known as trying to catch a Gurnard, fortunately my persistence paid off in some respects as I managed to land a bonus species the Scad, also known as the Horse Mackerel.

I hadn't really planned to catch this species at this point, but I was now pretty chuffed to get species 47 on the board. I had placed the rod I was using to target the Gurnards in one of the boat holders and heard a dink noise as the tip snapped randomly and cleanly and fell to the ground, yet another slice of bad luck in a whole cake of bad luck. Surely things must improve, and then Brian's float done the disappearing act as a shark tried to sneak off in stealth mode, no such luck Mr Blue as Brian was on the case, a good scrap followed and a nice Blue of 85lb was brought aboard.

I was really pleased for Brian to get off the mark and also to see a shark, it was an hour later, and Brian had another shark but this one rolled up the trace and straight through the mono main line. The same thing happened to Beau near the end of the day with a very good shark rolling up past the rubbing leader and through the trace. Day 2 was over and yet again no shark runs for me, this was shaping up to be my worst festival but who knows what the final day may bring. On our way in will pulled alongside another skipper called Dan and his boat Sowenna, they had been just out past us and managed 7 sharks which included 3 in the last 10 minutes.

Hard to work out these sharks but Sowenna is an older style Looe Shark boat and has a mizzen sail on her rear, this helps make the most of a small breeze and maybe the faster drift helped. Tonight's accommodation was to be with friends John and Caroline, as john was in the festival he drove me back to his place where I was once again treated like a VIP much to Johns disgust!

The final day was aboard Meercat and skipper Steve wasted no time in getting the kettle on, today Brian and I were joined by Kevin Tapper, Dave Stone and John Lock, an extra angler due to a breakdown on one of the other boats. This was a real motley crew, and Dave, John and I were all blanking in the shark stakes, so we really hoped something would happen today.

We got to the grounds and started the drift but despite the big tides the lack of any type of breeze once again curtailed a good chum slick. I once again resumed my daily effort for the Gurnard but the water was so thick with Mackerel I just couldn't get through them, once we had enough for bait I tried a single hook rig with a big bait this resulted in plenty of Whiting and once again it was a good old slog bringing Whiting up from such a depth, I then hooked a much better fish that battled pretty much to the surface, the result was a huge Whiting and new personal best, I even took a picture of this one to update my blog.

The tide was a bit strong for bottom fishing, so I had a rest while I waited for the tide to slacken off which was around 2.30 in the afternoon. We hadn't seen any sharks around the baits and even the shark alarm birds hadn't lifted from the water, a very, very quiet day. With the arrival of slack water, I returned to my task and in order to beat the mackerel I used a really heavy weight, the rig was a cut down set of feathers giving just two hooks, I baited these with tiny fish section in the hope the Whiting wouldn't notice and crossed my fingers.

The bait reached the bottom, so it made the gauntlet of Mackerel, there was no instant savage grabs from the Whiting the plan had worked. Around ten minutes passed, and the rod tip trembled gently, and this was followed by a few small plucks which I decided to strike, I could feel the odd small shake as I slowly retrieved the rig to the surface, but then a bar of stunning grey broke the surface and a pair of big eyes stared up at me. There waddling on the surface sat a Grey Gurnard, I gingerly raised the precious little fish over the gunnel and let out a yell of joy, shocking the rest of the crew. I forgot all the mishaps and bad karma of the last few days as this little fish meant so much to me, a real boost that was so needed, so there it was species number 48 the Grey Gurnard!

That would have probably been a great point to end my festival on but with 30 minutes left of the day my mind turned to the possibility of a Garfish as they had been around on the previous day. I tied a size 2 hook to 5lb fluorocarbon and cut a 2-inch slither of Mackerel belly for bait, I used a heavy swivel to act as a weight and trotted the bait back in the slick. Then about 10 minutes later I felt a couple of plucks on the braid, I had the line between my fingers feeling for bites when suddenly the braid pulled tight from my hand and line started pouring from the reel, a shark had taken the little bait.

Of course, it didn't stay on long and bit me off, I told the rest of the guys just as a really big shark swam right passed us, that's the culprit I exclaimed!

The shark swam deep and with seconds left on the clock grabbed Johns long distance bait, the fish made several long powerful runs and I was looking forward to getting my little hook back when disaster struck the hook pulled out! I really was gutted for John as like me he had bided his time waiting for that one opportunity and when it came he played the fish like a pro, it can be such a kick in the teeth sometimes.

 So that was the festival, great to get a few more species off the list and especially one of the more testing ones for me the Gurnard, I just need to get the other fish that has pushed me so close to the edge, the dastardly Blenny Henry! Mate John got his first and only shark of the festival on the last day, and with both John and Brian catching sharks in such tricky conditions it must surely be a result of good karma for doing a mate a favour and giving me a bed to sleep in.

Saturday morning and Chris has messaged me, "let's go get that Blenny", well it's a bit cheeky really, I've only just got home, and I don't think it's fair to even ask Mrs D, so I replied with I'm not sure. When my good lady returns she tells me to get my stuff and go and get that pesky fish, so its game on and attempt 6 at that little sea devil! Chris offers to drive which is great, I have a bit of a plymouthophobia, does my head in driving around there. Chris tells me on the way down that he has been quite sick all morning, he wasn't joking as through the afternoon he was so ill that I was really beginning to worry about him.

We turned up at the mark that Chris had named Dawes Destiny on account of the number of Blennies that resided there, he was quite excited to show me and as we climbed the wall his face dropped, the rock was dry. Chris was unaware that the mark ever dried out, but one thing was sure there isn't none there at the moment. We tried an area a little way along the coast but despite it looking prime for some Blenny action the area was in fact controlled by a pretty ruthless gang of Prawns, I managed to take out some of the ring leaders before we headed back to the original mark. It was around an hour before we got back to the rock and by now the water was lapping at the base of the rock, Chris however was too sick to fish and after being sick numerous times decided to go and get the car to park it closer. I set up my gear on the little rock and from the surface nothing appeared that exciting for Blenny's to make their homes. I flicked out a half ragworm and straight away a trebling bite signalled some interest, I lifted the rod to see the wriggling shape of a small blenny, yes, it then fell off, no!

Chris returned a slightly better colour and I told him I had one and it fell off, he cast his rod and promptly brought in the first Blenny, at the same time my ragworm bait was taken but this time by a pesky little wrasse Chris had to go for another wander to sort his stomach out and while he was gone yet another blenny fell from my hook as it dangled above the water. Chris returned just as another little nibble appeared on my rod, this time however I succeeded and that pesky, frustrating little pool demon the Blenny was finally mine, species 49 what a result!

Chris who was unable to fish managed to climb down the rocks to do the pictures and was clearly pleased that his prediction of Dawes destiny came to fruition. He then insisted we travel over to west hoe to try for a Tom pot Blenny the bigger more ferocious cousin of the blenny, I was a bit worried about his condition but agreed to give it an hour. We got around to West Hoe which was packed with people enjoying the sun, I found a gap and Chris crashed out on the ground for an hour. While I was fishing a young lad came over and asked me what I was fishing for and had I caught, I spent a little while explaining everything to the keen lad and when I caught a stunning little Corkwing Wrasse he was delighted to get to hold his first fish. His dad who was eating nearby with the family asked if he was in the way, no way it's great when youngsters are genuinely interested I explained.

The young lad's dad went on to ask me about my challenge and was keen to make a donation to the just giving page, I spent a bit longer showing the youngster the difference between the wrasses I was catching but soon he had to go off for his dinner. I hope this lad is another angler of the future and if not, he at least has an appreciation of those who do. So, despite the epic fail on the shark front I have still managed to get a few more species including two of my biggest nemesis, thanks so much Chris totally down to you today and I really hope that your are getting better. Thanks to my family for all the support lately and my friends at the Shark Club for rallying around in my hour of need, only 3 more species to go and I really would like one to be a Blue Shark and another the Tope.

## Chapter 32 Out of the Blue

With the various trials and tribulations of the shark festival 2018 now a distant memory, it doesn't take long to forget when your over 50, I've even got on and sorted my entry and accommodation for next year, I won't be worrying about Gurnard or Garfish then just 100% shark! Four shark trips done, and no sharks landed, I think I had this down as a green category for my challenge, meaning it should be one of the easier fish, that's why you should never take anything for granted. I think the biggest disappointment was not getting the Blue Shark during the festival for my challenge, it would have tied in nicely with the blog, and besides a lot better angler than me blanked and some worse ones caught, that was a joke John Doswell!

The Tope trip I had booked up in Minehead was cancelled Sunday afternoon due to a lack of anglers, crazy when the Tope fishing on the north coast has been sublime this year, this left me with a bit of a dilemma. With a lot of fish species now in the bag there's not many that are straight forward to go out and target, they tend to need a bit of planning, baits, rigs and venues etc. I was really banking on the Tope, and that has left me with one more Tope trip outstanding, next week on Pegasus with skipper Lewis, he delivered with the Black Bream so let's see how he does with the Tope. I was in a bit of a quandary to know what to try for, the day was booked as leave and I didn't want to waste it, then out of the blue I had a message from the skipper of Force 10, Pete Davis.

He had a trip sharking in the morning and a space had become available if I was interested, Mrs D took pity on me and sensing the end is nigh on the 52, gave me the royal approval. So, 6.30 am the next morning I am back in Looe with shark rod in hand to try and get number 50, and one of my most favourite of fish, the Blue Shark.

Pete had told me it would be an 8.20 departure, but I just couldn't help but get there early and try for something that maybe I hadn't had yet. I walked down to the rocks with a shark rod in one hand and LRF rod in the other, an old chap walking his dog looked quite amused by the size of my tackle, "What you after" he enquired " Dragonets" I replied, that clearly bamboozled him and he probably had visions of some fire breathing serpent that needed dragging from a sea cave. He wished me good luck regardless of believing me, and we both went on our way.
It was a lovely hour or so spent dragging tiny lures into ever more snaggy gullies and despite having the odd snatch on the plastic worm no fish materialised. It was time to head to the harbour and board the boat as the sun started rising so would the temperature, a flat sea looked inventible and thoughts of the doldrums that plagued the festival returned. Pete was running through his boat checks and it's only a foolish man that boards a boat before the skipper invites you, so I stayed harbour side until I knew the skipper was happy his safety routine was complete. The kettle was on and I had the feeling I was going to get a shark, last time I was out with Pete I caught the Devon Trophy winning shark.

Force 10 and skipper Pete have always been a good omen for me and I always try and do a few trips with Pete every year, after all I caught my first ever blue shark with him, my shark club qualifier with him and we even won the festival together so as statistics go it's a lucky combination. The rest of the anglers arrived, Mark, his dad John, and Gordon the kitchen fitter, crewing for us today was the hyper active Helen Small and what a great job she did. With everyone on board we were off, back out of the mouth of the river a sight I have seen more than my own front door lately, and one I will never tire of seeing! The sea as I feared was like a mirror, the surface only disturbed by the lifting of seabirds as we cut through the glass sea, like a wood plane sliding through cedar. Why couldn't we have a bit of a breeze, this stagnant sea doesn't create enough movement, our only hope that 16 miles away things are different.

Well the sea can be a beast of many faces and by the time we arrived things had changed with a strong blow now hitting from the southwest, rain heavy in the air and the boat rocking like a weak jelly on an uneven washing machine on final spin. The green mountain dew bottle was a sharking virgin, I had lost my original in a boating accident, and the new guy was finding out what it takes to become a fully-fledged shark float, as the waves crashed all around in the fast-developing squall. The slick ran out perfectly, flattening as much of the sea as it could, it really looked prime for sharks, we had caught plenty of fresh bait upon arrival so surely it was just a matter of time.

This was so different from the days of the festival and even completely different from 2 hours previous, Pete and Helen worked the bags tirelessly and regularly topped up with the sweet smelling rubby dubby that only shark skippers can create. Never stand to close to a skipper while he thrashes his sacks against the side of a boat, with the wind in your face it's only a matter of time before you have chum on your face, it stings your eyes worse than soap and lingers longer than the most pungent of garlic!

Then something strange happened, the green horn float got promoted, as a shark pulled it below the waves, a few clicks of the reel signified there was indeed life out there, the float had now returned and was travelling along the surface to our right. I reeled the greedy little shark in which had by now got involved with Johns line, making us think we had two sharks hooked up, we brought her in and Pete had her unhooked and washed for a photo in seconds.

This was no monster, but by god I was pleased to see this lovely blue girl, she behaved perfectly for the photo and was quickly sent on her way, I didn't worry too much about catching anymore, or bigger as that was species number 50. I am pretty sure I will catch some larger sharks this year, but that fish will be the fish in the gallery regardless, thanks so much Pete for your sharking voodoo, I know you wanted me to get a bigger one, but this challenge isn't about monsters, that's next year!

It's incredible when you start looking closely at these apex predators just how many senses and methods of dealing with their prey they are armed with, the eyes, teeth, nostrils and the small lines of dots that make up its electroreceptors combining to create a holistic view of the food source.

With the shark done I went straight into Garfish mode, and quickly set up the LRF rod with a small hook and strip of mackerel belly I trotted this back in the chum trail. The wind had receded, and the rain passed so fishing returned to a more comfortable situation, what's more I was getting plucks on the garfish rod.

I struck to find myself connected to a mini tuna, although only a mackerel, on 5lb line and light tackle these 1lb fish were stripping line and after landing 20 in ever increasing sizes I passed the rod to Mark to experience the sport. No Garfish appeared but I really recommend this light tackle fishing as opposed to feathers for these great powerhouse fish. Then Mark was into a shark as the far-left float was away, a good scrap ensued, and Pete tagged and unhooked a nice 70lber, sadly that was the last action of the day for us and the day had flown by. The journey in was made interesting as we passed by a huge aircraft carrier sat off the Cornish coast, I thought it might have been the USS Trump with him being in the country but probably far too small for that! Great trip aboard Force 10 with another great bunch of anglers, I am amazed how many anglers live not far from me and we have never crossed paths before, or maybe we have, and I forgot them.

The final act is to raise the shark flags as we cross into the harbour and although it didn't take an awful lot of raising, it has made me a dam sight happier. Thanks Pete for your hospitality and support for the challenge it's much appreciated, thanks to Helen for her hard work through the day, certainly give JD a run for his money. Now I am really scratching for species I don't know what I shall try for this coming weekend, but the alternative is gardening so might have to tell Mrs D I am out after The Averagely Spotted Eight Spined Mud Gudgeon. As an update for anyone who read of my plight with the Harbour Moon hotel in Looe and Expedia, I am pleased so say that Expedia refunded all of my money and are sending me a £25 voucher as compensation, well done them! the Hotel though I will avoid for the rest of my life!

Chapter 33 Can it be true, I have reached 52!

With the recent capture of my first Blue of the season and species number 50, I was thinking that every trip from now on had the potential to achieve the magical 52. The first trip that could have done it was another shark trip from Looe, this time aboard the huge Cat, Swallow 2 skippered by another of Looe's greats Murray Collins. The trip had been chartered by good friend Steve McDonald and I wasn't aware it was to be just the two of us until the day before, this meant we could have literally avoided each other all day with the size of this boat.

The morning arrived and yet again it was hot, flat and early, this had been my life lately, and I don't think I can remember getting out on so many trips in a row. I met Steve M in Launceston and I drove the final 40 minutes down to Looe, I dropped Steve off in East Looe and drove the car up to Hannafore Road to park the car for the day. The great thing about these Looe Skippers is they are most obliging with picking you up from either side of the river and sure enough Murray brought Swallow 2 over to West Looe to pick me up.

Now things were about to get confusing, as Murray's crewman was Steve Allen, this meant that 3 out of the 4 people on this boat were called Steve and so I became Steve 52. We stopped for bait a short way off shore and rather sneakily I kept my pink Gurnard feathers tight to the bottom in the hope that a Red Gurnard would start the day off in style.

The other Steve's were catching Mackerel, so I continued with my plan and sure enough I hooked something, I nervously wound in to see a red shape spinning up to the surface, could it really be the Gurnard? Unfortunately, not this time as it turned out to be red coloured Ballan Wrasse, this was followed by a Cuckoo Wrasse and finally another Ballan. With several fresh baits caught it was time to head off to try and find some Blue Sharks and fingers crossed a Garfish for my challenge. We arrived on the mark to be greeted by the same flat sea that welcomed us out of the harbour early that morning, the fulmars and gulls arrived and although not invited were most welcome.

Murray and Steve A, got the multiple chum bags over the side and the slick was off and running, it's always an adrenalin filled 30 minutes when the first bait is trotted down the chum trail. With the initial excitement now replaced by the creeping fear of the blank, it reminds me sharking is very often a game of two halves with the latter often consumed by that sick feeling that a journey in, minus a blue flag conveys. I was feeling positive and within an hour the feathery white audience bobbing up and down in front of us took off in unison, a sign that a Shark was in the vicinity. By now I was in full Garfish mode and despite doing so well on the Mackerel with the LRF on the Monday with Pete I struggled to get a bite. It amazes me that where fishing is concerned no two days are the same and fish are a true enigma, and like the famous code every now and then we solve a bit of the code and catch a few fish.

The birds returned but wouldn't relax and over the next hour were up and down more often than my beloved Newcastle United, we knew a shark was there but for now it remained hidden within the blue shadows. I then put in a music request to the skipper, thinking maybe that some Fleetwood Mack booming from the wheelhouse may inspire a shark or two.

Then one green bottle was no longer sitting on the wall as it disappeared beneath the surface, the ratchet slowly purred in a steady but satisfying way. I wound down and met the tension created by the departing shark which set the circle hook perfectly and it was game on. The fish wasn't huge but made a few short runs before skipper Murray brought her in for unhooking, the fish was between 40lb to 50lb and in stunning condition.

With a quick picture taken the fish was quickly released and swam off strongly to continue her incredible journey. So, with a fish in the bag it was hopefully Steve Macs turn and I was really hoping we would see something special come our way, Steve A then shouted, "Shark at the rear of the boat"! We 3 Steve's stared intently at the large fin rapidly moving towards the slick from the east and maybe it was shark fever or too much sun but none of us realised it was a Sunfish. Murray exited the cabin and stated with some degree of authority it was a sunfish not a shark, straight away we could then see it was a sunfish but a real big one and moving with real purpose.

These wonderfully strange half-fish love to eat jellyfish but also enjoy picking off parasites from the feet of seagulls, this particular sunfish had acquired a target, a fat herring gull bobbing on the edge of the chum trail. It approached like a missile and the gull clearly looking through the same spectacle's as us must have thought, Shark!! It exploded from the surface in the nick of time as the huge sunfish turned on a new target further away again, and it slowly shrank from view.

Suddenly, Steve Mac's balloon was down and out as a shark popped it, ate the bait and headed off with the rig, Steve's battle was shorter than mine and a shark of around 25lb was quickly landed and released. I carried on with the hunt for a Garfish in the hope that I could add another species to the list, but I just think they weren't there on that particular day, their time will come. Steve Mac had another smaller shark before it was time to head in and despite achieving no more species it was a truly great day and Murray has gone on to support my challenge which I am most grateful for.

That was the first trip done and the next outing was to be aboard Pegasus from Lyme Regis, skippered by an impressive young skipper Lewis Hodder. The target this time was to be the Tope, a fish that has been elusive only due to previous trips being cancelled, and quietly I was excited at the prospect having not caught a Tope for a few years.

Chris was joining me on this trip and surprisingly he had no obvious ailments other than the usual mindless ramblings 'of an ageing air drummer! It was my time to drive and as per usual it was the standard 5am ejection from the bed to pick up Chris at 5.45am, and yes, it was once again a lovely morning, if you like it hot, dusty and no breeze! We walked down the hill towards the harbour and I stopped to take a quick shot of the myriad of boats leashed like a pack of tiny white dogs waiting to be free, to frolic disobediently amongst the waves. With the lovely summer ramble down the hill complete, we found ourselves first at the boat, Lewis was going about his chores and told us to go on aboard. We have come to really enjoy fishing from Lyme and Lewis has got some wonderful fishing on his doorstep being less than an hour from home it's our closest charter. We gravitated towards the back of the boat and set up the rods with the feathers for the first part of the mission, fresh Mackerel!

A couple more of Lewis's regulars turned up and joined us at the rear of the boat, we ended up with 8 anglers and what a great bunch they were. There were 4 chefs from Beer, two of whom had recently believed Bite Adventures Skipper Chippy when he told them all new shark anglers have to eat some of the chum! Having seen the post on face book it was nice to meet the chum eaters in person, a great bunch, that it was a pleasure to fish with. We headed out on an almost tropical sea and an hour later we stopped for bait and were enveloped by a sea mist that dropped the temperature considerably, the Mackerel were scarce, and the bait box consisted mainly of small Scad.

We headed off for the final hours steam towards Portland Bill and I sat on my bait box actually shivering, something I didn't imagine id be doing when I left home that morning. I put on the only other layer I had with me a neck snood and covered up and dreamt of tope, I knew this trip could see me achieve 52 species if I got a Tope and maybe the Red Gurnard. We had also brought the LRF rods along, so we could end the day trying for a Scorpion Fish or Tompot Blenny, I was determined to get something on this day. We arrived at the Tope mark and the tide was pushing through to start with, so it was 1lb 8oz leads to keep in touch with the seabed. I was using my new Fin Nor rod and reel and was really hoping to test them on something other than a gert big lead weight. The whole Scad flappers were lowered into the clear water and the nervous wait began, it was about 30 minutes before one of the Beer boys hooked into a fish and the first small Tope made an appearance.

Both Chris and I missed a few finicky bites before I had a ratchet running bite, I struck to find an angry fish attached as the Tope I needed broke the surface. The tope was no monster and skipper Lewis grabbed the trace and the fish was released and gone, Lewis turned and said, "well-done on the Tope you needed ". I was temporarily stunned, I had forgot to inform the skipper that I need a photograph as proof for my species challenge, Lewis said don't worry you will get another! Then Chris had a great bite on his Mackerel head bait and he struck to find himself attached to a stubborn fish that hung in the fast tide.

The fish was clearly a ray and eventually kited to the surface, we could see straight away it was a stunning Undulate Ray also known as a painted ray. I was really chuffed for Chris as I didn't think I would ever see one of them, an incredible looking ray and a fish I was extremely envious of. The fish of 10lb 8oz was a personal best and nothing less than Chris had deserved for all his perseverance lately.

The fish were switching on now and I had another run on my double squid bait, this was clearly another small Tope and this time shortly after reaching the surface it was safely netted by the skipper. It was great to see this second Tope and a massive relief as there were only 4 Tope landed all day, so good fortune smiled on me. With the Tope done I asked Lewis how do I go about targeting this stunning Undulate Rays, I really wanted one having seen one in the flesh. The skipper advised me to go with a whole mackerel head, the same bait Chris had landed his on but apparently, they love them, so I removed the wire trace and replaced it with 150lb mono just in case and a fresh Mackerel head.

It was down on the bottom for literally a few minutes when a fast run developed and upon striking I knew I was into a ray, the dogged fight was quite impressive and gave the little Primal reel a good test. The stunning Undulate appeared on the surface down tide and the markings are truly amazing just like an elaborate dot to dot, I was so excited at getting one of these rays I forgot what it actually meant.

*My first ever Undulate Ray and species 52!*

The skipper congratulated me on hitting species 52 and then it dawned on me, I had actually done it, I felt strangely numb for a second then Lewis informed me the ray weighed 11lb 8oz, nice personal best. There were several fish turning up as another couple of rays made an appearance to the Beer boys, Chris was back into some ray action and this turned out to be his first Thornback of the year which made his smile even bigger. I then had a small conger and a few sandpaper sharks before my mackerel head once again attracted an Undulate Ray, I was really getting fond of this fish, being a ray fan.

A few of the guys had swapped over to Bream rigs and were wading through the onslaught of Poor Cod and Pouting, eventually getting Black Bream to 3lb. Chris sensing another personal best was on the cards added a small hook with a sprinkling of the finest green to his bottom rig, Bream love a bit of bright green it attracts them for some unknown reason. He wasn't out for long before a Bream took the little strip of squid and green wool, this was another first for Chris who was on cloud nine, alongside me of course. The fresh bait had been pretty much exhausted so the next pouting that appeared was going to be my next bait, sure enough I didn't wait too long to get the fresh pout I needed. With a fresh bait in place I hoped something different may appear, Chris was having an aggressive bite but managed to miss it and that cost him the last mackerel head. Then my pouting was grabbed by a fish that shot off and I assumed was a tope, it wasn't until the fish broke the surface that it was identified as another Undulate Ray, I couldn't stop getting them now.

With the ray in the net and the skipper dealing with another fish on the other side of the boat, I decided to remove the hook myself, I am fully aware of the ray's ability to project its mouth and furthermore how powerful those crab crushing jaws are. Still I made a careless mistake and grabbed the hook at the bend inside the ray's mouth, in a flash the mouth extended, and the jaws came together on my finger, it was extremely painful instantly and I wrenched my finger out but the damage was done. Chris in the meantime had baited with a large pouting and was now battling what he hoped was the tope he wanted, I on the other hand was nursing my injured finger and plunged it into a bucket of sea water, cures most ailments. The tope Chris was playing had changed into a conger eel and wanting to join the conger club Chris requested the eel join us on deck, having received a nasty leg wound from the last eel I had brought on a boat I decided to stay clear.

That was time over and Lewis had delivered yet another great trip and for me and incredible finale to the 52 species, during the journey in to the harbour I ran over in my mind all the adventures that I had gone through to get to this point. There were so many people that have helped, supported and donated to the challenge, I am eternally grateful to all my friends, family, skippers, guides and fellow anglers who have got me the 52 species. I fully intend to go on and try catching as many species as possible and hopefully keep raising awareness and money for the incredible charity and worthy cause. Chris wanted to know if we were going to try for a mini species when we got in, my answer was no we will sit on the harbour and eat fish and chips to celebrate, Neptune has been good to us let's leave it at that, for now!

I am taking a few days away from fishing now, not because I want to but because I am having a minor leg operation and I will off my feet for a bit. However, I have started the next phase of trip planning and booked a few interesting ones that will make a good blog or two. The harbourside fish and chips were sublime and fitting reward for a very good day at sea.

## Chapter 34 Bats, Prat's & Tiny Cats

The completion of the 52 species has still been sinking in and following my leg operation it's been nice to spend the weekend recuperating and spending time with the family. Having promised to take them out for a slap-up meal upon completion of the challenge, it was only right I honoured that agreement. I decided to let my daughter pick somewhere to go seeing as it was also a celebration for her doing so well at University for the last two years, fortunately she knows what a fuss arse I am and picked somewhere with little chance of me complaining. Absurd Bird, a new American style chicken restaurant based in Exeter, all things chicken that's a safe bet where I am concerned. It turned out to be a popular eatery so good job we booked, and if I had to moan about something I would say that the prices are probably on the top end of the chicken scale, however it was extremely good. The other thing that Absurd Bird highlighted to me was that there's not enough chicken in a glass, meals out there, the chicken in a glass is the modern version of chicken in a basket!

With my statutory duty completed I could once again think about the next species as my new target is 62 species, although I am not getting new merchandise to reflect this. Angling mate Sam James and I had planned to have a night targeting Wels Catfish, a fish I have spent many years home and abroad targeting. Sam was keen to catch his first to get some experience with them before a trip to France in 2019 where his path will cross with some bigger ones.

The venue we chose was Milemead near Tavistock, I had eel fished it many times when I was younger but had not fished it since catfish were introduced. Sam who loves his carp fishing had gone down earlier and spent a couple of nights on the carp lake, landing some nice fish to 26lb. My session was limited to a short overnighter and I had to be gone at first light to start work at 8.00am, Sam also had a near 2-hour journey to get back for work. I arrived at the complex around 6.30pm and setup in the swim next to Sam, this was also the outlet point of the lake and the deepest water.

The lakes have matured lovely over the years and the owners have done a cracking job of providing comfortable quality fishing, I can't say I am surprised they have always been working hard to create their vision. Sam had been pre-baiting a central area with pellet and with a live bait ban on the fishery I had decided to fish large bunches of worms suspended on my Dyson Rig variation over beds of pellet. This method is pretty good on commercials as it tends to dissuade unwanted species from picking up the baits and with 300 carp in the lake and only 30 catfish you really want to avoid Carp. I set up my two rods and gave Sam a spare rig to try for himself, I placed one bait in the right-hand margin and one out towards the middle next to a thick bed of water lily's. I baited both areas with a mixture of 10mm and 20mm pellets and within minutes the areas were bubbling as the numerous carp raided the free larder. We appeared to be the only anglers on the whole complex, but Sam informed me the large double swim next to him had been booked by a couple of anglers.

It was then my margin rod was indicating some interest as the bobbin pulled up sharply, this was repeated a few times but upon striking I missed, the only evidence being the ravaged worms. The hook was re-baited and dropped into the same spot, whereby the same thing occurred including the missed strike, more missing worms, was this some overzealous silver fish?

I stuck with it and once again the indicator rose, but this time line peeled steadily from the reel, I struck and hooked the little culprit. The 3lb test curve rod hardly indicated the battle of the little fish, but as soon as I saw the tiny whiskers I knew that despite its small stature it was indeed a big deal being the catfish we were after. What is incredible is how a small kitten like this can grow to over 9 feet in length and several hundred pounds in weight, they do not seem to get stunted by smaller waters and are governed by food source and water temperature's.

I have myself, landed Wels Catfish at the other end of the scale from this little predator to nearly 200lbs, and at that size they fear nothing. We needed a catfish for Sam now and at least it proved the choice of rig was working and kittens like this normally come in groups, so surely, it's just a case of when not if. With the rod back into position and another scattering of pellet it was time to sit back with a cuppa and enjoy the ambience.

Then the silence was shattered as Wayne and Waynetta Slob appeared over the grassy knowle, him carrying a naff tent and her holding an Aldi bag with one hand, while holding up her pink jogging bottoms up with the other. I quickly tried to dissolve into the camouflage of my Nash Bivvy, but they spotted me, " caught anything mate"? my answer was as limited as possible "nope", they then proceeded to tell me they had booked the double swim and had 20 kilos of the right stuff! I can only surmise that the right stuff, was either something home grown or tins of cheap beer.

They moved along to Sam realising that they would be neighbours, I knew for anyone else this would be a nightmare, but Sam has two things to help him with these sorts of people. The first, his laid-back attitude where nothing really phases him and secondly hearing aids which he can simply switch off! The pair of Prat's then returned to fetch their car, parking it directly behind me and just past the bloody big," no cars past this point sign"! If that wasn't enough, they then proceeded to blow up a double size inflatable bed with the loudest pump you can get, sounding like a Hornet with a migraine shut in a tin, for 30 minutes! With the bouncy castle of a bed blown up, they then decided to argue about the firmness, each taking turns to bounce on the flippin thing, I was tempted to go and have a go myself. Finally, with the bed firmness agreed and all of their shopping bags delivered they were out of my section of the lake, I could however still hear them arguing about what flavour pot noodle should be for tea and breakfast.

I think fishing should be accessible to anglers of all abilities and backgrounds, accept maybe those two, peg banging, bed blowing, carpark flouting, noodle munching Prats! There, rant over and to be honest I am not even sure they cast out, maybe they assumed it was a camp site. With some degree of normality returning to my swim I refreshed the baits with more worms and added a few more pellets to keep things bubbling, the night had now well and truly started to pull in and the witching hour was upon us. With the twilight came the Bats and I love bats, they go about, busy flitting around ridding us of all the insects that were previously hassling us. The number of bats though, resembled the Scooby Doo opening sequence as dozens and dozens filled the air above the water's surface. There must have been a significant roost somewhere nearby, a cave or old barn but they are incredible creatures that we are lucky to have. The margin rod was away again but this time it was an Eel of around a pound, nicely lip hooked though, which made for an easy release. This was followed shortly after by another Eel a bit bigger, then the rod in the middle tore off as a better fish headed out towards the gap between the islands. This could be the Catfish I was after and once I struck line continued to come from the clutch, I shouted to Sam that I might have a better one. He was ready with the net as the fish swam towards us then rolled, a darn carp, I couldn't believe it, especially as I had called Sam to come over. I was so disgusted I let Sam unhook the pesky thing which was probably a scraper double, so disappointing when you think you have what your after and it turns out to be an imposter. I put the rod out and got under my cover, quickly falling asleep, I awoke somewhat confused as to my location and in total darkness.

As my eyes strained into the inky blackness, two red eyes glared back at me like the legendary sasquatch, but only 2 feet tall, I then realised it was the Delkim Alarm lights that remain illuminated to show you where to place your rod.

The other alarm burst into life making the blue lights flash like the approach of a tiny emergency vehicle, time to move as the line was disappearing rapidly! The fish was on and this turned out to be Eel number 5 for the night, probably the biggest of the bunch being around 2lb, like all the rest perfectly lip hooked, looks like the Dyson / Bait runner system is effective with worm baits for the eels. I decided to try a change of method for the rest of the night as the eels were clearly not bothered by the Cats, I now put out large catfish pellets on both rods in the hope that it may attract one of the better catfish. Sadly, it wasn't to be, and the final act of the session was to make a brew and watch the dawn unfold over the lake, it's always a special experience.

Gutted for mate Sam, he has been so instrumental in helping me get many of the species in my challenge, I feel like I failed him a bit on this trip, I do know about catfish and we really should have had a couple. Next time I will be better prepared and spend a bit longer in scoping out the various swims, of course it could have been down to the Munster's emptying 20 kilos of the real stuff into the lake! So next Sunday I shall be out with Sicknote Chris and the Happy Danglers trying to hunt down a Greater Weaver fish or if I am really lucky a Megrim, one thing is for sure, Chris will get a Dogfish!

## Chapter 35 Things that go bump in the night!

With the arrival of yet another month it feels like our unusually settled (touch wood) summer is slipping away, with several summer species still to target, I have to grab every opportunity that presents itself. That's exactly what happened last night, shark club mate Alex Mckay and I have been discussing the possibility of catching a Sea trout for my challenge and last night was to be the night. I am sure purists will say that Sea trout are actually the same species as the Brown trout, *Salmo trutta*, and this is true, the sea trout is anadromous, choosing to spend most of its life at sea, but like the debate over Smoothounds for this challenge I aint a purist! The sea trout is also thought to be largely female and grows larger on a richer sea food diet, they return to freshwater to spawn during the summer, often sporting a silver scale pattern. I am not a Sea trout expert and must confess to having never tried to catch one, something I really hoped to change. Alex on the other hand does do quite well with the sea trout and having grown up fishing the river in question was most definitely the ace up my sleeve.

Like so many of my friends and fellow anglers, Alex has really been supportive agreeing to take me to his most precious of fishing spots, not even a mention of a blindfold! To be honest I wouldn't know where we ended up last night or how we got there, Alex told me it could involve a tad of jungle warfare, it certainly did. I made my way down to meet Alex and his best friend and fishing partner, Jack, a lovely Jack Russell cross, and despite his age was as mad as a box of frogs!

I pulled up in the south Cornish town with the night time rapidly approaching, sea trout are lovers of the dark and we had timed the trip to perfection. I parked my car up and jumped in the van with Alex and Jack for the magical mystery tour that included cameos by Badgers, and Rabbits, sadly they were mostly pretty flat, but the appearance of a bounding Deer and two Magpies was surely a sign. We parked up for an attempt at the first pool of the evening, both spots we were going to try were tidal and have produced Mullet, Flounder, Eels and Seatrout in the past.

I grabbed my light spin rod from the van and tied on a small hook to which I added a small split shot, that's it basic rig ready, I had the chance of 3 different fish and I had tied up some spinners with a single hook just in case a Thin Lip Mullet was spotted. Jack was off through the grass like a Tasmanian devil that had been slapped on the butt, the only sign of his frantic zig zagging was the shaking of the grass that covered him so well.

The valley we made our way across was silent and magical in the twilight, it just needed the screech of an owl to complete the scene. Alex explained that this pool wasn't the best of the two, but we needed the darkness to have fully fallen before attempting the second spot, he had watched more than a dozen fish in the second pool earlier in the day and was confident it would produce. I must admit that the excitement of targeting a new species in locations I have never fished far out ways the catching, which is the icing on the cake.

I know like many before him, Alex was feeling a bit of pressure to help get me the fish I was after, but fishing is fishing and if it wasn't a challenge it wouldn't be fun. We approached the tree line and my first glimpse of the river, which to be more accurate was very stream like, we crossed under and over the barb wire fence, only two puncture holes for me. Then it was time for the aforementioned jungle warfare, Alex isn't exactly small being built like a rugby prop, but he literally vanished into the Cambodian forest of twisted limbs, nettles and brambles. Jack kept bounding back for a giggle at this strange man dangling from several pointy saplings, eventually I fell into a small clearing. The pool reminded me of Cornwall's version of an Amazon tributary no doubt supporting a caiman or two, how Alex ever discovered this magical little place heaven knows but what a privilege to be taken there. The pool was very overgrown and as we were just about on high water it had the appearance of a pond, it was however very deep and moving very slightly. Fish topped just under the far marginal trees, but their identity was unknown. This is the sort of fishing that so excited me as a youth and I can understand that as Alex fished this as a young lad what memories it must hold, if not for this challenge I would have missed out on so many wonderful experiences.

I nervously baited my hook with a couple of worms and flicked them into the centre, holding the line between my fingers to feel any plucks. Within a few minutes the line was yanked tight and I struck to find myself attached to a strong fish that took me into a hidden snag, sadly that one got away and I just hoped it hadn't spooked the pool.

I re-baited and cast the bait further down towards the tail of the pool, once again I had some interest with small pulls and plucks on the line, I struck sending the worms at Mach 1 towards us. Strange little bites that Alex concluded may be flounder, I positioned the fresh worms in the same spot and once again tiny plucks, I waited this time which resulted in an escalation of the bite with the line once more yanked tight. I lifted into the fish feeling the reassurance of thumping pressure, Alex knew straight away it was a sea trout just as it decided to go berserk. The fish ran all over the pool, deep, shallow and along the surface before succumbing to a good bit of netting from Alex. The fish was gorgeous in the low light and we needed to work quick to get her unhooked and back to the river, a second quick picture didn't go quite as planned. Great first shot but the combination of me wetting my hands and the fish being like a bar of soap made the second shot a case of there it was, gone! Alex found this hilarious and luckily Jack had got his fish kissing ritual done before she disappeared back into the black lagoon.

What a start and we still had the banker pool to go, I tried another bait in this pool, but the excitement of that crazy fish had spooked the area, so time for extraction from the jungle. We got back to the van both still a little in disbelief, Alex explaining that sea trout aren't always as obliging as that. We pulled up in total darkness at the second area and we firstly done what all anglers do when confronted with a bridge, we peered over, down below in the dark, a large pool could be seen and right on cue a very big sea trout gulped down a water critter.

Wow, I thought this place looks the business, we grabbed the tackle and as stealthily as two old blokes could, we negotiated the overgrown trail down to the river. Splosh, another sea trout disturbed the surface of the by now emptying tidal pool, a large overgrown bush in the near margin was the honey hole with fish, Alex estimated upwards of 4lbs. We really were in stealth mode, creeping around whispering and only using red lights, Jack however was many years past being stealthy and stomped around like a dog twice his size, he stared frustrated into the black water, knowing full well what lied within its depths. I dropped the bait right on the money and with my heart pounding braced for impact, the instant bite never came. I spent 30 minutes trying different areas of the pool, twitching the bait back slowly and at one point the bait was grabbed and after some extremely subtle nibbling it was ignored.

Alex trying a few of the less favoured pools suffered the same fate and despite, perfect conditions, perfect bait and a pool loaded with fish we never caught another. It showed why sea trout can be so frustrating and just how fortuitous the earlier capture was, Jack seemed to take the second pool failure worse than us and whined disappointedly as we made our way back to the van. With the night at its darkest and our journey back through the spookiest of lanes, both Alex and I exchanged stories of things that went bump in the night during our many night time fishing trips. I think it was a good job we done that after we got back to the van, or the night may have been a tad shorter.

Thanks, so much Alex and Jack for sharing some truly wonderful fishing spots, a night of great company and a great result, I'd love to do it again, for a thin lip mullet next time! That's number 54 and I really hope I can get something different on Sunday but it's certainly getting harder now.

## Chapter 36 Golden fish & a golden child!

This week's blog relates to the boat trip we had yesterday from Penzance aboard Bite Adventures skippered by Chippy Chapman, most will know this boat and skipper for their incredible Shark captures, including the British catch and release Blue Shark record.

There is however a lot more to Penzance than just sharking, the incredible diversity of species that visit these waters makes it a sport anglers delight. The trip had been organised by Happy Danglers supremo and top bloke Nick Smith, it was booked as a species hunt which was perfect for my cause. As can be the case with trips planned in advance, there were the inevitable dropouts, leaving a couple of vacant spaces, Chris was keen to join us so that left one and with only a day to go it looked like the space wouldn't be filled. Chris then suggested that his nephew Elliot might enjoy trying boat fishing but having only fished once before at the lakes it may be a step to far. Well it turned out young Elliot was indeed keen as mustard to get out and try some boat fishing, so with a cracking day of sun and no wind predicted we were all set.

The morning was glorious and as we travelled west down the A30 the rear view towards Lyme Regis was illuminated by that ball of fire we know as our sun; however, our direction was bathed in a fog bank, creating an impression of islands poking through a slate grey sea

The fog appeared at various points along the journey clinging to the hollows like the set of a Hammer Horror movie, the higher elevations were already bathed in the sun's rays, highlighting what we were too, expect throughout the day.

Before long we arrived at the car park and despite leaving home at 5.45am we were still well and truly beaten by the rest of the danglers, who were busy trying to winkle out mini species from the harbour. The team today were Pete, Nick, Dave, George, Paul, and the three of us, those guys are pretty dam good anglers, so we were confident young Elliot would learn plenty, and some of it would even be useful. The skipper reversed the Cat, Bite Adventures up towards the steps and we all piled aboard with a real air of excitement, all of us having our own personal goals that we hoped to achieve from the day. Personally, I was looking forward to picking the brains of these guys who I have fished with on several occasions, but they still have so many tips and advice on several of the species I still want to catch. The boat headed out from a sun-drenched harbour towards a misty sea, that quickly diffused the sun and dropped the air temperature a few degrees, this was still an incredible site.

We soon punched through the mist into an area of clear skies and the flat sea resembled the surface of an inland lake with just a solitary dolphin to create some ripple. First on the agenda was the catching of the fresh bait, as I watched Chris advising Elliot it didn't seem 5 minutes ago I was explaining this to Chris on the very same boat.

The strange thing was that a memory popped up on Facebook that evening, of that very same trip, and it was indeed a year ago, many breakfasts and at least one rod have passed over the side, for Chris since then, now with his own sea legs he was passing on the joys of the sport to a future angler. The Mackerel were obliging, if not in particularly large quantities, and before long we were filling the bait box, I had tied on Sabiki's a tiny set of shrimp pattern feathers excellent at catching a variety of species as well as Mackerel. This quickly paid off as a new species was hooked and swung on board, another of the country's smaller species the Sardine, what a start 5 minutes fishing and species number 55. With the bait well and truly sorted it was time to try for a Weever fish and possibly a Plaice on an area of sand and stone, this quickly produced a Dragonet for species maestro and best dressed angler George. The drift was so slow that we hardly moved and that really ruled out the Plaice, we did get a few of the stunning Cuckoo Wrasse and I managed a male and female in quick succession.

Elliot who had already managed Mackerel and Sardine added a nice male Cuckoo Wrasse to his species tally and despite Uncle Chris's help was doing really well, a bit of a natural I think. With the drift not really producing the species we were after, Chippy decided it was time to head over to a tackle hungry section of reef for some mixed ground fishing. The method was a two-hook rig with the weight on the bottom, this was bounced in the hope that it didn't snag in the jagged reef, baits were Prawn and King Ragworm. The action was instant and a species carnage, as most of the time, most of us were playing fish, the bulk of the fish were stunning Ballan Wrasse in the 3lb to 4lb class.

The variety of colours and markings were incredible and with so many beautiful Wrasse to choose from it may have been hard to pick the most handsome, but I think Chris nailed that with a red and pale blue corker. Everyone was getting Wrasse, Pouting, Poor Cod and Pollack it really was a lucky dip to see what would appear next, exactly what you want from a species trip and it was shaping up to be a real red-letter day. I then picked up a Codling just as super boy brought in the trips first and only Bass, I had to grab a quick double shot with this future legend. That hour was probably the best wrassing I can remember, Pete, Nick and Chris tried hardback crabs to try to get through to the bigger fish clearly in residence, but the baits were grabbed instantly by their smaller brethren.

It was almost disappointing when the skipper announced we were off to try for something else and a quick stop for a Ling awarded Nick with a nice fish and the rest of us with some big pouts. Chippy kindly took us to an area where we could try for the Red Gurnard, a species that has so vexed me on a number of trips, I know how to target them now, having had several attempts and quickly had a small strip of Mackerel dragging along the sandy sea bed below us. The rod tip rattled violently, and I paid out a little line just to be sure the fish could eat the bait, the rod bounced more vigoursly as the fish was hooked, I tentatively reeled the fish to the surface and sure enough the bright red colour of the target gurnard appeared. Species 56 and more importantly the species that for everyone else was an easy fish to catch but when it's something you really need it just doesn't happen.

There was a few Red Gurnard landed including a huge one to Dave in the corner, Chris managed red and greys, but so too did the golden child, but I think by now we all knew he was to be top rod that day. With the gurnard caught we were once again on our way to a new area this time to anchor for a chance of Couch's Bream a stunning hard fighting member of the bream family that resembles the Red Snapper. The rigs needed to be strong for these powerful fish and 2 hook paternosters baited with whole squid was the order of the day.

The area was once again snaggy and started producing Ballan Wrasse even on the big squid baits, a few strap congers were also caught. Other than uncle Chris, Elliot was the only person I've known to be delighted to get a Dogfish, but by the second one even his admiration in the species had waned, but as this day was to be young Elliot's, he then added the only Haddock of the trip to his rapidly expanding list of species. Chippy pointed out that the area we were now anchored had produced some lovely little Rock Cook Wrasse to some anglers previously, I didn't need telling twice I really love the look of the colourful little wrasse and prepared to set up to catch one.

George then offered up one of his LRF shore rigs fitted with two tiny size 12 hooks, perfect for these tiny reef dwellers. I baited thc hooks with tiny sections of ragworm and dropped them down to the reef below, straight away the rod tip rattled as small greedy fish pecked frantically at the baits. Upon inspection I had hooked a couple of small Poor Cod one on each hook, I persevered with this rig in the hope it would eventually sort me that special fish.

Chris had set Elliot up with a tandem hook rig, baited with worm, and after a few small rattles the rod had bent over into a heavier fish. Without any fight it was a bit of a mystery to see what species the youngster had now lured from the depths, Chris was peering intently into the water and suddenly shouted " John Dory"! Incredible Elliot had caught one of the most amazing of fish and a fish that many anglers with years under their belts had not even seen yet alone caught. The fish weighed 5lb and was a stunning creature, despite my rod having frantic tapping little bites I just had to get some pictures of the JD, so left it bouncing. With the pictures taken and Elliot congratulated I returned to my rod, to reel in the pesky little critters that were no doubt attached to the line, I turned the reel handle and was suddenly met by extra weight. I continued to reel with the rod bent over clearly indicating something more than a couple of poor cod, I then remembered that I had a really light rig with tiny hooks on, so reeled as steadily as possible. Chippy joined me and asked if the fish had fought at all, but as it hadn't, he was sure it was another John Dory and was ready with the net, just as well as it was indeed another of these magical fish. The skipper didn't miss, getting it in the back of the net, I was stunned, what a fish for the challenge and without doubt, the most difficult to have even considered targeting.

I could see as I went to remove the hook, that the tiny hook was attached to a poor cod, that itself had been eaten, by the John Dory. It really seems that Neptune himself has decided to support my challenge as this fish really is a special one and needed a large degree of luck to have landed it.

*Above yet another first for me this year, a John Dory.*

Strangely the John Dory I caught lacked the same vibrant striping of the one Elliot caught, and I am unsure if there are differences in the male and females like so many other fish species. It was amazing how quick, rigs were set up complete with poor cod baits in the hope that a shoal of John Dory had appeared, sadly they were the only two, we were blessed with, and an incredible fish for number 57.

With the wind and tide conspiring against us and with an epic day under our belts we all decided to spend the last hour gathering some Mackerel baits for future trips. Heading in we were all shattered having a fun, fish filled day, it appeared that no one had told Pete at the back we had stopped fishing as he sat transfixed to his rod tips while we skipped across the waves back to Penzance.

I have to say a big thankyou yet again to Nick for all his organising for the Danglers, and the guys on the trip for their advice and support, skipper Chippy who proved once again there's more to Penzance than sharking. The true star of the day was young Elliot who on his first ever boat trip landed 12 species including a couple of the most sort after fish in the country, he is shopping for tackle this weekend and what an angler he will become. Not sure what I will catch next, but with some shark trips on the horizon my money is on a Garfish.

# Chapter 37 The sharks don't want to play, but a Garfish makes my day!

With two days sharking planned it would surely mean aching arms, plenty of shark rash and the scent of chum heavy in the air, the fishing gods had other plans though! First of the two sorties was back down to Penzance aboard Bite Adventures with Chippy, and I was feeling just a tad confident having never blanked on a shark trip down there. The trip was one of the three shark trips I have booked with chippy this year with the other two being September and October. Unfortunately, I had a few drop out for various reasons and I needed to find some other anglers at short notice or end up with an expensive solo day, having experienced a day of 78 sharks previously I didn't fancy that on my own.

Fortunately, Chippy posted the spaces on his Facebook page and I quickly got a crew together, Josh, Ash, Phil and Graham gave us five on the day a good number for a normal Penzance trip. Josh and Ash were travelling down from Kent through the night, I agreed to meet them at Okehampton services and drive the rest of the journey down to Penzance. Phil from Birmingham and Graham from Manchester made their way down the day before and stayed in Penzance meaning they should have been better rested. The day arrived and I was up at 4am to meet the guys at the services at 4.45am, when I arrived they looked like a pair of zombies having only cat napped for an hour, when they got their cool box from the car, I actually thought they had brought their own boat down, such was the size of it.

The two young guys looked like they could handle a 100-shark day, and that's not surprising, with Josh being a personal trainer, I remember when I looked like that, not! What great company these two were, when they weren't tag sleeping that is, and it's always nice to meet and fish with new people. We made the journey down in good time and arrived harbour side at 6.15am, Phil and Graham joined us shortly after, and we were on our way by 6.45am. The stop off for bait was hard work with just a handful of joey mackerel and Scad being all we could muster, it may have to be whiting from the shark grounds if we get through the bait we had. Bite Adventures then pushed out through Penzance Bay and out into the swollen Atlantic sea, it was a pretty rough ride out, no doubt similar to the experience clothing has, within a washing machine on a long wash, needless to say Chippy couldn't get as far out as he wanted to go.

We arrived at the shark ground refreshed and ready to go, we'll all except Graham, who had taken a tumble on the way out, poor old chap, not the best way to start a day's sharking. The chum bags were soon in the water and a wonderful slick instantly spread out smoothing out even the bigger waves, the shark floats quickly followed, and it was now the waiting game. Phil was up first, and a small shark was plucking frantically at the bait causing the float to bob up and down rapidly, Chippy stated "you could do with this one Steve, for your challenge as I think it's a small Porbeagle".

Sure, enough Phil hooked the little sea Rottweiler, and it was quickly unhooked at the side of the boat, unfortunately it was so lightly hooked it couldn't have been brought in for the photograph that Phil really wanted. Graham who had been keen to catch some whiting, to exchange for beer back at his accommodation, was getting plenty of fish every drop, he was then hit by something while reeling in his latest string of fish. Sure, enough upon inspection the biggest of the group of whiting had a nice bite mark that appeared to be made by a small blue shark. I think he may have been bitten off by sharks a few times during the day as several of his rigs seem to disappear suddenly! Then Ash was away on his rod and having not had a shark since the age of eight was getting the run around from this hyper active blue shark, after a good battle a nice shark was unhooked, photographed and sent on its way.

By now I had decided to try to target the next species on my list, the Garfish, chippy gave me some pointers on methods to target them, the sea was a little bit choppy for them, but they should still be attracted by the chum trail. Despite fishing for them all day, I had one solitary little bite, which could have been down to a small mackerel nibbling as it sped past. Normally they have some pretty awesome garfish fishing down there, and I really needed to get the garfish during these two days, so I could move on to something else. Another shark interrupted proceedings and Josh got to flex his muscles for a little bit making short work of a feisty little blue shark, once again quick photo and the shark was on its way.

The sharking by normal standards for this neck of the woods was slow and we couldn't really see a reason for it, good drift, plenty of chum and clear water, everything required for plenty of action, but even hot spots can have warm days. The weather was starting to look angrier as rain clouds formed just to our west, we could be getting a soaking shortly. Graham then had a shark which once again fought really well, and at least when they turned up they gave a great account of themselves, this fish was quickly released at the side of the boat. I had the next fish, which had taken the bait on the 12lb to 20lb class kit, and this blank saver was most enjoyable on this lighter outfit, the fish was unhooked at the side of the boat and shot off, clearly still full of beans.

Finally, Phil had yet another baby porbeagle, this time however the little guy was brought on board, so Phil could give it a quick cuddle, these little powerhouses need to be held tight, as they have the dentures to inflict a nasty wound. Incredible to think that in a few years this fish could be 9 feet and 500lbs a true British apex predator.

That should have been the end of that, but right at the end of the day, three thin lipped Mullet arrived around the chum bags, picking off particles that oozed through the mesh. I quickly ran over with my LRF rod to take a look and ultimately try and catch one for the challenge, in doing so I leant against my rod on the gunnel, crack! that was rod number three broken this year.

Chippy pointed out that the weight marked on the rod was in grams not stones! I was pretty attached to that little rod having landed several mini species with it, but there was no doubt that was the end of it, not a great finish to a tough day. To really rub it in Chippy was out the next day landing 41 Sharks and getting garfish on the mackerel feathers, fishing is like the sea plenty of highs and lows!

The second trip included within this blog is a trip out from Looe aboard Force 10 skippered by Pete Davis, the crew today was friends John, Roger and Nigel whom I've fished with on several occasions. The morning was sunny but fresher than I had expected, but that was something we really needed for a good drift, the journey out was full of a excited group of anglers and a somewhat shattered me, having not got back from yesterday's trip till 10pm. We were soon in position with the chum bags once again omitting their pungent shark aphrodisiac and as per normal the choppy sea was made flat for the full width of the trail.

We trotted our rods out, into our selected positions, and sat back for a bit of a chin wag and a few tall fishing stories. Eager to get the garfish, I had messaged Roger the previous night asking him to bring his garfish rod as I had broken mine, he had happily obliged, and I was now keen to have a go. I asked Pete if he had seen gars lately, unfortunately he informed me that, on only one day this season had garfish shown up, not the news I wanted to hear.

Despite this I wanted to persevere and decided to fish a small weight on the swivel in the hope the bait would be raised through the water column as the boat drifted finding the right layer for the garfish. Before I could get the rod in the water Roger had a take on his rod which was close to the boat, another hard scrap ensued before Pete pulled in, a nice skinny male blue shark. The fish was soon shown the door and we could all once again return to the sharking lottery in the hope it would be our rod that went next, I however had other plans, and got the garfish rod out, hoping one or two had by now arrived in the slick. The thin strip of mackerel belly fluttered slowly down through the chum trail until it was no longer visible, I then closed the bail arm allowing the rig to rise as the boat drifted.

I held the 8lb braid in my fingers feeling for the slightest pluck on the bait and sure enough it came, but no plucks a full-on yank as the gar hit the bait on the run. I tightened down causing the silver missile to explode out of the water like a miniature marlin, line poured from the tiny reel and a mini battle unfolded, with the garfish fighting every inch of the way in. So important was the fish that we actually opened the rear door to bring it aboard, rather than risk the light line parting on the gars serrated beak. The garfish is a wonderful looking creature, built for bursts of speed with all the power towards the rear like a pike, their long bills capable of piercing flesh in an instant. They are covered in tiny green scales that in the sun create a pure bar of silver, big eyes allow for spotting their prey, normally smaller fish. With the garfish landed that was species 58 in the bag, a great relief.

The garfish kept me busy for quite a while being addictive and after a couple of fish the size of the first, I hooked a real beauty, the garfish must have jumped a dozen times and repeatedly took yards of line from the reel in screaming runs. I knew it was a good fish as I had seen several times, and John carefully lifted it into the boat, the fish was a new personal best, I didn't weigh it but it was a meter long and thick as my wrist. The next garfish though, would need to be shark bait, there were so many out there that the sharks would certainly love to snack on them, plus I've done well with them as bait in the past. It didn't take long to get one for bait but before I could use it, Johns rod was screaming as a shark made off with his bait.

The fish was another feisty male and gave him a good bit of fun before getting quickly released, I had managed to sneak my rod in and re-bait with the garfish while Johns fish was being released. I had just put the rod back into the rest and walked away when it tore off, they clearly appreciated the garfish delicacy, another great scrap and the first female shark of the day was landed. I decided to grab a quick picture as the fish was calm and we were fast with the unhooking.

That just left Nigel to make it a fish for all four of our rods, and as luck would have it the very next take was on his rod, and he battled a nice little shark for a quick release at the side.

We were all hoping for another quick run of fish and Johns rod was soon off again as a small fish crashed the party, the last action was once again on Johns rod, but the fish rolled up the trace and went through the leader to spoil our 100% average. The wind had started to increase with the turn of the tide and it was all too soon time to head for home, I was however feeling pretty happy with how the day had gone, everyone got a fish and I got a personal best garfish. We steamed homewards and but by the time we reached the radar buoy the sky had become somewhat angry, and white horses quickly developed.

*Personal Best Garfish and species 58!*

Once we had finally escaped the claws of the approaching squall, we could see blue skies over Looe and Pete stopped in the calmer water to hoist the flags, to display the sharks caught.

Thanks to Chippy on Bite Adventures and Pete Davis on Force 10 for a couple of enjoyable days in pretty testing conditions, I think I am a bit of shark Jonah this season, but as long as I can catch something then every trip's a good one. Really enjoyed the company of Josh, Ash, Phil, Graham, John, Roger, and Nigel over the last few days, great banter. Things are going to get a bit trickier now, as I target more difficult species, and Saturday night sick boy and I are getting the beach casters out, thanks to some advice from a darn good chap.

## Chapter 38 It's a dry Wye, but we'll have a try

Apologies for the delay in writing a blog for those that do follow my ramblings, but I've been busy with work and getting the book ready on Amazon, so I can publish in December. I have managed a couple of trips over the last week cumulating in a wonderful road trip to the gorgeous Wye Valley in Hertfordshire. Our first effort was to try once again for the Spotted Ray, I have tried several times this year for one of these little rays via boat and shore. This trip was to a pier mark that had produced a number of spotty's to fellow dangler Paul Lorimore, he very kindly gave me a ton of info on the mark and where to target the rays. The afternoon was spent in the kitchen making homemade Pasty's plus small squid and Sandeel wraps, that way both the family and Rays would be happy. I drove the 1.5hr journey up to the mark in north Devon and the weather was far from inspiring with driving rain and a blustery wind. We pulled up in the car park to find it fairly empty apart from a couple of drongo's spinning round the car park in their pimped up Corsa, complete with spoiler and fandango wheels.

The rain eased enough to get set up and walk the short distance to the mark, both rods were cast on the hotspots and baited with the perfect little wraps, Chris put one rod out for ray and one for conger. We were fishing the last of the ebb tide and the water on the Bristol channel rises and falls with incredible speed, this leads to a few moves up and down the pier. The rain had returned and great sheets of it shimmered in the lights of the harbour, after such a prolonged bright spell the rain was a novelty, well initially.

Chris's conger rod rattled angrily as an eel mouthed the mackerel head, sure enough the strike resulted in resistance and a strap conger was hoisted aboard the pier.

Great start, we both thought this was the beginning of some frenzied fish feeding.

Well 2hrs passed and that novelty rain had become a proper pain in the rear end, added to this fact was the incredible stillness of the rods, even the intrusion of the bait robber crabs had long since ended. I had one bite during the whole session and even that fish decided it didn't like the taste of the bait, maybe I should have swapped the pasties with the Sandeels. With the flood tide well under way and work in the morning we decided that once again the spotted ray had eluded us, better to sleep and fight another day! Well another day, was the following Saturday morning and the rain had departed, but with a few days of good heavy showers we decided to go out to the lakes and try for a crucian carp in the golden lake.

The crucians had only been stocked the previous autumn and were only a couple of inches long, but another species is another species regardless of size so that was the challenge. The method was size 18 hooks 2lb bottom and swim feeder for me, Chris opted for float and was quickly rewarded with a brightly coloured Orfe. I was missing more bites than I could afford too and that's the problem going from a beach caster to a light feeder rod, it's a question of scale, poor eyes and slow reactions also compound the problem.

The next bite however even a giant Galapagos 'tortoise would have reached in time, the rod tip doubled over, and a strong fish made for the abundant lily beds. Steady pressure won the day and despite the tiny hook and trace the fish was safety netted, a lovely golden tench. Still no sign of a crucian but with plenty of bubbling going on in the swim, it would surely only be a matter of time. Then Chris's float dipped slowly beneath the water and the first crucian carp wriggled on the surface, not huge but bigger than they went in. The coloured water had caused them to lose their lovely buttery golden flanks but I'm sure as the water clears, this will once again return. We fished on for another hour but that was the only crucian that appeared, so that was now two trips in a row that my target species had eluded me, the frustrations of fishing.

With the weekend over, it was now time for the main event, a road trip for a couple of days fishing the river Wye. I have tried for my first ever Barbel on a number of occasions even joining Barbel supremo Des Taylor for a guided night trip, such is my bad luck with the species that we blanked that night. I should add that the trip with Des was to target double figure fish and that was always going to be a tough challenge. For the purpose of my charity challenge I really wanted to catch a Barbel off my own back, both Chris and I had spent a great deal of time learning the ways of the Wye's whiskered warrior. I had booked us a few days, staying at the Red Lion Inn, Bredwardine, Hertfordshire, they own around 4 miles of the river wye in some truly stunning countryside.

The plan was to travel up early Monday stopping at Woody's tackle shop in Hereford for maggots and to pick local expert Woody's brains, it's always great to support these local tackle shops, when there gone, there gone, and you won't get local knowledge mail order! Chris and I loaded the Popemobile Sunday night and headed off at 5.30am sharp, we were having breakfast at the café next to the tackle shop by 8.30am, having had a perfect trip up. With the delights of a fresh cooked breakfast safely packed away, we had a stroll around Woody's tackle emporium, picking up a few spare feeders, boilie needles and plenty of maggots. I explained to Woody what we were doing and my challenge, he then offered to put us on a few good spots Wednesday morning if we failed on the Red Lion beats, anyone visiting Hereford pop in and support Woody, he is a top bloke. We had a stroll down to the supermarket to get a few supplies and I noticed an amazing sculpture on the roundabout made of scrap metal, I simply had to grab a picture, we first thought a Kingfisher but on hindsight maybe it's a wood pecker either way I loved it.

With the SAS stronghold of Hereford visited it was now time, to get up the road, get checked in and down on the river, the day was slipping away. It was only 10 miles from Hereford to the Red Lion Inn and we weren't able to check-in to our room before midday, so a quick stop at the iconic bridge on the road up to the pub was in order. I love my bridges, working with them every day, and this bridge from the 1700s is a wonderful example of superb engineering, built to join the two neighbouring hamlets it's as good today as it was then.

The Red Lion itself is an old coaching Inn from the mid-1700s and the whole area is steeped in a rich tapestry of history and folklore. We could quickly see that despite the recent heavy rains the river level was painfully low and the flow at the bridge was hardly moving, there was however still a tinge of colour. We pulled up at the pub and while Chris ambled off to find some life in the seemingly deserted inn, I went and checked out a small feeder stream in the hope of a minnow or two. The stream was virtually dry but next to it sat a lovely map of the valley we planned to explore over the next few days, this really is a beautiful area and I thoroughly recommend it for a visit.

Chris returned, having found the owner Mike at the rear of the building, he was happy for us to go straight in the room as it was all ready, and once we were settled he would run through the fishing beats. It took us literally 5 minutes to chuck the stuff in the room and decide who had the big bed, before we were in the pub nagging Mike for the information on the river. Clearly Mike has done this a thousand times but for us it was exciting to put all our research into practice and the challenge of a new species in an alien environment is both exhilarating and thought provoking. Mike produced our own personal map, which he quickly marked up with the most productive swims for our list of species, he stayed clear of giving any specific details opting to suggest we stay mobile in order to find the fish. As good as the above map was, it neglected to mention the huge emotionally challenged, black bull residing in the field, patrolling many of the beats.

I have now included the animal to scale on my map, to prevent anyone else falling foul of this grumpy bovine, unfortunately as I wasn't driving I became the designated gate opener stroke bull wrangler. With daylight burning we jumped in the car and headed off through the myriad of gates, fields and tracks to the last car compound. Our plan was to fish with cage feeders loaded with ground bait and pellet hook baits, using just one quivertip rod each to enable a roaming approach. The first look at the river clearly showed the remaining water was confined to shallow glides punctuated by a sprinkling of deep pools with little to no flow. It can be tricky picking the best time to visit the Wye and all around us was the evidence of the extreme levels the river can reach, many meters above where we were standing. The first pool we stopped at was a mixture of rapids, into a slow glide cumulating in a pool several meters deep, our theory was, that this section had a bit of everything. Despite my overwhelming desire to catch a Barbel I was also here for a number of species and opted to change to the maggot feeder with maggots on the hook, in the hope of getting a Dace.

The first cast over to the far bank resulted in a plethora of sharp bites and upon striking the maggots had been sucked to death, this process was repeated several times before a change was needed. With the arrival of a handsome pair of swans I was once again fishing, having scrounged a small hook from Chrissy Crabtree, who settled into the role of river roamer very quickly, landing the first chub.

With the scaled down tackle now back in the swim, I felt I was in with a greater chance of connecting with one of the little torpedo's, sure enough the changes resulted in my first fish of the trip, another of my favourites the humble Gudgeon. With the first fish on the board the next one quickly followed and this time, it was one of my target species, the flighty little Dace making species number 59. Chris also managed several Dace having swapped to maggots, just so we could enjoy the fun of this amazing river, by catching a fish a chuck. Reluctantly we decided we needed to see more of the beats and moved on down river to another nice looking area, sticking with the maggots produced yet another of the species I was after, the Minnow, this abundant little fish form into great shoals, pouncing on any food items that drop into the river, like toothless piranha, species number 60.These are the fish that have adorned many a child's jam jar, while undertaking their first river dipping adventure, their appearance is a sign of a healthy eco system.

With the first afternoon slipping into evening we came across another angler staying at the Inn, the section he and his wife were fishing was the best section of river we had seen, and we surveyed the water with envious eyes. This was compounded further when he told us he had managed a small barbel and 4 decent Chub that afternoon, he was however now leaving if we wished to jump in the section. We didn't need asking twice and Chris fetched the car, so we could bring down a second rod a piece, and try for the fish we were really after, the Barbel.

This swim had a lovely fast, shallow section, pumping oxygen rich water into a steady glide with large willows and black thorns overhanging the far bank. The section went on for several hundred meters and the depths looked around 3 to 4 feet over the far side, perfect in the present condition's. Our new best friend wished us luck and headed off for a slap-up meal in the pub, no doubt washed down with a pint of the local cider, to us a Barbel was still more appealing. The method I had opted for, was one rod fished carp style with a small meaty boilie coupled with a method feeder, the second was a quivertip, cage feeder and double 8mm pellet. I then introduced a catapult full of pellets every 10 minutes, this resulted in several fish topping in the swim and loads of line bites on the fine quivertip.

Chris had gone similar but with luncheon meat as a hook bait after hearing that's what our friend had been using all day. With the dusk approaching and a real feeling of confidence building the rod tip arched round and I was into my first decent feeling fish, the lightish tackle was great with the river being so low. The fish tried to get back to the overhanging trees but lost the battle, Chris scooped up what was clearly a personal best Chub. The fish would have probably been in the 3 to 4lb bracket but I remember being slightly disappointed it wasn't the Barbel I so desired, that I didn't even weigh it, very poor on my behalf. It was then Mr Crabtree's turn and he also added a Chub to the proceeding's that was no doubt his personal best, we added several more of these greedy Chub in the next hour and started to wonder if there were any Barbel in the swim.

Finally, I had a take on my rod that didn't just pull the tip over but the rod out of the stand, upon striking the line started disappearing as the fish shot off downstream. Sometimes fish make errors of judgement just like us anglers and this Barbel turned around and came back upstream towards me, it was just a case of steady directing and the fish was in the net. At last with several attempts at Barbel from a number of rivers the curse was finally broken, and in the net, was species 61 a gorgeous river Wye Barbel. Well I say gorgeous, it was in fact slightly bent with some sort of banana effect on its tail, I however, considered it a thing of beauty and punched the air in excitement. The fish wasn't huge by Barbel standards weighing 6lb 1oz but in difficult conditions and caught by my own fair hand I felt it a real result, after a quick picture I spent 10 minutes with the fish getting it re-oxygenated before it swam off strongly.

Big fish like this should never be let go straight away while the river is in the conditions like it is, they could easily belly up further down the river. By keeping the fish well oxygenated in some faster water until you feel them kicking it ensures they are strong enough to get back to the main river. We stayed on till 8.45pm but there were no further bites and as I was starving and with the thought of our swim buddy tucking into some pub grub weighing heavy on my mind we headed back across the fields. As we reached the penultimate gate a huge black wall blocked our way, the Bull had appeared, it took a step to the side and as I went to open the door stomped its feet and huffed aggressively, " looks like we are stopping here then" I stated to Chris.

I had no intention of getting out to open the gate by moving the great cape water buffalo that blocked our way. Chris however can be just as pig headed as that beast and climbed out to move him along, the creature reluctantly moved but turned and looked me straight in the eyes, I knew it was thinking if I catch you, I will kill you! I had a sudden urge to order the biggest of steaks that evening, thus creating my own act of defiance. We arrived back at the pub after last food orders thanks largely to Bullgate, but Mike kindly arranged for the chef to knock us up some scampi and chips.

We entered the bar and it was one of those slaughtered lamb moments, with a strange array of locals spread around the room, cauliflower Colin sat in one corner telling the tale of how he discovered the joys of cauliflower cheese after his third wife left him. The stool at the bar was occupied by Pat the poacher who was not only dismayed at the lack of rabbits but that he was only on his second divorce. Mike sat on the big chair and undertook the role of judge and jury dealing out the odd verdict as and when he saw fit to do so. The bar maid stood aimlessly filing her nails only punctuated by the odd request for a drink, or too boost the morale of the clearly insecure chef, Lionel, with the odd food-based compliment. As you can see Chris and I fitted in a treat, and after a hearty meal and a couple of warm ciders I was off to bed, Chrissy Crabtree however was with his type of people, staying behind to spin a few yarns. I was soon asleep in the strait jacket like bed, so soft that it literally started to eat you, and unless you woke every 10 minutes you would be in too deep to climb free.

When I woke I was greeted to the sound of a traction engine going through a long tunnel, it would then pause before starting up even louder. This was in fact the sound of newly named Combustion Chris, throat bellowing, I was never going to sleep with that racket going on and needed to think of something fast, as a tired me isn't a happy bunny. The plan I came up with was maybe a little basic and involved going into the bathroom and filling my ears with rolled up toilet paper in an effort to create my own DIY noise cancelling system. Upon re-entering the bedroom Chris had woken and asked why I had toilet paper sticking out of my ears, but because I could no longer hear correctly my reply was more of a yell, " BECAUSE YOUR BLOODY SNORING IS KEEPING ME AWAKE". Now, that didn't come out as tactfully as I had hoped, and once I climbed back into bed I noticed the skulking silhouette of Chris, slipping out of the room like a scalded puppy.

That was the last I saw of him that night, and I felt really awful, well I felt really awful until I fell into a deep relaxing sleep without a care in the world. The next morning saw the puppy return and I did apologise, especially as I found out he slept in the car all night, and there I was thinking he had bunked up with new mate, cauliflower Colin. The breakfast was excellent, and we were soon finished and ready for the second day on the river, the plan today was fish until 1pm then return to the pub to meet up with midlands maestro and long-term mate Nick Rose. Nick was coming down for a few hours float fishing and to meet up for lunch, nice little catch up with the benefit of a beautiful river back drop.

We were soon fishing again in another nice section of river and my worm bait was grabbed by the mother of all Minnows, this was clearly another personal best, but I don't have scales small enough to weigh this slab of a Minnow. With the excitement of the Minnow over with, it was a morning of the usual suspects, we caught plenty of Dace, Chub and Gudgeon but no Barbel, the river had in fact dropped further and cleared. We walked several pools and glides, but none had the perfect combination of the long stretch, we decided as we were staying on later tonight we would visit that beat again. We packed up, so we could be back at the pub to meet Nick for 13.00, the journey through the fields was bull free and we made it back bang on time. Nick text me from the front of the pub, simply saying "oh bugger, the pub is shut", sure enough, turns out Tuesday the Red Lion doesn't open lunchtimes. Fortunately, Nick had been to the area a number of times and new another pub that served good food, this also turned out to be closed Tuesdays, what is this some sort of inconvenient tradition, are Tuesdays Witch burning day! Nicks final plan was to drive to Haye on the Wye in the hope of finding a chip shop, for anyone that hasn't been to Haye on the Wye I can sum it up by saying it's a Librarians Shangra la! Every shop is a book shop. I have never seen so many book shops and the worst of it was, Nick knew it was wall to wall book stores, and I may be speaking out of turn here, but poets, authors and scholars don't strike me as the kebab types. Of course, we never found the greasy spoon we so desired and had to make do with the smallest Spar shop I've ever been in, literally it required a give and take system to move down the aisles.

I made the mistake of getting caught between a pair of rather rotund librarians sifting through the bargain basket, I couldn't back up as a young mother had illegally parked her pram in front of the cheese section and gone off to the cold meats. I needed to get out of this hell hole, so with a medium white sliced loaf and pack of cooked turkey I squeezed through to the checkout and extradited myself. We all had purchased some type of food too sustain for the coming night and headed off back to the river for the start of the evenings fishing. When we arrived at the gate the mammoth was once again blocking the way, but with Nick following behind I decided to face my fear and open the gate, he stomped he's feet and snorted but I pushed the gate towards him, upon turning around I noticed Chris leaning from the car window, waving a red towel at the animal, what a dirty trick! I managed to survive and now I didn't feel so bad about the snoring complaint, the rest of the drive to the river was monster free.

Despite Chris waving the red rag to the bull I let him choose swims, he chose the swim where I had caught the banana Barbel from, I went above in the faster water, Nick went below to trot a stick float through the lower section. I noticed a Trout jumping in the faster part of the rapids and decided to cast a lobworm right on it to instigate a bit of action, a perfect cast resulted in an instant take and the fast juddery fight must be the result of a feisty little brown Trout, no, it turned out to be a little Barbel just to wind Chris up even more. Nick was getting a Dace every trot and the river was packed with so much life it's incredible to see, plenty for the kingfishers that constantly sped passed with their shrill whistle and electric blue plumage.

Nick then had a nice little Chub on the stick float and despite his reluctance I forced a photo out of the old geezer, the smile though was extra.

*Nick Rose & I with a nice little Wye Chub*

Before we knew it, the darkness fell around us and the distant squark of the departing Heron signified the witching hour was upon us, the river itself seems to come alive in the darkness with the babbling water almost having its own language. The Chub went on a bit of a feeding spree and we caught several in quick succession, their aggressive bites clearly visible on the rod tips silhouetted against the purple sky. Chris managed one of around 3lb 8oz but with this being the final evening he was desperate for his first Barbel.

I recast a pellet covered with paste somewhere out into the gloom, it splashed, so it was in the river somewhere, I placed the rod on the rest only for it to be yanked violently down, I was attached to another Barbel. The fish swam upstream and just stayed in the centre of the river head into the rapids, Chris waded out in the now ever shallowing water with the net. My non- fish spooking red head lamp just wasn't producing enough light and Chris reluctantly switched on his 10'000 lumen headtorch, instantly a million midges surrounded his head and we opted to stick with the red light. The fish was once again expertly netted by the man with the midge covered head. I unhooked the fish then went to grab the camera while Chris and Nick weighed it, 6lb 2oz was the agreed weight, this got me a bit suspicious and a quick look at the tail revealed it was indeed the banana Barbel at 1oz heavier, a new personal best, just 24hrs after the first

With that fish landed I decided to call it a night, Chris was determined to catch and decided to stay on by the river, Nick was heading back to brum and agreed to drop me off at the hotel on the way. I really hoped Chris got something during the night for his efforts, as to my mind he had worked his socks off and payback was required. After a shower, coffee and sandwich I was off for a good night's kip, this was interrupted by a text from Chrissy Crabtree, was this the news we had been hoping for, not really, he had just lost a Barbel after the hook pulled out, sometimes it just doesn't happen. The next morning, I was up and packed ready to leave following breakfast but with no sign of Chris it was clear he did indeed spend the night on the bank. I gave him a quick text to ask if he was coming back for breakfast, he replied he was on his way.

Turned out he lost a second Barbel in the night that snapped the line after running down river, this pushed his despondence over the edge and he packed up opting to sleep on the grass under the stars. We of course had plan Z, this was to head to Woody's tackle shop in Hereford and see if he could point us towards one of the smaller more abundant Barbel in the town section. Breakfast was once again delicious, and we settled up with Mike and thanked him for some wonderful hosting, although Chris paid for two nights bed & breakfast without actually using the bed. We got to Woody's about 9.30 and purchased two-day tickets which included a free bit of Woody info scribbled on the map, we managed to drive around aimlessly for 30 minutes before giving in to the lure of the sat nav.

Eventually we pulled into the car park next to the river, by sheer luck we bumped into the bailiff, another wonderful guy that directed us to a swim where we might get a Barbel. We planned to leave for home at 14.00 at the latest, and with 10.30 approaching we had 3hrs fishing time to try for some Barbel. We were only permitted one rod on the tickets and opted for the quivertip, these having been the most suitable for the conditions. The swim was a narrow section with some thick overgrowth on the far side, a nice rapid section entered the stretch from the left and another section of rapids exited 50yds downstream. Immediately we were aware of the more industrial feel of the river with road saws and excavators clunking in the distance, a pair of swans brought over their cygnets for a look at the strange men.

We were also seeing a lot more Kayakers on this section and Chris kept quoting it's a bit like last of the Mohicans here, I will say that of the numerous kayakers we encountered, all were courteous and kept clear of our lines, this was reflected in our own behaviour with a polite thank you. The bailiff had recommended luncheon meat as the bait doing the business at this time, Chris went with the advice and I stuck with what had worked for me previously, pellet covered in paste, combined with a cage feeder and ground bait. I think it's good to try different things so there's more chance of stumbling across the right combination. I fired out a couple of catapults of pellet and sat back in the chair, the rod butt nearly hit me in the head as the tip was pulled down with such force. I grabbed the rod as a powerful fish stripped line and headed down towards Chris, I couldn't stop it but eventually it changed direction and shot off upstream.

Chris came over net in hand and really couldn't believe I was attached to another Barbel, " you really are a lucky sod with the Barbel he exclaimed". Where this may have been true for this particular trip it has not been the case on many other attempts, I believe I once spent 3 fruitless days for Barbel on the Hampshire Avon. This fish was a much better fish than the little rapid runner or the banana Barbel, and as it slowly kited towards the slacker water in the margins its great coppery form grew visible. Once the fish broke the surface it did look very decent and I really thought I had caught my first double figure Barbel, Chris squeezed it in the net on the second go and we were both blown away with the pure quality of the fish.

We weighed the fish quickly and despite my best attempt it didn't quite make the double, coming in at 9lb 6oz, I got some quick shots before wading out for the 10-minute check with the fish.

*Above 9lb 6oz of stunning River Wye Barbel*

Chris just needed a slice of luck, that couldn't be the only Barbel in the swim and we tried everything to try and induce another take, but it really came down too being in the right place at the wrong time. If we were on this swim for the evening, then I really think another couple of fish would have come our way, I've learned a lot in a short time and will be trying for a double in the autumn on the River Severn and maybe this time Chris will have his red-letter day.

The only species on my list for this trip I didn't get was the Bleak and they were there, I just got a bit too distracted by the wonderful Barbel to get out the whip and size 20 hook. Thanks Mike at the Red Lion for a wonderful stay, and thanks Nick for driving down and taking us around book world. Many thanks also to Woody at the best of Hereford tackle shops and Hereford Angling Association for running a first-class stamp of waters. Much thanks to Chris though for driving, netting, photographing, snoring and putting up with me, I have my fingers crossed that Tuesday you get a Shark to pay you back for all those efforts. Finally, to my wife and kids that have been so supportive through this year, I promise next year I will only fish half as much as this year, but twice as much as the previous one.

This weekend it's the Penzance species festival, should be a bit of banter, the Happy Danglers put on a boat driven by Captain Howell what can possibly go wrong! I will be trying for the greater weaver and dragonet but may have to settle for a John Dory.

# Chapter 39 Watch out Beagles about!

Having just returned a day early from the Mounts Bay annual sports charity comp I can understand why day two was cancelled, what a difference a day makes. Yesterday the day was hot with light north westerly winds and today driving rain and strong south westerly gusts, but at least day 1 went ahead. The competition is spearheaded by Robin Chapman and raises money for the excellent Children's Hospice South West a great cause for all in the south west. The competition is entered on an individual basis and has some incredible prizes from many great sponsors, so it's not surprising that around 60 anglers signed up to fish.

I had booked up with a group from the Happy Danglers, Nick, Pete, Paul, Simon, Dave and Jordan as per usual it would be a banter filled trip. The boat we were booked up on was none other than my shiny headed Falmouth favourite Andy Howell and his charter boat Anglo Dawn, I knew we were in fairly safe hands! The other guys had travelled down from Falmouth on the Friday with Andy undertaking a shark trip on route, this had been quite a challenge in itself. The weather on the Friday was pretty extreme and the rounding of the Lizard peninsula was described by all as a squeaky bottom experience. Despite this whitewater journey to the shark ground, fresh winds and large swell the guys managed 7 Sharks with a couple of bonus Megrim Sole thrown in for good measure. When I arrived at the harbour in Penzance first thing Saturday morning Pete was sat in his van wearing his storm suit with the engine running no doubt still trying to dry out.

The sunrise on this particular morning was stunning and the sea had become as still as a lake, no signs of the previous days storm or the one set to arrive. Pete filled me in on the perfect storm they had survived and how Nick had spent the whole day somewhat green and huddled in the corner. The competitors were soon arriving, and Chippy fired up the barbecue for the breakfast rolls that we were being treated to, just a donation to the charity pot and a hot coffee and bacon roll was yours. We all signed on and paid up the fees giving us our entry form and lucky number, this number could win you a great prize if you attended the Sunday presentation. Unfortunately, when we signed up for the Al a Carte baps we were unaware of the dodgy chef, this turned out to be none other than our own Nick Smith who actually done a pukka job, good on you mate!

With the food, signing on and social mingling underway the boats started appearing against the harbour wall, our boat Anglo Dawn still looked like a new pin, not really surprising following the previous days natural power wash. Skipper Andy arrived and started sorting out some of the carnage left over from the shark trip, he also signed up for the competition seeing as it was for charity. The eager competitors started loading their boats and before long we were all bobbing around in the harbour waiting for the signal to start. With the 9am start time reached Bite Adventures made her way through the flotilla of boats to signify the start, as the harbour entrance was passed all the engines roared into life and the myriad of boats erupted into the open sea.

Andy powered the boat towards the area we hoped to gather bait from and we all readied our feathers to get some fresh baits to accompany the ragworm and squid we had brought. Within 20 minutes we were at the bait area and all busy jigging the small lures, this led to several Mackerel, Poor Cod and Scad being landed giving us plenty of baits for the day. Little did we know the Mackerel would follow us all day and become somewhat of a pest. It seemed that everyone knew where to gather the bait as the mark was soon full of boats of every size and colour all seeing who was on the money. With enough bait we headed off to the first mark and a go at the John Dory's, Dave had set his stall out for a Dory and would be targeting them all day.

I had decided to go small and go for some of the mini species over the course of the day, starting out with tiny hooks and small bits of ragworm. We struggled to get baits down through the Mackerel and Scad, a quick look at the sounder showed shoals from top to bottom, it really was frustrating although Nick did pick up a possible Scad to weigh in. Eventually once we got baits down a few Cuckoo Wrasse started being caught and I managed a nice little female plus more Poor Cod. There were several Gurnards landed and I managed a nice little Red Gurnard before Dave pulled in a nice Tub Gurnard on a live bait. Andy decided to move to an area of sand where we would drift for some Plaice, Dabs and possibly a Weever, this was the fish I was after, so I set up a flattie boom rig with one long trace baited with a strip of mackerel belly and a shorter trace baited with worm.

A few fish started appearing with Plaice, Dabs and Grey Gurnard making up the numbers, I finally had my own enquiry as the rod tip rattled violently. I wound down slowly to find a little more weight and the odd kick of a hooked fish of unknown origin, the bright blinged up rig was visible first, then the mottled sand of a Turbot. That was a fish I never expected and a tough one on my list making species 62, not a huge one but another in the bag, quick picture and I dropped the fish back to grow into a specimen. With a couple of drifts undertaken Andy decided to put the hook down to see if any Dragonets, Rays or Weevers could be landed, I scaled my hooks down to size 12s with tiny bits of worm to try for that Dragonet. Then jammy Jordan who was having a day like young Elliot did a few weeks ago reeled in a lovely female Dragonet.

We all had a good look at this stunning looking little fish, but it is the male of the species that sports the most amazing colours and I am yet to see one in the flesh. The bites were really lacking on this particular mark and I think when it came time to move we were all ready for a change, this time we were going over a section of rough ground before hitting the Wrasse mark I call the Mumblestone. The section of rough ground produced a Pollack, Wrasse and Pouting before Dave hooked something on his live poor cod that could well be his target. Sure, enough I got to see yet another John Dory as a lovely fish popped up onto the surface and was quickly netted.

Really pleased for Dave that the plan worked he had fished a live bait since we started and was finally rewarded for his efforts with this iconic fish. With a few drifts completed we headed to the Mumblestone to battle the mighty Ballan Wrasse the action can be frantic and unforgiving on tackle. Within minutes of arriving Pete was into the first nice Wrasse, bright red and angry looking, was how I would describe the skipper at this point! Wrasse were being landed all around the boat and despite a few nice fish we couldn't get through to anything over 4lb.

The fishing is consistent at this location and we spent a while enjoying these powerhouses before departing for another area of less snaggy ground. The area though did have a few pinnacles that have produced some nice Ling in the past, I made a trace of 80lb mono, 7/0 hook baited with a whole joey mackerel. This produced a fast rattling bite that turned out to be the only Dogfish of the trip, I guess that gives me the wooden spoon. I re-baited with another whole mackerel and lowered it to the seabed, once again I was soon receiving a bite, I wound the bait in and felt there was something on the end like a dead weight. I carried on slowly winding joined by Andy who enquired what I had on, then about halfway up the rod was yanked down hard, and line poured from the reel. I think it has woken up I stated, but it would appear that a Porbeagle was now attached and after a minute or so the fish was up and visible in the gloom, a fish in the 60lb+ class. This would be perfect for my challenge and just the right size for a photo, the skipper was ready with the net but as the fish dived again it bit through the mono trace.

The fish then came and took Dave's live bait so Andy quickly got me a wire trace which I hooked up with bait and dropped down unfortunately this was one beagle that wasn't going to make the same mistake a third time. I must admit to feeling absolutely gutted, I really want a Porbeagle to be included in this challenge and I seem to keep missing my opportunities', time is running out on that one now, but you never know. We moved on to a wreck for a proper go at some ling and I kept the wire trace and mackerel fishing just above the wreck in the hope another Porbeagle was lurking. Jordan continued his lucky streak landing the best Ling of the day at 15lbs, Pete and I however got into a mass tangle leading to me needing to cut the skippers new shark trace, he's head was already too red to see if he was even angrier but I know I won't hear the last of it so I will need to get him some sort of treat. That was the last of the fishing and at the weigh in we had Paul and Nick both putting in weighable fish, but the real disappointment was Dave's John Dory was 1gram under the qualifier weight and couldn't be entered.

Despite day two being cancelled it was a wonderful day 1 and I am sure a lot of money has been raised for this great cause, a really well run, well supported event, I look forward to supporting this again. Thanks to Chippy and the organisers for running this event, the danglers for their superb company as per usual, and of course skipper Andy for doing what he does well putting us on the fish. I really look forward to Tuesday week when we are out on his home turf chasing something I haven't had yet and many other things for everyone else.

Just need to wish skipper Kieren Faisey a speedy recovery after contracting sepsis from one of the sharks he has handled. I hope I am fishing with you Tuesday mate, this means you would have recovered and I have another chance at a Porgy.

## Chapter 40 Fishing just for fun.

This last week has included some of the most enjoyable fishing I have done for a while, no pressure trying to hunt down this or that, just getting out with people enjoying the sport, regardless of what comes along. The first of these grass root sorties was back down to Lyme Regis aboard Lewis Hodder's Pegasus, our initial trip Sharking, aboard Lo kie out of Penzance was cancelled due to the skipper becoming ill. Skipper Kieren Faisey had for the second time picked up sepsis from handling sharks, this is a serious poising of the blood and fortunately he has recovered fully and is back in the saddle. Lewis had advertised a few spaces fishing the inshore marks which meant Bream, Conger and possibly Hounds, nothing I needed for the species hunt, but I just fancied going there for some sport. Chris was keen to tag along despite going to a rock gig in Southampton the night before, he planned to drive back through the night and feast on a breakfast of redbull, washed down with lashings of ginger tea. I had opted to go light on the tackle front, to get some sport from the feisty Black Bream as for their size they really pack a punch in the power stakes.

To complement my light rod and reel I also included my recently repaired LRF rod, I had managed to carry out a pretty impressive repair using the spigot and shaving the tip section down. I planned to use the LRF gear in the harbour before we went on the boat in the hope I could catch something I hadn't had yet, I was secretly hoping for a Scorpion fish or Dragonet.

I picked Chris up at 6.00am and straight away realised he was going heavy with the type of tackle that gives no quarter, the two rods also could only mean one thing, he intended to fish two rods. We arrived at Lyme with plenty of time to spare and ambled down to the harbour at the start of a stunning day, the seagulls screamed like excited children only drowned out by the robotic wine of the reversing refuse truck. Lewis was sorting out the boat when we arrived and invited us aboard, the bait was included in the trip, this gave us plenty of ragworm to have a go in the harbour. I set up the LRF kit and baited the tiny hooks with small ragworm section then flicked it out towards the structure that the little fish tend to dwell amongst.

It was then the rest of today's anglers started to arrive, a lady and her male friend climbed aboard and bid us good morning, they were followed by a guy and his small dog called Reg. It soon became apparent that not only was this Reg's first boat fishing trip but that he actually hated the idea and slipped his collar before legging it, the owner frantically shouting Reg, Reg REG! Chris and I found the whole think hilarious and named the comical canine Reluctant Reg. Shortly after reluctant Reg was reunited with his collar and ushered aboard with two young lads who were part of Reg's group along with their father. With the chance of a photo, of the super cute reluctant Reg, Chris whisked him from the floor and held him aloft like a prize fish, it was at this point that Reg done an amazing impersonation of Star Wars character Yoda!

The two lads quickly started asking Chris and I questions probably due to the fact their dad had told them we were professional anglers, a good ploy no doubt to give him some free time. It turned out that one lad was his son and the other his sons best friend, the young lads were a real credit to their families, polite, keen and very respectful, the polar opposite of us then. They noticed the bite on my LRF rod before I did, and their dad told them to stand back so they didn't impede my strike. The rod bounced vigoursly and I swept it sharply upwards only to see the tip section fold straight down with a crack, looks like the super dooper repair was pants! Still it could have been worse, there could have been an audience of impressionable young future anglers watching, even Reg winced, and I knew he was thinking, awkward.

I continued to reel the line in by holding the tip and butt section together and managed to land the rod snapping culprit, a Corkwing Wrasse. The pretty little wrasse at least restored some degree of dignity and the two lads were impressed that the fish had been so powerful it broke the rod, I did have to explain that the rod had actually been repaired before, badly. With everyone aboard we headed out to the reef a few miles offshore, the youngsters were keen to ask us many questions but also took a genuine interest in my charity challenge. With the anchor down the first fish started appearing instantly, the inevitable pouting and poor cod, it was just a case of fishing through them. With the scent in the area it wasn't too long before the first bream arrived, with the lady on my left landing a nice starter fish.

Lewis pointed out that he had caught some nice Bass at this mark recently and maybe a large fresh bait may pick one up, although you can't actually keep Bass this year, I still hadn't had one for my challenge. Chris spotting an opportunity stated, what we shall do is chuck out his spare rod with a big bait on and take turns on it, this seemed like a good plan and pretty dam sporting of my old Mucka. Sure, enough the fresh chunk of Mackerel on the bonus rod was soon taken and Chris dropped his first rod and struck the second, connecting with a Conger eel of around 15lbs. That was great and the spectators on the boat were impressed with their first sight of a writhing Conger, the rod was re-baited and once again it was quickly showing some interest. I went to position my rod in the rest for my go and heard the woosh of a strike as Chris was once again reeling in a conger of similar size, it wasn't till about the fourth conger that I realised that, what Chris actually meant by sharing, was that he would use the two rods! The good news is though I am not bitter about it, and I even took a picture of Chris playing one of the many eels he had on our shared rod!

With just the one rod to worry about I decided to get on and catch some Bream, that was what we had actually come for. I tied up a single hook running paternoster that included the Breams favourite enticer, some finest green, better known as green wool. I baited this with a whole small squid and fished it 2 feet off the bottom to avoid the pesky pout and the new combination worked a treat as I quickly started getting a few Bream.

The young lads inspired by rod hogger hodgson's antics had managed to convince Lewis to set them up to have a go for their own leviathan's, Lewis quickly obliged and before long they had some Conger interest. The youngest lad was pretty soon attached to an angry Eel and while we all assumed he was making a mountain out of a mole hill, stating it's really pulling, none of us expected a 30lb+ Conger to come in over the side.

Well-done to both lads who both managed to get good Congers, totally by themselves and they loved every minute of it, it was so great to see the joy in their young faces that angling can bring. The lads continued to fish well all day, landing plenty of Bream, Pollack and Conger all the time looking for tips and advice to help them catch more or different species of fish. With the tide dropping off, the bites eased, and Lewis signalled that we would be heading west shortly for an hour hunting Plaice.

The Bream had been steady but as with any fishing you always want just one more and this was the case today, I just wanted one last Bream to finish on, fortunately my luck was in and upon dropping my whole squid the rod bounced frantically. I hooked the final Bream and relished the frantic little battle on the light gear with the fish making a number of line peeling dives, fantastic sport fish indeed. The anchor was pulled and as we made the journey to the Plaice ground, I decided to gut a few of the Bream that had been taken for people's tea, the two youngsters watched intensely.

They asked after watching for a while if they could prepare the ones they had caught because they wanted to have caught, prepared and cooked their own fish. I found this attitude quite inspiring and once again a credit to their family's for bestowing these values on their kids, all children should understand where their food comes from and how it is prepared.

The two lads both gutted and prepared the fish they had caught, and I held the spines while they trimmed them off, so they didn't get injured but everything else they done themselves. They washed their hands and stated they were looking forward to cooking and eating them that evening, a fitting tribute to the fine fish I feel. At this point I think I should explain the difference between the area I was fishing on the boat and the area Chris was fishing, while my section still sparkled pristine and white, Chris's area looked like an explosion in a squid factory, skippers beware Chris is a messy git, just saying!

We arrived at the Plaice mark full of the usual anticipation and straight away the lads were asking what do they look like and will we definitely catch one? The first fish to make an appearance however was a Jellyfish as a giant pale shape appeared from the gloom, a giant barrel jellyfish. I had a little tap tap on the ragworm and landed a lovely looking Brittle Star, a fragile type of starfish that can carpet the sea floor, one of the boys brought over a goby to show us and I got a quick snap of the two together for prosperity.

There were a couple of nice Plaice landed including one by the youngsters, much to their pleasure, they did however return that fish, claiming they already had enough for tea. Chris and I however blanked on the Plaice front and this is a bit of an enigma on this bit of ground as it's the second time for both of us. As we headed back to Lyme the couple fishing next to me all day were quizzing me about my challenge, both having been affected by Strokes in their lives, they both gave me a cash donation on the boat and I am so grateful for their support. Unfortunately, unless I write names down my diminishing brain quickly forgets so I put their donation on my just giving page as the couple on Pegasus. Before we walked the great hill to the car park Chris must have suddenly remembered it was my turn on the rod and bought me an ice cream of my choice instead. Yet another great trip aboard Pegasus with young Lewis and what a wonderful group of people to spend a day with, really enjoyed a simple days fishing.

The weekend was planned to go to the lakes Saturday morning, undertake any chores and check water levels etc, the afternoon I planned to spend a few hours stalking a Koi Carp from Anglers Eldorado. Sunday was to be something different as I had been invited by Wayne Thomas and Coombe Martin Sea Angling Club to their annual fun afternoon at Ilfracombe Pier. First trip was to the Sanctuary Lakes and after checking the fence and all the lakes I noticed a group of red, white and gold coloured fish sat on the surface of the bottom lake.

This was unusual as there are no ornamental fish in this lake other than 4 Koi Carp that we hadn't seen in two years. I fetched a light float set up and cast out a small pinch of bread flake directly behind the group of fish, this caused them to scatter into the murk. The float however slowly dipped, and I struck to find myself attached to one of the golden immigrants, I swung it ashore and could instantly see it was a Goldfish. I have no idea how these Goldfish got there but not sure if I fancy their chances with Mr Esox this autumn, but who knows they have survived this long.

With the jobs completed It was time to head off to Anglers Eldorado and try for species number 63 a Koi Carp, I have had one this year a real beauty but as it was from France it doesn't count, but hopefully today I could get another. I picked up my ticket from the tackle shop at Anglers Paradise which was strange as I used to be a member of the Anglers Paradise 5Cs syndicate and spent many weekends at the complex. With my ticket in hand I was off to the day ticket Eldorado, upon arriving I couldn't believe how busy it was with no space in the car park and a dozen bivvy's spread across the lakes. I had only arrived with a rucksack and a new LRF rod that I was keen to try out on the hard fighting Koi. Fortunately, the Koi lake is pretty small, weedy and doesn't contain any monsters meaning it was devoid of other anglers, perfect for me and I quickly picked a swim where the weed wasn't quite so dense. I fired out some dog biscuits that floated slowly on the green surface, as they reached the edge of the dense lily beds Koi Carp slowly emerged and began slurping them down.

I continued to feed the fish steadily letting them gain confidence and slowly pulling them away from the security of the lily beds. Once I felt the chances were edging in my favour I threaded on a small clear float and tied a size 12 barbless hook straight to the line. The float was fixed in position by a rubber band and gave just enough weight to cast out my hook bait, this was a cork ball threaded on the hook leaving the bend of the hook clear. I then using scissors trimmed the cork ball into a dog biscuit shape and the deception was complete, finally I cast towards the lily pad and waited. It didn't take long as a bright orange Koi sucked down an adjacent dog biscuit before turning and slurping down the forgery. The strike was met with a water explosion as the Koi smashed the surface in rage before plummeting into the thick weed, the LRF rod preformed excellently and despite the numerous weed beds the fish was soon netted.

A gorgeous bar of golden Koi and species 63 in less than 20 minutes, it was so simple, yet so exciting back to basics to trick one of the smartest of fish. With the water disturbed I moved to another area and gradually gained the confidence of another group of fish, its lovely to sit and watch these stunning coloured fish going from nervous to sparring with one another to get the free offerings in just a matter of minutes. As I sat on the grass keeping a low profile I was surrounded by a symphony of electronic wizardry as the multitude of anglers fiddled incessantly with their motionless alarms, why do they need them set so loud, they are literally feet from them in the middle of the day. Once again, a Koi brought me back down from my soap box as it munched the cork ball and sped off towards another set of water lily's.

A great battle from another beautiful looking fish and I have to say with the fish of this quality on a lovely sunny afternoon with just a mobile approach this really did feel like an Anglers Eldorado. With this swim now spooked I returned to my original spot and fired out a carpet of biscuits then sat back on the soft warm grass to eat a sandwich and drink some tea. I then noticed what looked like a draft excluder, just like the ones my Nan used to have at the foot of the door, this one though was walking steadily towards me along the grass. It was a large and quite colourful caterpillar and I wished at this point I knew what it would turn into, my initial thought due to the size was maybe an Andean Condor.

It's quite incredible how much you actually do see, while you're out angling, and the important thing is to not only take time out to notice these things but see them as part of the whole experience. From the Kingfisher to the Storm Petrel, and from the Mermaids Purse to the Caddis Larvae all this life creates the perfect environment for us to enjoy, if you prefer to stomp around with your alarms up high, squashing bugs as you go, then you are not a true angler. If, however your excursions to the water's edge is enlightened due to the wildlife you have encountered then you are made of the right stuff. With the departing of my friendly condor larvae my eyes were drawn to the antics of a Moorhen on the lilies at the edge of an island, it stepped from leaf to leaf like a contestant on total wipe out, except the large footed bird hardly caused a ripple.

Now with a break in the antics of the various wildlife I was back in fishing mode as several more Koi appeared and began feasting on the dog biscuits, time to fish I think. By allowing the water to rest and feeding without casting I could catch a fish every time I tried, and that's just down to building the swim. Sure, enough the little chunk of cork was soon eaten by another Koi and yet a different colour pattern although still on the orange / golden theme.

This last fish created a bit of splashing at the wrong time, as an angler from the world of stealth is what you wear not how you act, spied me netting it. Soon after two camo clad soil stompers appeared brandishing rod pods, I cringed at the thought of what my little bit of nature will now endure. Sure, enough 3oz leads were hurled at the island along with copious amounts of brightly coloured boilies hitting the water like bouncing bombs. I moved around the lake as far as possible away from them and still managed to land several smaller koi before giving in to hunger and thirst. A really enjoyable afternoon and the icing on the cake the two bods with pods caught nout!

The finale to this blog was the Coombe Martin Sea Angling Club's fun afternoon and seeing as this was aimed at encouraging youngsters and non-anglers into the sport I took the whole family along with me. Wayne had asked if I'd like to come along to explain my challenge and answer any questions on Strokes and also to perhaps gain a few donations.

I didn't really know what to expect from the afternoon but any excuse to get the word out there and highlight the issue of Strokes while still doing a bit of fishing can't be a bad way to spend an afternoon. I was surprised when my daughter Phoebe also asked to come along, and I am so glad she did, it was so nice to have my whole family alongside me fishing.

*A family effort on this afternoon*

The event started at 2pm and Wayne and fellow club member Nick had arranged a few other guests to attend, two members of the coast guard and angling writer Dominic Garnett who also works for the angling trust, to promote angling. Dominic is a super guy with a ton of patience and was a joy to watch him engaging with young and old alike. www.dgfishing.co.uk

With the event underway I soon realised that some of these kids had arrived determined to catch a fish and plenty of friendly rivalry was taking place. The lower section of Ilfracombe Pier was quickly taken over by eager youngsters and Wayne, his son and Nick were busy logging down the captures as soon as they were landed. I entered Phoebe and Matthew into the comp and set up a couple of rods with two hook rigs baited with prawn, straight away Matthews rod signalled a bite and he was in. He reeled the fish in and it turned out to be a little pouting, he was delighted to have some points on the board but as far as he was concerned that was the fishing part of the day done.

Matthew with his fascination for the emergency services then wandered over to the lonely coast guard team to investigate why they thought they needed a blue light on their vehicle. Child number two however, doesn't quit that easily and she went and caught a small Pollack, and followed this with a Poor Cod, there were plenty of bites and with a spare rod I thought I would have a go for something unusual. I noticed that fellow dangler Paul Lorimore and his daughter were fishing just up from us and it looked like she was thrashing her dad.

Everyone around were having a great time and it was a case of if you saw a child wandering around with a fish hanging from their rod, you just unhooked it, re-baited and told Nick or Wayne to record it. Phoebe then added a Pouting to her species collection and I was impressed with her angling skills although she has always caught fish, when I have ever taken her.

The event was to end at 5pm and with just one hour to go I had managed a couple of small Pollack and even when they are tiny you can tell they are a sight-based predator. The aquarium people had arrived with a few buckets of sea water in the hope they could add a few of the mini species to bolster the numbers in their exhibit and I quickly obliged with a nice little Poor Cod. I then swapped to a tiny section of rubber worm which I jigged slowly alongside of the structure, I felt a few taps before the worm was grabbed ferociously. I wound in to find a new species of Goby, with the worm wedged firmly in its mouth, a quick check with the expert from the Aquarium and I had species 64 the Rock Goby, furthermore this little critter is now on display at the Ilfracombe Aquarium.

With the tide nearly at its lowest and a Cormorant waiting to pounce on any stragglers the bites dried up and the 5pm deadline arrived, we all made our way up to the top of the pier for the presentation. Wayne asked me to say a few words about my species challenge and the charity, he also had an amount of donated tackle that he said people could take if they popped a few quid in the Stroke Association box. With my rambling out of the way the prizes were awarded, and I was really proud of daughter Phoebe for winning a prize with her 4-fish catch, think I might be getting a pack of lures for Christmas. Thanks, so much Coombe Martin SAC for the invite to this really enjoyable family fun event, I will try and make this a regular expedition. Thanks Wayne and Nick for all the support and for pointing any donations my way, the Stroke Association South West will really appreciate the donations.

To end a perfect family day out we called into the Dolphin Fish and Chip restaurant in the town, the meal was fantastic, and I thoroughly recommend this chippy, when I went up to pay, the waitress informed me the boss had told her to knock off 10% of our bill, as we were raising money for charity. What a wonderful gesture and yet again, while carrying out this challenge I have witnessed real generosity, that I feared had gone from our country, thank you Ilfracombe. With this multifaceted blog finally coming to an end I can honestly say I have loved the last few trips, seeing the next generation of anglers embracing the sport and receiving support from so many strangers, but the icing on the cake was having the people I love the most, alongside me, and that doesn't mean Chris before anyone asks! Couple of boat trips on the horizon with the first being our very own Captain Pugwash, Andy no more cookies Howell, let's hope for an ocean oddity to appear.

## Chapter 41 It's a long drive for species 65

Tuesday was a chance at another species and every trip now requires a game plan that gives me a good chance at something new, the species trip aboard Falmouth charter boat Anglo Dawn was a good bet. Having done two previous trips aboard her this year I knew the ageing, yet cantankerous skipper Andy Howell would pull something out of the bag, especially as he had put me on 7 species already. The trip had been booked at the start of the year and over that time a few of the guys had pulled out, part of the territory when you arrange charters and that's why this is the last year I ever charter boats. I am just going to boat fish on other people's charters or individual spaces, trying to fill spaces at short notice is both stressful and costly, it's a shame because I love to support our wonderful charter skippers many I consider friends.

Any way back to the blog, good mate Nick Rose drove down from the midlands on the Monday evening, so we could leave early the next day, we did nip out for a quick pint with Chris at his local. Nick asked me what I wanted, and to soak up the pint of cider I asked for a bag of pork scratchings, little did I know that scratchings now come in an assortment of flavours, nick shouted from the bar, " what flavour do you want"? I was a bit confused but answered with, pork please, but apparently that wasn't accurate enough as there were a multitude of sub-flavours.

When I was a lad the pork scratchings came in just two variety's, shaved and unshaved, I opted for ready salted which tasted like standard scratchings to me. Chris thought it would be a good idea to test Mr Roses's midlands pallet and served him a single, super-hot volcanic scratching which was washed down with a slightly potent slug of Rum at 88% proof! The vindaloo veteran hardly raised an eyebrow as he polished both off in an instant, Chris would need to try harder next time, I fear Chris may suffer another level of heat on our next midlands road trip.

The bad news was that we had tried everywhere to get fresh ragworm and finally secured a pound from Lizard Tackle and Bait, this meant an early start to drive round to the lizard then back to Falmouth. So, our mini pub crawl was swapped for a bag of chips and an early night and Nick was asleep and snoring within a minute of lying on the bed chair.

The morning arrived way to quick and before we knew it the Popemobile was loaded and straining under the added weight of our man from the midlands. Chris did a sterling job of the driving and we soon arrived at the bait shop run by Tony Portas, Tony kindly let us pick up the bait at 7.15 in the morning, that's a pretty dam good service and the worm was top notch. Finally, we arrived at the marina and loaded the trolley, I noticed Chris didn't put anything in the barrow and I can only assume he was worried he might have to drive that too.

Andy was waiting for us at the gate and looked like he had been spending a bit of time in the Gym, well that's if the gym force fed you cream cakes, made you wear oversize wellies and slapped your head on the way out! I know that previous sentence will cause me pain at some point and I do love to wind the old bugger up, that's why I boarded his boat wearing another charter boats merchandise, just to see how long it took him to spot it! With the skipper now in a much better mood it was time to go and catch a few fish, and if he got me a new species I would change the shirt to the Stroke one! The crew on board Anglo today was Chris, Gary with his son Fin, a customer of Andy's whose name I forget but I will call the Rag worm rustler, and finally spicy Nick and I.

We drove a little way along the river Fal and anchored close to the main channel, this may have looked strange to the passing small boats, seeing a top-class charter boat stopping so close in, there was method in this madness and despite being far from perfect, skipper Andy knows how to track down species. Sure, enough the ragworm rustler had the first bite and the first fish was swung aboard, a female Dragonette, a species that was now high on my list, Andy sat grinning in the cabin. The next bite was deep sea diver Gary's, and would you believe it, a Bass another fish on my list, the skipper now had to pass on his smugness, " I told you they are there, I've put you on the spot, if you can't catch them I can do no more"! I hadn't had a bite yet and I reeled in added a fresh Ragworm and fired it out to the middle of the channel, it had just settled when I felt a fast snatch on the line I held between my fingers, I struck and connected with a dynamic little fish I assumed was a Bass.

Andy who can give the impression, he only moves like a Sloth, sprang into action with the net, " that's a Couch's Bream", sure enough the stunning pink shimmer confirmed his initial statement and the gorgeous little warrior was scooped up. Andy had mentioned there was a chance of getting one of these wonderful bream and I had set up my rig accordingly, however I have never even seen one in the flesh and to say I was happy was an understatement. This fish was day made for me and the small stature of the fish was more than made up for in its appearance, it did manage to spike me as I released it over the side just like every Bream I've ever caught has, their spines are like needles.

With the tide ebbing and lots more to try we headed out of the river towards the lair of the Red Band fish, tiny Sabiki feathers were rigged up and I for one couldn't wait to be reacquainted with the bright red pulsating ribbon fish. We stopped on the mark and straight away we could see on the sounder a huge ball of bait covered the Red Band mark, Gannets dived like missiles striking at the dense shoal of Mackerel and Pilchard. We couldn't get our little sets of feathers past a few feet below the boat as string after string were brought aboard, Nick was filling the bucket with fresh bait. It was then I noticed Commercial Chris as Andy pointed out he perhaps should have a long line type reel as he pulled a full string of about 10 mackerel on his 20-foot line of feathers. It was a great 20 minutes from the perspective of bait collection but completely scuppered the Red Band fishing, I did get through the bio-mass once and straight away had a trembly type bite so reminiscent of the Red Bands, this turned out to be a lovely Red Gurnard.

We tried another mark for the bands but once again the vast shoal of mackerel spoiled any chance we had and to be honest they were a pain in the rump all day long. I started to think we were cursed but soon the culprit was clear to see as yet another episode of Bananagate took place aboard this vessel, skipper Andy throwing caution to the wind and scoffing the cursed fruit in broad daylight! I guess this was more penance for the T-shirt incident and as John the fish Locker found out on a previous trip Banana banter doesn't pay! We stopped on a bit of broken ground for a drift in the hope of a Tub Gurnard for me and anything for everyone else, there were several nice red gurnards caught especially by the Ragworm Rustler who had a knack with them. My large strip of fresh mackerel finally got a bit of interest and upon reeling in I found myself attached to my first Cephalopod of the year in the shape of an Octopus. They are a crazy creature taking on surrounding colours in an instant combined with their superb suction they are a true ocean oddity. Strangely I always have an overwhelming urge to fling them towards a wall to see if they would stick, I should add this has never become a reality and will remain the case, I think. It seemed the octopus were in a shoal or whatever a group of Octopuses are called, possibly Octopods, as Nick landed one right after mine, noticeable by the squirts of water hitting the side of the boat. We then headed off to an area of rough ground, so Commercial Chris could get his Wrasse fix, and instantly the Wrasse were hitting the fresh ragworm. Chris, still keeping with the commercial theme was bringing them in two at a time and I managed a few nice female Cuckoo Wrasse. Nick was keen to catch his first wrasse and as soon as he changed to ragworm baits he was straight in to a fish.

With everyone having several Wrasse it was time for another move and this time anchoring for the chance of a Dab or Ray, the small tide resulted in a distinct lack of rays with only none turning up, their cousins the Dogfish turned up but even they were more of a pair than a pack. The final effort of the day was to try a bit of reef for Conger and I opted to have a gamble for a Red Bream on hindsight probably not the smartest move. The problem was the anchor kept tripping and we just couldn't hold on this section of reef, this meant a short journey to another area and at this lump of rock we did get the hook to hold, curse of the banana! Once we dropped our lines I started getting plenty of bites which resulted in the capture of Wrasse, Whiting and Pouting. The other guys fishing for Conger were missing some good bites as the congers seemed a bit finicky but eventually the ragworm rustler managed to hook a low double.

The final fish of the trip was another Conger to Nick who had persevered in his effort to get one, not huge but with the Congers being so fickle it was a target fish. That was trip done and despite the fishing being tough for a number of our target species we all had a really enjoyable day, plenty of banter. With the huge pile of quality ragworm left I said to Chris we would have to go fishing the next evening to make the most of it, but whilst on our journey back Chris informed me he had given all the worm to the guy I subsequently named the ragworm rustler. Many thanks Andy for getting me yet another species and despite the bent fruit and unsolicited assault on my shorts the double choc chip cookies and Couch's Bream just about made up for it.

Great bunch of guys to fish with and it's that sort of camaraderie that can make a tough day memorable. Cheers commercial Chris for driving all over Cornwall to get us some bait, next trip might be for something small but rare in our neck of the woods.

## Chapter 42 It's not the slick that made Nick Sick!

Epic fail this weekend on the species front, but I did try hard, and with my daughters 21st birthday party taking centre stage I couldn't expect too much. The only trip I had any chance of a new species was aboard Sundays shark trip aboard Bite Adventures, alongside the Happy Danglers. With Sharks being the target, I maintained my diminishing hope for the Porbeagle Shark but with only a couple of trips left this year I think that's clutching at straws now.

The weather had been forecast to give messy conditions, but the sun was breaking through and the winds diminishing so everything looked good. Craig and Nick had kindly agreed to pick me up on route and with a departure time from the harbour of 8.00am it meant a lay in until 05.15, lovely jubbly. The guys were already at the meeting point when I arrived and a perfect run down the A30 got us to Penzance harbour by 07.15, plenty of time to get sorted and to the boat. Skipper Chippy had told us the Mackerel were in good size shoals not far from the harbour entrance so get the feathers on asap. The 6 anglers Dave, Aaron, Pete, Craig, Nick and I were soon loaded aboard and eagerly attaching various sparkling bait catching strings of tinsel.

The sea was flat, and the rising sun created a golden glow to herald the start of another adventure, fingers crossed none of us blanked everything else is a bonus.

We soon stopped as the fish finder showed a dense shoal of bait below the keel, sure enough the brightly coloured attractors, journey to the sea floor was abruptly stopped midwater as the massing mackerel grabbed them instantly. The deck was soon shimmering with a multitude of the beating fish as everyone swung in string after string, 10 minutes and our shark bait was collected, onwards into the fray. It was about this time that Chippy's young prodigy Kieren done a drive by in his boat Lo kie, great to see the young skipper back on his feet after his second sepsis episode.

It was over an hour in a swollen sea before Bite Adventures engines fell silent, Nick for the second trip in a row turned into the incredible Hulk with his colour turning green. The chum bags were readied and thrown over the side to commence the slick, but it was by now too late for poor old Nick as the curse of the sea had a good grip on him.

Touch wood I have never suffered from the cursed seasickness, but I really feel for anyone who gets struck down by the affliction as it really ruins your day. The other issue is it makes you a target for everyone not affected to show just how supportive the cant be! The first rod was put out and while it was running back in the tide it was taken by a Shark, Aaron was on the rod and playing the first Shark, which was also his first Shark. Nice to see someone get their first fish and also to find out that Blue Sharks do pull a bit, the fish gave him a good little work out and once to the side of the boat was quickly t-barred off.

It was a little wait for the next Sharks to appear but soon a couple arrived in short succession giving big Dave and Grandpa Pete a bit of fun as these 60lb class fish fought well on the 12lb to 20lb class tackle. These fish like all of the fish through the day were released at the side of the boat, but if we had managed a monster then a quick pic would have been taken. I was position 5 and therefore set up my own rod to try and get another species for my challenge, we were in really deep water but it's amazing at the variety of species that reside in the desert like area of the big blue.

My rod soon bounced frantically as a Whiting grabbed the bait, this was followed by several more whiting before a small Gurnard created a change. We were then witness to a depth charge explosion of water, only 20 yards from the stern of the boat as a passing Tuna decided to breach out of the water.

It is mind boggling how such a fish, clearly heading towards a thousand pounds in weight can be so agile, we were left temporarily stunned and in awe of these creatures. With the excitement over Craig was now connected to a powerful Blue shark his first for 20 years and at around 80lbs a new personal best by some distance. The Shark really showed him the ropes and I think Craig will admit they warrant a bit of respect when they approach the ton mark. It was now my time on the rods and soon I managed my first fish, unfortunately without commercial Chris on hand to take any shots I have nothing to post of me, so I will have to post a picture of Nauseas Nick preparing for his turn on the rods!

With my go out of the way I returned to the bottom bouncing having noticed Pete and Dave getting a few Haddock, sure enough the Whiting had been replaced with some lovely little Haddock. I soon had a few under my belt and as this is the first year I have ever caught Haddock they are still a novelty, plus they are a cracking looking fish. Nick was forced to fish as a Shark continued the no sympathy theme and made off with the bait, he was soon back in the groove and playing it like a chundering champ. He did manage to get the fish to the side without any additional chum contributions and I think this bit of fishing perked him up.

We all caught another round of Sharks with Pete setting the boat record for the smallest blue shark of the year, and strangely Aaron landed a lesser spotted dogfish at the same time that was bigger! I managed a Shark of around 50lb and Craig had managed to send me a shot of me playing this one.

Unfortunately for Nauseas Nick no Shark arrived, and we headed inshore for an attempt at a Red Bream, skipper Chippy suggested there may be a chance of one and as I needed one of these I was keen to try. We dropped down over a wreck with our small feathers baited with ragworm, I soon connected with a rattling bite but knew the lack of fight equalled a Pouting. We didn't connect with any Bream and the skipper felt that the lumpy sea may have moved them off the wreck, this was backed up by the sounder with very few marks showing.

We decided to catch some bait for our various autumn fishing excursions, I like to have some for the Pike to eat at the lakes also. Within 30 minutes of fishing we had enough for what we needed, and the skipper had his baits for the next day. Despite not picking up a new species it was as usual with this bunch a thoroughly enjoyable day and despite Nicks illness he is still a legend for all that he does. Thanks Craig for the lift and the information on a species I will be targeting in the next couple of weeks, and to skipper Chippy Chapman for giving us a great day out. This coming weekend I am sharking from Looe, if Neptune really wants to make an old man happy send a little Porbeagle my way and I will send a shiny 5 pence yours!

## Chapter 43 Time for a bit of Sole searching

That's another week flown by, and it seems that the writing of these blogs is coming around quicker and quicker as the year slips away, mid-way through September and I guess the year is rapidly approaching its conclusion. With my new target of 72 now seeming a little tricky, especially having missed several species that I tried for, and now with only around 14 weeks until the close of play, the pressure is on. I have a list of the remaining species I want to target, and there are a couple that I am pretty confident in getting, but there's no such thing as a certainty with angling so I will just have to keep the fingers crossed. That's why when there's a chance of something species wise I hadn't previously considered, I need to get out and go for it, makes for some exciting fishing.

A chance conversation on our recent shark trip, sowed a seed in my head that within 48hrs was bordering on an obsession, the fish in question was the Dover Sole and call me naïve, but I had always assumed they resided in the waters around Dover a bit like Kentucky Fried Chicken. Bristol channel angler, Craig Willis had kindly tolerated me picking his brains numerous times during our Happy Danglers trip, with one of my query's focused on the question of Sole. Craig had told me that there were a few areas that I could try for one and went on to give me advice on baits and best tides. When I got home I began the research, which is so important when targeting a new species, I read, watched and digested as much information on this fish as possible over the next few days.

Without wishing to wait any longer for the best tides as advised by Craig, I decided to take a chance and go on a bigger tide that would mean I couldn't fish all the way up to high water, the weather was also not great, with a stiff westerly blowing, not great for angler comfort. With my mind set on going, I tied up some rigs with the first being a 4-hook setup, comprising light mono snoods and size 6 hooks, this was pinned flat with a weight at both ends and a swan shot on every hook link. Everything I have read about the Sole points towards the importance of the bait being fished flat on the bottom, there was no doubt this would remain flat. The second type of rig I had prepared was a 3-hook rig comprising of 3 weighted booms, the hooks were larger being long shank size 4s and the rig also had weights top and bottom.

I had ordered some King Rag to arrive on Thursday, sure enough Solent Baits didn't disappoint, with some quality worm in pristine condition. I had the car pre-loaded so once I got back from work it was a quick bacon sarnie courtesy of the lovely Mrs D, and I was off on my solo Sole mission. Commercial Chris, was busy, being a quirky quizmaster at his local pub and couldn't join me, it's a shame as Mrs H, had been shopping for him last weekend to buy him some new outfits, I think she considered him not fit for purpose in his current attire. He had then turned up at work every day in a different shiny new outfit, ranging from a French Onion seller, to one of Captain Nemo's sailors, ending with a nice retro Val Doonigan look. For anyone too young to have heard of the great Val Doonigan he was like a modern-day Justin Bieber but sat on a stool by a fire.

I am sure Chris would have had a new outfit for fishing, probably along the lines of a set of Burberry dungarees and flat cap. I steadily trundled the 80 miles up to the mark on the Bristol Channel and thanks to information supplied by Nick Smith, I went straight to some free parking adjacent to the beach. My first look at this beach and it seemed windswept, cold and muddy but once I was down amongst it, I soon realised it was in fact extremely windswept, bitterly cold and bloody muddy. The westerly breeze really felt quite bracing and glancing in both directions highlighted my madness even further as no other anglers were present, in fact no humans whatsoever. I started with the smaller rig, and one ragworm managed to bait all 4 hooks, the plan was to wade the rig out and place it, then walk back paying out line. I had read that if you fish your Sole rig at only 40 yards then your fishing 20 yards too far, the speed with which the channel water comes in, is staggering and you really need your wits about you.

I waded out in amongst the thick chocolate soup, squelching mud and rafts of weed, carefully placing the bait in about 3 feet of water, before slowly walking back while letting out line. This isn't the sort of mark that you take too much kit, everything gets covered in mud, I had opted for my big plastic bucket, cheap tripod and single rod. If you like slop, weed and chocolate water then this is the place for you, but what these conditions do attract are the Sole that I so desired, Bass, Rays, Conger and Cod. The Bristol channel is a truly awesome fishery and Chris and I will be spending a good deal of the winter up there this year.

With the rod in position it was soon obvious that the biggest issue was going to be the amount of weed floating in the surging water and my line was quickly draped in various clumps like eco-friendly Christmas decorations. The weed built up to such a degree that the gripper lead was pulled free from the bottom, the lack of casting probably added to its poor embedment. I wound in the rig and removed the copious amounts of weed noting that two hooks had no ragworm on anymore, something was clearly feeding as it certainly hadn't been cast off.

Once again, I waded out and placed the bait, and with the tide now pushing in strongly, by the time I walked back to the tripod the water was already there. This time I kept wading out and clearing the weed, to leave the rig in the water, by doing this I was able to give the baits a chance to get a bite, I also managed to keep the line slack and rod low helping get the baits hard on the bottom. While waiting for something to happen. I noticed some trembling on the rod tip and despite the strong breeze it clearly looked like something was nibbling the baits, another snippet of info I read was if a Sole begins to bite have a cup of tea before striking, they are finicky feeders due to their tiny mouth.

I turned away and poured myself a steaming cup of coffee, fighting the urge to investigate the bite, the rod still showed signs of plucks although they had become less frequent. Now I was concerned I might have given it too long and that once again they had scoffed the worms, the coffee was downed, and it was time to check out the baits.

I lifted the rod sharply freeing the gripper weight and flinging the most recent clump of weed skyward, there did feel a little more weight, but it could be weed that had travelled down the line. I walked down to the water as the leader knot reached the tip eye, I freed the blob of weed to allow the retrieval to continue, and there skimming along the surface like a tiny leather paddleboard was the object of my desire a pristine Dover Sole.

I lifted the rod triumphantly upwards to see another on the bottom hook and for some stupid reason shook the rod to dislodge the weed on the rig, instantly the bottom fish fell back into the water and was gone. Fortunately, the other fish remained, what a disaster that could have been, if that had been the only fish and I had shaken it off, sometimes a moments lapse of concentration can cost you dearly. Luckily, I had been blessed with two of the little wonders and this Dover Sole, species 66 made me so happy I had to do a little mud jig, much to the little fish's disgust I imagine. Having never seen a Dover Sole up close I examined the little flatfish, they are extremely slippery to the touch a bit like a bar of soap, their side slung mouth is indeed very small, and I can understand why it may take a little while to consume a section of king rag.

I carefully and quickly set up my camera on the bucket using the bait board as a platform to take the pictures with the self-timer, the fish was then, like its fellow escapee released back to the chocolate channel to grow and prosper. With the target achieved I immediately changed to the 3 hook bigger rig in the hope of perhaps getting a bigger sole or another of my targets, a Bass. The best time was now approaching as the Sole is an avid nocturnal feeder, although it's probably pretty dark all the time in the channel, the tide was racing and having clocked the numerous gully's to my rear I knew that there was a real danger of being cut off. At one point I moved to the other side of a rapidly filling gutter, but my rig was on the other side of an exposed island of mud, I wouldn't have been able to reel that in until the tide covered it.

The sun began to set with an amazing display of colours and patterns and being alone on a beach as the tide rises and the sun falls is a real privilege, photos never really do it justice as I am sure all anglers will testify. I started to get some sharp rattling bites that just didn't seem the same as the subtler sole nibbles, sure enough I wound in a couple of small Whiting, one of which went out as a bait. It was only 10 minutes later when the rod thumped over sharply and sprang back, as some unseen assailant ripped the whiting from the hook, probably a Conger. Of course, with my interest in a bigger fish now pricked, could I catch another Whiting for bait, no way hozzay, despite my best efforts no more turned up.

With the darkness well and truly all around me I watched intently as 3 strange glowing pink hoops spun in circles further down the beach, like UFOs skimming the surface of the mud, they then stopped before heading directly towards me. It looked quite spectacular almost CGI like but when they had closed to around 40 yards I could hear the loud panting of big dogs, " oh bugger". I was suddenly surrounded by 3 German Shepard's and I don't mean Bavarian Sheep farmers! The huge dogs although menacing, seemed a little bit camp with their glowing pink necklaces, I didn't think it was the right time to mention that. Somewhere off in the distance a lady's voice shouted out the names of the dogs, Slasher, Smasher and Basher! Actually, I made them up, I couldn't actually hear their names above my own screams, but fortunately they could, and they turned and bound off, leaving me only seconds from a fate worse than being smashed, slashed and bashed.

That wasn't the last canine visit I had that night as right near the top of the tide with the dry land rapidly disappearing, I spotted eye shine heading towards me along the beach, the culprit this time a Fox who bounded past without even a side glance, right under my rods and off into the dunes. The tide as predicted finally beat me and with my back to the wall, I had to make my escape via the steps or face a muddy bath. The near two-hundred-mile round trip, putrid mud, relentless sea weed, bitter wind and driving rain would soon be forgotten, my first ever Dover Sole would not. Thanks Craig and Nick, true gents of our angling brotherhood and if not for your advice I wouldn't have got that fish.

This Blog, like one of my old school reports has its highs and lows and if the first part was the positive part of one of my old reports, the Art lesson bit, that stated Steven is showing an artistic flair and an aptitude for creating. The second part of the blog would reflect my Maths and PE section of the school report, Steven lacks any comprehension of this subject and must try harder, and Gym, "who is Steven"? he seems to be absent from all rugby training!

The second trip was a day Shark fishing out of Looe and as it transpired with regard to my shark fishing this year my Maths and PE teachers were spot on! The trip was aboard Force 10 and with skipper Pete Davis, normally being my lucky talisman, I hoped that my curse of the sharking Jonah would be lifted. The trip was organised by good friend and shark festival team mate Brian Copeland, also including his best mate and sharking virgin Dave, plus son in-law James.

I decided as I still had some ragworm left I would get to Looe early and try for a thin lip mullet over at the Millpool, I rigged my LRF rod with a Mepps spinner and single hook, so I was ready to roll out of the car and cast. The morning was surprisingly chilly, and the car temperature gauge showed 6 degrees but with a stiff breeze blowing off the moors, it felt more like 5.5 degrees. The journey down was largely uneventful other than the fact that I felt Sting was largely responsible for our plastic bottle on the beaches epidemic, having made it cool to put a message in a bottle during 1979, it's sad what a long journey, grumpy git and Police's greatest hits album results in.

I pulled into the Millpool car park and disembarked from the vehicle like a navy seal, reaching the water's edge in mere minutes, only problem, no water. The tide hadn't pushed up this far yet and despite having thin lips the mullet still had fat bodies and would take another hour to squeeze up to this point, I decided to go with plan b which meant dropping off the gear at the boat and doing some LRF on the rocks at the end of the day. I arrived at the harbourside and could see skipper of Swallow 2 Murray Collins busy cleaning the boat deck, I think he could do with a ride on polisher for that deck, I bid him good morning and asked if he would keep an eye on my gear while I drove up to Hannafore to park up. I decided to leave the light rod in the car for my return later as there was some great rock marks close by, as I walked back to the river I spotted a group of huge Mullet picking algae of the new concrete slipway, darn it why didn't I bring the light rod down with me. Once I reached the boats, Pete had arrived, and we transferred my kit to the boat and had a bit of a catch-up before picking Brian and the guys from the other side of the river. We headed out briefly stopping for Mackerel but with only a handful of joeys caught we headed straight out to the shark grounds.

With the hour and a bit journey completed Pete dropped the chum bags while we tried to get a bit fresher bait, soon a few nice Whiting were caught and sent down the chum trail for the sharks too feast on. I had decided to put out my shark rod and carry on bottom fishing to try and get something different and soon had a lovely little Red Gurnard, and a plethora of Whiting that arrived in hungry hordes even taking mackerel heads.

Brian who had been religiously feathering shouted that a big garfish had followed his feathers to the surface, I didn't need telling twice and I just had to have a go for one of these silver missiles.

The instant I dropped down the thin slither of mackerel belly it was hit by a garfish and after a short energetic battle I swung it on board for a quick picture. The gars have been a bit short on the ground this year and strangely I had just asked Pete if he had seen any since my last trip with him where I caught several, he had replied they had seen none. Now back on the boat a month later and I winkled out another Garfish, this was however the only one that day, which in itself is strange they don't normally travel alone. James was then away on the long-range rod and a little Blue Shark capitulated and swam in with less fight than my Garfish, but a Shark's a Shark and these pups are our future qualifiers.

Then Dave's float submerged, and another pup made an old man very happy, as Dave had tried several times for his first ever shark and this little male had made his day, great to see. An hour later James was in again and a bit better blue made him work a little harder, James was hoping for his qualifier, but this fish wasn't it and was quickly released. Next Brian was into a shark and again a feisty male punched well above its weight, although Brian probably made the most of it, it's important to enjoy them when you finally get one.

With my Shark curse hanging over me I tried different baits, different depths but no Sharks even accidently bumped into my line, last year I could do no wrong but now with my mind focused on every other species they have shunned me. No time to contemplate as the newly promoted Shark wrangler Dave was in again and this fish was a much better fish and no doubt the biggest of the day, a moments lack of tension on the rod and the fish was gone. The final run was once again to James's rod and his biggest of the day, but the highlight of his day was when he captured his first ever Octopus. Despite my Shark blank I still had a fantastic day with top notch company, a great skipper and a west country sea looking radiant, only two Shark trips left this year and only one of these is in this Shark club year. With the trip over my mind turned to an hours fishing off the rocks, I had 4 king ragworm left and a need to catch a fish or two. Mrs D then messaged me a picture of a bucket of fried chicken, that was a sneaky move although it wouldn't be going anywhere so I fished on with impunity.

The sea was rising and the gully I wanted to fish would be cut off within 30 minutes, no fish is worth risking your life or the lives of rescuers for, and I planned to fish the gully for 15 minutes only. The first drop of the mini species rig resulted in an instant bite and I struck to find a wriggling black goby on the bottom hook, this fell off clearly only holding on to the bait via pure aggression. The next drop and the light rod rattled sharply, this time my old adversary Blenny Henry was the culprit and a fine looking lenny he was too, incredible camouflage on these mini preds.

A quick check of the water level to my rear and I was still fine with my exit strategy, so I once again dropped the rig, this gully produced a few more Blenny's before I was departing to some safer ground. The next rock mark was a bit of a deeper hole in-between some thick beds of weed and the first fish humbled me in the weed bed and got off, clearly one of the wrasse species.

The next drop I was better prepared and pressurised the fish as soon as the take took place, a good little scrap and in came a nice little Ballan Wrasse, this was followed by a couple more before the light and tide created hazardous conditions and it was time to stick my head in a bucket of chicken. A couple of mixed result trips but one thing is for sure a poor fishing trip still beats a night in front of the box hands down, the Sole is one of my highlights of the challenge so far and fingers crossed there's still a surprise or two left in the year. A few big Conger trips coming up which won't add to the species list but if I get a P.B eel that may make me a tad happy. Thanks for all the support this week everyone that helped and hopefully Commercial Chris the crazy outfit wearing quizmaster will return for a bit of one sided character assassination in the next blog.

## Chapter 44 Mini monsters make my day.

Its pouring with rain as I write this latest blog and that long hot start to the summer seems a long time ago as the grip of autumn begins to take hold. Of course, with the weather becoming less predictable it is inevitable that boat trips will be cancelled, this Fridays hunt for mega Conger aboard Kevin Mckies huge charter boat Size Matters was such a trip.

The forecast for strong westerly winds and heavy rain is not the best recipe for a long-haul trip, where precision anchoring is critical to a successful trip and in my mind, this was a good call by the skipper. With the trip off, both Chris and I needed another option for the day, I looked at my dwindling list of targets, the tides and the strong winds, opting to target a couple of the mini species that have so far eluded me.

The two fish I needed were the Tompot Blenny, the bigger cousin of the infamous Blenny Henry and the deadly sounding Short Spined Sea Scorpion, a small fish with the look of a dragon. My initial thoughts were to go straight to Plymouth and fish a few of the sheltered shore marks that are largely protected by the breakwater, Chris was keen and that was the plan. I messaged mate Nick Smith to see if he wanted to join us and knowing how great he was at targeting the mini species, his experience would be invaluable. Unfortunately, Nick wasn't able to join us, but we did discuss various other options that would be better with the storm that was forecast, however I decided to go with the original plan and head for Plymouth.

Chris picked me up in the Popemobile, but he needed to be back by 18.30 as his boy's band had a gig that evening, this would work out well as high tide was 16.20 and that gave us 6 hours fishing. The mark we arrived at was a large carpark bounded by seawalls looking out to Plymouth Sound, Nick had advised me it didn't fish well over low water and would be better 2hrs up to high water. The area was well sheltered from the wind and the sky was blue with the great yellow orb shining brightly, a perfect day, however looking across to the pier at Mountbatten we could see the waves crashing against the rocks, a different world.

Chris reversed the car towards the railings and when the up and over boot door was raised we had a perfect shelter to fish from the back. I had opted to bring my freshwater quivertip rod and fish a two up 1 down rig created from an old sabiki rig, this was light snoods sporting size 12 hooks and the feather material removed. I baited with king rag section and dropped the rig over the edge of the railings and into the water that was only a couple of feet deep at this stage of the tide. We had decided to try here for 20 minutes which could have been a mistake as the mark fishes best with more water in front of it, however as I tightened down on the rig the fine quiver tip shot down and I had a fish on instantly. The little fish kicked to show it was indeed attached and the great thing about this sort of fishing you never know what will turn up, and that's not revealed until they swing in over the railings. This turned out to be a lovely little Goldsinny Wrasse and the last time I fished this mark was during the Conger festival and on that evening, I had landed a Goldsinny for the challenge.

This wasn't on my list this time, but as with all Wrasse, they are all uniquely patterned and can be quite stunning. With the first fish in the bag it heralded a pretty nonstop session and the baits were hit as soon as they touched the bottom, we missed plenty as the superfast rattling takes cleared the soft ragworm in seconds. The 20-minute deadline passed and neither of us wanted to move to another mark and leave feeding fish, Nick had informed me that the two species I wanted do get caught from this mark, so it was just a case of fishing through the other species. I decided to cast out onto the sand about 30yds out to see if there was anything different from the Goldsinny's that were at the toe of the wall in large numbers. The bite took a little while longer out on the sand but after 10 minutes the tip trembled as something discovered the baits, I struck and wound in to see a small goby of some description.

This turned out to be the Rock Goby, a species' I had already had when I fished at Ilfracombe Pier with the family, still great to see these little guys. Chris also managed a Rock Goby his first ever so that was great news for him, it's great to get so excited over these great little fish but there is another undersea world going on where these mini fish really are kings. The water was rising with the incoming tide now pushing in strongly, I decided to try tight to the wall again, as I was sure this would be where the Tompot Blenny would be found. As before the bite was instant but this time the fish gave a great little scrap so typical of a stocky little wrasse, sure enough a stunning Corkwing wrasse was swung over the rail.

The Wrasse had a huge Sea Louse stuck to the corner of its eye, I quickly removed this parasite that feeds on the fish's mucus and blood, that was my good deed done for the day, hopefully I'd get rewarded for that act of mercy. I've caught a lot of Wrasse with red sores on them and I guess it could be these types of parasites, doing that sort of damage. Chris was then hooked into something decent as his rod hooped over and for the second time during this challenge year he landed a fishing reel, the previous year he was letting the sea take them from him. Just a shame all the gear he salvages is a load of tat, but I'm sure whoever fishes out, his lost rod and reel will think the same.

He did get to keep the lead weights that were attached to the barnacle covered mess, so that at least made him smile. The Wrasse were on the feed and both Chris and I were on the receiving end of a couple of good Ballan Wrasse taking us to ground, eventually taking the hooks in the process. I did manage a couple of smaller Ballan's including a stunning dark fish, once again proving the diversity of the species and their colouring.

Chris decided to go up to the end where a stone platform jutted out further into the sea, at this point there sat a decaying set of steps that Chris felt could produce something different. The end was occupied by a group of youths who in-between casting their sets of feathers thought it hilarious to dance and balance close to the edge of the wall. When Chris returned having seen enough, he informed me the group were drunk and still drinking, total dimwits who not only risk their own lives but the lives of others.

With the tide came hordes of tiny Whiting and at first, they were confined to the sand 30 yards out but soon they moved in with the Wrasse and became a real pain, quickly snaffling the pristine ragworm. With no sign of either of my target species I was starting to get itchy feet, there were a ton of marks within an easy walk and as much fun as the Wrasse were, I wasn't here for them. We decided to give it 10 more minutes and I started readying my kit for some hiking, a little bite tight to the wall though resulted in the fish I was after and a cracking Tompot Blenny made me very happy, species 67.

With the photos done and half of the target achieved we were keen to stay where we were and finish the session off on this mark, there after all was still time to winkle out something special. The Tompot is a really cool looking fish with its bug like antennae making it appear to be a fish / insect hybrid, if they grew to a 200lb they would be man-eaters, they have a rather aggressive disposition.

It turned out that the little Rottweilers had moved in to take control of the bottom of the wall and once I dropped back down the bait was ambushed by more of these bolder bullies, and now they were in gangs. I had tried several times for these great fish and I was making the most of getting amongst them and so I continued to catch them while they fed so aggressively, I even had one take both hooks. So, the Tompot Blenny was well and truly out of my system, I now needed to try for the rarer Scorpion fish, a fish I've never ever seen, all I knew was they had been caught at this mark and they were very predatory.

I decided to try twitching the bait across the bottom in the hope it would instigate a predatory reaction, it did but from the wrong species as a Corkwing Wrasse pounced on it. Then it was grabbed by another Rock Goby which for a second fooled me into thinking it was something I hadn't had yet, these little fish come in so many shades and colours that a positive id can sometimes be tricky. So, all my plans for the scorpion had so far failed and we both decided we couldn't end our session on a tiny Whiting, and I changed my rig to a single size 6 long shank baited with a small whole ragworm. Chris had done the same and managed to catch his final fish which was a nice size Corkwing Wrasse, I had put my bait, danger close, at the foot of the wall where it was quite snaggy.

With the high tide nearly upon us and everything packed up except my rod, the fat lady was about to sing, I picked up the rod and twitched from the bottom and it was instantly hit by some minor assailant. I wound in the last fish of the trip and clearly my kind deed of removing the parasite had impressed Neptune so much he gave me exactly what I wanted in the final seconds of the trip, a Scorpion fish. Both Chris and I were equally excited to see this little water dragon, its armour-plated head complete with dragon ears and if it had blown a flame from its mouth I wouldn't have been surprised, species 68 in the bag. The scorpion was small, but they don't grow huge it had however managed to engulf the whole ragworm in its initial strike, I just love the look of them and photos just don't do them justice.

*The Short Spined Sea Scorpion*

That was a great way to end the session and what a great 6 hours fishing it was, I even managed a couple of prawns, one Chris used for bait the other I stepped on in my excitement! Thanks Nick for all the tips and advice, also Chris for driving, getting the bait and for sharing the excitement of that little dragon, great memory's and at least with your latest recovered reel, your tackle value has doubled! I have just found out that the second of my Conger trips has been cancelled and fortunately I have had a few eels this year, but I guess the new P.B will have to wait until next year's trips. I have said it before during this challenge, but since starting in January I have gained huge respect for the mini species that I previously wouldn't have given a second glance too. Hopefully I have highlighted via my pictures and blogs just how amazing our inter tidal species really are, colourful, alien, and thriving, all the more reason to tread carefully and replace what you move, when next visiting the shoreline.

Next week is my penultimate Shark trip, down at Penzance and this will be Chris's first and last Shark trip of the year, so hopefully things will improve on the sharking front and we will get a few. I am not even going to say what I am secretly wishing for but starting to think I've used all my Neptune's favours up. Stay safe if you're by the water this weekend, and tightest of lines anglers.

## Chapter 45 Multiple trips, seatbox slips & portions of chips.

The Autumn seems to have arrived early this week with a huge full moon bringing the first frosts and it highlights the speed of this year's passing, it just doesn't seem 5 minutes ago I was putting on the frost prevention screen. This has also signified that the summer fish species will soon disappear and that I have missed several opportunities to add crucial fish to the challenge. The first trip on the cards for this blog was to be a Shark trip with Bite Adventures, this would normally be a dead cert for a back-aching day of multiple Sharks, however with my Shark mojo at an all-time low, combined with the recent storms I was strangely lacking confidence.

The powerful sea storms can result in disturbed water and murky seas, coloured water I have learned can be the kiss of death for catching Blue Sharks. I was up at 5am and as we were finishing boat fishing at 4pm, I chucked the quivertip in the car to have a go for a Golden Grey Mullet. The car was well iced over and as I hadn't taken the precaution of adding the frost deterrent screen it was a case of running the engine and waking the neighbours, and more alarmingly Mrs D. I still managed to pick Chris up by 5.45am and with a great run down to Penzance we pulled onto the harbour wall at 07.15, just in time to watch the sun creep up over the Mount across the bay. We kitted up with some warm clothes knowing full well we wouldn't be needing it later, at this point the scantily clad figure of Alex appeared at the end of the wall, in his standard shark attire of shorts, bare feet and sandals.

We bid each other good morning and chatted about the day to come, it's always great to catch up with fellow anglers, exchange a few tails and generally have a whinge about lost fish, or other people's big fish. Chippy arrived and started running through his boat checks as our final team member arrived, Martin, a nice lad from Somerset who was looking forward to just getting out fishing.

 The skipper reversed Bite Adventures back to the steps and we climbed aboard feeling lost on the large open deck, the kit was stashed, and feathers attached to the rods. The Mackerel were in dense shoals and the trick was to get through the joey mackerel at the surface, as below them were some proper ones, we filled a barrel in 10 minutes, with pristine baits and were then on our way. Below Alex contemplating the days fishing.

We travelled considerably further than I have been from Penzance and ended up around 10 miles off the Scilly Isles, this was a valiant attempt to find clear water. When the engines fell silent the water still looked the colour of Chris's ginger tea, and Chippy could not hide his disappointment. The chum trail was started, and the rods sent out with fresh mackerel flappers set at a range of depths going from 20 feet down to 200 feet, we were in over 300 feet of water so a pretty deep area. The skipper knowing, I needed a Porbeagle told me to set up a bottom rig with a circle and heavy mono leader, this was to have a whiting flapper hooked up and fished hard on the bottom.

Chris set about catching me a fresh whiting but was getting nervous as his braid on the reel disappeared rapidly, due largely to the depth of the water and strength of tide, bigger lead needed. With the feathers now baited and sporting a 1lb lead Chris reached the seabed but the only fish being caught were Poor Cod, far too small for a Porbeagle bait. Chris then started getting Haddock although these were too big for a bait, they allowed Commercial Chris to swing into action, he became a fish refinery, catching and processing the fish as he went. With everything quiet on the shark front and plenty of fish down on the bottom I decided to have a go myself, quickly catching a nice Red Gurnard, followed by a Haddock. Fortunately, Chris finally got me a nice big Whiting and the skipper flappered it up and I sent it to the bottom to entice that elusive Porgy. Unfortunately, after an hour the rig snagged on something on the sandy sea bed and I lost the lot, the skipper done me another trace and with no other Whiting showing I hooked up a half Haddock, much to Chris's disgust. I added a big lead to keep it down in the strong tide and there I stood like a coiled old spring, rusty and seized, waiting for some shark interest.

This was on my 12lb to 20lb class tackle, so any shark would make for some exciting times, however after several hours I was becoming a little despondent. Alex had managed to catch the first and only Blue Shark of the day and a couple of others had stuck their heads up through the murk but disappeared again.

Its days like this that skippers clearly suffer as much as the anglers on board, they are in the business to find you fish and believe me they share in the angler's disappointment. As I sat watching commercial Chris and Martin giving themselves a deep-water workout, by checking their baits in the murky abyss, I started wondering if my half Haddock was actually still attached. Boom! that question was answered in an instant as the rod was nearly yanked from my hands, the braid emptying from the spool at such a rate it burned my thumb, I had it on the spool to keep it from pulling out as the big lead bounced.

I lifted into the departing fish and Chippy got me to the other side of the boat, I needed to check the clutch as the line was still emptying, the skipper concurred the clutch was fine. The fish decided to turn and head towards the boat, but in that instant, it was gone, when we retrieved the rig, the back of the bait was gone leaving just the head. Gutted was an understatement and even now 24hrs after, I am still going over my actions piece by piece, this is the second Porbeagle I have lost this year the first biting through the trace. This time I can only surmise that the instant and savage nature of the take, didn't allow for a good hook hold, but the fish was certainly powerful and covered a lot of distance in a short space of time. With that bit of excitement over, the trip soon came to an end and we headed for home with the Scilly Isles still visible to our rear. On the way in I quizzed Chippy about the Golden Grey Mullet that frequent the harbour, he offered me plenty of tips and the other species I asked about was another mini-species, the Sand Smelt, also residing in the harbour.

We docked and disembarked but before I left the boat, Chippy gave me a huge donation to my charity challenge, I am so grateful to everyone that has not only supported the Stroke Association through monetary donations but with the overwhelming help and advice I have received, my donations are now over £800! Chippy also chucked a little chum around the steps to aid with attracting the Golden Grey Mullet, he then took Bite Adventures off to her berth for the night. Chris and I swapped the tackle over and as per the skipper's recommendations I set up a light pencil float rig, and size 8 hook, baited with a small piece of skinless Mackerel flesh. The advice was to fish this just off the bottom which meant a 12-foot drop under the float.

Chris sticking with the commercial theme, used a giant mackerel float that wouldn't have looked out of the way attached to a lobster pot, no doubt he was hoping to fool the shy feeding mullet into thinking no one would be daft enough to try and catch us with that. I was getting several sharp bites which cleaned the hook in an instant and I decided to reduce the hook size further, borrowing a size 14 from Chris, this resulted in the capture of a Blenny, which was followed by another Blenny.

We did notice that small fish were shooting up from the murk and grabbing fish particles from the surface, these must be Sand Smelt. With the Mullet not playing ball and the call of the KFC growing louder, I needed to get something from the trip, Chris suggested going shallow with the float and a tiny piece of squid tentacle.

As soon as the shallower set bait drifted downwards a group of little fish surrounded it as if it were a new kid at their school, but it was quickly rejected, and the gang sank from view. I then baited with a tiny piece of fish flesh which again the little fish gang mobbed around, this time however one of the bigger boys of the group stepped forward and sucked in the bait, I lifted the float from the water with the little gang member hanging on the end. I knew straight away this was a Sand Smelt, and although small it was a stunning little fish with its pearl like scales shimmering in the sunlight. I thought it would make a better shot to take it on the steps next to the water where I had caught it, great idea until I realised just how slippery they were.

The first shot was luckily a good one, so well-done Chris, the second however was of the fish leaving the scene to return to the water, another potential disaster. Chris thought the whole thing was extremely funny and I just don't think he appreciated just how tricky to hold these little guys are, wait until he gets one I shall see how well he holds it! Anyway, this little beauty made species 69, and saved the day from a challenge perspective, I have had to accept the fact that the Porbeagle Shark isn't appearing in this challenge other than as the one that got away, twice! The next time I was too wet a line was down at Looe, I needed to drop the shark club trophy back to John Mac, so it made sense to kill two birds with one stone. The night before I had spent the evening polishing the trophy back to its sparkling glory, can't believe how much they tarnish, still, on the plus side no polishing for me to do next year!

My plan for this little sortie was to try for a Sandeel in the harbour, it was loaded with them the last time I was there, then I would try over at Millpool for a school Bass and maybe a Thin Lip Mullet. For the Sandeels I had got a set of the Tronix pro micro feathers, these are designed for Sandeel with size 16 hooks and a very fine feather made up in 6 hook rigs. For the Mullet and Bass, I had a modified Mepps spinner with the treble removed and a small trailing size 6 hook with a small rubber worm threaded on the hook. Really this should have been fresh ragworm but as I didn't have any I substituted the real thing for a bit of silicon after all it works in other scenarios. Just as I was about to leave Mrs D asked if she could tag along with Matthew as it was a lovely evening, wow I never expected that but it would be great having the family there.

We got down to the harbour by 17.45 and I went straight over to start jigging the micro feathers, however I couldn't see a Sandeel anywhere. John popped down to pick up the trophy and we had a quick natter after which he told me that there could be some Sandeels up by Pete's boat, we said goodbye and I headed off to fish next to Force 10, maybe the lucky boat would bring me a bit of luck. I tried really hard to instigate a bite but there were no Sandeels anywhere, I was fast becoming despondent, even Mrs D told me to cheer up and catch something, the plethora of flags behind signifying someone had done rather better than me, and now I not only blanked on the boat but next to it too.

With none of the little snakes making an appearance I worked my way back to the car trying at every gap in the moored boats, finally I spotted a target. A large raft of weed hid a rather special fish and despite my best efforts I couldn't get Mrs D as excited about it as me, a rather large 15 Spined Stickleback. The fish blended perfectly with the weed, darting out every now and then to inspect something floating past his lair, my micro feathers only seemed to terrify him, I guess a tiny shoal of synchronised feathers are somewhat scary. I really wanted to catch this fish it would have been one of those red species but with no bait and no size 18 hooks it was never going to happen. Having wasted too much time in a fruitless effort I needed to get over to the millpool before high tide. We drove over to the car park and I set off to find a spot while Mrs D and Matthew went off to hunt sausage and chips. I positioned myself on the outer wall of the pool and tried caster inside and out, I started having a few tentative plucks on the river side and eventually spotted the culprit as a Bass was following a few inches behind the lure. I then noticed my feet were getting wet as the rising tide breached the pools outer wall, I jumped up on the steps and just 5 minutes later water gushed into the pool bringing the hungry Mullet with it.

There were by now bow waves appearing all over the pool from the excited arriving fish, but there was no way the Mullet were falling for that plastic ragworm method. Mrs D arrived with a large portion of hot chips and we sat and watched the rising of the fish and the tide, wow those chips tasted good with the sea air to wash then down with.

The darkness enveloped us and all to quickly it was time to head for home, it may have been a blank, but time spent with the family is never time wasted, so no complaints.

It's now Saturday and the missed opportunity with the saltwater stickleback reminded me I had a chance to fish for the freshwater version, the 3 Spined Stickleback, a much smaller cousin. I knew about a wildlife pond where these little guys were rumoured to be, it's a bit of a trek and a tad of a commando mission but worth a shot. I decided to use the pen rod and a size 20 hook to nylon with little maggot for bait, no float as I planned to watch the maggot, the pond was shallow and clear. With the trek completed I could see a few of the little fish sat motionless under the surface weed much like the sea stickleback was. A couple of maggots were dropped in and I watched as they seemed to dart around in different directions, like shooting stars in the night sky, and clearly too big for the mouths of the voracious little fish. I sorted out a smaller maggot but found the maggot skin more effective and after a first frustrating hour managed a number of these little fish, shame they were not in their breeding colours as the males have stunning red bellies at that time. Anyway, these tiniest of our freshwater fish made species number 70, and although not as mighty as a Shark or Blonde Ray they do rule their little world.

The final attempt this week was a two-pronged approach, part 1 being to try the River Taw in Barnstaple for a Bass or early Flounder, part 2 was over to Ilfracombe pier and have another attempt at a Spotted Ray.

We would fish two tides at two venues surely, I could nick something from this 14-hour session, good weather, sociable tides and quality bait. We left home at a reasonable 6.30am and pulled up alongside the river by 7.30am, the area we had chosen was just upstream of the new bridge and an area that fishes well for Flounder during the Autumn. The fresh ragworm baits were cast out to the channel and a couple of other anglers who had been there since 5am told us they hadn't had a single bite. We were using carp rods for this first mission, they are much more sensitive for the rattling bites of these smaller river fish, but still able to put out a 5oz grip weight if required. Before long the river was in full flood pushing in large rafts of weed and various other flotsam and jetsam, the rods were taken out numerous times, but we persevered. Unfortunately, venue 1 failed to produce and it was maybe a tad too early for the Flounder, but the school Bass should have been moving through.

So, it was onwards to the next venue and as the best chance of the Rays would be during the evening flood, the afternoon would be spent having fun with the mini species on the LRF rods. When we first arrived the main area of the pier was still underwater, and we had to fish from the higher area, I was joined by another fisherman who clearly felt I had a better chance than him. This was a young Cormorant, a pain when they turn up on the lakes but here by the sea is where they should be, so he was welcome to sit by me. The downside was that every tourist wanted to take a selfie with him, the result was a barrage of questions aimed at me about the darn bird, as if it was my pet that I took fishing.

We finally got down onto the lower pier and setup on the middle section where a short cast gets you on to a nice sandy gully, this was information supplied by a friend who has caught a few Spotted Ray from this area. The far end of the pier was taken over by a group of eastern Europeans and one of them was a man mountain whom Chris, secretly named Shrek, it was clear Shrek was in charge of the fishing party as his two mates, Donkey and Pinocchio were clearly clueless. Don't ever judge a book by its cover but these guys really were fast food fishermen, clearly hoping for something to put in a soup, and both Chris and I had to snigger when Donkey thought he hooked a monster. He was so convinced it was a leviathan, that he put down his beer and spat out his cigarette, the handle turned frantically, and the clutch screamed, after 5 minutes he didn't seem to be making any head way on the unseen foe, but he kept reeling and reeling. Both Chris and I could see he was snagged in the bottom at the foot of the pier, and unless he found a hole 300 feet deep, the clutch was too loose, eventually Shrek ambled over and tightened the clutch. It was only now Donkey appreciated the gravity of the situation, he was about to lose some of Shreks tackle, a man capable of quite literally popping him, fortunately Donkey was the man with the beers, so a deal was struck. It goes to show just how quiet the fishing was that we looked to other so-called anglers for some form of entertainment, they just went from one disaster to another. The funniest accident of the day was reserved for good ole Commercial Chris and just as the pier was at its fullest with tourists, families and other anglers, he fell extravagantly from his seatbox and lay on his back, feet in the air with a loud crash.

Why do you never have a camera ready when you need one, I know that one of those many visitors will no doubt have it and post it somewhere at some time. Back to the fishing and I had just noticed the rod with a Bluey section bounce violently, nothing else materialised so I decided to check the bait, hanging from the trace was a Shore Rockling. I love Rockling and I am still chasing the bigger cousin of this guy, the Three Beard Rockling, unfortunately this wasn't it, so a couple of pics and back he went. Chris then hobbled over, still smarting from his fall, " what's this" he asked? on his trace was another Sand Smelt, amazing I had one from the south coast just days ago and now Chris had got one from the north. You need a photo I told him, secretly wanting him, to find out just how tricky to hold these Mexican Jumping Smelts really are. He started with the gentle pinch, but I told him to try in his hand, sure enough the fish did its stuff and sprung clean out of his hand, " not so easy now is it"! The mini species fishing was as per usual pretty good and we were soon getting the usual suspects, Ballan Wrasse, Common Blenny, and Rock Goby's but nothing I haven't already had, great sport on light tackle though.

With the flood tide came strong winds and a large swell was already forming, white horses pushed into the harbour mouth and the whole thing didn't feel fishy, time to move to a more sheltered section. We tucked ourselves in around the corner, and on one of the lower decks, it was like a different world and being so close to this amount of structure we decided to focus our efforts on a Conger. I prepared a couple of baits and changed over to heavy mono traces, the rigs would then be lowered to the base of the pier, hopefully to entice an eel from its lair.

Chris then offered to go and get some chips which on this by now rather chilly evening seemed just the ticket, you can't beat hot chips by the sea and for the second time in this blog, I ate alfresco chips with a big dollop of sea air. With the chips rapidly consumed we just need to add the fish, and we both started getting bites on the light rods, mine transpired to be Pouting but Chris hit the jackpot with a fish I've hoped to get on numerous occasions, the Dragonet. Fishing is a strange old game and both Chris and I have many highs and lows during our excursions and as much as I really wanted one I felt that Chris deserved one more than me on this trip. What a lovely little fish to end this blog with and as the night fell on that evening that was indeed the very last fish, our Conger baits stripped bare by the numerous crabs. With 70 species now in the bag and things getting harder I'm not sure if there will be enough material to even compose a blog, so they may have to be less frequent. I have it in my mind to try and get to 75 species and then wrap things up, but without a few more of the tricky ones gracing my net, that isn't going to happen. Thanks, as usual to everyone who has been so supportive with information, donations and also for taking the time to read and like the blog, keeps me going. Lovely to spend time fishing with the family, Mrs D please feel free to join me anytime but if you think you're having one of my rods in Thailand, I am not risking it, your far too good an angler. Well done once again to fishing buddy Chris, other than me I can't think of anyone I'd rather see, fall of their seatbox, I actually mean catch a Dragonet. However, if you keep rubbing it in I shall be forced to give new friend Shrek, a case of beer to pop you!

## Chapter 46 Fanbasstic

Here we are again another week gone and another blog created, this week I had a few chances that I was unable to take and one, that the weather scuppered. I was busy at work this week, but Chris and I had Friday off to try and track down a Grayling, a bit of research had thrown up a couple of venues for this species. I then had a message from a friend saying there was a space on a trip targeting big Congers on Wednesday if I wanted to join them, I know this skipper gets plenty of good eels and was desperate to jump aboard. Unfortunately, I had some important meetings that day and it's also the day Mrs D works, and I have to be around to meet Matthew from the bus, this led to me declining the trip. I knew I'd regret that and sure enough the guys had blinding day landing 80 eels to 60lb plus plenty of Ling, I could have kicked myself and after last Sundays species fail I could have done with a bit of sport.

I did have a trip booked on Saturday from Minehead fishing with Scott Shepard but the forecast for Saturday looked horrendous and this just added to my frustration. I was banking on the Bristol channel trip, to try yet again for a Spotted Ray and I just knew that it would be cancelled, I really needed something exciting to do, a little treat. A boat I have been following on social media is Silver Halo charters, based in Torquay, the reason it stuck out, it was a smaller style charter boat aimed at smaller groups of anglers, targeting specific species etc. Part of my love of boat angling is trying new ports, boats and skippers it can be both exciting and educational, every skipper I have ever fished with has taught me something new.

It's also incredible not only how diverse our various shorelines can be, but also how different the tides, depths, seabed and fish species can be. For example, Dartmouth with its close proximity to the Skerries is great for Plaice, Lyme Bay for Black Bream, Falmouth for Red Band fish, Looe for Shark and Minehead for Cod, obviously much more can be caught from these areas, but it highlights the opportunities we have. I think largely because of this challenge I have tried different areas and different skippers and it's been not only productive but enjoyable, it just confirms how fortunate we are to have so many hard working, quality charter boat skippers available. I would say though, that most of these guys are really working hard to carve out a living and the costs associated with running a charter business mean that a long spell of bad weather can be crippling.

Silver Halo skippered by Matt Forrester is a new 7.9m Cheetah Marine Catamaran that has been constructed around angler Matts specific requirements, and I was keen to have a go on this compact style vessel. I was to get my chance as Matt posted a Bass fishing trip for the coming Friday with spaces, the method was to be targeting big Bass on the inshore wrecks with live baits. This definitely was something exciting to do and the poor old Grayling was relegated to another day, I contacted Matt and booked a space, Chris was just as keen as I, and booked up too. The day before we were due to go I had a message from skipper Andy Howell asking if I was free Friday to try for the Porbeagle I was desperate for, another opportunity that I had to turn down, I was extremely grateful to Andy for thinking of me though.

The day of the trip arrived, and we left in the dark at 5.15 and arrived at Torquay Marina still in the dark at 6.15, time to have a wander around admiring the plethora of boats that adorned the marina berths. Before long Matt arrived and introduced himself, the other angler who was out with us was one of Matts regulars Dan, we shall refer to him as fish pan Dan. Dan was a chef who along with his wife another chef ran their own restaurant in south Devon, Dan seemed to have a recipe for every single species and was happy to cook any fish, hence fish pan Dan. He was though a very good angler and superb company, so I have no doubt he makes a mean fish dish, although his claims that Pouting were tasty are maybe a dish too far. We followed Matt through the marina maze to the berth that housed Silver Halo, the skipper invited us aboard and the well-designed craft was like a sea tardis, everything was designed for angling. There was a lot of space and dozens of rod holders, collapsible seats at the rear of the bait table were a delight for a couple of ageing anglers with dodgy legs. The live bait tank was pride of place and large, proving that this was an important item of kit, for this boat's method of fishing, the twin 115hp Honda engines looked capable of quite literally getting the boat airborne. Speaking to Matt it quickly became apparent this boat was his pride and joy and he had invested heavily to get her to this stage, it is however no good owning a Zonda if you can't handle it. The skipper was however more than qualified as a proficient seaman and just as importantly an excellent angler, both of these crucial for successful charter boat success. We headed out through the harbour with the darkness departing rapidly, Chris and I both commenting on our many trips to Halden Pier.

I told Chris one of my last trips from Torquay was when I took my then fiancé Mrs D on one of the tourist Mackerel trips, I had sneakily put a bit of bait on the bottom hooks on our feathers. Then little Mrs D told me that she had something on her line that was hard to pull in, I told her not to make a scene and just pull it up, it was just a string of Mackerel. That turned into a massive egg on face moment, as a near 20lb Conger appeared on the surface attached to her bottom feather, the boat full of tourists thought she was a god, I however thought, she was indeed marriage material. The skipper opened up the engines and we skimmed the mirror like surface towards the bait fishing mark, as the engines stopped the air fell eerily silent as we drifted into a mine field of black barrels. The barrels were a vast mussel farm and the whole thing felt strangely surreal and I couldn't help but feel that if we touched a barrel it would explode, like a giant game of battleships.

The area however was a very good fish attractor as is the case with any structure in the sea, the bait fish roamed in spasmodic shoals amongst the mussel covered chains, and that is why we were there. Fish pan Dan was first into a fish and would you believe it, a lovely Tub Gurnard a fish I needed, Dan was already planning the recipe for that one. Then Chris and I both started getting our target bait fish, the Scad and these were dropped quickly into the fish Jacuzzi at the rear of the boat. We went on to add some large Mackerel to the tank and 20 minutes later headed off to the first wreck, the tides were small and live baits should be a better option to the lures in these conditions.

Chris had forgotten to take his seasickness tablets, so I prepared myself to grab pictures of any suffering he may endure, however he was fine all day more proof he had grown some sea legs, makes the blog a tad less colourful. We soon arrived at the first wreck and skipper Matt had tied up a few Portland style rigs that were combined with an 8-foot fluorocarbon trace and 5/0 Mustad circle hook. I fixed this rig to my light boat setup and attached a Scad, this was steadily lowered to the wreck some 30 meters below. I asked Matt how we should be fishing this technique and he explained to let it hit the bottom then wind up two turns, which I did, he then said if a Bass is approaching the bait will start to panic and bounce the rod tip, this incredibly then started to happen. Matt continued, then the Bass will grab the bait and try to dive, the rod then arched over as a Bass indeed hit the bait and dived towards the wreck, this literally happened as he said it. I was now however attached to a very strong Bass and on the light outfit was excellent sport, it stripped line repeatedly in its attempts to get to the structure, but luck was with me and the stunning bar of silver soon rolled on the surface.

I haven't done much Bass fishing and I knew the fish was clearly a personal best, it was bouncing around 7lb on the scales but was long and lean. Chris and Dan hadn't even dropped their lines yet and we had our first Bass, what a start and for me species 71, a truly stunning example of the Bass, I am still so delighted with this fish. This was proof, that listening to the advice of the skipper will help you put those special fish on the deck, ignore them and rest assured you will miss out.

Personal Best Bass

Chris kindly done the pictures before getting his own bait down, straight away he was also into a good Bass and with the fish nearly at the surface another big dive caused the line to part. Such a shame when that happens but all you can do is get set up and start again, this is exactly what Chris did and soon he was back in the feeding zone. Fish pan Dan was now attached to a Bass and they really were fighting well on our balanced kit, this turned out to be a fish of around 5lb, again another beautiful example. Another boat arrived at the wreck, and this seemed to be full of a group of shirtless anglers targeting pouting, they were clearly happy pulling up string falls.

As the Pouting pirates drifted only yards from the stern of Silver Halo, my rod started to show a trembling bait, slam the bait was smashed by a Bass and line was once again pouring from the spool. The other boats sumo like crew looked on as the fish battled in front of their very eyes, the skipper netted another Bass of similar size to the first much to my delight. The fish was released over the side facing the Pouting pirates, and you could hear them exclaim " that was a Bass"! I started to get the feeling if they spotted us land anymore Bass they may very well board us and steal Chris and the fish. With that, yet another boat arrived, and skipper Matt suggested we move to another wreck as there were plenty to try, we all agreed and soon we powered off further east, leaving the cast of the full Monty to their Pouts.

We arrived at the new wreck and I tried a joey Mackerel bait for something different, while Chris opted for a go big or go home approach with a big Mackerel, both baits were soon taken. Chris was into his second Bass and the fish around 4lb stayed attached for long enough to get netted this time, it just proves how big a bait a Bass will engulf. I however, maybe should have not taken the Michael out of the bare-chested boat stalkers as the fish that engulfed my live joey Mackerel was a blooming big Pouting, reap what you sew I guess. Dan added another Bass to his total with a bit smaller fish of around 3lb and we all caught a few more of the voracious Pouting, maybe this information leaked out because steaming towards us was the Pouting Pirates. We moved on again, such is the abundance of inshore wrecks there is really no need to be sat in a pool of boats, with the nippy Silver Halo reaching each wreck in 15 minutes it was no hassle to move.

This wreck produced a new best Bass to Chris of around 5lb and the fact we both now had personal bests proved we had been right to shelve the Grayling this week. Of course, Chris couldn't go the whole trip without causing some sort of drama and the fact the bait pump kept cutting out was initially a mystery, until we realised Chris kept sitting his fat backside on the pipe, crushing it flat, hence the flow stopped.

We were also visited by a pod of Dolphins and no matter how many time these wonderful creatures cross my path I will never tire of seeing them. The lack of tide was definitely affecting the fishing and the powerful slams of the morning Bass takes were replaced by cautious plucks and stolen baits as slack water arrived. We had used no more than 6oz leads all day which is great for light tackle fishing, but the fish become lethargic and more suspicious of the rigs.

We did try various options and a few more wrecks but the fish really switched off, however we were all delighted with the day and anything else was a bonus. Chris nicked another smaller Bass that he didn't know was even attached until he retrieved his trace and Fish pan Dan added another species to the fish pie as he landed a nice Pollack on the last drift. I cannot recommend Matt and Silver Halo Charters enough, a super skipper that will give you a great days fishing. Check him out if you fancy a trip with a smaller group from the Torquay coastline.

As I suspected Saturdays Ray trip was cancelled and I spent the day with the family. Sunday was another chance to wet a line as Mrs D wanted to visit her mum, this meant I could have a couple of hours checking the lakes were okay, and consequently have a little go for a Crucian Carp. I knew with a little manipulation I would get another chance to add to the species list, and although I didn't have maggots I decided tiny cubes of Luncheon meat would suffice. I dropped the family off and headed out on what was a lovely sunny Sunday afternoon, I was welcomed at the gate by a stunning Red Admiral, and despite the recent frost the summer was clinging on.

I set up with a quivertip outfit and size 18 hook with a 2lb link, this was baited with a tiny cube of meat and cast out between two lily beds. Straight away I started getting line baits no doubt due to the bed of pellet and corn I had just put out, a few minutes later the tip swung round, and I hooked the first fish, a lovely Golden Orfe. This Orfe was the first of several as the greedy fish seemed to get to the bait before anything else, clearly, they have bred several times already. I stuck with the meat bait and trickled in micro pellets that eventually lead to the swim beginning to bubble as fish dug amongst the bottom silt, the next bite was something different and I netted a lovely Golden Tench, now they were in the swim the Orfe had been pushed out and I had several Tench before the swim went quiet. I introduced some bread dispersals to try and draw in the Crucian Carp, but the bubbling had stopped, the sun had become shrouded in cloud and a cold breeze blew across the lake.

I was beginning to doubt any further fish would make an appearance and started to think about making a move. Then the tip shot round and I struck to find myself attached to a small fish impersonating a Marlin, as it breached twice from the water, I struggled to identify the species but once netted I knew exactly what it was. This was an Albino Grass Carp and I was unaware that they actually fed on Luncheon Meat, assuming they ate water plants and insects. Well a bit of a result really, as it certainly wasn't a species on my list and that was species 72 not what I had expected. I had just slipped the little fish back when my parents turned up for a walk around the lakes, I knew this would mean that their crazy whippet, Shadow wouldn't be far away and sure enough he bounded over.

He was surprisingly well behaved and didn't eat too much of the luncheon meat, he actually sat and watched the water no doubt waiting to see a fish that never came. They soon had to make tracks and I remained for a while longer to feed the Carp with some bread and the Pike with half a dozen Mackerel. It was an enjoyable unplanned few hours and resulted in a surprise capture a great way to finish the weekend, next weekend it's a road trip up to the midlands as a guest of Mr & Mrs Aldridge, no pressure Carl!

# Chapter 47 Surging Storm results in Siberian success

This week's blog covers a 500-mile round trip in the middle of a storm for a day session with a guy I had never met face to face, on a lake that I had never heard of, and for a species I had never fished for, what could possibly go wrong!

 If I rewind several months to when fellow shark enthusiast made the offer to try and help get me a Sturgeon for my challenge, I am not sure either of us ever thought we would get it sorted. But with the weeks rapidly ebbing away, Carl and new bride Wendy managed to get a weekend that suited us all booked in our calendars. Carl and Wendy Aldridge have been extremely supportive through my whole charity challenge, they have their own reasons for helping support the Stroke Association.

The plan was to travel up to Carl and Wendy's place then we would travel on to the lake and spend the day trying for one of this Midlands Stillwater's Sturgeon. Why travel so far, I hear you ask, well Sturgeon although once permitted to reside in still waters are now considered as an illegal invader that should remain with the ornamental pond market. I am not going to argue the why's and wherefores' of CEFAS permissions but as far as I understand these non-native sturgeons cannot breed within a Stillwater environment, so the risk must be confined to escapees entering the river system. Anyway, there are virtually no waters that contain these fish and following a bit of research Carl had found the venue and spoken with the owner to find out if was achievable.

The weekend arrived and before I headed north I needed to sort a few things, first of which was to track down some appropriate wine that would appeal to both Carl and Wendy, fortunately I think I nailed it with a cheeky south African number that Sharkaholic Carl would love. Next it was prep the rigs and baits, I had decided to fish one rod carp style with pellets but incorporate a longer trace and hair to allow the Sturgeon to pick up the bait with its large underslung mouth. The same applied to rod two, this was a free running rig with a long trace and size 6 barbless hook to be baited with a large chunk of luncheon meat. Next, I prepared a tub full of PVA bags of pellets which were soaked in halibut oil, so for once I was super organised and would be ready to fish within minutes of arriving.

This Friday Storm Callum arrived, and this was probably the first proper storm of the autumn, I got soaked loading the car and literally had to dodge items hurled at me by the angry wind, a bit like a contestant in a game of Dodgeball. With the car loaded it was a case of waiting until 2am to depart, I had managed to grab an hour's shuteye during a particularly disappointing episode of the Chase. I said my goodbyes to Mrs D and set off in the teeth of the storm, the rain was outdriving me, and the violent gusts rocked the car from side to side making me question my sanity. Carl had asked earlier if I still wanted to make the trip with the conditions as rough as they were, but its fishing and a storm called Callum wasn't spoiling this party. Fortunately, as I approached Bristol the rain eased and consequently so did the spray, a quick coffee stop at good old Michael Wood services and I was re-energised for the final 100 miles.

I pulled up to Carl's place just as the clock struck 5am and credit to Carl he did exactly what he promised and made me a top-notch bacon sarnie for breakfast. With the breakfast consumed we loaded my car with Carls kit for the next part of our journey. The rain had again started, and storm Callum was hanging on like some needy teenager. We spent the next 40 minutes talking sharks although I didn't have a lot to add from this year's season, Carl however had made an impromptu visit to Looe courtesy of some SACGB members and had his best day ever with part of a 21 fish catch. The postcode Carl supplied took us to a housing estate and must I admit to feeling a little concerned, however after only another 15 minutes of trying, lanes, gates and paths we located the padlocked gate to the fishery.

Carl had been insistent we get to the fishery for 7am in time for opening and to ensure we get some good swims. We were at the gate for 7am and another car arrived with a few local anglers, Carl was out of the car and quizzing the guys for some info, once he explained what I was doing they were extremely forthcoming and were confident we would get one. The gate was opened, and we followed the two lads down to the lakes car park, to my horror the car park had at least a dozen cars already parked up and I could see several Bivvies dotted along the closest bank. I got out of the car and our new fishing buddies informed me that this was a quiet day, I am not used to seeing this many anglers but Carl was unfazed and keen to get started. He grabbed a few items and headed off to talk with the occupants of the nearest dome tent, I followed with my brolly and rucksack.

We walked around the lake until we came to a bay with two islands that was devoid of any anglers, this looked good to me and we dropped our kit and headed back for load number two. The miserable weather had kept the dawn from breaking and it was still quite dim, I set up the brolly and chucked everything underneath so at least we had some protection. The advice of the locals had been to fish luncheon meat in the margins over a bed of pellets, rod number one was done exactly like that and I lowered it carefully at the edge of a stand of rushes. The second rod was fished with a pellet covered in paste accompanied with a pva bag of pellet which was cast to the tip of my nearest island.

The traps were set and with the light improving I could now see the lake was a typical commercial although it lacked designated swims or platforms, it was fairly sparse and probably not many years old, the water was chocolate also typical of a water containing a head of Carp. Carl was fishing to my left and he had decided to fish rigs considerably more refined than mine, his thinking was that if the fish were a bit more finicky, wary or clued up the finer trace and hooks may get some action, it's always wise to try a few different things. We were now both set, and it was just a case of seeing if the gods of the fish deemed us worthy of some rewards. Then the right-hand rod in the margin signalled a bite, the indicator rose steadily and upon reaching the rod the bait runner ticked steadily as line disappeared from the spool. The bait had only been in the water for a few minutes and I wasn't expecting such a quick start, however the strike resulted in a good bend in the rod.

I glanced round for the net, but super keen Carl was already there net in hand, it was then that a large shark like tail broke through the surface and waved at us before disappearing into the murk again. Both of us looked at one another without saying a word as we now both knew what was on the other end, a nice big Sturgeon. It was a nervous few minutes before nets man Carl scooped our prize and instantly offered his outstretched hand, "you've only bloody done it" stated the man with the Cheshire cat grin. We shook hands, punched the air and then set about getting the photos done, I was in state of numbness, the journey, the weather had all been forgotten as I stared at the beautiful fish on the mat before me. I hadn't even had time to train Carl on my camera so to get the pictures he did shows just how careful he was in getting it right. The fish was a wonderful slate grey, armour plated dinosaur that really has got the traits of a shark, it's only the whisker covered head and suction mouth that differs.

*Above a superb Siberian Sturgeon*

This species was a Siberian Sturgeon and number 73 on the list, did this mean it was time to go home? I had missed a few bites on the pellets as I was still walking around like a zombie, lack of sleep combined with a sudden adrenalin rush will have that effect on you. Carl had told me I needed to try for the other species of Sturgeon in the lake the Diamond Sturgeon, that would be the icing on the cake. Then Carl was in and a spirited fish appeared to be the first Carp but as it rolled just out of range it was in fact a brightly marked Diamond Sturgeon, but one more dive caused the hook to pop out.

I was gutted for Carl, but he was still grinning about the one I had landed, it turned out Carl had been really worried that I may have not caught and as it was his suggestion he felt he would have failed me. I however would never see it like that and fish never read the script, so the fact Carl had treated me to the days fishing was a wonderful supportive gesture.

Carl was in again on his upgraded luncheon meat, he had added a bit of spice which certainly seemed to be working, this time yet another Diamond Sturgeon but I managed to net this one first time. Lovely looking fish the Diamond Sturgeon and I got a picture of the man himself. Now I wanted one of those, earlier I wasn't too worried as I had managed a Sturgeon and anything else was a bonus, but now seeing one in the flesh I had to try harder.

Fresh bait needed and instead of the pellet was now putting in a few handfuls of chopped meat. The effect was fairly rapid as yet again the indicator on the margin rod rose steadily, I raised the rod swiftly into another nice fish and like the first Carl netted the fish first time and once again it was a handshake moment as the bright white pattern of a nice Diamond Sturgeon reflected in the recently arrived sunshine.

That really was it now I was made up and Carl's Cheshire cat face was back on the scene, he even managed to start taking photos from different angles such was his confidence in the camera, species 74 in the bag. Now we were just fishing for fun and with sun out, the big grin out and a good job done we just enjoyed an afternoon catching whatever came along, and that meant several Carp and although not huge it made for fun.

Carl did however slip into his coarse fishing alter ego, the Bream Whisperer and he must have had a dozen of them even offering to give me some tips on how to catch them, I however was quite happy to let him intercept them before they reached me. We heard a lot of squarking and quacking as Donald Trump the Duck turned up in the swim, couldn't believe the duck had a proper trump hairstyle, funnily the duck didn't know how stupid it looked either.

 As can be the case I had one more chance at a Sturgeon as the luncheon meat was again taken and yet another Diamond Sturgeon seemed ready to give up when the hook pinged out, but I wasn't to disappointed and that was a great point to end on.

We packed up at 4pm, the lack of sleep was now weighing heavy on me and I still needed to drive back to Carls. We got back around 5pm and It was great to finally meet Wendy and son Kyle, they made me feel like one of the family. I was treated to a lovely Chinese meal that even a fussy person couldn't complain about and we raised a glass of wine to their recent wedding and a successful day for the challenge. I was so tired I crashed out on the couch after they all turned in and was in a deep sleep in seconds, I was however woke during the night by what I thought was Donald Trump Duck squarking again, and as I strained my eyes in the darkness towards the direction of the noise I was hit by a blast of pure flower extract. The blast was so pungent I felt it was going to lead to death by Pot Pourri and I coughed sharply and quickly recoiled to the safety of the duvet. Apart that incident I slept like a log, and upon waking in the morning I could see the vapour culprit was one of those fabreeze powered air fresheners, now I was wondering did it discharge on a timer or if it felt something smelled bad.

Anyway, I did raise the matter with my hosts and they confirmed it does just go off and perhaps they should have disarmed it. Well that was the trip over and I was meeting my daughter for lunch in Bristol so needed to load up and hit the road, the rain had started again and once again I got soaked loading the car. Carl and Wendy have been my Facebook friends for over a year now and despite Kyle being a little concerned I might turn out to be a serial killer, seeing as I was a guy off of Facebook, we all got on like a house on fire.

On Facebook they come across as a super warm-hearted couple, who go out of their way to make peoples day a little happier and I am so glad to say they are exactly what it says on the tin, Salt of the earth people. Thanks guys for all your support this year, your donation to the charity cause, and for playing a key part of putting two more species on the bank, both fish, being personal bests, look forward to catching up soon.

*The Bream Whisperer Carl with a Diamond Sturgeon*

# Chapter 48 Ancient Lakes, finicky takes & a few mistakes.

Early on in the year I travelled to the Midlands to try for a variety of species with the help of good friend Nick Rose, one of the species I caught on that weekend was not a target and although I got it I really didn't want to count it. The fish was a small Zander caught in a canal and the reason for my reluctance to include it within the challenge was that I had already been offered a trip to try for a personal best Zander for my charity challenge later in the year. So, although I had put the little Zander on the gallery I had always hoped to replace it with a proper Zander and even better a personal best. Before I knew it the day of the Zander trip had arrived, and good friend Steve McDonald had kindly offered me an all-expenses paid trip to Old Bury Hill Fisheries in Dorking in support of my challenge. I have really wanted to fish this 200-year-old estate lake ever since I first witnessed it on one of angling legend, John Wilsons programs, all these ancient lakes have an air of mystery and legend.

The other issue that really excited me was to try Zander fishing on a Stillwater, I have had them from canals and rivers but never a Stillwater so there was lots to look forward too. Steve Mac had, had his first and only Zander at this very lake 16 years previously so the trip would add a touch of nostalgia for him and give him a chance to reacquaint himself with the lakes Zs. The trip was only a day after I returned from the Midlands, and that great trip courtesy of Carl and Wendy, this meant I dropped one lot of tackle in the house and grabbed another set.

Steve Mac had planned to pick me up at 7.30am to get to the lake for midday and be fishing by 13.00, he had negotiated with the owner for us to stay on the fishery until 21.00. With the Zander being largely a nocturnal feeder, we would be fishing a prime time, we were staying over in a hotel and if it didn't go well on the first session we had scope to stay until lunchtime Tuesday for another attempt. The morning dawned with a thick mist and light drizzle, Steve picked me up on schedule and we started the long trip to Dorking, the mist followed us for the duration of the trip. We reached the venue and entered the drive, the long estate road was shrouded in thick woods and this combined with the low light, mist and drizzle it felt very like a Hammer Horror. This feeling was increased further as we past the huge old estate house and entered the fishery carpark, a cabin sat on the edge of the road housed a tackle shop and a chap called Dave.

We parked up and sidled over for a chat with Dave, he gave us a wealth of information on the lake, and what to use and where to use it, he even made us a cuppa while we sat and explained my challenge. Like so many times on this adventure I have been fortunate to meet so many wonderful people, and although some may be strangers they have gone out of their way to help me get the target, Dave was indeed such a character. With more information than we would ever need, rigs and baits sorted it was time to head off and get started. My first look at the old lake was just how I imagined, a truly ancient sheet of water that has given 200 years of angling history to several generations of anglers, I felt privileged to enjoy the same experience.

The lake was typical of an old estate lake, huge island, thick lush woods adorning the shorelines and the boathouse, although this was in the process of being converted to a dwelling for the owner. The rods and stands were assembled, and it was now I realised I hadn't picked up my rod pod or more importantly my rollover indicators, the indicators are perfect for these resistance shy fish. This vexed me considerably and I paced around scratching my head for a while until one of the remaining cells fired up and delivered a cunning plan, I used a couple of red foam balls that I use for popping up dead baits with a hook to hang on the line. This made a super sensitive bobbin and although when these were combined with the wonky storm poles they looked naff, but I knew it would work, a carp angler would have been pulling their hair out. Steve's set up was just as awkward and strangely sported the same type of bobbin, if only the fairy liquid bottle top was still available.

My left-hand rod was a free running rig with a wire trace and size 6 barbless hook baited with a Lamprey section, the Lamprey is an eel like fish that sucks blood from a host fish and is basically like a swimming black pudding, although greyer. It does contain large amounts of blood and that attracts any predatory fish, so the Zander should home in on it, the second rod was baited with Roach section. The Lamprey was cast left towards the tree line and the Roach straight out towards the middle of the bay, Steve done the same but with Smelt section and a small chunk of Sprat. It was now a case of sitting back and hoping we could nick a bonus fish before the evening witching hour arrived, the overcast skies did still give us half a chance.

My left-hand rod alarm screamed as the bobbin flew to the top and jammed against the rod, I struck but connected with thin air, the bait was re-cast and I sat back down. It was only 20 minutes later, and the same rod was beeping again as a steady climb of the bobbin indicated something had grabbed the bait. I struck to the right, away from the treeline and the rod immediately bent over and line started to pour from the spool as the fish powered towards the centre of the lake. The fish seemed too strong for a Zander and now changed direction back towards the snaggy sunken trees, I put as much pressure as I could, but not only did it not stop it, the fish took even more line. Eventually the fish won the day and made it to the trees, now I could feel the grating line and the branches furthest out were shaking indicating the fish was stuck.

Steve headed off into the overgrowth brandishing the net, after 5 minutes of jungle warfare he got to the water's edge, the fish however was still a long way out. Steve shouted through the darkness of the undergrowth " it's a good Zander", darn it, I sort of hoped it wasn't what I was after as the fish was surely lost. The fish sensing Steve had crawled within scooping range, splashed frantically on the surface sending waves from the trees to the bank where I stood, I was now thinking I am going take a swim for it. Then the fish popped the hook free and disappeared just as Steve reached the branch holding it in place, he shouted those sickening words " it's gone mate"! I immediately pulled for a break knowing the fish was gone and stood staring into the now calm waters surface rueing the fact I had swapped from my 3lb TC rods with 8010 bait runners to my 2lb TC rods with smaller bait runners.

I just know a more powerful rod could have stopped that fish. I had felt they would have been to OTT for the type of Zandering I was doing, anyway chalk that up to experience. I set up again but instead of wire went with 45lb quicksilver trace, mainly because I had no Dorking Dave traces left and I've always done fine with quicksilver, I did however cast further away from the tree line to give myself a better chance. During the course of the afternoon I had several takes on Roach dead baits all on the quicksilver traces, I only managed to connect with one fish that managed to spit the hook fairly quickly, Steve's rods on the wire trace remained still. It had got to about 5pm when one of Steve's rods signalled a steady take and he was hooked into a Zander, his first one for 16 years. With the photos done I was bemused as to why I had got so many aborted or dropped takes, the bobbin was really light, and I was on it before it reached the rod butt, I then thought about my Eel angling.

When I first started eeling I used light leads, less than an ounce and as the fish moved off with the bait the lighter leads used to move slightly changing the lines resistance, this was then very often dropped. Here I was in the same situation, fishing light leads for a resistance savvy fish, I changed my leads over to 2oz on run rings to allow easy passage of the line. The twilight had arrived, and it was now feeling like the witching hour, this would be the period the Zander should start to prowl. The next take I had was to a freshly cast bait and I had reduced the bait size to just a small Roach head, this was hooked through the mouth and up out of the nose.

I cast, set the bobbin, then sat in the chair as instantly the bobbin began to rise steadily having no time to relax I was instantly ready with the strike, which resulted in a strong fish pulling back. The fish also tried for the tree line, but I wasn't falling for that again and applied maximum pressure, this changed the fish's mind and direction. Now it headed over towards Steve's lines as if to teach me another lesson, fortunately it was by now up on the surface and no harm was done, Steve done a great job of netting the fish. With the fish unhooked I could have a decent look at this wonderfully adapted night predator, its eyes glowed bright red in headlight and the multiple fangs glistened as a warning to anyone getting to close. This lovely Zander was now my fourth personal best fish species, in the last 3 trips, highlighting what had been a wonderful couple of weeks fishing. It's a shame that night time photos are never as good as the daylight ones and where Zander are concerned they really don't do this beautiful species justice, it does highlight their super reflective eye shine.

We kept the fish upright in the net close to the margins, to let it recover fully, like a lot of predators they may seem tough, but the truth is they are fairly fragile and need to be handled carefully. Within minutes Steve's rod was away as another Zander struck out in the darkness, this was another good fish, but the barbless hook came free and the fish was gone. It was now 19.30 and there was a lot of activity out on the lake with Carp crashing in the back bay, Zander striking fry on the surface and the deep screech of a departing Heron, I love night fishing, it's when the intrusion of man recedes in favour of the creatures of the night.

Suddenly my right-hand rod was lit up as the bite alarm burst into life, the indicator climbed as the Zander took the bait, I stuck hard, only for the spool to whirl violently, I hadn't disconnected the bait runner before striking, text book bad angling! That cost me a Zander for sure and I reeled in the baitless hook, as Steve shook his head in disapproval, and rightly so I may add, I should have known better. I re-cast a new bait and as I set the bobbin the left-hand rod beeped causing me to jump, however as I was stood by the rod I wasn't going to miss this time and sure enough I had another fish on. This one was only a small one and we quickly netted it, I thought I would grab a quick picture but as Steve took the first picture my other rod went again, I instantly released the first fish but in the few seconds that took, I missed the second fish.

Despite fishing next to each other and using the same baits and virtually the same rigs, I was getting a lot more takes, the only difference was I had quicksilver and Steve had wire. We fished on to around 20.30 and I had packed up my alarms having just a rod on the platform when I noticed the spool spinning wildly, another take that I managed to miss. That was the first session done and dusted and I could certainly have done without the school boy errors, but we achieved what we set out to achieve, so happy days. That evening it was a celebratory Chinese meal and a few beers, that's two celebratory Chinese meals in a week I could get used to this, I guess it will be vegetables and salads for a few weeks now! With the Zander session yielding a result we decided to try another lake on the complex, Milton Lake, this smaller water had several nice Crucian Carp and even the possibility of a Ruffe.

We left the Dorking Travel Lodge at 6.30am stopping for a quick bacon baguette on route then it was off to the lakes. Dorking Dave didn't work on Tuesdays but fortunately another helpful chap was in the cabin to offer advice on the new lake, it appeared that the fishing was tricky, and we would need to scale down. We grabbed some maggots and headed off for the 15-minute walk over to Milton Lake, this more recent water looked like a perfect Crucian Carp water with thick lily beds dotted randomly across the whole lake. The early morning mist rose from the lakes surface similar to a recently run bath, a moorhen called out in its gurgling shriek, it was a lovely morning to be out by a lake. I set up next to a large bed of lily's and my rig was a fine float coupled with a 2lb hook to nylon with a size 18 hook, baited with a tiny cube of luncheon meat, Steve went similar but tried the maggots.

This lake also had some incumbent water birds, and none were more spectacular than the spectacular Kingfisher, although the bird didn't come over to us I managed to use the zoom to get a few shots of this most handsome of anglers. Another of this lakes inhabitants that I simply had to take a picture of, was an Egyptian Goose much better looking than the monotone Canadian honking grass gobbling goose. There were many of these Geese at the complex and to me somewhat like the Coot there is a large degree of novelty, even more amazing was the flock of Green Parrots that flew over us, didn't manage to get a photo of them though. I had been steadily feeding the swim micro pellet, chopped meat and corn and finally tiny pin bubbles started to rise close to the float, any bite now would need to be taken seriously.

Then the float lifted flat and slid slowly away, I struck and felt the fish for an all to brief second, then it was gone, the only evidence a cloud of slowly rising silt and a shaking lily leaf. An hour then elapsed, and I felt I had missed the opportunity, Steve however was getting a Perch a cast and I thought it was time to try a few maggots. As soon as the maggots reached the lake bed they were gobbled up by the feisty Perch, still good fun when things had been so quiet and there was always the chance of a Daddy Ruffe. After catching several Perch, I caught a couple of Roach but still none of the species I was after, the lake was strangely quiet and with the sun out it had become quite hot. The great thing about being at the water's edge is there's always something to sit and watch and while sat there Dragonfly's would approach and hover perfectly still like a biological Apache Helicopter, I really wanted to capture that amazing sight but every reach for the camera sent them darting away. I did manage a few shots, but these were blurry until I altered the shutter speed, still couldn't get the shot I wanted though. The time reached midday and that was our cut off to ensure we cleared the M25 in plenty of time, so it was a quick pack up and hit the road. It had been a thoroughly enjoyable couple of days and I can't thank Steve McDonald enough, for his generous support and excellent company, we achieved the main objective, but the Crucian eluded me. So, to answer my friend Simon Ward's question from the last blog, see I do blank mate! Next weekend I am off to Scotland for our friend's wedding and unless there's Salmon on the menu I am not going to see any fish, time is running out now, so I need to try and squeeze a few more trips in somewhere

## Chapter 49 Release the Kraken!

Things are getting decidedly tougher on the species hunt now and the last week has been a series of highs and lows, culminating in the Shark Club presentation evening. Our return from a great weekend in Scotland was somewhat marred by the deterioration of our beloved pet Husky, Nooshstar, and within days the tough decision was made to let him go peacefully. Pets become so engrained within the family that after 14 years it really feels like a part of you has gone with them. With morale at an all-time low I struggled to think about going fishing and if it wasn't for a kind offer of skipper Andy Howell I probably wouldn't have bothered, Andy had offered a day on Anglo Dawn for Chris and I, to try and get me a Tub Gurnard. This was just the tonic I needed, especially as possibly the final Porbeagle trip of the season aboard Force 10 was to be scuppered by the weather on the Friday. The trip aboard Anglo Dawn was scheduled for the Thursday and being confined to the river Fal meant it was possible in all but the worst of conditions.

We were to be joined on the trip by friend John Locker and he was bringing along the son of some friends, young Tide Mills, the entertainment was of course to be supplied by old smiler himself, Andy the Christmas Grinch. The morning arrived and the Popemobile was soon outside the house engine throbbing, at 5.30am we headed off, the journey to Falmouth was a breeze and both Chris and I were looking forward to a day on the river. We all met at the marina gate for 07.30am and with the arrival of Tide we headed off to the boat, 20 minutes later we were on our first mark and fishing for a Tub Gurnard.

The sunrise was a cracker and it felt good to be on the water with the sea air once again filling my lungs, who cares how the day went it was just great to be there. John was in full mentor mode and was careful to explain every process to young Tide, this polite young man was a model pupil absorbing all he was told, with a keenness that is lacking in many of his age. The Gurnard failed to show and after an hour we moved off to try for Huss and Rays at a mark further down the river, with the anchor down the skipper put the kettle on and produced the chocolate chip cookies. Andy very often, kindly supplies biscuit's and it appears that the quality of the biscuit defines how fond of you he is, so if you get a Ginger Nut you know you may need to try harder. Through hard work and sucking up to him, I had managed to work my way up to double chocolate chip cookies, but I think the fact I drag Chris along has led to me being downgraded to simple choc chip cookies. We had decided to raise the game by bringing our own offering in the form of the Triple Chocolate Chip Cookie, surely the highest of tributes.

With the baits in the water for around 15 minutes the first signs of interest started to appear in the form of a dogfish to Tide, who was delighted with the little spotty, John then opened his account with one before I added a small Huss. The dogfish whisperer was strangely quiet and without his token dogfish I couldn't take the mickey about his doggie pheromones, normally the pied piper of the Rock Salmon world he must be losing his touch. Then, like a medieval Trebuchet Chris launched into a strike that if not for the soft rod would have flung the fish a mile inland, fortunately the blow was cushioned by the wibbly wobbly spinning rod and it was fish on.

Chris clearly feeling he was connected to something decent milked the fish for all it was worth, however the Fish Locker to his right skimmed in a Bull Huss while Chris battled on. It was only when the knotted shape of a dogfish popped up on the surface did Chris realise he had been duped by the sandpaper shark, even trying to shake it off before we noticed! So, with normal service resumed Chris could try for something other than a dogfish but with the tide slackening it wasn't to be and we tried a few more marks for Tub Gurnards, once again we were all shown how to do it by a youngster. Tide hooked a cracking Red Gurnard and, on the light, tackle it gave a good account of itself, the young angler dealt with it admirably and with a bit of coaching from John held the fish perfectly for some quick photos.

The final mark we were to try was quite a way up the river and I know from a previous trip the area produces, Dragonet, Couch's Bream and Bass so a productive little area. Chris had wanted his Wrasse fix, but it wasn't to be and like my desire for a Tub Gurnard it would need to wait for another day. Tide was soon into another fish and this time he got the fish he had come for, a Bass, he really had done well today and hopefully he will continue to fish now he has humbled a few old timers. Chris and John both caught Bass and I was starting to think I had no bait on when my ragworm bait was finally hit by a typical bass strike, and I too had a little schoolie. Chris was now on fire and landed a nice little Dab, but my latest tentative bite resulted in a personal best Starfish, amazing creatures if not a little lacking in the fight department.

Then the strangest thing happened and if I ever wanted to swap rods with Chris it was now, as I hooked a Ballan Wrasse and he hooked a Tub Gurnard, fishing can be so cruel sometimes! That was the end of our trip on the river courtesy of Andy but wait, it wasn't over yet, we had booked up on the evening squid trip aboard Anglo and it was just a case of changing the rigs to the squid lures. We dropped John and Tide off at the marina and welcomed the new bunch of anglers hoping to tangle with the cephalopod's.

We pushed out of the river to try various squid marks, the squid had been fairly sparse off Falmouth this season, but they should appear at some point, why not tonight. As we suspected, the going was tough, but Chris managed to get his wrasse fix with a nice female Cuckoo falling to a baited jig, an Octopus also made an appearance to one of the other guys, think that made his night. Andy pushed out a bit further to an anchored tanker in the bay and we drifted a reef now in darkness, the perfect time for the squid to attack.

Then at last a squid was landed, from the front of the boat, this inspired us to try working the jigs harder, the ground was extremely snaggy and it was tempting to keep the jig high above the rock but that's not where the squid were. I bounced my twin jig rig right amongst the reef and the bravery was rewarded as a squid struck, the pulsing of the rod tip signalled the unique fight of a squid. carefully I drew the squid towards the boat and the waiting net. It was no Kraken but welcome nevertheless and Chris took a few pictures before hooking a squid of his own, unfortunately it escaped on the way up.

Andy took the boat round for a couple more drifts and on the last drift over the same section of reef I hooked a much better squid, this one actually took line on its initial strike. Once again, all too aware of how soft the squids hold can be I retrieved the squid steadily stopping only to submit to the creature's powerful surges, the bright shape of a big squid appeared on the surface. Now another unusual event took place, Andy Howell a skipper of great experience managed to knock the squid clean off the jig with the net, he literally released the Kraken, I tried the, that was my children's meal sob story, but he remained largely unemotional. It did however prove he was indeed human and also gave me ammunition for use on another day, so not all was lost. That was it for the evening squid trip and the squid just haven't arrived in numbers yet but when they do I will try for another monster.

Saturday night was the Shark Angling Club of Great Britain's annual presentation and meal, it's always a great evening and one I can share with Mrs D. We had booked into the Jolly Sailor for the night and as I was also booked with them for next year's festival I was keen to check the pub out. As soon as we arrived Zoe & Garry were perfect hosts and despite busy organising the evenings Halloween party they still showed us all we needed to know. I am a great lover of interesting stuff and boy this pub is interesting, firstly this is one of the country's oldest pubs opening its doors in the 1500's, I just can't imagine how many pints have been served during that time. Also, the main beam above the bar was taken from a captured French ship in the battle of Trafalgar, no wonder the place is haunted!!

Our room was incredible and just as you would imagine a member of the Blackadder dynasty would have, the first four poster we have ever encountered, very salubrious. With the room checked out and in, we made our way to the Portbyan for an evening of good food and company, celebrating our fellow members great achievements. Our table consisted of great friends Pete & Helen Davis one side and Libby & Brian Copeland the other, great company as always.

I did actually manage to have a quick chat with angling legend Andy Griffith, a real inspiration to so many anglers myself included, but incredibly nice with it, can't wait to see his next achievement. The meal as always was fantastic and professionally served by the staff at the Portbyan Hotel, John Mac once again organised a wonderful event.

There were a few real poignant moments during the presentation, none more so than Dave Stone emotionally explaining his granddaughter's remembrance award, the Iris trophy. I had to grab a shot of Billy Whistance collecting the new Carl Aldridge trophy on behalf of Martin Shipp, as I knew Carl couldn't make it and it was a great thing for him to have donated. Of course, Andy Griffith couldn't have gone without recognition for his mind boggling 5 Threshers and catching the big four, Thresher, Porbeagle, Blue and Mako from the U.K. He was awarded the IGFA Certificate and the Mako Tapestry by John Mac, in a word Legend! No silverware to our table, but with an agreement to try harder next year it certainly cannot get any worse, can it?

Before we knew it, the evening was over, and we retired to our haunted house (pub) still in the throes of the Halloween party, with horror classics booming out like, The monster mash and Oops up side your head! I planned to get up at 6am to have a quick fish in the harbour, maybe the 15 spined stickleback was still there. So, with the early start I didn't need any spooks, ghouls or even a sleep walking Mrs D haunting me through the night, happily for both of us, nothing went bump in the night. The alarm went off at 6am and I really struggled to leave the comfortable four poster bed, it was just so dam high, my little legs just didn't touch the ground. Eventually I managed a controlled fall and the cool air rushing into my face as I plummeted to the floor helped to wake me up, fortunately my airbags are permanently deployed, and the landing was soft. I then set about getting dressed as noisily as possible in the hope Mrs D would wake up and feel implored to join me on this chilly morning sortie, it did indeed wake her but only in so much as she was able to say bye, have fun.

That was it I was out the door and alongside the harbour wall in under a minute, the sun was rising slowly and in the famous words of Debbie Harry the Tide is high. I decided to use a Sabiki rig baited with Thursday's ragworm which were more like a bunch of brown jelly, however they would have to suffice, especially as I was up now. The crabs were rampant this morning and were happy to climb the rig to extract the brown goo from the hook, eventually my persistence paid off and the rod tip trembled sharply as a Blenny tucked into breakfast.

Despite my best efforts I couldn't get the elusive extra species and it was pretty dam chilly stood by the river, so I headed back for my full English breakfast. The breakfast was just as good as I hoped, and landlords Zoe and Garry run an excellent B&B that we will be returning too next year. So that's that for this blog, sad times, fun times and inspirational times isn't that what life is made up of and as long as good times can out way the sad / bad times then we can soldier on. So, I remain on 74 species and next weekend I am off chasing a couple of bucket list fish that will take me halfway round the world, but if I get them it will all be worth it, I will of course put a Blog upon my return if and when that is!

# Chapter 50 Red Sky at night Amazonian delight!

It's been a while since I created a blog and this one won't even count towards my species total as it refers to a foreign expedition, but I still managed to promote the Stroke Association and my challenge. A few of my friends know how much I have been wanting to catch an Amazonian Red Tail Catfish, a species on my bucket list that I was beginning to doubt I would ever get an opportunity to fish for. This species of voracious catfish naturally resides deep in the rivers of south America and as the name suggests frequents the mighty Amazon, to explain the fish's credentials it eats Piranha, say no more. I am a huge fan of catfish and to me this is the most beautiful of the many sub species, its banana coloured flanks, speckled head only superseded by the incredible red tail. With the fish making its home deep in the jungle rivers of some of the most dangerous areas of South America I knew I couldn't put the time, money and physical effort to realise my dream. Fortunately, there was another option as the species had been introduced into a few still waters in Thailand where it had thrived in the tropical climate. This created another problem, Mrs D wouldn't give me her blessing for this one, I think she feared I might be pounced on by the numerous angling lady boys. So, every year I would ask can I go to Thailand? and every time the answer was the same, No, stop asking! I have fished a lot of the world and been on many fishing holidays with my wife's blessing and this was the only one she has ever put her foot down too. The problem with having a passion to achieve something it never goes away and on the contrary it festers, changing from a dream to an obsession, as was the case with the Red Tail Catfish, and I even started painting them.

Then while out boat fishing with Pete Gregory I happened to mention my predicament, I knew Pete fished in Thailand quite a bit and he might have some advice. Sure, enough he told me to have a look at Gillham's Fishery in Southern Thailand as he had been going there for several years with his wife, the resort was perfect for partners. I hadn't even considered taking Mrs D, knowing that sitting in a swamp while I spent days looking longingly at my rods would drive her insane, but maybe this resort was the answer. When I checked out the website I knew straight away this was the perfect solution, luxury bungalow's set in landscaped gardens, Spa, pool, a restaurant serving English and Thai cuisine. The fishing was the stuff of dreams with a collection of some of the worlds most wanted monster fish from all corners of the world, Mekong Catfish, Arapaima, Sting ray, Alligator Gar and of course Amazonian Red Tails.

Once I showed Mrs D the answer was a resounding yes, not willing to give her time to change her mind I booked up straight away. Due to our circumstance with our son we were only able to spare a week away in total and with the travelling it meant that I would only have a maximum of 4 days fishing, hopefully enough time to get my Red tail. The year flew by mainly due to my challenge taking up so much of my time and before I knew it November had arrived, and it was time to pack for the trip. I had managed to get info from Pete and Glen Patterson as they had both caught Red tails before and both concurred that Luncheon meat, or Pepperami fished in the margins was the way to go. I packed 5 tins of meat, 15 packs of Pepperami and my trusty travel rod, complete with tackle.

I hoped that if I managed my target I could try for a Snake Head or one of the stunning Julian's Carp. Friday morning dawned cold and as we loaded the car Jack frost had created a little gift in the form of some frozen tropical style leaves across the windscreen. The journey up to Heathrow should have been 3 hrs but with road works, accidents etc it ended up being closer to five and boy did I enjoy that pint of cider in the airport hotel that evening, holiday started!

The next day was the start of the big journey and neither Mrs D or I are good flyers but if you have to fly, then the Airbus 380 is the craft to do it with, it's a monster and I wonder just how big commercial airplanes will get. Once on board I could quickly see why Singapore Airlines are so highly rated, amazing media equipment built in to the seats with top movies, hundreds of albums, games etc. The seats are comfortable, but they need to be if you're sitting on them for 14hrs, the service is sublime from the start to the finish. I did get a telling off from Mrs D when I tried to take a quick snap of the drinks being served, not sure what was wrong with that, not my fault the lady holding them was stunning.

I've always hated aeroplane food, normally ending up with everyone's plastic cheese and crackers as my fussiness has made me reject everything else, however this flight we had a Prawn Cocktail for starters and Chicken Kiev for main. Weirdly when the pudding arrived it was nice to get a little taste of home as despite being on a Singapore Airlines flight bound for Thailand our ice cream came from the Salcombe Dairy, and a quality ice cream it was too.

This was fast becoming the best flight I've ever been on and being handed a cold Tiger beer by a beautiful attendant, while watching Avengers Infinity War and on my way to fish in Thailand was like a dream. The beauty of the blog is I can now skip the 21 hrs of travelling it took to reach the resort and we finally pulled up on the Sunday afternoon having departed home mid-day on the Friday. We were met by host Sean at the resort bar where first job was to have a nice cold Tiger Beer, we were given the low down on the lake, fishing and accommodation but by now were literally walking round like zombies. Head guide Chris popped in to have a chat at our lakeside bungalow, asking me the most important question, what are your target species?

That was a simple one to answer, Red Tail Catfish please! Chris explained the lake had been hard fishing the previous week and he would put me in a swim where the margins could produce the catfish I was after. The swim was probably the furthest from the accommodation, but I really didn't care if this is where I needed to be, Chris had told me to get to the swim at 7am Monday where a guide would meet me to run through the methods. We were both really tired but as we had just booked a half day Elephant experience for us to go on, reducing the fishing days even more I really wanted to have an hours fishing. The elephant trip was on Mrs Ds bucket list and would give her the chance to meet Elephants up close and personal, it was great for her to do something for herself during this trip. Sean had kindly said I could go on the top lake to wet a line and guide Chris dropped off a light rod setup at the bungalow, so I could achieve this.

We chucked the clothes quickly in the wardrobe and set off around the main lake, truly stunned by the incredible views of the resort. The calm blue green waters of the lake were constantly rocked by leviathan's erupting on the surface, sending waves in all directions. Huge rock monoliths reared from the earth surface like giant dragon's teeth, higher than skyscrapers and partially covered in lush jungle growth. The whole scene resembled the first view of Skull Island in the film King Kong and who knows what creatures resided outside the complex perimeter fence. We finally found the top lake, and once again despite our heavy eyes, we could not fail to admire the stunning vista, it was more stunning than I could have imagined and even Mrs D was impressed.

We found ourselves one of the little fishing huts that contained a couple of chairs, unhooking mat and landing net, time was running out as darkness fell at 6pm and it was already 5pm. I didn't really know what to target and the rod was setup with an inline lead and hair rig trace, I baited with a couple of 14mm meaty wafters I had brought along. I dropped this in the margin and sprinkled a handful of the pellets supplied as part of the trip. The rod tip was soon bouncing, as fish moved into the baited area and soon the bait runner was whirring violently as some unknown creature tore off. I struck but the fish was gone, the baits were fairly mangled, and a quick refresh was in order, this was once again placed in the same spot. As I walked the rod back to our hut the rod was nearly pulled from my hands, a fish had instantly grabbed the bait and was now hooked and running.

The fish was incredibly powerful and stripped line in run after run, the best thing was that I had no idea what species it was as the lake contained 30 different types. Eventually the constant pressure won the day and my first ever Julian's Carp rolled ready for netting, this species are simply stunning with their golden flanks, vivid stripes and bright red eye, probably a bit like our eyes at that time. I was a bit shocked at the capture of such a fish that quickly and decided with only 30 minutes of daylight left to try for a Red Tail or other type of Catfish, by using double Pepperami baits. This was in the water for only 10 minutes when the rod was nearly pulled into the water by a savage take, I struck, and the line continued departing the reel as a strong fish made off across the lake. I managed to slow the fish down and pump it back towards the margin at my feet but despite the fish sulking for a few seconds only a rod length out I couldn't get it to the surface.

This was clearly a decent fish and the fight was clearly that of a catfish and most likely my target fish, it was then the fish decided it was leaving and tore off on a run I simply could not stop, the fish crossed the whole lake in one powerful run eventually reaching a snag. I tried every angle and applied pressure, slack line but eventually the line parted and the fish escaped, my first encounter with a Red Tail, I was sure. The darkness was nearly upon us and we still needed to have our dinner, so I called it a night, satisfied with that wonderful personal best Julian's. We got back to the room, unpacked properly then dressed for dinner, the restaurant was lovely with its lakeside position and we were soon tucking into some wonderfully fresh cooked Thai food and cold beers.

We certainly slept well and the 6am alarm soon came round, I jumped out of bed like a child at Christmas, desperate to get to my chosen swim, my wonderful wife also got up and joined me like she did on every day of this holiday, there were many wives staying but only one out with their husband at 6.30am, what a legend. We walked around the lake exchanging pleasantries with all the other anglers setting up for the day ahead, huge Siamese Carp crashed on the surface spoiling the serenity of the morning. We reached our little hut and Mrs D approved, no mud, no swamp but instead a concrete floor, ceiling fan and charging point, hard to believe the jungle was just a hundred meters away. An English guide appeared at our hut, to explain everything and despite my determination to fish for Red tails set one of my two rods up for carp. This rod was baited with a complex boilie on a hair rig and I cast it 50 yards to an area suggested by the guide, the second rod was set up with half a tin of luncheon meat on a coil rig that was dropped into the margins. The guide explained the fishing had been slow and by fishing one rod for Carp and one for Catfish I had more chance of action, I understood the logic, but I really wasn't interested in the Carp. There were around 15 anglers on the lake, but the swims are designed to keep everyone separate and with a total of 26 swims on the lake there were options to move. We were then visited by the Iceman and not the pilot from Top Gun but the little Thai man with a barrow full of ice, he fills a cool bucket in your hut for your water bottles and puts more ice in your bait box. With temperature's reaching 31 degrees this ice was very welcome, I did think that by the time he got all the way round the last anglers may only have cold water for their buckets.

Next visitor was the breakfast man on his insulated scooter, he appeared every day at 8.30am to take your orders then delivered them around 9.00am, everything from a full English to omelettes. We couldn't believe how well thought out the whole thing was, and it really was fishing in luxury, the coffees arrived in thermal mugs and even ice-creams were delivered still frozen. The other important thing you are supplied is a whistle, this you must keep around your neck and upon hooking a fish you are required to blow the whistle to alert your guide. Each guide covers three anglers and all fish on this lake must remain in the water, the guides are required to enter the water to land the fish in the specially designed nets. Anglers wanting a photo of their fish must also get into the lake, these are large valuable fish and their care is paramount, they are also medically treated by the guides should they have any wounds or sores.

My left-hand rod on the boilie indicated a bite as the bite alarm wailed, before I had a chance to blow my whistle Thai guide Dac appeared from nowhere, Mrs D told me he jumped out of a tree. I was playing my first fish on the main lake and once again I had no idea what it was, short powerful runs didn't give me any clues but guide Dac made biting gestures with his hands and stated Pacu. He then slipped into the water with the net and walked towards the fish nearly up to his neck at one point, these guides are top notch and the fish was straight in the net, sure enough it was indeed a Pacu. The Pacu is a member of the Piranha family although it is a vegetarian feeder, it does however possess a set of teeth similar to that of a human and an incredible bite force.

The species even made it on an episode of River Monsters where they were found to be the culprits of a spate of attacks on people washing in the waters of Papa New Guinea. I didn't realise just how big the Pacu got or how hard they fought assuming they would be like a common bream, a pretty impressive fish and one to keep your fingers clear of. I decided as the carp rod was now in, I would change it to another catfish rod and baited it up with meat then lowered it into the left hand marginal weeds. The guide Dac asked me why no boilie? I told him I want to catch a Red Tail and that was the most important fish, he laughed and gestured towards the sun, clearly pointing out it was too bright for the predatory catfish. The rods remained silent for hour after hour and I found myself taking selfies with Mrs D and even doing a crossword with her.

Then a whistle sounded from a swim on the far side virtually opposite me, the angler was clearly into a big fish and I watched in awe as his line passed me by, heading off down the lake, the word went out Mekong! This is not what you want to hear if you're not attached to it, the mighty Mekong Catfish can fight for many hours and travels with impunity from one end of the lake to the other and there's nothing an angler can do about it. The guide came over and told me I needed to reel in, not sure it would have caught my lines as they were only 3 feet from the bank, but I still wouldn't want to cost someone their fish of a lifetime. This particular fish was spotted on the surface after the first hour and the guides reported it was foul hooked and swam out and unhooked it, that was a tough one for the angler.

With the all clear given the baits could be re-positioned and once again I was fishing just as the lunch man arrived on his scooter, turns out he was the same guy as the breakfast man, Chicken, chips and cold tiger beers were ordered and 40 minutes later that's exactly what arrived, top service. The whole area is rich in wildlife and I love seeing new critters of all genus, the first was a type of lizard, the Many Lined Sun Skink was a stunning bronze coloured reptile that appeared once the sun was up, they were not shy and actually came within a few feet of us, chasing insects.

The other critter that visited us on that first day were the nectar feeding birds, they were extremely fast but not quite Hummingbirds, I was determined to try and capture a picture but as if they knew you were pointing the camera they quickly shot off. I did manage a couple of blurry ones but to do them justice a tripod and fast shutter speed would have been better.

The fishing generally around the lake had been quiet with only a few whistles being heard throughout the day, I must admit to feeling a little nervous, fish are fish and are more than happy to spoil the party and with the lake out of sorts there was more than a chance I wouldn't get that fish I so coveted. The longer I sat watching the motionless rods the more doubt crept in, then one of the guides appeared and excitedly told me to come and see what the angler further up the bank had caught. As soon as I arrived in the swim I could see the bright red tail of a lovely catfish, it was a double-edged sword, lovely to see but it was caught out in the middle on a fruit boilie, typical!

I returned to my swim even more determined to get one and with the evening approaching I felt that the darkness may offer the best chance, it gets dark at just after 6pm and you can fish until 8pm so those 2hrs could be golden. It was starting to darken when Thai guide Dac arrived, he knew my desire for the Red Tail and set about improving my chances. He made me reel in both lines, he then set about baiting one with some fresh Luncheon meat the second rod was a Dac special, luncheon meat, Pepperami and a fish head cocktail. Then he jumped into the water and swam my baits along the margin actually disappearing under the floating water plants to place them in the best spots possible, what a legend. He climbed from the water and gestured to the left-hand rod, "Red Tail Catfish for sure" he stated, that's exactly what you want to hear, and now I was super confident. The witching hour had arrived and now this was the time I had waited all day for, Mrs D had gone to the restaurant and filled our thermal mugs with coffee for the evening, then she sat in the dark alongside me while a multitude of flying bugs fed on our exposed skin. The time hit 7pm and as if the fish was waiting for that exact time the Dac cocktail on the left-hand rod was taken and the alarm was squealing. I was on the rod in seconds and hit the fish that was on a mission and kept on running, nothing I could do even with the big Shimano and 6lb Cat Tamer rod, once the initial run stopped I was able to get the line back and although it had gone through the deepest of vegetation the fact it is floating meant I could keep the rod tip down and pump the fish back. The fish made a few more runs and I hadn't even noticed another Thai guide was climbing into the water, young trainee guide Bel, I forgot to blow the flipping whistle in all the excitement.

With Bel in the water and the net poised I felt confident the fish was going to be landed, I was internally praying for that Red Tail to appear on the surface and sure enough a rod length out in the darkness the unmistakable form of a Red Tail Catfish appeared, Bel stepped out to meet it and scooped my prize up first go. Yes! Yes! I couldn't contain my joy the fish I had dreamt about, painted and travelled halfway round the world for was sat safely in the net, Mrs D gave me a celebratory hug which was also one of relief. I stripped off and jumped into the warm dark water, I reached into the sunken net and lifted the fish like the trophy it was, it grunted loudly a trait common with the species. The fish was even more stunning in the flesh, the cream of the body adding to the red vibrancy of the tail, its head was like concrete and I wouldn't want to be rammed by one.

The guide gave me 35lb for an estimated weight but to be honest it was irrelevant, my trip was made although Mrs Ds comment of can we go home now, was maybe a tad premature. With the fish safely returned Bel was about to help me get the rods back out but for me I wanted to go and celebrate with my wife, we had a few ciders to sink and I didn't want to be greedy. The rods were wound in and we went back to change for dinner, I couldn't stop beaming, all anglers know the feeling when you have that fish that has haunted you for so long and you can finally move on. The next day was I ready to move on, was I hell I wanted another one and I wanted one in the daylight, what happened to all I need is one more, well I wasn't ready to give up on the Red Tails just yet.

So once again I defied the guides advice and fished catfish baits in the margins from 7.00am ignoring the chance to target the Siamese Carp, I planned to fish until lunchtime then go to the top lake for the afternoon to try for a Cat in the daytime, finally returning to the main lake for the evening session. The morning mist rose from the jungle and shrouded the hills giving the perfect atmosphere for something to happen, sure enough a whistle pierced the silence, followed by the words of doom, Mekong on! Fortunately, my margin fished rods were not considered a risk and they were able to remain in the water, the Mekong did venture up our end of the lake at least twice, but my lines remained intact.

The normal routine ensued with Iceman and Breakfast guy doing their stuff, the skinks visited but were strangely nervous and soon disappeared completely. The reason soon became apparent as a large Cloudy Monitor Lizard appeared in our swim, it climbed the tree overhanging the left margin and eventually he came towards us across the grass, incredible looking beasty. The monitor lizard was the highlight of the morning, plus the Mekong to the day angler which eventually he landed after 3 hours, not fun in that heat. We were also hit by a huge thunder storm and got a little taste of what a tropical storm can be like, the thunder, lightning and rain were all extreme and fortunately over quickly. It was time to head off to the top lake for a few hours and see if I couldn't winkle out a Red Tail in the daylight and luckily the rain had stopped, and the sun was once again shining.

As we approached the top lake I spotted a huge snake that turned and slithered into the thick vegetation around the lake, fortunately Mrs D had not seen it as I wouldn't get her to run another errand if she thought snakes like that were residing here. I later found out that Cobras are quite common and that a huge King Cobra once had to be removed, now that's a snake and a half. I set up the rod with a 14mm meaty boilie and dropped it in the margin, it didn't take long to get some interest and sure enough it tore off as a Julian's Carp once again took a liking to the smaller bait. These fish are awesome fighters but to be honest most of the fish seemed to be like that in Thailand. The carp was soon netted and Mrs D once again done a great job with the picture taking, she was fast becoming a valuable fishing asset.

I had been observing the Arowana hunting insects on the water's surface down on the bottom lake and now they were in front of me on the top lake, they are another of the Amazons oddities with their upturned jaw and small barbel on their nose. It was a fish I had decided I wanted to catch although I know they can be quite hard to specifically target, I had been told that they have a soft spot for Pepperami and that was to be the next plan. Hair rigged Pepperami was dropped into the margin and I sat back and waited for a bite, I spotted an approaching Arowana which did appear to sink down over the bait, a finicky bite followed before the rod lurched round. There on the surface was the fish I had been hoping for the Arowana, Mrs D sprang into action and netted the spirited fish just before it threw the hook.

With two species landed I set about getting myself a Red Tail, the rig was baited with a large chunk of Luncheon meat and dropped just off the marginal weeds. It was literally 5 minutes before the rod shot round and line poured from the reel, I struck as a powerful fish shot across the lake and after a powerful battle Mrs D managed to slide the net under the daytime Red Tail I really wanted. I decided for the final 30 minutes to chuck on a resort bait and try for something else and after missing a hat full of bites I finally connected with my first ever Tilapia, a pretty fish but with nasty spines not unlike the Black Bream. It was time to head back to the main lake for the evening session, especially as the next day was the elephant trip. The rigs were readied, and a new guide arrived to help position the baits for the evening, French guide Bud was very keen to make sure everything was correct rig wise, bait wise and location wise, we had half a tin of meat on the left rod and 3 sections of fish on the right-hand rod. Like Dac the previous night he swam the baits into position and explained that under the vegetation on the left-hand side was a patch of gravel that was the place to put the bait. Once again, I felt confident with good baits in perfect positions and like clockwork at 7pm the left-hand rod was once again screaming for attention, even better I got to blow the whistle, Bud appeared in seconds as I battled the fish in the darkness. He slipped into the water and done the honours with the netting, another beautiful Red Tail was in the net I was really starting to get the fish out of my system. This time however I decided to fish on until 8pm and the rod was once again positioned on the gravel patch with another half tin of luncheon meat, 20 minutes later and it was taken again.

This fish powered out to the centre of the lake and tried a multitude of dirty tricks before I finally won the battle, Dac went in to land the fish and the fish looked a lot bigger than my previous fish and at 45lb it was to be my best of the trip.

*Amazonian Red Tail Catfish, bucket list fish*

I did have a bit of a scare when I thought the whistle round my neck was some form of critter crawling up my chest, screaming like a child, briefly. That was that night over and tomorrow I would try for a few hours in the morning before heading off for the elephant trip and if we got back in time I would squeeze in a few hours in the evening. The next day was quiet on the lake and only 4 or 5 fish were landed before lunch I did get a few shots of the dragon flies that perched on the rods every day, amazing insects.

It was time for Mrs Ds adventure and after lunch in the restaurant we were picked up and taken to the elephant reserve, as we pulled into the park we were greeted by a couple of elephants approaching along the road. It was incredible to see these magnificent creatures up so close, they had no leads, ropes or chains but simply carried their driver / rider they also carried up to two people on specially designed saddles. We rode on one of the 40-year-old females who had a mind of her own stopping constantly to pull plants from the jungle, she was not encouraged to stop by the handler and it was a case of waiting until she was ready to continue. It was quite humorous when the elephant pulled a branch from the tree to use as a fly swat, this was constantly swatting the wife, something I have only dreamt of doing. With the ride over we were introduced to one of the junior members of the family an 8-year-old female who loved bathing in the river.

We got to spend some time with this amazing elephant and clearly this was the highlight of Mrs Ds trip, so we both achieved something special. I was impressed with how the elephants were respected by their handlers and the villagers that owned them, the whole excursion was well run, and nothing was pushy or hurried. We returned to the lake to hear it had been a quiet afternoon, so I hadn't missed anything, and I was still in time for the evening session, however this evening the lake was dead, and no bites were forthcoming. The next day was my last day of fishing and I decided to spend the day after the Siamese Carp, I had plenty of bait left so it was to be a big baiting day. The morning arrived, and I seemed to have Thai guide in training Bel with me all day, I didn't have a problem with that the young lad works hard. We baited the rigs with wafter baits, PVA bags loaded with crushed boilies and pellets, when I cast Bel would pepper the area with pellets. We kept this system going and Bel had rigs baited and bags prepared for quick changes. Finally, the carp started topping in my swim and I cast to the area and the bait was instantly taken, I was connected to a big Siamese Carp and line streamed away when the hook pulled. Bel indicated to me to re-rig and get another bait out which I did, and once again it was taken instantly, like before the carp tore off right and yet again the hook pulled. We checked the hook for sharpness and it was fine, extremely frustrating, even more so when they turned out to be my only takes of the day. We returned to our bungalow and I must admit to feeling a bit down as it would have been nice to end on a couple of fish, I did find it amusing that our German neighbours had saved their patio chairs with towels as if they would be nicked.

We had our evening meal and chatted with Sean about transfer times the next day, then Mrs D asked if it would be ok for me to have a couple of hours on the top lake before we left, he agreed no problem. She really was a star on this holiday, and her reaction to insect bites had left her with more bumps than a skateboard park, a real labour of love. The last day dawned and I had kept back a single bit of fish to try on the top lake maybe for a Snakehead or different type of catfish. Of course, this was in the water for only 5 minutes when it was taken but the fish shook the hook, I put on the remaining half a fish and placed it in the same spot, it went again. This time the fish was well hooked and powered off across the lake to the thick water vegetation, I clamped down on the spool, but the line still emptied eventually the fish stopped and everything was solid.

Mrs D went off to find a guide as I didn't want to leave a fish snagged up, she soon returned with French Bud who swam out to sort the problem. It turned out the fish had got behind the big pump spewing water into the lake and left the hook snagged while it escaped. It seems that I wasn't destined to land anymore fish and with only 30 minutes left before we had to go and check out I opted for the complex boilie with a few handfuls of bait over the top, fished in the margin. Bites were instant with the first fish being another Tilapia. The next fish was something new and led me a merry dance with its incredible turns of speed I finally netted it but had no idea what it was, I have since found out it is a Mad Barb or Sultan fish. I then spotted another fisherman high above the lakes, circling impressively a White Bellied Sea Eagle, what a great sight to finish with.

With the last 5 minutes approaching I hooked the final fish of the trip another Julian's carp although this one was a bit of a warrior and looked like its tail had been bitten. That was an exciting last 30 minutes and a great end to a truly incredible trip, it had always been a tall order to travel all that way for 4 days fishing, but the gamble had paid off, we had a great time and it was lovely to share it with my wonderful wife. The staff and owners of Gillham's were all fantastic and instrumental in making our trip so special, it truly is an angling paradise. The Red Tail Catfish I've spent so long hoping to catch, has finally been caught and it's time to move on to the next fish on my list. Thanks go to my mother in law Ann and daughter Phoebe as without your help this wouldn't have been possible, and to my wife who managed to remind me every day why I was so lucky to marry her. Thanks also Pete Gregory and Glen Patterson for the pre-trip Red Tail advice. I've been a zombie since I returned and slept for 12hrs straight it's also to darn cold to think about fishing but by the weekend I should be acclimatized.

## Chapter 51 The Lady of the stream

Despite having a few great trips recently, I haven't increased my species list for a month, if I had chosen to include my foreign species I would have hit 80 by now, but I seemed to be stuck on 74. It was always going to be tricky towards the end and now with the autumn really tightening its grip, several of my target fish have to be considered as missed opportunities. One of the species I really wanted to get this year was the Grayling affectionately known as the Lady of the Stream, a lover of fast water and shallow rivers. The Grayling in my home county of Devon are fairly sparse, and I had a few offers of help to catch one throughout the year, that for one reason or another never materialised. Having researched the species a number of times, including contacting the Grayling Society, who I might add didn't ever respond, I narrowed the likely spots down to a few waters in Somerset. The river I finally decided upon was the River Tone and the sections in particular being the Taunton Angling Association run beats. Like with all my plans they are constantly being re-jigged if I feel that another species offers a better opportunity and as the Grayling is a fish of the autumn it has been pushed back a number of times. On my recent Zander trip, mate Steve Mac and I discussed fishing the Tone to try and get a Grayling, Steve having fished there before, had landed several Grayling. We arranged a date in November and stuck to it, the concern was the river levels but as luck would have it they were just about perfect with a slight bit of colour and good flow. The day arrived, and Steve picked me up at 8am which gave us an hour to get to the tackle shop, Taunton Angling, for the day tickets and maggots.

The proprietor of this excellent local tackle shop was extremely helpful and took the time to explain the best swim and methods to get a Grayling. Fortunately, Steve knew his way around Taunton and to the river, it was only 10 minutes later, and we pulled up at the padlocked gate. The shop had given us the code but what they had failed to mention was that there were around 10 different padlocks on the gate, so I had my very own Crystal Maze challenge to undertake. Finally, we arrived next to the river and I was surprised to see just how small the river was at this point and how built up it was in the surrounding area, it still had its own type of beauty. We headed off to the swims recommended by the tackle shop and I plonked myself in the first swim under the weir, it really looked prime for the target species and I was excited to get started.

Steve was going to let me have the prime spot while he roved other swims targeting whatever came along, it's a great stretch of river for the mobile angler. Having not trotted rivers with stick floats I needed a quick lesson from Steve, he also lent me a few floats and explained the shotting pattern to get the bait down quickly. With all the info digested I started feeding the swim with a steady stream of maggots before doing the first trot down the swim. Straight away I could see that despite the narrowness the river in front of me had various speeds and depths, with the far side being the quickest water and my margin hardly moving. The first lesson I learned was that when the float entered the slack water it was in the realm of the Minnow and they would quickly grab the double maggot, enjoyable for the first 50 times then a tad annoying.

Steve had dropped in the next swim down and his first run through saw him connected to a feisty fish that looked good fun on the light tackle, of course it had to be the fish I was after, and he netted a stunning Grayling. I wound in and went to have a look, taking a few photos of the fish to remind me what they looked like. Now back in my swim and feeling positive that the Grayling were around I continued with the plan, trot the faster water and avoid the slack section. This was now starting to pay off and the next species I started picking up were Dace, another of the rivers smaller species, although somewhat better than the Minnows. The Chub would take the bait if the float reached the overgrown tree, and I was really starting to understand how the fish were all positioned in this little weir pool, just the Grayling to find. The Chub were really on the feed and although they started off around 8oz they were gradually getting bigger with fish approaching 2lb giving a great scrap on the light float rod, the mouth on a Chub is a real bucket.

I now started catching Roach amongst the Chub and it was really wonderful fishing as every run through the swim produced a fish of some type, unfortunately none of which was the fish I needed. With a few Gudgeon also thrown in I was already up to 5 species and all from a river only 20 feet across and 3 feet deep, I felt like that child angler I once was, and this was one of the most enjoyable days angling I had done for a long time. Sometimes the back to basics style of angling is all that's needed to remind you why you fell in love with the sport and what ignited that passion for angling.

Then the float dipped sharply in the Chub zone and a powerful fish shot off downstream, I had no idea what manner of beast it might be but, in the flow, and on light tackle it took a bit of time to get the fish back to the net. Finally, a nice big Brown Trout was safely scooped up, another surprise from this pool, what would be next I wondered. I had decided to stop feeding the swim with maggots as it may be that the other species were bullying their way to the bait and pushing the Grayling to one side. After a few more Dace the swim definitely went quieter until finally I hooked the fish I was after as a Grayling spun vigoursly just under the surface. This was no monster but instead a dainty example of the handsome species, but did it matter, certainly not, I was delighted and messaged Steve to come back up river to take a quick snap.

With the Grayling landed I could now try for a bigger one and surely, I now knew how to get them, of course this was fishing and what actually happened was I managed to lose two stick floats in a row in the trees. I tried for a while on the quivertip, but this seemed to pick up a plethora of Chub and lacked the refinement of the trotted float. I had managed to catch a heap of fish plus the species I was desperate to get so I thought I would call it a day, I packed up and went and watched Steve trotting the river with his closed face reel setup. I was intrigued to have a try having not used one before and this type of reel was perfect for this style of small river trotting, I may need to get one. Steve passed me the rod and I caught a couple of Chub using it, so I am converted for certain situations. Steve informed me he had also filled his boots with a variety of fish including some cracking big Roach further down river.

Strangely we only had the two Grayling all day, but the bailiff explained while checking our tickets that it was still a bit early for them, a few more frosts were needed. That was the end of the day and a massive thanks to Steve Mac for showing me the way regards river trotting and without whose advice I wouldn't have caught that Grayling. Also, thanks to Taunton Angling for the advice, we all need to support our small tackle shops they are gold dust to travelling anglers, helping with tickets and advice. I fear that the high street tackle shop is becoming extinct and it will be a sad day when they are all gone.

Saturday night Chris and I decided to start our Conger campaign off with a trip up to the Bristol Channel, plenty of eels coming out at the moment so it seemed a good option. First mistake was to follow Chris's satnav and he must have it stuck on sightseeing mode as it took us all over Somerset, over hills and valleys, past castles, gorges and speed cameras. The upshot was we took over 2hrs to get to the beach and another 30 minutes to hike to the spot, the only thing that made me feel better was the sight of Chris carrying a catering flask of coffee. We dropped our tackle and finally felt the full bitterness of the cutting easterly wind, last week I was sat in 31 degrees and now I was sat in a blast freezer. We got the gear sorted and I went straight for the big baits, whole Bluey on one rod and joey mackerel on the second, the conditions were tough as the wind created a large bow in the line that the huge boulders quickly rolled across. It quickly became a tackle graveyard and combined with the greedy crabs was a real struggle to fish, I reeled in for an hour and lay on the beach in the darkness looking up at the amazing natural planetarium.

I spotted 5 meteors', 4 Satellite's and one UFO, I also warned Chris that if you ever see a UFO while fishing, never, ever flash your torch at it! A group of 4 Canadian anglers had made that very mistake while camping in the wilds, a UFO flew across the lake they were fishing, and they flashed and waved their torches at it, 5 minutes later they were all abducted and given the stereotypical alien probing! Chris just laughed it off and stated, they probably just flashed the wrong car in a car park, I however won't be flashing UFOs, ever! With the tide now flooding and the wind increasing we toyed with the idea of heading home, instead we decided that fortune favours the brave and we would stick it out.

I had put out a whole cuttlefish that was finally getting some interest as the rod tip bounced and line slowly pulled from the reel clicking the ratchet loudly. I left it a few minutes to let it develop and when I finally reeled in, the bait was chewed badly, and the trace spun into a mess, a sign of a strap conger. Next action was when the sandpaper sharks turned up and we caught a few after they whittled down the baits, it's amazing what size bait they will chow down on. With the time 1am and us being down to our last leads we decided to finally give in, and as good as the previous river trip had been this trip was the polar opposite, absolute pants! Very often when I blank or as in this case almost blank, I can at least say, well it was nice just being there, but not last night. We do have to take the rough with the smooth but in scales of rough that was more like being dragged naked over coral, while systematically whipping yourself with a bunch of brambles.

Hopefully our next Conger trip will be a bit better and next Sunday it's a day out with the Happy Danglers chasing Cod, or in my case that dastardly spotted ray. Not sure what if any the next species will be, but hopefully a Flounder will be an option in the next few weeks.

## I'm Floundering in Mud & Blood!

This week I have mainly been messing around in mud, very often in the pursuit of fish you have to go through a bit of pain for that ultimate gain, this week was definitely that. The first trip was back up the Bristol channel to Burnham for a spot of Thornback Ray and Congering. Chris hadn't experienced the joys of the channel mud and during my last trip up there for Sole I had put out a Whiting bait that was quickly ripped from the hook. The night before what was to be an all-day trip I had prepared all my baits, bluey sections wrapped with squid, extra oil was added, and the tub re-froze, I then discovered I had broken the eye on one of my rods, darn these cheap eyes. I picked Chris up at 9.30am and we set off up the M5 to the destination, the wind was a brisk easterly, but the beach should be fairly sheltered. I parked up and we strolled down the steps for a quick look at the beach, Chris was concerned he could see no water, I pointed out the chocolate stream in-between the lighter brown slabs of mud.

The tide was still retreating, and high tide was predicted for 18.30, this would give us the final 2 hrs of the flood in darkness, perfect. With the bitterly cold wind and the plan to stand out in it all day, I had taken the gamble and put on my thermals, as I added the rest of the layers and my waders, I felt it had been a wise choice. We loaded ourselves up for the 15 minutes yomp to the water's edge, the first hundred yards was a pleasurable experience and we spoke of the strange beauty that radiates from Burnham light beach.

Then we hit the sludge and I learned that no two trips to the Bristol channel are the same, my last trip the mud had been firm and easy to walk on, this time each step was like escaping from a vice of silt. The sludge was not content with just gripping your legs, it also threw in deep undulations, that were filled with liquefied slime to try and make you slip over. This area of the beach was the domain of the sludge monster and I am sure many an unwary angler has been sucked down into the primordial ooze. We then reached the third zone, the sloppy, slippy mud, whereby only the top 2 inches were soft, this was like stinking brown ice that could quickly put you on your back. We reached the sea and were already plastered in muck, the bitter wind drying the goo, causing it to set on the rods and tackle. I know that after a good storm this beach is considerably more pleasant as the soft mud is washed away exposing the harder core, clearly, we hadn't had a storm for a while.

With the ground around being so treacherous everything you do has to be considered and done steadily, any rash or sudden movements would instantly result in a Burnham Beach Bomb. We got the rods baited and cast, finally able to relax and look forward to getting that first fish under our belts. Chris managed to break one of his tip eyes on the first cast, so we both now had broken rods, can't wait till Christmas when Santa brings me my Tronix! The sea was at this point just a river as the low tide was still 45 minutes away, and the rapidly ebbing water brought large clumps of weed with it, consequently the lines were quickly covered. I had brought in my rods for the third time to clear the clumps of weed and decided to wash the muck of my still intact bait at the water's edge.

I walked to the edge of the water where I had waded out safely only 10 minutes previously, took one step into the chocolate soup and slid straight down into the sea. The shock of going under the freezing water was instant and fortunately I had been wearing my fishing floatation vest that prevented me from staying down. I managed to dig my fingers into the mud on the seas edge and drag myself back onto the beach, water poured from every item of clothing and I struggled to get my breath in the cold clothes. Chris was now helping me up the beach and urging me to strip off, not for the first time I might add! My main concern however was my phone that had been in the pocket of my flotation vest, I retrieved it and placed it in the sun before removing all my top layers. My trousers were wet in places and I could feel water around my feet in the waders, but they had largely sealed me from water ingress.

My top clothing however was drenched, and I removed it all and rang it out, Chris kindly giving up his hoodie to give me at least one layer to put on. The sun was shining, and I necked a couple of steaming cups of coffee to get my internal temperature back on track. Chris stated right we better pack up and get you back home to dry out, " no way pedro" was my answer, " we came here to fish, and we will be staying to fish". Sometimes you really need to know when it's time to go as bloody mindedness is no good to you when you're in hospital with pneumonia. Anyway, I had made my decision and we fished onwards, it wasn't long after that Chris succumbed to the brown ice, doing a triple twist on the way to the ground. He was now looking like a potato in gravy but at least his hoody wasn't covered in mud!

Fortunately for the second trip in a row Chris had brought along his catering size flask of coffee and as the sun dropped so did the temperature making Catering Chris's flask choice a wise one. The tide was now pouring back into the area and the shallow gradient requires a constant retreat, walking backwards across the sludge fields was precarious to say the least. I did say to Chris that the vast sludge flats were quite stunning in the setting sun almost like a perfectly iced chocolate cake, he however was uninspired and in no hurry to return. We still hadn't had so much of a bite and with the baits coming back untouched it was just another frustration in a pile of frustrations, bloody fishing!

I had decided to put out two big perfect baits and leave them there while we retreated, these baits ended being out over 250 yards at the end of the tide. Despite our suffering, hard work and determination to stay to the bitter end, we never got so much as a line bite. With the darkness enveloping us I was suddenly aware of how dam cold I was, my feet had long since become numb, my body shivered uncontrollably, it was time to head home. We packed up concerned we may get in trouble for taking home this much beach with us, the mud caked everything, and fishing in mud is something I wouldn't be doing anytime soon. I decided to get KFC on the way home as despite the heater being on the volcanic setting I was feeling really cold and needed to shower, change and eat as quick as possible. We spun round the drive through in Exeter and were back onto the M5 within minutes, 5 minutes later we were stopped by a barrier of brake lights, an accident only a few hundred yards from our junction.

This lead to us sitting in the dark on the M5 for over 2 hours waiting for the road to clear and there are only so many of Chris's amusing anecdotes that are actually amusing. Eventually we got home cold, tired, hungry and vowing never to fish in mud again, or at least for a good while.

The next trip was scheduled to be back up the Bristol channel this time though from the safety of a boat, aboard Osprey alongside some of the Happy Danglers, the target Cod but for me a Spotted Ray. The forecast had looked iffy all week with strong east north easterly winds reaching 30mph, however Nick Smith sent the message to say it was on in the morning. I spent Saturday afternoon preparing baits, tying rigs and getting the kit ready for the morning. However late that evening Nick messaged to say the weather had taken a nose dive and the trip was off, frustrating but safety must always come first, I for one didn't want to find myself back in the Bristol Channel, it's too darn cold! So, plan B was needed, and I knew exactly what I wanted that to be, I just needed to convince Chris. We were going to have a go for Flounder up on the river Taw in Barnstaple, this was a species I needed for my challenge and I knew a few had been coming out. Chris was fine until I mentioned we may need to dig a bit of bait, this of course meant once again scrambling around in mud. Chris was keen to purchase some Ragworm rather than dig it and to that effect he was happy to drive to Summerlands tackle at Westward Ho! first. We bought £10 worth of King rag and made our way over to Pottington Industrial Estate, in Barnstaple where the river is close by.

Surprisingly there were several anglers fishing up and downstream and rather than scrawl down in the mud close to the river we set up on the concrete meaning a longer cast. The group to our left in the deepest of the mud were catching consistently and even the anglers to our right reeled in the odd fish, our rods remained painfully still, and this was becoming the norm on our trips. We were then approached by a couple of anglers who had planned to fish the area, but as it was busy they would move on, I recognised one from our trip aboard Bluefin earlier in the year. He enquired how my challenge was going and offered advice, which included the point that it might be worth using the smaller ragworm abundant in the river. They took Chris away with them, must be crazy, and helped gather us enough fresh ragworm for the rest of the trip, really great guys who's help we greatly appreciated, apologies for not remembering your name.

Chris returned like a child with a new toy clutching a writhing mass of gooey worms, he reeled in to re-bait only to find a flounder had hooked itself. This being Chris's first ever Flounder he was suitably excited and just as importantly it had ended our run of poor results. With that fish landed it created a bit of positivity in the area we were fishing, however the guys to the left were still getting several fish, eventually packing up having landed 10 flounder between the 5 of them. Despite the thick mud both Chris and I knew what we had to do, get over to that mark and wallow in the glory of hitting the target species. I grabbed my tackle and moved across to the new swim, the concrete slope at this point was covered in green slime and slippery as an eel, I left the box on the concrete and took the tripod and rods into the muck.

With everything set up in the new area and being so close to the water's edge we could see just how shallow the channel was becoming and there were surely only a few feet at the deepest point. I had decided to check my baits every 15 minutes, I was paranoid about the crabs steeling them or indeed casting the soft ragworm off the hook. I started reeling in the right-hand rod and I noticed it was kiting right and the rod tip knocked every now and then, sure enough the Flounder I needed splashed angrily on the surface.

That was it, species 76 and it was so nice to get a bit of reward for a quite a lot of effort over the last 3 trips. I recast the rod and hoped we could extradite a few more before calling it a day, after all we hadn't fallen in, or broke anything on this trip.

With the tide still ebbing away I wasn't too sure if the flounder would continue to feed but then as if to answer my query the rod tip bounced vigoursly as a flattie pounced on the worm bait. I lifted into the fish and the second flounder of the afternoon was landed, a quick photo, then it was released to fight another day. Chris had noticed a wading bird walk past his baits indicating he was actually fishing in less than 6 inches of water, a quick recast was in order. This paid off as Chris's rod bounced indicating some interest, he too brought in his second flounder, happy days. The sun was beginning to set, and the haunting warble of the Curlews echoed across the mud flats, it really did feel like autumn.

We decided to call it a night the darkness was upon us and the area was quite treacherous to move around on, especially the slime covered slope. Chris had managed to break his unbreakable flask and it was surely only a matter of time before one of us took that tumble. As I returned to retrieve my second rod from the tripod I slipped on the last bit of green concrete on the slope, falling straight onto the rocks below. I had put my hand out to cushion the impact and in doing so caught it on the rocks, I was covered in mud and so too were my hands however the blood still found its way through. At first, I thought I had broken my wrist as the pain was like getting freezing fingers hit with a hammer and my whole hand throbbed. Chris packed up my kit and then shouted gleefully from the water's edge, " I've got another one", if my hand wasn't so sore I might well have put that flounder somewhere Chris wouldn't have wanted a flat fish to be! I washed my bloody hand in the muddy water and knew I needed to get it cleaned properly sharpish, fortunately Chris had a first aid kit in the car and a few alcohol wipes had it nice and clean in no time. We packed up once again covered in mud and in my case tears, once again taking solace in the local KFC, a few lemony wet wipes cleared a bit more of the wound, I could now see I had taken the top off my nail also. What this has taught us over the last few trips, as you get older falling over hurts a dam sight more, fishing with a mate just might save your life, and always carry a first aid kit with a way of clearing a wound, otherwise infections are inevitable from dirty water. When I fell in the channel I was kept upright by my flotation vest but if I had failed to grasp the bank I would have been taken in the swift water out to sea.

Tragedy takes seconds to happen and a lifetime to get over, we all need to be careful out there and take nothing for granted. These last few trips have really taken it out of me and maybe I have been trying a bit too hard as the species options dwindle, 80 would have been great but I may have to settle for 76. If anyone has a suggestion for a species that is still catchable please let me know, Spotted Ray and Dragonet are still a possibility and so too is the Tub Gurnard.

## Chapter 53 Darn Dogfish Dampen December

It's the 1st of Jan I am writing the final blog summing up what has been the hardest month of the challenge, I fully intended to do this yesterday afternoon and post for New Year's Eve, but I could hardly talk let alone type. This wasn't due to the obligatory alcohol consumption expected on the eve of the new year but due to exhaustion and lack of sleep, the final push for a glorious ending had been extreme and fruitless.

Going into December I was feeling positive I had just received a wonderful donation from a group of Skittle players from Holsworthy, this is an annual event to win my father in-law Denzil's memorial trophy. Every year my mother in-law Ann chooses a charity to support and all proceeds from the event go to that cause, this year she chose my challenge. I was too ill to play but supported my wife Lisa who done pretty well but was ultimately bested by a professional none the less, a great evening and I was particularly impressed when my significant other explained my fish-based challenge to a crowd of people who didn't have a clue what she was talking about. I am so grateful to all concerned for their support not only this year but on every year to support the event, Dad would have been proud as punch. The total raised for my challenge was £160, taking me through the £1000 barrier, fantastic! With my monetary target exceeded for the second time I guess I could have bowed out on a high, after all 76 species is far more than I ever hoped for.

Unfortunately, the angler in me wanted me to catch just one more fish, just like the one more cast scenario we anglers are hardly ever satisfied, pushing for more fish, bigger fish, till our bodies finally divorce our mind and refuse to function. So, what did I have left that would still be a viable target, top of the list was the fish I has spent many, many trips across the year targeting, the Spotted Ray, I was told on numerous occasions it was the easiest of rays to catch. This had been far from the truth and with 6 attempts drawing a blank I was fast believing this fish to be merely a myth, however I set my sights firmly on this fish, being a lover of rays anyway. With several boat trips booked in December I knew I had several goes at the little nemesis and it would be nice to finish with a fish that vexed me so much this year. Well the Gods of the weather conspired, and a combination of strong winds and heavy rain kyboshed the first 2 boat trips and made fishing a truly miserable experience. Searching for something to fish for I tried out the lakes in the slim hope of getting a Crucian Carp, the wind and rain were relentless, the quiver tip wouldn't stop quivering the float couldn't float and I got drenched, result, blank!

Finally, a gap in the weather up on the north coast resulted in our trip out with the Happy Danglers being good to go, this was with Minehead skipper Steve Webber and was a great chance for a Spotted Ray. The day of the trip arrived, and it was an early morning sortie, but Chris and I had a plan B should I fail to catch the Ray from the boat, we would go straight to the beach and try for one. The trips with the Danglers up north are always filled with Banter, Bacon and Bullhuss, the sort of trip where the fishing is secondary.

We arrived at the harbour as per the scheduled departure time and everything looked perfect, the weather was settled, check, the guys were all at the harbour, check, we had plenty of bait, check, the boat was sat ready to go, check, the sea was lapping gently at the steps, wait a minute where was the darn water! Fortunately, the tides are swift up on the channel and after 30 minutes the water was deep enough for Steve to bring Osprey over to the disembarkation zone, we were off chasing the legendary Spotted Ray for me and Cod for everyone else. Chief Dangler planner, Nick Smith was in fine form and when you add Paul Lorrimore into the mix it makes for a laugh a minute, Nick even managed to kick his recent chunder habit.

With rigs tied, baits banded and hopes high the anchor was dropped, this was only a short half day trip, so we had to make the most of every minute. It didn't take long for the first sandpaper shark to appear and like a bad case of Delhi belly, everyone suffered their constant intrusion, a waste of bait and time. I did manage to catch a Whiting that was quickly returned to the seabed on my second rod to find me a monster, it was out for minutes before a Conger of around 15lbs took a shine to it. The Whiting went on to catch me another Conger before its final journey ended in the belly of Dogfish of equivalent size, such was their determination on this trip. Chris then hooked into some sort of behemoth which not only showed it was not coming up without a fight, but it wasn't actually coming to the surface full stop, the hook came free. Nick's son in-law Jordan was top rod landing a good Huss and a Conger topping 20lb but generally the fishing was tough and before we knew it we were heading in.

Chris and I were straight off the boat and swapping the gear over at the car, we got some tips from Nick, Paul and Mikey Webber before heading down the beach. The beach at Minehead is strewn with ankle breaking boulders and having already suffered a few painful falls this year I clambered carefully and soon reached the water's edge. The sea was retreating, and we planned to fish the dropping tide until low water at 6pm, this would lead to regular re-casts to ensure we were in enough water.

The sky was becoming angry and soon we were hit by heavy rain and a sharp cold wind, the early start was taking its toll as I now felt tired and cold. A rainbow appeared high in the sky and just maybe there was to be a fish scaled pot of gold at the end of it, and yes there was in the shape of a plethora of Dogfish, they must have followed us back. We battled through the hordes of doggies in the hope that a rogue Spotted Ray may beat them to the bait, it wasn't to be and as darkness fell we trudged dejected back to the car for the long journey home. I really felt it was a chance missed and every trip seems like a giant game of Jenga with another block removed and the tower close to falling. Frustrated by my depleting opportunities I booked a guided session with Minehead shore guide Craig Butler of S.S Angling in the hope he could point me in the direction of a Spotted Ray, like Jansen Teakle's excellent Gambling Angler guiding service, Craig also knows his area and techniques. A shore guide maybe frowned upon by some I cannot recommend them enough, a couple of sessions with these guys can give you the confidence to go out and catch fish safely, while using the best of methods.

I arrived at my second home Minehead Harbour as the sun was rising on what was a splendid morning, the meeting place was outside the tackle shop Craig runs. Unlike Debbie Harrys famous lyrics the tide was low, and we would be fishing from low tide up, before long Craig arrived, and we yomped off to the mark Craig recommended. Strangely this was yards from where Chris and I had our attempt recently but under Craig's tutorage I must admit to feeling a little more confident. We discussed methods, baits and tides that favour the species and Craig went on to tell me they were one of his favourite Ray species and despite their small stature they punch well above their weight.

I learned a great deal in a short time and like Jansen had given me the tools to target Thornback Rays, Craig had left me more confident in targeting the Spotted Ray. I caught several dogfish on our session and despite being at the right spot, with the right methods and bait the little Ray didn't show. Craig had to make tracks to his sons Christmas nativity but set me up on a highwater mark before he left. We made our way back across the rocks and just before I made it to the safety of the grass and during Craig's anecdote about an angler who slipped and couldn't get back up due to his huge rucksack, I once again slipped and fell to the ground this time landing on my wrist and bending my fingers back. I am sure Craig was relieved he had got me to sign the insurance waiver, but it was my pride that was hurt more than my throbbing hand. Craig made sure I was okay and got me set up on a much safer mark before bidding me farewell.

Once again, I stuck it out to the death, fishing on into the night until the high tide, the rain had become torrential and I gave my new waterproofs a proper work out, the prize for my efforts 2 dogfish and a Whiting. This month was harder than I could have imagined and the thought of December being the only month that I didn't add a species was fast becoming a reality. The next trip was to be a real Christmas social aboard Anglo Dawn with skipper Andy Howell, Chris, I and mate Steve McDonald were all determined to make this a fun day out. Despite the social side of the trip Andy had used his contacts to find a Spotted Ray mark, thus putting me back in with a chance. Once again, the weather spoiled the party and strong easterlies scuppered this Christmas eve party, Chris and I headed over to the lakes for some crusting Carp consolation. I have managed to get the Carp to take floating breadcrust every month of the year and hopefully Christmas eve would be no exception. Sure, enough the Carp obliged, and we managed to get a few fish to brighten our spirits, it was nice to get something other than a darn Dogfish, as it was fast becoming Dogfish December.

When I got home I managed to grab an individual space aboard Mike Webbers Teddie Boy, again from Minehead and on boxing day, I was out on a planned trip with Mikey on the 29th December, but a bonus trip could be just the tonic. The trip was scheduled to leave at 10.30am and get in around 19.00, my plan was once again to fish the night on the beach should I fail to get the Ray again, only 6 days left so I needed to pull out all the stops. I left home boxing day at 8.30 and the morning was still and warm very unlike December of late.

I pulled up outside the pub near the harbour securing one of the much-coveted free spaces, today was going to be a good one, this was my first trip with Mikey having had previous trips cancelled by the weather. I have heard good things about Mike and as Steve Webbers son he would have certainly been raised with the sea in his blood, at 21 he is another of the West country's next generation of skippers, like Lewis Hodder, Kieren Faisey and Looe's two Dan's are the future that will keep our sport alive. When I got to the boat despite being early I found I was still the last there and I quickly climbed aboard and bid everyone good morning.

The 5 other anglers were all friends, but such is the comradery of the angling brotherhood I was quickly made welcome, I was in-between Clem and Biff which I found out was like the rose between two thorns. The two guys trading humorous insults all day was entertaining to say the least, Mikey backed the twin engine cat out of the harbour and turned her seaward. We were soon cutting through the calm seas heading westwards back to Devon, passing the various shore marks I have yomped too recently. Soon the anchor was released into the coloured channel water and the engines fell silent, Teddie Boy swung round on the rope into her position and Mikey yelled "okay lines down"! I had tied up new up and over traces using Craig's rigs as a template these were to be baited with Sandeel / Squid wraps and fished uptide. The bait was cast uptide and the 6oz lead dug into the sand perfectly leaving the fine tip of the uptide rod curved sharply. I decided unlike everyone else I wouldn't put my down tide rod out but instead concentrate on the uptider with small Sandeel baits.

We were supping our first hot cuppa of the day when my rod sprang back sharply, I wound down rapidly until I caught up with the fish. The fish was fighting well in the tide and gave a few short sharp runs before Mikey netted the first fish of the day, a pristine Spurdog my first of the winter. I recast as Roy at the back of the boat was also into a nice spur, they do go well using the tide to their full advantage. A few more Spurs appeared around the boat some biting through the trace at the boat, I then hooked a good fish that went off wide of the boat but managed to bite through my 80lb 10x trace, no doubt a Spurdog. I changed the trace to a stronger 150lb mono but this meant changing up the hook size too as the heavy monofilament won't fit through the 2/0 long shank hook eyes, added to this the stiffer trace is more rigid and doesn't flutter in the tide. The spurs seem to disappear allowing the pesky sand paper sharks to fill the void, skipper Mike quickly deciding to move to a deep hole that fishes well over slack water. Mike did tell me that a spotted ray is more than possible from this mark so once again I crossed everything, the compact Sandeel baits were suffering at the hands of the dog squad and while everyone else were hitting good Conger and Huss on big baits I had to question my sanity. The Huss were getting bigger with Roy landing two personal bests in a row to a best of 12lb 8oz, I do love Bull Huss and I must admit to feeling frustrated sitting it out for the Ray. I had posted on Facebook that I was on my 9th attempt at the Spotted Ray and the support I received during the day is what kept me focused, top rod Jon Patten even offering to take me out for one if today remained fruitless. Biff and Clem either side of me both landed nice Huss and I simply had to join everyone else and bring my down tide rod into play.

I set up a 200lb mono trace and 8/0 hook baited with whole Herring then lowered into the depths of the hole, it was hit instantly, and I struck into a good fish as the rod bent and juddered. Just before the surface the fish was off, it had spat out the bait a trait common place with the Huss, I re-baited and sent the fresh bait back into the gloom. I checked the uptider only to find yet another blooming dogfish hanging from the hook, how long had that been there I wondered. No spurs had been taken from this mark and as I was casting away from the hole I decided to go back to the 80lb trace and smaller hooks, a fresh Sandeel / squid wrap was hooked up and the rig cast well uptide. I sat back to enjoy a fresh cup of coffee courtesy of the skipper when I noticed the downtider rattle sharply, this rattle changed to an aggressive serious of pulls and It was time to investigate. I struck to find the reassuring weight of a good fish on the other end and this time the Huss wasn't letting go as the skipper netted it. The Huss was followed by a small Conger before everything went quiet, it was then Roy at the back hooked something special as the fish battled for several minutes taking yards of line on several powerful runs. We were all straining to look through the chocolate water for the first glimpse when the line fell slack, the fish was gone, the skipper felt it was a good Tope but like the answer to the question how did trump end up in the Whitehouse, we shall never know! The skipper announced 5 more minutes then we are moving to the final mark to try for a Cod, everyone sounded their approval, all except me, I knew that was curtains for the Ray again and also meant a cold lonely night on the beach. I packed away my downtider and as I rolled the trace onto the foam holder I noticed out of the corner of my eye the other rod pull downwards very slowly.

I watched the rod tip intently and it sprang back as a fish pulled the grip lead free from the sand, I wound the reel frantically to catch up with the running fish. Finally, the line tightened, and I could feel a fish nodding in the tide, the fish swam uptide and Clem told me straight away, " that's the fish you're after boy". Mikey was next to me with the net and he too said, it's got chances, sure enough out of the murk appeared the most wonderful sight, my own Yeti, or loch ness monster the Spotted Ray. Mikey didn't miss with the net and the beautiful male Spotted Ray was safely aboard, the other guys were made up for me, but I honestly felt elated. I quickly stripped off to reveal my Stroke T shirt, Biff was getting concerned as I removed my layers thinking this was some type of strange ritual I did.

I was so happy I posted the picture straight on Facebook, not something I normally do as I tend to save it for the Blog, but this was the culmination of a lot of time, effort and advice from fellow anglers like Ian Hooper, Paul Lorrimore and of course Craig Butler.

This fish was species 77 and meant I had managed to catch species through every month of the yearlong challenge. We went to the Cod mark for the final hour but alas no Cod appeared, I sort of hoped they would for the rest of the boat to get the fish they really wanted. I of course didn't do the night on the beach opting to go home and celebrate with the family. Was this the end, well maybe it would have been if I hadn't worked out that although I had achieved 77 species I was now also on 51 sea species, one more sea fish would take me to 52, I had to try. I decided my last effort would be directed towards the 3 Bearded Rockling, a species that may just be possible from the shore or boat.

I received some great information from North Devon angler John Shapland on areas to target the species in Ilfracombe and Minehead. Chris and I would put a maximum effort into this attempt which was to be all day Saturday the 29th December. We arrived at the mark only to find another angler already in the spot, this angler though was only interested in stealing our bait and Chris gave the Cormorant a dam good telling off! We fished the tide down with no luck and I decided to message Paul Lorrimore to see if he was around, he told us to pack up and move to a different mark for the low tide. We met him at the new spot and he gave us some further tips and methods to target the Rockling at this mark.

This spot and the habitat that Rockling love is snags upon snags, the rougher the better which equals tackle losses, Paul also brought a spare rod down for me to use which was dam decent of him. Chris then hooked a fish which dropped off right on the edge he told me he was positive it was a Rockling, I then hooked a fish that got me into the snag again we felt it was the target. Paul had to make tracks, it was his wife's birthday and they were off out for dinner, dam decent of him to even pop down. With the darkness now upon us I hooked and landed a small Conger Eel, I followed this up with another small Conger, but still no Rockling. As the tide started to push in I landed two Pollack on chunks of herring which I really thought were the target. The tide had risen to the point we needed to move, and we made the decision to make tracks back to the first mark where it was safe to fish the flood. We sat eating a portion of chips while the sea crept up the beach and it really was a lovely evening to be out, I managed another Pollack and a Pouting.

Then I cast a bait a bit closer to the abundant rocks, this resulted in rod wrenching bite that I couldn't stop before it got to safety of the snags, that was a decent fish. At the same time Chris landed a better Pollack and we thought things are starting to switch on, despite sticking out the whole flood nothing else happened and the species eluded me. The boat trip we had again with Mikey on the 29th had been re-scheduled for New Year's Eve with a departure time of 3am it was a real red eye trip, to make matters worse I had a cunning plan to get to the harbour by midnight and try for a Rockling or Gilt Head Bream. This meant when I woke up at 9am on Sunday the 30th I wouldn't get anymore sleep until New Year's Eve afternoon over 30 hours later. When we arrived at the harbour at 23.50 I already felt knackered and I really felt I may regret this plan, we set up the LRF gear and tried to catch that last species. I had a good bite that turned into a little bit of a battle on the light gear, once again the darn Dogfish spoiled the party, however on light stuff you know they are there. Chris then tested his LRF gear further by hooking a Conger Eel which lead him a merry dance fighting right up to the steps, I added a further dogfish before conceding it wasn't going to happen from the shore. Mike arrived to fetch the boat and once everyone was on board we were on our way for my last trip of the challenge, despite being full of confidence the day was really tough and consisted of hundreds of dogfish and strap conger. Chris did hook a good fish that took line, but such was our luck that the only decent fish we had got away, I ended the day with my last fish of the year being yet another darn Morgay, Rough-hound, Small-spotted Catshark, *Scyliorhinus canicula*, or as we know it Bloody Dogfish!

My face just couldn't hide the disappointment of the final effort but as my wife reminded me 77 is a long way past 52 so I should be satisfied with that, if I wasn't an angler I probably would be. So, despite my best efforts and a big bunch of help from my fellow anglers my challenge ended on 77, UK species, 51 of which were sea species and 26 were coarse. Also, during the course of this challenge, I managed 43 personal bests if I had included my fish from Thailand it would have been 49 personal bests, a total I never expect to replicate again. The biggest misses of the year would have to be the Porbeagle Shark, losing two was a real blow and also the Dragonet. If I include the journeys undertaken by Chris and I the mileage would exceed 7000 miles, the costs of bait, tackle and trips were extensive with two trips a week being the norm regardless of weather. I have asked a lot of my friends, family and fellow anglers and the fact there is over £1200 on my just giving page is testament to the generosity and support of great people. I do feel fished out, exhausted and glad it has reached its conclusion, I had great times, sad times and have hurt most of my body at some point.

I have made new friends and great friends, I have been moved by the generosity of strangers and humbled by people with little to spare, so many skippers have gone out of their way to support me both via donations and trips. I have not named people individually but for everyone who has donated, supported me, given advice or simply liked and read my blogs you are all great, great people and I cannot thank you enough and I am proud to call you friends.

I do have to say a big thank you to Chris, I really couldn't have done it without him, sharing the driving, splitting the bait costs, taking my pictures and wrapping me in Vinegar and Brown paper when I have fallen, yet despite all this, I still took the mickey out of him at every opportunity and with very little right to reply. Finally, I must thank my wife and children who donated the most precious of things, time with their Dad / Husband, again I couldn't have done this year without their total support I am truly blessed.

Due to the fact that during this challenge, I fell into the Bristol Channel, slipped on rocks several times and fell down a slope gashing my hand, I was given some very sensible gifts for Christmas by my family. I know the RNLI have been running a campaign to encourage anglers to wear a life jacket I have always been concerned about the bulkiness of such items, however the Crewsaver sport165 is perfect and leaves an angler with no excuse not to wear one. This has been combined with Snowbee Rock Hopper boots to ensure I don't slip as much next season. Apologies for the health and safety interlude but having experienced several accidents during the course of this year it only seems right to highlight ways to mitigate the hazards as much as possible, although the biggest safety device you can have is a fellow angler, fishing alone is just too risky. So, what happens now? Well hopefully I may get a few more donations now the challenge is complete, thanks to the 36 donators so far, some have remained anonymous, so I cannot thank you personally but thanks so much. I am going to organise a date for the cheque photo with the Stroke Association and hopefully Andy Adams down in Looe, and in the next two weeks the book should be complete.

Thanks to the following boats, skippers and Shore guides for putting me on fish this year, in no particular order.

African Queen, Alan Hemsley
Anglo Dawn, Andy Howell
Bite Adventures, Chippy Chapman
Pegasus, Lewis Hodder
Force 10, Pete Davis
Swallow 2, Murray Collins
Lo kie Adventures, Kieren Faisey
Reel Deal Charters, Dan Hawkins
Osprey, Steve Webber
Teddie Boy, Mike Webber
Silver Halo, Matt Forester
Bluefin, John Barbeary
Meercat, Steve Brenchley
Top Cat, Andre Theoret
Borlewen, Dan Gunnow
Tamesis, Roy Strevens
S.S Angling, Craig Butler
The Gambling Angler, Jansen Teakle

Also big thanks to the people who took the time out to guide me to some of their local species

Carl Aldridge, Coventry Sturgeon
Steve McDonald, Zander Dorking, Grayling on the Tone
Nick Rose, multiple species, various waters, Birmingham
Sam James, Plaice and Rays Cornwall
Nick the Magnet Duffy, Eels Kent
John the Fish-Locker, Black Goby Falmouth
Also a thanks to Wayne Thomas for his media support

*The following three chapters are taken from an Eel book I wrote they should however appeal to all anglers.*

The Quarry

During the 80s, I was juggling Art College, girlfriends and becoming a New Romantic. Fishing time was limited, and so once again, I turned to the mysterious Eel to meet my angling addiction. I was now armed with a 49cc Vespa, so the world was my oyster but, as a student, fuel was a premium, so local lakes it was. The lake I carried out most of my 80s eeling adventures on was an old quarry and at that time I still believed the stories that it was bottomless. The lake was surrounded by steep jagged rock faces, typical of a West Country Quarry, the water dark black and menacing like a gateway to hell. During the day and with strands of sunlight permeating the thick tree canopy, the Old Quarry seemed like an oasis of nature almost like a lost world. The nights drew in quickly at the quarry, even during the height of summer, by 8pm the darkness cloaked the banks and the temperature would drop, most nights a mist crept in at dusk heralding the arrival of the night crawlers. I have fished thousands of nights over my lifetime, and in that time only a few places have given me the creeps, this Old Quarry was one of them. The bulk of my fishing is done alone. I do have good fishing friends and I like fishing with them, but I have my own goals and plans, many of my trips are gut feelings and if it feels right I have to go and fish. The other thing that makes me fish alone is the importance of being nomadic. I like to move if I don't think the fish are in front of me, socials tend to restrict this crucial part of catching fish.

My friends would say I am an unsociable git and for the reasons stated above I would happily agree. My fishing at the Old Quarry was spasmodic and, despite the super creepiness, I had to fish nights as Eels are nocturnal hunters or, so I believed at this time. Most trips would involve me arriving around 6pm on a Saturday evening, the farmer would be given the obligatory fiver, which seemed to be the price whenever you arrived and however long you stayed.

This particular trip was a little more creepy than normal and took place around September 1985. My Vespa was loaded up, like a petrol driven camel, it coughed and spluttered as I drove it through the puddle covered canyon that led to one of the quarry's only fishing spots. As I pulled up on the small grassy bank, I could see the lake was deserted as usual, most trips I have the place to myself, but I always secretly hope someone else would be there even though swims were extremely limited. I quickly disembarked the state of the art kit I had amassed growing up; first job was to replace the skid lid with my fishing hat sporting the Angling Times Rodbenders Club badge of honour. I was at this time an active member of the Rodbenders, and had achieved Bronze, Silver and the much-coveted Gold Award for specimen fish.

Once the hat was in position the gear quickly followed and back then fishing shelters were the same size as flat screen televisions are today. I put up my brolly and overwrap, and setup the deckchair ready for the impending darkness. The two rods were different makes, and different sizes, it didn't seem to bother the Eels or me, as long as they did the job.

The reels weren't bait-runners, not sure if they were even around then but, once again they did the job and I fished bail arm open anyway. The free running ledger rigs consisted of a weight with a split shot a foot from a size 12 hook baited with worms. These were both cast to the middle of the lake and placed on rickety rod rests, the front ones containing bite alarms. These were a massive step forward to my fishing and it was because of this early Eel fishing that I felt they were needed. The left alarm was a family special, built and designed by my cousin Bradley big brains, who was an electronics wizard, I simply told him what I wanted, and he made it. Unfortunately, after my prototype was such a success he wanted to charge me for the next one, so I took my business elsewhere and bought a commercially available indicator. This indicator worked on the same principle of: the tightening line pulling the two connectors together resulting in a squawking strangled duck sound, and the lighting of a dim red LED, sometimes.

These early alarms on the face seemed ground breaking but, in the middle of the night in pouring rain and gusting wind I think many were sent to Davey Jones Locker. I know one lake that contains a reef constructed entirely out of BiTec Vipers. Once the rods were placed on the alarms and the slack line tightened, the bail arm was opened, and the line trapped in an elastic band on the handle, the final part of the trap, and one of the best pieces of 80s fishing tackle, the fairy liquid bottle top was added to the line. I cannot overstate the influence the fairy liquid bottle top had on my early fishing, we all had them they were simple cheap and extremely effective I have toyed with the idea of 3D printing them for old time's sake!

With the traps all set it was time to slip into the German army tank suit, that I classed as a life saver, I didn't have a sleeping bag and instead, sat in the deckchair between the rods usually nodding off and waking with a dreadful pain in my neck! The Bivvy was only really fit for Hobbits and Womble's so, unless it was raining, I wouldn't be testing out my claustrophobia issues. The German tank suit was heavy and like most things German well made, it did though; highlight just how cold German tanks must be. I retrieved the lunchbox from my bag and the weight felt reassuring, my mum had prepared the usual of chicken nuggets and cheese rolls, I was sorted for several months should I somehow become trapped there. The evening seemed pleasant and warm, all my experience on the bank told me I was in for a nice night, an hour later as I cowered from the driving rain under the collapsing brolly with thunder and lightning all around I decided not to trust my bankside predictions again. Under the leaky overwrap I managed to fall asleep despite the perfect storm occurring all around me. Somewhere in the distance, unspeakable torture was being carried out to a water bird, the screeching wail got higher and higher surely the poor thing would die soon I thought, suddenly the realisation dawned on me it was my alarm. I climbed from the now flat deck chair and scrambled towards the wailing noise, slipping down the bank in my effort to rendezvous with the rod. The surface had been turned to a mud bath by the thunderstorm; I managed to scale the bank from the water's edge. When I reached the rod, I could see line peeling from the spool the LED had given up as it did in the rain, but the god-awful sound hadn't, in fact it was gurgling like it was drowning, I quickly ended its misery by picking up the rod.

I closed the bail arm and struck widely in the wrong direction being totally disorientated by the unexpected take, I wound down and soon met resistance as the rod hooped over and the familiar reluctant bounce, bounce, of an Eel indicated its presence. This felt like a really good Eel my previous best at this time was around 1lb 8oz, as I tended to go for quantity not quality, but this one must be erring on the side of quality. Opposite my swim on the other side of the lake there was a small shingle beach caused by the cascading of a waterfall against the rock face, years of turbulence had pulverised, the stone to shingle and this had been pushed up to form the beach. I stood battling the Eel and although it was dark, there was enough moonlight to make out a large dark humanoid shape, stood on the beach staring at me. I tried to focus better and use my experience of the landscape to try and get some sort of scale on the object but strangely it remained blurred. The Eel suddenly dived for the bottom and the abundant snags that litter the quarry bed; I returned my attention to the battle and quickly gained control.

When I glanced back to the beach the mysterious shape had disappeared and, just as I thought I must have imagined it, I heard the sound of falling stones from the goat track leading from the beach. I was quickly brought back down to earth as the Ecl burst onto the surface and straight away I could see it was a new best, the Eel went 2lb 4oz when weighed and after a quick photo it was returned. I then sorted out the carnage that accompanies landing, weighing, and photographing an Eel in the darkness.

The rods were recast and with the sky looking angry and my forecasting in doubt, I decided to reconstruct the collapsed brolly and overwrap. Shortly after, I was in a deep sleep with no more thoughts of strange shapes lurking in the shadows; only dreams of even bigger Eels filled my head. It was around 2am when I woke, I wasn't sure why I woke other than the obvious lack of comfort and warmth but then, I heard a branch snap which at 2am in a quarry sounded like a gunshot. The sound had come from behind my little shelter and was followed by a shuffling noise and another twig break, I had convinced myself that the noise was just a vole or water rat but there were now definite dull thudding footsteps.

I edged further in towards the back of the bivvy in the hope that 3mm of nylon would form an impenetrable barrier to this creature, maybe, if I kept as quiet as possible, it would walk on past. It seemed like an age, but the footsteps seemed to be moving off when suddenly "SQUARRRK" the flipping alarm went off as another Eel made off with a worm supper.

The angler in me kicked in straight away and I was on the rod in a flash, a quick strike and the Eel was on, as I started battling a very strong Eel I felt like I was being watched, I knew if I turned the creature would be revealed. While keeping a strong grip on the rod I gingerly turned my head to be met with a dozen Friesian cows looking down at me from the high bank, mystery solved they were walking behind my bivvy and one must have walked down to that beach earlier to drink.

I felt a bit of a plonker and was annoyed that I let my imagination get the better of me, I continued with the Eel which managed to throw the hook right at the net. That was all the action that night and in the morning the farmer asked how I got on, I explained how the cows had scared me half to death especially when one was lurking down on the beach. He then replied that the cows can't get down that side of the lake he blocked it off years ago after a man had fallen to his death over there, my heart sank. Many years later I returned to the old quarry and achieved an Eel catch that will go down as one of my greatest eeling achievements I will return to this story later.

☐

## The Carp Lake Monster

The 80s came and went and I got married and targeted other species, I never forgot my passion for the freshwater eel, but I needed to broaden my horizons. I was now heavily engrossed in carp fishing which took me to waters home and abroad, I began writing articles for Carp magazines and field testing for a bait company. One of the lakes I was fishing was a 40-acre silt bowl on the Devon, Somerset border, this water had a national reputation for 20lb Carp and contained some stunning fully scaled mirror Carp. I had, like many of the lakes I was now Carp fishing, fished this water as a youngster and on one occasion had quite an Eel session although it was not planned.

I had arrived at the lake nice and early and managed to pack all the necessary equipment on my Suzuki 125cc trial bike, it was a bit precarious down the narrow lanes, but I made it. The plan was to target the lakes large Bream population and the chosen method was quiver-tipping using maggot filled feeder. The swim chosen was near the end of the dam, an area which offered the deepest water in the lake and produced Bream in the lakes regular matches. A few hours into the trip and only one solitary slimy slab had graced my net, I started to second guess my swim choice and nagging doubts crept in. I was considering a move to the opposite side of the lake, when a voice croaked from behind me, "morning". The fishery Bailiff Cyril Hooper appeared from the foliage at the back of the swim "any luck" he asked in his gravelly tone, "just the one Bream" I replied. He checked my ticket and asked if I fancied earning a free days fishing by having a go for a trapped Carp in the overflow pool at the bottom of the large sluice.

This pool was about the size of a double garage and around 6 feet deep, the Carp must have gone over the sluice in the heavy rain and was now stuck. I was keen to undertake the mission, and the free ticket was secondary to getting on the right side of Paratrooper Hooper, as he was known by the fisherman.

Cyril who was in his 70s had indeed been a Paratrooper and some believed that he had progressed to the SAS, which would explain some of the techniques he used to carry out the role of fishery bailiff. It has been rumoured that the man has appeared from beds of rushes face blacked up to catch fish poachers, and that he once dropped from a tree on a rope scaring a couple of twitchers who were disturbing breeding grebes. I had even had my own near miss with Paratrooper Hooper when I and a friend, fished the river that joined the Higher and Lower Lakes.

The Higher Lake was stocked with rainbow Trout and occasionally like the unfortunate Carp, they got washed over the sluice, these fish found their way into the small river, we had decided to exploit this bounty. We assumed this overgrown boggy area would not be patrolled by Paratrooper Hooper as we had never observed him there. We both wore chest waders to deal with the brambles and boggy ground, before long we had a several plump rainbows on stringers and were making our way back to the Lower Lake. We then heard the barking of a dog heading in our direction, Paratrooper had two Labradors, Monty and Churchill, and if they had located us we were in danger of capture and integration military style.

Quick thinking was required and so the rods were stashed, and the Trout deposited into our chest waders, not pleasant but the lesser of two evils. We then shouted out "help, over here" the dogs were on us in seconds and typical Labradors their wagging tails indicating their lack of malice. Directly behind them a camo dressed Cyril emerged clearly disappointed by the over friendliness of his two faithful hounds. The dogs now got the scent of fresh Trout and jumped up trying fruitlessly to open the waders and reveal our deception, "Down Monty you bad dog" growled Cyril, the dog was clearly confused but obeyed. "What's going on lads" enquired Paratrooper, we explained we were baiting up swims for Carp and got disorientated in amongst the high rushes then became stuck in the bog.

Cyril bought the story and was visibly pleased with his apparent rescue; he then blazed a trail through the overgrowth with a machete he produced from his backpack. We reached the road and thanked him then made good our escape, I still wonder if the crime had been discovered, would we have been chopped up and buried in that bog. My kit was quickly packed up and I made my way down towards the overflow pool, I could see the water was a thick brown soup colour from the constant tumbling of the silt. It felt a bit daft setting up to fish something not a lot bigger than a garden pond but at least the target of the mission would never be far from the bait. I decided to keep it simple, one split shot on the line with a size 12 barbless hook and three maggots; I cast out and placed the rod on the flat concrete, on the edge.

The tip sprung round, and a fish was on, I swung it in and was amazed to find an Eel of around 12ozs, I released it, into the river below the pool and recast. The split shot must have just reached the bottom when the bait was taken again another Eel was swung in and released this continued relentlessly until, as the sun was setting. I reached 110 Eels caught and released. I have never caught a greater number of Eels than that afternoon session and although none were giants it was fantastic to see, I also didn't catch the Carp and I had my suspicions that it might have been devoured by the pit of Eels. This lake was also the scene of my only Cryptid sighting and for the uninitiated Cryptozoology is the study of creatures that have not been proven to exist yet, despite many sightings such as Sasquatch and Nessie. My particular Cryptid is more than possible as it exists in many other parts of the world and, like most witnesses to something strange, I know what I saw. The creature sometimes known as the Beast of Bodmin was a large Black Panther type cat that was spotted a number of times in the vicinity of the lakes one September.

I was 2 days into a Carp fishing session with good friends Prat the Tat Hodgkinson and honorary water bailiff Teddy Tiddler Taylor, their names are sort of self-explanatory, with Prat covered in tattoos and Teddy catching tiddlers. The lakes owners, Water Trust South had pensioned off poor old Cyril the Paratrooper Hooper to be replaced by free honorary bailiffs, anglers who for a free season ticket, carried out the role of bailiff. It was very handy being mates with Teddy as we always got a good swim and new exactly where the Carp were feeding, in return I was sharing the latest bait I was trialling.

During the night we had been woken by an ungodly scream and between us were unable to identify the perpetrator but settled on a Jurassic barn owl trapped in a grain silo. The next morning, we were all sat in front of our bivvies' enjoying bacon sarnies and steaming mugs of coffee, prior to getting an angry wet slapping from the sacked carp we landed during the night. I noticed our conversation was getting louder as we were combating an ever-increasing din from the sheep in the adjacent field; I reached for my binoculars to examine the irritating animals. I could clearly see that all the sheep in the field were huddled in the top corner, using the binocular's I scanned around the field but could see nothing to cause the fear that was shown in the sheep. Prat pointed frantically towards the bottom left corner of the field "What's that"? We all stared as a large black shape slinked along the field side of the stock fencing; it disappeared behind some foliage as if it knew we were watching. Teddy was groping in his rucksack for a camera as the creature reappeared, it reached the corner of the field and bounded completely over the fence and entered the tree line. "Let's go" barked Teddy camera now in hand, Prat sprung from his chair and grabbed a storm pole, "You stay and watch the rods" added Teddy I wasn't arguing I didn't fancy being dragged up a tree by a panther.

The two fearless anglers made their way around to the bottom of the field and I could now see that the fence came level with six-footer Prat's chest, the creature had sprung that in one bound. The two now disappeared, shrouded by the dark woods that encircled the lake, I sat waiting, wondering if they were being savaged out there in the woods.

Before long I started eyeing up the array of Carp equipment and wondering how my fishing would improve with these guys kit if they should fall to the beast today. Then for a second, I had a terrifying thought, what if they flushed the creature out and it doubled back behind me! I reached for the catapult and some pebbles I wouldn't go without a fight. After what seemed like an age, two shapes emerged from the forest pausing to look over the fence the beast had leapt, once back they explained they had seen some prints, but the creature had been swallowed by the thick overgrowth.

We now sat back and for the first time discussed what we had witnessed, this was unanimous a large black cat the size and shape of a panther. The way it moved keeping flat to the ground, the ease in which it bounded the stock fence, the long tail, and the reaction of the sheep all pointed towards a big cat. We decided with the lack of evidence not to go public, plus did we really want loads of thermos carrying monster hunters descending on our peaceful Carp water, setting up thermal camera traps and planting pheromones to attract all sorts of nasty's.

Three weeks later and I was doing a night session camped in a swim called the swamp, the previous night had been the first frost of the year and there was to be another tonight. I got all the baits in position and was troubled by a couple of Bream, on Carp gear they are a bit of a pain; the net was coated in the slime which they are well known for. I changed to 22mm boilies to hopefully reduce their interruptions and an hour later it seemed to have worked as the rods remained silent.

It was sometime around 2am when the left-hand rod bleeped, I opened my eyes but couldn't see the latching light then it became visible. I worked out something had obscured my vision, so something had been stood between the bivvy and the rod, there was a loud rustling and a clang noise followed by something large running off through the rushes. I lay in my bed silently listening for any further sounds but after 15 minutes all was quiet, the left-hand rod beeped again as the indicator dropped slowly, a bream had managed to whittle down the golf ball bait. I clambered from my comfy warm bag into the cold frosty night and proceeded to reel in the bream that was now sulking on the lake bed, I reached for the net, but it was no longer leant up against the rushes. The Bream slid into the margin like a Frisbee and at around 6lb would have been quite a fish on the right tackle, I managed to slip the hook and return the fish without the net. Lucky it wasn't a Carp I thought, I would never have landed that without a net, I switched on the head torch and preceded to grid search the immediate vicinity, but the net couldn't be found.

The net was a 42-inch specimen net with an alloy spreader block, net float and 6-foot solid handle making it a large unwieldy item, I set up the spare I always carried and retired to bed now trembling in the cold night air. The next morning, the October sun rapidly thawed the overnight frosty coating that covered the bank and everything on it, I decided to have a good scout for the net but was rapidly coming to the conclusion it had been pinched. I had to wind in the rods to re-bait, so I reeled them in and placed them against the rushes then zipped up the Bivvy door.

I grabbed a storm pole to use to poke around in the undergrowth and headed over to the last known position of the net, I could see that the rushes were flattened off to the right of the swim and decided to head in that direction. As I walked deeper into the beds of rushes they started to form a jungle tunnel and along the ground there was a definite drag trail, after 200 yards I discovered the net handle and finally the net itself.

The net handle was splintered just below the spreader block and the net was shredded, obviously the net had been taken by an animal most likely attracted by the Bream slime. When I cast my mind back to the previous night I recalled the latching light being obscured by a large shape then the crashing noise as the net was pulled down and dragged off, had the beast returned to the lake?

The question was answered sooner than I thought as Tiddler Taylor turned up doing his rounds, he started by saying "You'll never guess what"? "what I answered" "Gerald Tamsworthy the local farmer has been telling people he has seen a big black cat stalking his animals, apparently the police are investigating as it's the third report this month". We both stood, looking out at the lake knowing the cat was out of the bag, excuse the pun, "What should we do" I asked, Ted replied "I'll go to the police and give our report and if they want to speak to us they can". I never heard from the police on the matter and I moved on to fish other waters and as far as I know there has been no further reports regarding this creature.

Coming back to the real subject of the story the eel, I need to go back in time from the incident with the beast to the previous summer where once again I was doing a Carp session with a few of my mates. Prat the Tat again, Strangely Slim Tim and Rodney the Rod breaker were all camped along the shingle beach swims, this was a proper social and we had brought along the Barbie to cook up a feast. The weather was stifling, a proper August day and the Carp were milling around bathing on the surface, sniggering at our attempts to induce them to feed, there was a large patch of bubbles breaking the surface by my right-hand rod. I watched the expanding bubble patch and awaited the inventible Bream drop back, it however never materialised. I managed to motivate myself into reeling in and trying a rig change in an attempt to catch the bubble maker, I swapped to a running rig with a size 8 hook and a boilie chopped into a tiny cube was then soaked in an amino acid compound. The rig was cast into the latest patch of bubbles and the rod set back in the alarm to wait for a take, sure enough the indicator rose slowly, and the bait-runner ticked steadily.

I swept the rod upwards in the standard striking arc and met a healthy resistance, so I could quickly rule out the bream; suddenly a large fish snaked across the surface, tail walking like a mighty marlin. I knew immediately which species I had hooked; as I had experienced them tail walking in the past but the size of this one was mind blowing. The rest of the group had turned up wondering what had interrupted their afternoon siesta; surely none of the resident carp had fallen for these basic refinements. "It's a bloody huge Eel" I yelled, trying to contain my excitement, having seen the fish jump from the water I was right to be excited.

The Eel was now taking line and the power was incredible, the rod juddered as it changed direction heading straight for me at high speed, I managed to catch it up as it went straight passed us and along the margin. Soon she was in front of me, and the huge head stuck out defiantly from the water, while the powerful body reversed seemingly gripping the water and somehow getting purchase to pull powerfully back. We were at stalemate and it was time to take the net to the fish, and Strangely Slim waded out and done the honours, sliding the large net under the eel, at the third attempt the Eel stayed in the net. We placed the Eel on the mat and stood back to admire the biggest freshwater Eel I had ever seen; the girth was huge, and I was truly speechless. The hair rig had worked perfectly finding the side of the Eel's mouth and the barbless hook popped straight out, the Eel was weighed and pulled the scales to 5lb 1oz smashing my personal best by over 3lb. The photos were taken and once again this huge eel amazed, with the way I was able to handle it for the photos, no wriggling, spinning, slime flinging, common with the smaller Anguilla, this fish lay still and calm and swam away strongly when I slipped her back into the water.

The Eel made my season that year and sowed the seeds of a future campaign, dedicated to chasing monster eels and to this day that Eel really opened my eyes to just how impressive large freshwater Eels are. Strangely several years down the line, I returned to this water as part of a campaign to target the Eels on this lake, I could not catch eels over 3lb although there were hundreds of 2lb Eels in there just like peas in a pod.

## Winter Wonder

The late, great, John Sidley was a true inspiration to my eel fishing. I have read his book over and over and although many things have progressed, he really was a pioneer. One of the things that Sidley did on a number of occasions was, to catch Eels in the winter. Several of these fish were caught after he noticed picky bites while Pike fishing. Carp fishing was once considered to be a summer pursuit, nowadays winter carping produces some of the better fish, and carp are considered a year-round target. I decided that I wanted to continue eeling all year and in particular I wanted to catch a big Eel by design, while in the middle of winter, another of my goals and a pretty tough one. October of the first year chasing a winter Eel was mild and I did catch several eels to just over 3lb.

The weather was sunny and warm, this isn't winter and really December, January and February are when it counts. The plan was to concentrate this first winter on the local canal, my thinking was, that the canal was constantly churned up by boat traffic and maybe this would keep the eels moving. I was doing nights in some likely looking swims with evidence of structure and depth variations. This canal was a bit hairy at night with a lot of drunks and weirdo's skulking around. I didn't bother taking a bed chair as there was no way I was sleeping, I would have probably woken with a plastic bag over my head, so it was just a brolly and seat. I managed a few Pike during these nights, but no Eels made an appearance. February, I changed venues to a canal by the sea. This canal was a few degrees warmer and hardly ever froze, it was also considerably safer, and I could park 10 feet from my swim, luxury really.

I managed a few bootlace Eels using maggots and these were caught in pretty harsh conditions, but they were a long way short of a specimen. The first winter ended with a total of 5 bootlace Eels, 3 Pike and a nice Perch, not exactly what I was after but as with all angling you always learn while spending time on the bank, it's never time wasted. The second winter and I started on the coastal canal as it had at least produced Eels for me previously. December threw up 3 bootlace Eels and I needed a rethink, as I couldn't see a specimen eel coming from this venue. On my return from the latest canal trip I had a message left on my answer phone from Murray Mathews, the owner of an ancient old lake I had been trying to get access too for several years.

The message simply stated that if I still fancied eel fishing the lake, to give him a call because there may be an opportunity to fish in January. I was convinced this was a lucky omen, just when I was going back to the drawing board on my winter eeling campaign, this drops in my lap, happy days. To put this opportunity into context, I first visited the water 2 years previously in the summer, when two of my Carp fishing mates had the place booked for a week and invited me down for a look at the place. They had waited several years for their own chance to have a crack at the lakes huge common Carp topping 40lb, and a real historic strain, a much-coveted venue where money really didn't talk. The owner Murray would meet for a chat, and if he felt a good vibe and you were someone who loved fishing to experience the whole environment you would make it to the guest list, at some point Murray would call.

He was known as 'No Hurry Murray' as it may take several years before you received that prestigious phone call. If you shunned the offer you were dropped from the circle of trust quicker than a snitch from a gang. This lake, of around 10 acres, was located deep in a deciduous forest with many ancient old oak trees towering above the thick canopy, their roots creating humps and bumps all along the bank. The lake was only stocked with 30 Carp, and the clear shallow water aided their ability to avoid capture, the eel population was completely unknown, but I just knew they were there. When I first looked around the lake I was in awe of the natural beauty and peacefulness of the place, a real credit to Murray and the calibre of angler he recruited.

The guys had done a few days without a twitch from their sentinel like rod set ups, pods set perfectly, and the indicators positioned to react even if a Carp farted near the bait. Despite the inactivity the guys were relishing every second of the atmosphere, created by this 200-year-old lake, it really was paradise and I longed to fish there. We sat around the camp having a barbecue and were joined by Murray, who relayed some of the history of the lake, including the ghost stories that were ingrained in local legend. Apparently, during the early 18th century while the rest of the country was preparing to accept an act to prevent the burning of witches, the villages here continued. Frog Toed Lil, so called because of the toes on her right foot being webbed, was accused of witch craft and the fact that her deformity had left her shunned by the parish, added to her eventual condemnation.

She was found guilty and burned at the stake in the very wood that surrounds the lake, her ashes were scattered into the water in a bid to overturn the curse she claimed would befall the forest and all that entered. The lake had also been used to dispose of the bodies of sacrificial offerings by the once abundant druids; a stone monolith in the forest is still revered by pagans and devil worshippers. Murray continued that the whole place has a paranormal undercurrent, and many anglers had reported strange phenomena including screams, lights and splashing sounds like someone drowning. It all seemed really interesting, and in the warm glow of that mid-summer evening not scary in the slightest and besides, I wasn't actually staying the night. I bid the guys and Murray farewell and headed off for the 10-minute hike through the wood back to the car, little did I know it would be so long before my return.

"Hi Murray, its Steve, the Eel guy, just returning your call." I had rung first thing the following morning to ensure Murray knew I was still keen. "Nice to hear from you Mr Anguilla, I was thinking you weren't interested anymore, when you didn't answer." Bloody hell, I'm not Batman. I don't sit by the phone waiting two years for you to get of your arse and ring, I thought. Murray explained that it was my time for a shot at the lake and although the winter wasn't ideal for eel fishing, he would ensure next time I got a summer slot. I knew this was a test. I felt the lake would be hard in the summer so to expect results in the winter was crazy. I couldn't turn it down for the reasons previously mentioned and besides if I achieved Murray's criteria, I would be back in the summer.

So, the slot I had was a long weekend at the end of January, arriving on the Friday and departing Monday lunchtime. I wasn't too keen on winter session, fishing one night would normally suffice. When I was younger and a keen Carp angler I had no such reservations, waking on several occasions to find my rigs frozen under the ice and my rods stuck to the alarms, crazy days. I did have concerns that temperatures may plummet prior to the trip, but I needn't have panicked, although night times it dipped below zero, the days were a tropical 7 degrees. I pulled into the gravel car park as the last of the weak winter sun sank below the tree line, my breath was already visible in the chilling air, but the walk to the lake would no doubt get the blood circulating. It was going to be a single journey. I loaded the Carp porter, then my body like a giant game of buckaroo. I was determined to carry everything, regardless of my physical ability. I managed to get half way before the first item was discarded and shortly after, a trail of items littered the path down to the lake. I had once again, discovered those stunning mighty oak roots, as I went arse over tit and found myself pinned to the forest floor by my 100-litre rucksack, my mouth now full of decaying leaves and beetle juice. Why do you never have a handy-cam filming you when you need one? That would have been a definite £250, 'You've been framed clip!' I managed to struggle back to my feet and resumed the journey. The swim I chose was the same double swim I visited two years previously, and it was also the closest to the path so that settled it. I reasoned I could always move the next day. With the remaining gear deposited unceremoniously to the ground, I set off back up the forest path to retrieve the breadcrumb trail of tackle I had dropped along the way.

It's not until you're searching for something that you realise just how useless the beam of a cheap head torch really is. I was trudging around in the crispy leaves, scanning the ground without realising I had deviated onto a different trail. It wasn't until the path ended that I realised my error. The torch beam caught a glimpse of a timber wall, in a clearing to the side of the path. I walked nearer and could now see a ram shackled timber cabin. Closer inspection showed the windows were boarded, and the door had been propped shut with a stake. It really looked like it was done to keep something inside; it reminded me of the cabin at the centre of the horror movie Evil Dead. The air seemed colder here and once again, the vapour of my breath became visible under the weak head torch beam. I felt uneasy and had a compelling desire to flee. I backtracked along the trail and recovered the bits of kit I had dropped; the cabin had soured the air of anticipation I had arrived with. The next few hours the construction of my camp focused my mind, and by the time the rods were cast, I was once again relishing the opportunity to be at the lake. The rods were baited with sand Eel sections, soaked in winterised fish oil, this seemed to work for the canal eels and Sidley had some crackers using it, so it would be my starting point on this unknown venue. I was in the bag by 9pm, absolutely shattered having worked all day and overexerted myself carrying the gear. Not sure I even made it to 9.15pm before I drifted off into a deep sleep. I woke with a start, my face was numb from the cold night air, my eyes focused on the motionless rods and the realisation I was fishing grew clearer. I pressed the light on my watch and the time showed just after 3am. A scream echoed across the lake, but I couldn't pinpoint the location.

Once again, a scream like a tortured woman, this time, from behind. I had heard this type of scream on many night fishing trips, and still find it incredible that an owl can create such a horrific screech, never the less an owl was surely the culprit. I drifted back off to sleep, hoping the owl would not decide to perch close to the tent, as the thought of that scream reverberating around my camp was, in itself a terrifying one. I awoke to a white carpet of hoar frost, with the previously bare trees now sparkling and shimmering, cloaked in an icy skin. Wow, what a view to wake up to in the morning and despite the disturbed sleep, lack of bites, and unnerving feelings the previous night, this felt like paradise. I was checking the other swims further around the lake and decided that the only other spot that looked good for Eels stank strongly of bonfires. I guessed Murray carried out some maintenance nearby and the aroma lingered. Back at the double swim, I decided to swap the sand eel sections for smaller hooks, and a bunch of dendrobena worms. This would be fished flat on the bottom and not suspended. I added a small PVA bag of fishy ground bait and maggots to prevent the hook fouling in the bottom debris. To complement this finer set up, I adjusted the bobbins to be as sensitive as possible, figuring any bites may be confined to twitches rather than full blown screaming runs. I was now once again confident, and willing the indicator to beep, surely something would bump into the line at some point. The bright blue sky signified another chilly night ahead and I planned to fill the flask with coffee, and sit out under the stars, while absorbing the atmosphere and who knows maybe land an eel or two. I cooked up a few rounds of bacon sandwiches and washed them down with some piping hot oxtail soup.

Fed and hydrated, I settled down for the evening. When you are out under the stars on a really clear evening, far away from any chance of light pollution, the night sky is truly a thing of beauty. The number of stars is incomprehensible; it looks like a creation in a Disney sky scape. It was around 10pm, and the last of my coffee flask was still piping hot and doing its job. I was watching the sky when, from the left I noticed a slow-moving light coming from the west and heading east. The light was yellow in colour and larger than the usual satellites, asteroids and space stations. It had no flashing lights and progressed steadily, it appeared out of the ordinary. Then the weirdest thing occurred, the light divided into two separate objects with, one heading towards the ground. Before I could study the objects further, something equally strange occurred, the alarm started wailing. I was extremely slow to react, having spent so long dormant; it was a tall order to regain the same rapid reactions that support my summer fishing.

The rod was eventually struck. Straight away I knew the fish was a good one and strangely, I had a concern that it might be a carp. It would seem incomprehensible to many that, I would rather hook an eel than one of the rare Carp that reside there. To me, I was so focused on my goal that catching another species would seem like a kick in the teeth. The fish at the end of the line was not, however, a Carp. The fish although sluggish, had the characteristic thump, thump, of an Eel shaking its head; I felt vindicated there were Eels here and this most certainly felt like a specimen, my goal was within reach. With the Eel under control, I once again glanced skywards but the two objects were no longer visible. The fish then stopped as everything went solid.

I kept steady pressure on the rod and the eel was inching towards me when, suddenly ping, everything seemed to go light, the snag had gone, and it was just the Eel again. Just the netting procedure to go, and I sank the net in anticipation; the Eel was drawn steadily towards the nets spreader block, its broad head protruding from the water. I swept the net upwards just as the rod twanged straight, it was either in the net or gone. I could hardly bear to raise the net, and as it rose releasing the trapped water, I knew by the weight it was indeed empty. How could it have escaped? It was defeated and well hooked. A quick check of the trace showed the Eel had bitten through the 25lb quicksilver.

I could hear the words of an old eeling friend, who had little time for the modern braided hook link and swore that unless you used a wire trace, one day you would lose the Eel of a lifetime. It may not have been the Eel of a lifetime, but my disappointment at this moment, felt comparable. I hate using wire trace and would normally be using 45lb quicksilver as a hook link, a material that has never failed me. I scaled down for the winter eeling and without a doubt, it cost me the fish I so coveted. Nowadays there are some superb wire materials that can be knotted and are extremely supple, I use these for any eeling I do now. I think I stood motionless in the darkness with the rod and net in hand, for a full five minutes, as two winters worth of effort diminished along with that 4lb Eel. How can the angling gods be so cruel? As per normal, I pulled myself together, re-rigged, re-baited and cast the rod into position. No longer wishing to sit out and spend the night wondering what I could have done differently, I turned in.

The alarm was screaming could it be true, another run. I jumped from the bag and ran bare foot towards the rods, the normally bright run light was sadly absent, and the bobbin was motionless. Had I been dreaming? I checked the watch, it was 3.05am, and another scream echoed across the lake. It was a repeat of the previous night. This time I was up and noticed the red glow flickering through the trees on the far bank. I really couldn't determine whether the red glow was pulsating or was it a trick of the light. It wouldn't take me that long to go and check it out, but I couldn't find a positive reason to do so. I was here for the fishing, not to investigate things that go bump in the night, and I needed to exorcize my own demons and catch another eel. Positive action in the form of a re-bait and recast was carried out before returning to bed. That was the only action that night and the mysterious disturbances caused me to sleep until 10:00 am. It had at least thawed out by this time, and was once again, a pleasant day with clear blue skies. After a sausage bap breakfast, I decided to have a wander, and reeled in the rods to ensure there would be no missed fish to add to my woes. I grabbed a sturdy bank-stick to act as a pacifier and trudged off around the lake. I arrived at the swim opposite mine and once again the bonfire smell was pungent. I walked deeper into the woods until I reached a black scorched circle that was clearly the source of the smell, and no doubt last night's flickering glow. I knelt down and lowered my hand, just above the ash expecting a surge of heat, it was however stone cold. It must have been just dying embers last night, from the first night's fire. I carried on a bit further and entered a clearing devoid of tree growth. In its centre, sat the stone monolith or as it should be called, lump of un-extraordinary granite.

I went to the centre and rested my hand against the stones flat lichen covered surface, I felt no aura, no Zen and no more fertile than earlier. All claimed effects that the Monolith can apparently create. Maybe sceptics are immune or perhaps it requires the slaughter of a virgin goat to fire it up, either way it was best left to the druids, pagans and dogger's. Not sure what I would find around the next corner I walked on. Eventually arriving at the Evil Dead cabin, darn it, I didn't really want to see this again but as the sun was shining, and I was tooled up a quick look couldn't hurt. As the first evening had indicated, the place was in lock down with all the windows boarded. At the rear, there was a covered veranda, complete with a rotten rocking chair. The rear door was not only free from boards but was ajar, and I used the storm pole to open the gap wider still, the sunlight exposed a large hanging charm in the entrance, I now know to be a dream catcher. This is the bit in the movie where I would normally be saying, 'don't go in there, it will lead to certain death', and like the cheesy horror hero, I carried on, past the dream catcher causing the attached chimes to clang nervously. "Hello, anyone there"? Stupid question, but carrying on the stereotypical horror theme, no one answered. And furthermore, the light switch failed to function when I flipped it back and forth. At this point, I pulled the door wide open and sunlight flooded the single room. If Murray splashed around some wood stain, and lay a bit of laminate, he could rent this out in the summer. True, they would probably need to be axe wielding demons, raised by chanting verses from a book, covered in human skin, or a group of college kids with a talent for stupidity, that find such a book, anything is possible.

As for me, there was nothing more to see in the house, unless I counted the strange writing, scrawled in blood red across the cabin wall, *'This was the home of Frog Toed Lil, burned as a witch but she dwells here still, she cursed these woods to forever burn bright, as she wails and screams every winters night.* That didn't sound good, of course it could have been a plan by Murray to teach people a lesson that broke into his shack, especially if he had spun them the yarn beforehand. It suddenly dawned on me, I have sussed out the mystery. This is all part of the great Murray suitability test. If I leave terrified I fail, but if I stick it out, I get a future summer slot. He must really take this selection process seriously, to go to the trouble of lighting a fire, and creating the screaming. I have had weirder initiation ceremonies, but that story is for another day. The journey back to the swim was full of suspicion; I was expecting something to jump out, or a scattering of skulls to be placed along the path. Murray must be slipping; he would need to do better to scare me. Back at camp, I set about getting the rods out for the final night sortie and the plan would be, worms again backed up with the dissolving bag of maggots. With the rods out, it was time to chill. The solving of the mystery had the effect of allowing me to relax. I don't mind admitting, I had been getting a little spooked and I was close to failing the test. It was 11pm and I was sat by the rods admiring the stars again, when the light appeared. This time moving from east to west the opposite of the previous night. The speed was the same but this time it stopped moving, before heading north. This was not the actions of an eccentric fishery owner, and I wouldn't even begin to know how this could have been hoaxed. To me this was a UFO and the paranoia had returned.

I started thinking ever more ludicrous scenarios, was Frog Toed Lil an alien that would certainly explain her webbed feet and did her telepathic powers and anal probing raise the suspicions of the 18th century village. I didn't want to wake to find Frog Toed Lil brandishing some ungodly surgical instrument, before discarding my still twitching corpse to the dark water of the lake. Beeeeeeeep, the alarm burst to life signalling time for me to return to reality. Once again, I battled an Eel, this time a much smaller one but when the net folded safely around it, I punched the air as if it were a monster. The fish weighed 1lb 12oz and meant so much to me after the trials and tribulations of winter eeling. I released it straight away, concerned about the dropping water temperature in the margins. I baited and cast the rod to the same area, then turned in for the final night's sleep; strangely, I automatically woke at 3am and waited in the pitch darkness for the tick, tock, of my watch to reach the time of 3:05am. The scream rang out across the lake and I pulled my bag over my head and tried my best to ignore it. I didn't want to be involved in Murray's game or an alien invasion. I was too tired and very content with my achievement. The next morning, I was up early and keen to make tracks. It had been a strange and eventful session; I had lost a good eel, landed a trip saver and beat the test, a summer session surely loomed. As I loaded the last of the kit in the boot of the car, a range rover pulled up with a roof box and bikes strapped to the rear. It was Murray, his wife and kids. He lowered the electric window, "Sorry Mr Anguilla, I haven't had a chance for a chat, we've been away for the weekend and only just got back." I felt a sickening feeling in the pit of my stomach.

There had never been any test, Murray hadn't even been there! I bumped into one of the Carp guys a couple of months later and told him I finally got to fish the lake. He asked how I got on and when I said, just the one eel he interrupted. "No, how did you get on with Frog Toed Lil?" I laughed it off, but I have no doubt that the stories whispered between anglers, have some terrifying aspects of truth and furthermore, that Murray selects candidates with an ability to deal with everything that this haunted lake might throw up. That was it for that winter's Eel fishing, the session at Murrays had lessened my appetite for winter night fishing, and like a jumbo éclair they are very dark and very long. Next winter it would be day trips on deeper waters, my thinking behind this cunning plan, was that the temperatures in the deeper water would remain more consistent, and the darker depths may allow more confident feeding. The type of venue I would need should be a quarry somewhere local that I could get to for shorter trips. I suddenly remembered the Old Quarry. The Old Quarry had its own share of scary apparitions but as I was fishing days, I felt I would be able to avoid the night terrors. I had also landed Eels here in the past, so it wasn't such a gamble. This quarry had been good to me as a youngster producing many small Eels, Perch, Bream and Trout. Also, the fact I had never blanked there sealed the deal, the Old Quarry would be next winters target venue.

It was December on the third year of my winter eeling campaign, and I had arrived at the Old Quarry for my first trip. The method was to be suspended dead baits, fished a foot from the lake bed in 30 feet of water. I was hoping to use natural fish baits, as opposed to the sand eel sections I had used in the past, previous experience at the quarry had pointed towards fish as the eels preferred diet.

My plan was to catch some of the lakes Rudd or perch, and use them as fresh bait, maggots float fished in 12 feet of water usually did the trick. On this occasion the only interest shown was a small brown Trout, which was dispatched and sectioned for hook baits. The rods were cast, and the wait began. It is amazing how the seasons create so many different vistas from the same location, lush woods become fleshless bone yards, exposing sites previously unseen. I love our country's changing seasons, each bringing their own beauty and beast, from the summer's mist clad dawn to the winter's shimmering blanket of snow.

The price for such wonders comes in the shape of autumn storms and spring floods, the latter events being random and unpredictable, yet growing more inevitable. It sometimes takes a hobby that involves the great outdoors to remind you, just how amazing our world really is and that it should never be taken for granted. The Old Quarry in winter was a moonscape with the walls of dark rock lacking any atmosphere, the lakes surface black and still being shrouded by cliffs on three sides. In contrast the summer Old Quarry was mysterious and inviting. The thick emerald foliage creating a lake surface of green punctured by the abundant rings of topping Rudd. What I would have given for a topping Rudd at the moment, the trout bait failing to attract a single applicant in that first day session. The next trip was Boxing Day and having received the superb attx-v2 remote system I simply had to get out and use it. This did mean sacrificing the afternoon sloth session, stuffing turkey sandwiches and watching Chitty Chitty Bang Bang.

When it comes to remote alarm sounder boxes, I quite simply detested them, believing they lead to anglers wandering miles from their kit, with the strong possibility of a fish reaching snags or other anglers lines. This preconception changed, while Eel fishing a Carp syndicate lake. The abundant Eel population caused my alarms to be going off all night, much to the annoyance of the super stealthy carp boys. If I had been using the sounder box I could have fished the alarms on silent and had the box by my bed, allowing the carp hunters to snooze undisturbed like they did most nights. So, like bait boats, there is a use for them providing they are not abused and like so much in life, it's normally a bad element that spoils it for the rest. I have even witnessed the ludicrous rule, on one water, 'Carp fishing prohibited' not sure how you could enforce that one.

Having justified the need for a remote sounder box, I then convinced my wife that if I had one, I would become a more understanding and sensitive individual, the same line used for my birthday presents! So, I was now on the bank alone, during one of the biggest family days of the year. I really am an unsociable git, with a family I don't deserve. The rods were ready and once again I struggled to catch any bait with only a small perch to show for my efforts. The tiny morsels were hooked and cast into the depths. The new remote system was fitted and activated but as I was only sat 2 meters from my rods, it was somewhat farcical. I spent the first hour inventing methods of simulating a bite to test the system. This involved throwing stones at the line, prodding the rod with a stick and the worst of all, dragging the float from the bait rod over the line, which ended causing it to tangle into a knot.

The system passed all the lab tests, but really needed the genuine article before I could give it the seal of approval; this was not going to be the case today. So, this was another blank, and the trend continued through January with a total of 6 blank day trips at the quarry, despite various rigs and baits being used. Blanking and fishing to my mind go hand in hand and I am a strong believer in the fact that, if you put the effort in, eventually it pays you back. The many great trips I've had over the year's bare testament to this fact. I was though by now, rapidly coming to the conclusion that winter eel fishing was not a viable pastime, and this should probably be my last winter in pursuit of this goal, in favour of a more predictable winter species the Pike. With the arrival of February came a change in the weather going from, frosty still nights to frequent snow showers with strong winds, at its worst the snow was settling to a depth of 6 inches and deeper in the drifts. I think everyone who specimen fishes. longs to have a picture of their favourite fish with a background of fresh snow, nothing typifies dedication more than this type of photo. So, what better time to try for the big winter eel and technically it made sense, the actual temperatures had risen with the onset of the snow front. The route to the Old Quarry had been ploughed, being a main route to a nearby settlement but the farm track to the lake was still under a blanket of snow. I decided to leave the car and carry the kit down to the lake. It was an incredibly nice day and the first one the sun had managed to make an appearance on, the blue sky highlighting the twinkling in the snow as if externally powered. Unfortunately, the grass around the lakes only fishable side had thawed under the bright sun, melting the previous days snow.

The swim I chose was the Wonky Willow, a nice flat area with an old tree whose branches extended to the waterline, a great summer Eel swim.

The depth under the tree was just 12 feet created by a stone plateau bordered by a ledge that plummeted to 35 feet. I had avoided this shallow spot in favour of the more consistent deeper swims. Today though, the snow had really forced my hand, with this swim being the easiest to reach on foot especially as I used the shortcut across the field. The vehicle track lead to the other swims further around the lake. I went through the motions of setting up the kit and was once again fishing suspended rigs with the baits positioned a foot from the lake bed, the rod under wonky willow would be positioned in 11 feet of water. The next task was the frustrating job of bait catching but to my surprise as the float drifted under the tree, it slowly dipped resulting in a plump 4-inch Rudd. This amazing feat was repeated a further 5 times, ensuring a plentiful supply for the day. With such a bounty at my disposal I decided to fish live baits on both rods.

This had been a devastating summer method, leading to rapid and aggressive takes on numerous venues including this quarry. Around two hours later the rod on the left signalled a twitchy take that, at first, I put down to an overactive live bait, but the subsequent steady peeling off of 2 feet of line pointed towards a take. I excitedly struck and was met with minor resistance as a handsome stripy Perch of just less than 2lb floundered on the surface, the Rudd tail clearly sticking from the bucket like mouth. I was pretty chuffed with this fish and made the effort to do a few pictures before releasing it further down the bank, in an attempt, not to see it again that day.

The rod was baited and recast, and it was most definitely celebration coffee time. That fish combined with the brightness of the day, had inspired me with the confidence to catch some more. It was now midday and I was munching on the chicken tikka baguette my wife had lovingly prepared for me, when the wonky willow rod started twitching. The alarm didn't make a sound, but the bobbin was definitely quivering, as the Rudd's lateral line signalled the approach of a predator. Its vain attempts to flee; adding to the distress signals it was emitting. I placed the remnants of my spicy snack on my chair and walked over to inspect the rod. Beeeeeep, the alarm was wailing, and line shot from the spool, this was no Perch. I grabbed the rod with my heart pounding and closed the bail arm but was unable to strike, such was the ferocity of the run, the line instantly went tight, and the drag let the lines departure continue. This really felt a good fish. It was still taking line and had clearly dived over the side of the ledge, fearing the line would part on the sharp side of the ledge; I leant out taking the rod tip past the drop off. The line now went straight down; as the fish stopped running it had obviously reached the 35-foot lake bed with its extensive debris. Steady pressure resulted in the fish calmly rising up towards the light. The fish broke surface and I couldn't quite believe that it was indeed, a massive Eel with an incredible girth, a real monster. My joy was short-lived as the eel made another bid for freedom, taking line under pressure but not quite achieving the same depth. Somehow, I remained calm and persuaded the Eel up towards the net. The netting process was text book, with none of the stress and silliness that previous big eels had caused. With the net lifted clear of the water it was air punching time.

Once I composed myself, the stunning Eel was weighed and pulled the scales down to an incredible 5lb 2oz. The eel behaved perfectly, most likely due to the freezing air temperature. The photos were quickly taken, and the beautiful creature released carefully. Three winters of scratching for bites, freezing nights, spine tingling mysteries and miles of travel, had finally cumulated in one of the highest points in my angling career; a result I felt was earned. I still find it incredible, that the Old Quarry had never produced an Eel anywhere near this size, and furthermore has never done so since. Despite my best efforts, it would seem that the greatest mystery of all is the mystery of fishing itself.

*A Winter wonder 5lb 2oz Eel*

## The conclusion

This year has passed in a blink of an eye, I am proud of myself for sticking relentlessly to the task, although at times I really questioned my sanity. There were so many great moments, frustrating trips and hilarious mishaps and for once I have them all recorded. For as long as I have been an angler I have planned to keep a detailed account of my fishing year, at last I have finally done it. I was determined to keep this account real, so the highs and the lows were all recorded as it happened. The start of the year couldn't have gone worse, cancelled trip, broken rod and lost kit, the end wasn't much better with a near biblical plague of Dogfish. Fortunately, the middle improved and ending up with 43 personal bests will surely be one of the highlights of my 40+ years angling.

I still ask myself could I have done better? Well, probably, after all I lost a few fish I needed and let Chris catch a few, from right under my nose. However, I could have also done a lot worse, the John Dory was gifted to me by a supportive Neptune, a Short Spined Sea Scorpion on the last cast and a lone Grey Mullet gulps down the breadcrust throwing caution to the wind. Yes, I did have some luck, but I also persevered to get some fish, the Dab, Blenny and Spotted Ray testing my resilience to the bitter end. Tracking down a Wye Barbel was proof that homework, research and boots on the ground does pay, a fish I have coveted for many years, and what a year to make an appearance. Like a successful movie the person in front of the camera may get many of the accolade's, behind the scenes however, are so many supportive people that are integral to any success.

This was the case with this challenge and the fact that I exceeded my targets for species and money is totally down to the comradery of the angling community. So many of the species were down to skippers, guides and anglers going above and beyond to help me out. To every last one of you, I salute you, it's been a pleasure fishing with you. I must not forget the core reason for the challenge and that was to raise funds and awareness of Strokes, Stroke Association and support for the families of Stroke Victims. I was shocked to find out Strokes effect so many children and babies, you can never read this acronym *FAST*, enough so here it is.

**F**acial = weakness
**A**rms = weakness
**S**peech = problems
**T**ime = ring 999

www.stroke.org.uk

I have been asked, what was my favourite species of the year? That's a difficult one as all the fish have been part of the overall Jigsaw. I think for pure elation it would probably be the Spotted Ray, so much effort and such a fitting way to end the species count. The sad thing is, that fish didn't even make it into the book, but the costs of printing meant some harsh picture editing. The final part of the challenge is to arrange to hand over the big cheque to the Stroke Association. I am planning to do this alongside Andy Adams down at Looe, and if everything goes according to plan the final page of the book will contain the photo of this event.

So here is the money shot, so delighted to top £1300, thanks so much to everyone that contributed via, donation, boat time, guiding, local knowledge and supporting the blogs. The man pictured below, Andy Adams was inspiring before his Stroke, he has taken it to another level with his grit and determination, I salute you my friend.

As can be seen in the picture Andy has been exercising his right arm with a bit of Guinness lifting! It was a great afternoon down in Looe with the family, thanks so much Pete & Helen Davis for making the presentation possible. Also, thanks to Hayley Ali from the Stroke Association for travelling down from Bristol to receive the cheque and meet everyone. It felt a little bit sad today knowing I've finished and despite what I achieved it's a drop in the ocean for the amount needed to truly support Stroke Victims and their families. What is good though is that by creating and publishing this book, I have hopefully created a legacy that will keep raising funds for the Stroke Association even though my challenge has ended.

The final picture shows my wonderful family who supported me through the whole challenge, also Andy, Hayley, Helen and Pete.

I hope everyone that has kindly purchased the book has enjoyed reading it and feel it's something they will pick up and read again.

The End

Printed in Great Britain
by Amazon